THE 1973 METS – YOU'VE GOT TO BELIEVE

Len Ferman - The Sports Time Traveler

THE SPORTS TIME TRAVELER LLC

DEDICATION

To my wife Heather who always believes in me, who inspires me every day, and shares my love of time travel stories.

To my three amazing adult children and their incredible spouses. I am in awe of all of you.

To my parents, Arlene and Stanley, my cousin Sandy and all my best friends from New Jersey including Glenn, Greg, Charlie, Bill and Mark, for reading all my stories and encouraging me to continue this journey.

To my nephew Ben for his valuable advice that got me started sharing my stories.

And finally, to my young grandson, who I hope one day may enjoy reading and listening to my stories.

Contents

FOREWORD

By Ted Kubiak

Going back in time with Len Ferman, "The Sports Time Traveler," to re-live the 1972 and 1973 New York Metropolitans' baseball seasons, culminating with their loss in the World Series to my Oakland A's team in 1973, was a welcome reawakening for me, not only because it took me back to some wonderful memories, but Len's diligent research uncovered articles about me that I'd never known existed. His overall coverage of the Mets history is a fascinating read for anyone unfamiliar with baseball fifty years ago and the plight of the New York Mets and their surprising season in 1973. It fascinated me and I lived its reality.

Any written word about a New York sports team generally enthralls the public. After all, New York is New York! In his book Len has "traveled back in time" to give us the experience of following day-by-day one of the Mets' greatest seasons. You have to admire not only his ingenuity to begin such an undertaking, but the time and effort he put into the research for this fascinating book.

With Len's book "The 1973 Mets - You've Got to Believe," you will experience America's pastime when it was still America's pastime, a time when baseball was baseball, a time before it was interpreted by velocity, spin rate, launch angle, trajectory, distance, and a slew of alphabetized categories such as RC, FIP, WHIP, DRS, UZR, and my favorite, PECOTA. There is no way I would even attempt to explain that one, or the biggest and most important one, WAR, that no one can explain let alone agree on how it should be interpreted.

Baseball can provide enough history and stories to keep any fan mesmerized for as long as he or she wants. I don't see that happening with what the game is giving us today. Numbers and endless statistics don't make for interesting stories no matter what they reveal, but that's all the game is now. Baseball's appeal used to be its players and their exploits. It was fun to argue about who could do what better than everyone else.

As an example, New York City had, at one time, three of the game's greatest centerfielders, Willie Mays in the Polo Grounds, Duke Snider in Ebbets Field, and Mickey Mantle in Yankee Stadium. Who was the best of the three was the topic of many arguments. Book after book has chronicled each of their exploits, but Len does something unique, he gives you an inside look at the end of one of their careers. He tells you about the final days on the ball field for the "Say Hey Kid," Willie Mays, who played his last two seasons as a member of the New York Mets. How could that not be of interest to any baseball fan? It excited me. I knew something about Willie but nothing about his tenure with the Mets. And, ironically, Len wrote that the first day Mays wore a Mets uniform was May 12, 1972. I was born May 12, 1942. Coincidence? Omen? Luck? Was there any significance to those dates? Not really, but it was a lot more interesting to have learned that than knowing the launch angle of any of Willie's home runs!

What "The Sports Time Traveler's" stories help us do is re-live times when sports were magical. His focus on the Mets "almost" World Championship season of 1973 was during an era considered by many to be the best that major league baseball has ever given to its fans. "The 1973 Mets - You've Got to Believe" honors America's pastime as it used to be played. It also honors Len's passion as a baseball fan, not only as a ten year old at the time of that fateful 1973 Series loss, but then fifty years later having to relive it through his research. That is a true fan!

But this is not just a book about the New York Mets because Len made me a focal point of his research. He found out and told me things that I had not known about myself. It was an enlightening experience to have my own history re-lived and snippets of my career revitalized. Never close to being a standout, I was an average every day major league player, but Len discovered articles about me that had me looking at myself in a different light, and for that I cannot thank him enough.

The Mets were a franchise that could not have started any more disgracefully than the team that was put together in their inaugural season of 1962. But they were loved, really loved, by New York fans who embraced their ineptitude. Magically, before the end of the decade of the 1960s, the Mets rose from perennial bunglers to World Champions in 1969. This gave them something on which to build, and another miracle season in 1973 found them, once again, in the World Series.

The Mets played my team, the Oakland A's in that 1973 World Series.

We were in the middle of an incredible string of back-to-back-to-back World Series titles in 1972, 1973 and 1974. A unique group of individuals, we did not have the greatest players, but with enough very good ones and a strong supporting cast, we were a group that was focused and dedicated to winning in a way that is hard to explain. We played the game with a workman-like precision. One day was no different than another. We had a job to do. Every player, no matter their stature or role did what they had to do, no more, no less. And that never wavered. I'd been on bad clubs and good clubs, but the A's were different. There were no ups and downs. Sure, we had winning and losing streaks, but the focus and commitment from a group of guys, for a period of several years, was remarkable.

Then in 1975 something changed. I don't know if we'd worn ourselves out, or if pending free agency had anything to do with it, but the team had a different feel in spring training. Something was missing. It was strange, but very noticeable. And that was borne out by me being traded to San Diego early in the year. Not a great cog in the grand scheme of things, I nevertheless felt my role on the club was very important. With my trade, I believed the team was on its way to being dismantled. But that's for another time.

In keeping with "The Sports Time Traveler's" journey, I am going to take you on what could be considered my own journey. It may not provide the same enjoyment as those days that Len recalls, but it will give you the background as to why I was requested to write the foreword for Len's work.

As a seven and eight year old, whenever school was out, I could not wait to get to the playgrounds to play baseball. In our little town of Highland Park, New Jersey, I, and a group of maybe 15 or 20 friends, would get together, choose sides, and play until either the playground closed, or we had to go home for lunch or dinner. I loved the game.

One good thing about Highland Park was that it had very healthy sports programs for us kids to keep us out of trouble. There were baseball leagues for every age. I played Little League, Junior League, and made the best of a spurious Senior League, considered so because I never knew if enough players would show up so we could have a game.

I was a good baseball player as a kid, not outstanding in my view, but was always thought to be one of the best. I definitely had my shortcomings. Even at an early age I was honest with myself. I knew I wasn't a great hitter, and though I had an idea of what I should have been doing, I did not have the physical ability to do it. But I got by. High school baseball was just another hurdle. It seemed way more than I could handle. Never one to give myself enough credit, I one day found myself awakened out of the boredom of a high school assembly to hear my name called out as the "Most Valuable Player" on our team during my senior year. No one was more surprised than me. I was literally shocked. With that honor, my baseball playing days were over, or so I thought. Never, absolutely never, had I ever considered becoming a professional player, and with a scholarship to study architecture at Pratt Institute in Brooklyn, I was preparing for college.

Life, however, has its way of telling you what it is that might be best for you, and my world was about to be turned upside down. Sitting on the bench in between innings of a high school tournament game during my senior year, someone tapped me on the shoulder. I turned around and was face to face with a gentleman I did not know. After a brief and quick introduction as to who he was, his only question put me on cloud nine. "Would you like to attend a tryout camp for the Kansas City Athletics?" Those few words changed my life!

It wasn't easy, but I had the good fortune to play professional baseball for the next 16 years, including 10 years in the majors, and then spend another 26 managing and coaching in the minor leagues. I grew up in the Kansas City Athletics organization in the 1960s. Reggie Jackson, Catfish Hunter, Sal Bando, Joe Rudi and Bert Campaneris were all my teammates. We were not very good. In 1967, the team's last year in Kansas City, we lost 99 games, In 1968, Charles O. Finley moved the team to Oakland, and we improved to 82 – 80, and in 1969, to 88 – 74 while contending for the division title well into August.

Prior to the 1970 season, I was traded to the Seattle Pilots. The Pilots were never financially stable. Forced to file for bankruptcy after only one season in 1969, the franchise was sold and moved to Milwaukee a week before the 1970 season began. I was an everyday player that year for the first and only time playing for the Milwaukee Brewers, a team that finished the year two runs shy of scoring the least amount of runs of any American League club.

Two years later, in 1972, the A's brought me back "home." I was traded back to Oakland from Texas and reunited with all my former teammates, who by then had matured, and we began what was the greatest run by any team in the decade, as we won 3 consecutive World Series titles in 1972, 1973, and 1974. It was a truly remarkable experience that I was very lucky to have.

I did not follow baseball in the press or read about the Oakland A's games during those championship years, especially as they were covered in my hometown newspaper in New Jersey and across the country. Len, on the other hand, has religiously read the newspaper accounts of each game of the 1973 World Series from different locales, and has watched, listened to, and analyzed the tapes of the games to capture the full experience of what it was like to be a Mets fan of the 1973 team.

I usually made it a point to immediately forget whatever it was I experienced during a game; I don't really know why. It was just my nature that as soon as one game ended my focus had to be on preparing for the next game, not analyzing the past one. Because of that I missed remembering some special moments that Len's research has brought to light. His look back in time revealed things about my own playing career about which I either had no prior knowledge, or knew very little of what had really taken place. He found interesting stories about me that I never knew existed at the time, like his second-by-second account of how I scored the winning run in game 3 of the 1973 World Series – one of the highlights of my career.

Another story that featured me was that Pete Rose thought I was out of position when I threw him out at first base on a high bouncer he hit over the mound with a runner on third, to end the first game of the 1972 Series and secure the victory for the A's. Upon learning about Rose's comments, I thought it was a bit of hubris on Pete's part to think the ball even had a chance of being a hit. It was a very easy play. Maybe he thought he could have or should have beaten it out, but history says otherwise. Still, I loved that Len found the articles that he did about that game that put a new light on the play for me. I'd spent the last 50 years thinking it wasn't that great a play.

As a player, the 1973 World Series was a blur. The excitement during a World Series week is incredible. You can imagine how hectic it might be with the media coverage, traveling from coast to coast twice, playing nearly every day, the stress of the games themselves, traveling with your family, accommodating relatives and guests while trying to get enough rest. In addition to all of the normal proceedings, controversy was swirling around our club during the Series because Finley tried to fire one of our players in the middle of it and, on top of that, A's manager, Dick Williams, told us he was quitting; he'd had enough of Finley's interference. Our minds were everywhere but on the games. We came back to Oakland down 3 games to 2, but somewhere in my mind, knowing the guys we had, I honestly thought we'd win the next two home games and the Series. I guess "you gotta believe."

Any fan of the history of the game of baseball has to marvel at the "The Sports Time Traveler's" findings. Baseball tends to lend itself to so much history, more so than any other sport. Everything that has ever happened in a game has been documented. I've already mentioned some of what Len has found out about me and added to his book, but he has also been sending me articles from time to time about something I'd done, or about something that has been written about me in some paper somewhere across the country. He has brightened my days with what he's discovered. And, whether you enjoy momentous happenings or the "inside" scoop on something, he has provided both for you in his book "The 1973 Mets – You've Got to Believe."

I've marveled at the tenacity Len must have to recreate what it was like to follow the New York Mets day-by-day in 1973. The story, as he tells it, is truly fascinating. I found myself engrossed in what he'd written. Even for someone who had first-hand knowledge of the 1973 World Series, Len's retelling of the everyday happenings of each game held my attention. And, probably because I did have a working knowledge of the game, it made what he's reported even more captivating.

The losers of a big event are easily forgotten. My 1973 World Champion A's team have received more attention than the 1973 Mets. But it was only one game that turned the tide. We won four, they won three. If they had won four, and we three, Len may have never made this journey. And according to Len, that could have very well happened. The 1973 World Series could have been very different but for a play or two here and there.

Take Len's journey. Read this book. Whether or not you are a baseball fan, even if you are not a Mets fan, you will enjoy the ride. It doesn't matter who you root for, what team might be your favorite, or what players you like, the experience of the Mets' 1972 and 1973 seasons will make "going back in time" well worth your time.

INTRODUCTION

WHAT IS A SPORTS TIME TRAVELER AND WHY DID I WRITE THIS BOOK?

Isaac Newton never played sports.

But Isaac Newton is a giant to me, just as much as Wilt Chamberlain, Jim Brown, Babe Ruth, Jack Nicklaus, Muhammad Ali, or any of the other great sports heroes from 50 – 100 years ago.

During the plague in England, from 1665 – 1667, Newton used his years in isolation to develop the laws of gravity. They were so brilliantly posed that they were not updated for 250 years when Einstein revealed the framework of space-time in his theory of general relativity.

Reflecting on his life achievements, Newton famously said, *"If I have seen further, it is by standing on the shoulders of giants."*

It was Newton, not all the great athletes, whose shoulders I stood on in *discovering* sports time travel.

I say that "tongue in cheek," as I don't really believe sports time travel is a scientific invention, nor do I contend that as The Sports Time Traveler™, I actually go back in time.

But by just thinking a little outside the box, I designed a way to simulate time travel so that I could go back in time, virtually, and have the experience of following my favorite sports teams and athletes as they played decades ago.

I do this by systematically following the sports each day in newspaper archives – and never looking ahead.

I usually pick a specific time, precisely 50 or 60 years ago, to which I travel, and once I get there, I stay in the moment, mimicking the cadence of real life, by reading the newspapers one day at a time. I have found this is the key to generating the feeling that I'm back in time, and it's what makes sports time travel so fascinating.

In my newsletter & podcast, The Sports Time Traveler™, I share my sports time travel experiences whenever something is so exciting, so compelling, that I just have to return to the present day and tell someone about it.

Sometimes I'm traveling back to experience events I never knew anything about. In other cases, I'm re-living great sporting contests that I remember when I was a kid.

This book is about the latter. I wanted to re-live one of the most cherished episodes of my childhood, precisely 50 years after it had happened. I wanted to follow the 1973 New York Mets, day-by-day, during their iconic "Ya Gotta Believe" season.

It seems unbelievable to me that no book on the market exists, to my knowledge, which is dedicated solely to the 1973 Mets.

The 1969 version of the team, which is known as the "Miracle Mets," have had at least 10 books published for which they are the main topic. I attribute the lack of literary output regarding the 1973 team as being due to the simple fact that they did not win game 7 of the 1973 World Series. That single game separates them from the enduring label of world champions. Losing that one contest, on the road, has seemingly put a damper on the accomplishments of a team which made a historic, some would say miraculous run, in a frantic 6 week stretch leading up to the 1973 World Series.

There are just as many, and maybe even more fantastical, magical stories from the 1973 team as from that Amazin' Mets 1969 team But in our winner takes all society, the lack of a World Series title has left the 1973 team with an inferior legacy, one that no prior author seemingly wanted to touch.

I take personal offense to this.

The 1973 Mets were "my team." I was 9 years old in the summer of 1973. It's the perfect age for a baseball fan. I was old enough to fully understand the game and immerse myself in all the statistics. I was at that impressionable time in a boy's life where the players were my heroes. And I was still a pre-adolescent, so baseball mattered more than girls. The Mets were my whole world in that summer of '73.

I became a Mets fan in the summer of 1970, at age 6, and quickly learned that "my team" had won the World Series the prior year.

And that I had missed it.

I was too young in 1969 to notice the Miracle Mets. In that summer I was only 5 years old and not yet even aware of baseball.

1973 was my chance to experience Mets magic and magical it was.

You don't have to be a Mets fan to enjoy the story of the 1973 team. Their story transcends ballclubs, it even transcends the sports world. It's an inspirational uplifting human-interest story that anyone can appreciate.

For starters, the team included a transcendent player in Willie Mays, an American icon, who was in the final days of his legendary career.

The team was managed by another iconic figure, Yogi Berra, who continues to be quoted to this day (in jest) by people that have never even watched a baseball game.

The story of the season reads like a Hollywood movie. Yet if it was a fictional screenplay it would have seemed so preposterous that the script would likely have been dismissed as being utterly absurd.

And yet it did happen.

And sadly, it's little remembered, even by many of the die hard Mets fans I've met.

For those who want to know the arc of the story right now, and can't wait, it's about a team that was mired in last place for most of the summer before making an improbable drive to the top of the baseball world - the 7th game of the World Series.

If you're not a Mets fan, or if you actually hate the Mets, forget about their uniforms, this is a story about a group of people facing a nearly impossible climb, and then having a miraculous run to the summit. It has a nearly mystical theme as well, as some of the events in that 6-week run to the World Series defy natural explanation.

And for a 9-year-old kid in New Jersey in 1973, the Mets provided some of the greatest thrills of my entire childhood, while also teaching me some of the most valuable life lessons I've ever learned.

As we approached the 50th anniversary of the 1973 season, I decided it was time to travel back to the time of my childhood and re-live this experience once more, all the way from start to finish.

This book contains the highlights of my trips into the past to experience the 1973 Mets.

I started my journey back in time by pointing the sports time travel machine dial an extra year earlier, to a seminal moment in the spring of 1972. I wanted the beginning point in my experience to be when the Mets brought Willie Mays home to New York.

In this book I share the highlights of the journey with you. The structure of this book is that there are over 100 individual stories. Each of these stories was written precisely 50 years after the events happened. I have not included a story for each day. I've only included a story when there was something so compelling that I just had to share it with you.

Sports time travel might not be a real invention, but there is true excitement in being a sports time traveler. And while I might not be changing the world like Isaac Newton, my hope is that I'm making a tiny contribution to spread happiness with my stories.

And now let's begin the journey together.

NOTE: The date of each of the stories in this book is the date of the newspaper accounts during my virtual trips back in time. I do this to keep track of exactly where in time I need to travel to find the stories of the games. The actual games will have taken place one day earlier.

CHAPTER ONE

The A-MAYS-in Mets

PHILADELPHIA - May 22, 1972

The Sports Time Traveler™ is in Philadelphia, precisely 50 years ago, virtually, where yesterday the Mets played the Phillies.

I've been back in time, in 1972, for 11 days now ever since the Mets made a big trade that got me so excited, I just had to jump into the sports time travel machine and go experience what happened.

It's been a tumultuous time in the spring of 1972, for the Mets and their fans.

Beloved manager Gil Hodges, the mastermind behind the Miracle Mets of 1969, died suddenly of a heart attack, at age 47, just before the season was scheduled to start last month.

Then baseball's first ever players' strike delayed the opening games by over a week.

Yogi Berra, a 3-time MVP with the great Yankees teams of the Mickey Mantle era, was named the new Mets manager.

And then a week-and-a-half ago, on May 11, 1972, a trade took place.

41-year-old Willie Mays was brought back to New York.

And magical things immediately ensued.

The Willie Mays trade was possibly the first of its kind in baseball history.

Never before had a player sat at the table during trade negotiations.

At the core of the transaction was a spirit of commitment from both sides to help secure the financial future for the legendary Mays beyond his playing career. The Mets were in a position to do that. The Giants were not.

Still a deal had to be struck that was acceptable to Giants' stockholders. The bargaining almost broke down when the Giants insisted on getting an infielder. But they finally settled for minor league pitcher Charlie Williams and cash. And thus, an agreement was reached.

In a way it was a little sad. The great Willie Mays' trade value had been reduced so low that he didn't even fetch a major league player in return.

But this trade was about much more than what Willie could do on the field for the Mets.

Dick Young of the New York Daily News wrote a heart-warming piece, on May 12th, about the trade that helped explain what it meant to the city of New York. Here's my favorite part of the article, *"The wonderful thing the Mets have done is give their fans Willie Mays in a Mets uniform, for however short a time, for whatever contribution he can make. Having Willie Mays to root for is something special. Something that a whole generation of young fans in New York had not experienced."*

The Mets were not expected to be contenders in 1972. The National League East was owned by the powerful Pittsburgh Pirates, the 1971 World Series champions, and winners of the division the past 2 seasons. But Mets fans could now at least relish the fact that they had Willie Mays on their team.

Red Smith in the New York Times wrote an equally stirring piece about the Mays trade that included this passage: *"Not since Abner Doubleday converted a cow pasture to unnatural uses has baseball witnessed anything like the deal that brings Willie back to scenes of his youth... There are some pleasures in life whose value can't be easily expressed in monetary terms. For a considerable body of baseball fans in New York, watching Willie Mays play is one of those pleasures. And if the Mets fans haven't earned such a pleasure, no group has."*

Mays himself said, *"It's a wonderful feeling coming back here. I've always loved New York and I liked San Francisco, but this is like coming back to paradise. I'm very thankful I can come back to New York. I don't think I'm just on display here. There's no doubt in my mind I can help the Mets if I'm used in the right way."*

Baseball fans, and even Willie Mays himself, must have had reason for doubt about Mays actually being able to help the Mets however. At 41 years old, Willie had started the season batting just .184 for the Giants, with no home runs in 49 at bats.

On Willie's first day in a Mets uniform, May 12, 1972, the back cover of the New York Daily News had a banner headline that read, *"Willie Mays Is Back."*

The Mets hosted their largest crowd of the season up to that point. 44,271 fans came out to Shea, most of whom were chanting, *"We Want Willie,"* during the game. The opponent was the San Francisco Giants, Mays's former team for whom he had played his entire career starting way back in 1951.

Manager Yogi Berra resisted putting the .184 hitting Mays into the game against the two right-handed Giants' pitchers Steve Stone and Jerry Johnson. But the Mets sent the crowd home at least somewhat satisfied when Jerry Grote singled with the bases loaded in the bottom of the 9th for a 2 - 1 win.

Writing about the next day's game, Joseph Durso of the New York Times started his article with this: *"On the second day of the Willie Mays era the New York Mets defeated the San Francisco Giants again yesterday 1 - 0, and for the second straight day Willie Mays watched from the bench."* The Giants had started righty Juan Marichel, so Berra kept Mays out of the game.

Willie's First Game Playing for the New York Mets

Willie Mays' first game playing for the Mets was like a fairy tale. 35,505 fans came out on a Sunday afternoon, May 14th, at Shea Stadium. The starting pitcher for the Giants was "Sudden" Sam McDowell, one of the top strikeout kings in baseball. McDowell had been acquired from Cleveland in an offseason blockbuster deal for Gaylord Perry. McDowell was also a lefty. And this meant that right-handed hitting Willie Mays would get the start in Yogi Berra's platoon system.

Mays started at first base in his Mets debut. He was also the leadoff hitter. In his first plate appearance against McDowell, Willie fouled off the opening pitch, which was a fastball. McDowell then lost his control and walked Mays.

The next 2 batters, shortstop Bud Harrelson and center fielder Tommie Agee, also drew walks. This brought up the clean-up batter who was another Mets recent acquisition, Rusty Staub. Staub, unlike Mays, was in his prime and was dealt from the Expos to the Mets in the offseason for three promising young players, in an attempt to add power to the Mets lineup. No Mets player had hit more than 14 home runs the prior season in 1971 and the team as a whole had only clubbed 98.

Staub delivered, belting the ball over the fence in right center for a grand slam.

What a start! Mets 4, Giants 0 and Willie Mays had reached base and scored a run in his first time up as a Met.

There were still no outs in the bottom of the 1st, but McDowell suddenly turned things around as he struck out the next 3 Mets batters in a row, Cleon Jones, Jim Fregosi and Teddy Martinez, to retire the side.

McDowell also retired the Mets in order in the 2nd inning including a strikeout of Willie Mays in the 'Say Hey Kids' 2nd plate appearance. And McDowell was sharp in the 3rd and 4th allowing only one base runner and compiling a total of 7 strikeouts through 4 innings.

Mets starting pitcher Ray Sadecki was even better as he sailed through the first 4 innings, allowing no runs. But in the top of the 5th, the Giants scored 4 times, capped by a 2-run homer by Tito Fuentes.

The game was now tied when Willie Mays stepped to the plate in the bottom of the 5th. Don Carrithers was the new pitcher as McDowell had been taken out for a pinch hitter in the top of the inning. Even though Carrithers was a righty, Yogi Berra kept Mays in the game.

Willie worked the count to a full 3-2. Carrithers threw a fastball on the payoff pitch and Mays slammed it. His rising line drive went over the fence in left field for a home run, his first with the Mets and first of the season. More importantly, it gave the Mets a 5 - 4 lead.

You can watch Mays' home run at this link:

https://www.mlb.com/video/willie-mays-homers-in-mets-debut

Or you can find the video by typing in this search in YouTube: Willie Mays 1st Mets Home Run.

The rest of the game was uneventful. The Mets and Giants both went down quietly in their remaining turns at bat. Mays came up one more time in the 7th and drew a walk. He then was caught stealing second base on a play in which there was a missed signal. Jim McAndrew threw the final 4 innings for the Mets and struck out Bobby Bonds to end the game.

41-year-old Willie Mays had reached base safely in 3 out of 4 plate appearances and hit the winning HR in his first game as a New York Met!

Since the lead never changed after Mays' home run in the 5th, his blow was the winning hit in the game.

In the locker room Mays discussed his home run, *"That was my first hit as a Met, and my first hit as a Giant was a home run too."*

Willie went on to remark that, *"It's a strange feeling to be batting against the club I played with for 20 years. You look up and see 'Giants' written on their shirts and feel you should be out there."*

It was a story book first game for Mays. The New York Times called it, *"a far fetched soap opera."*

The Daily News commented that now Willie will *"be stuck for an encore. That unique problem might worry a lot of performers, but don't bet it'll faze Willie. He'll think of something. He always does."*

Mays picture took up the entire back page of the May 15th Daily News with the headline, *"Willie's HR Wins It."*

The New York Daily News comment about Mays needing to provide an encore turned out to be prescient.

Something magical was happening to the Mets now that they had Willie Mays. Even though he wasn't playing every day, the Mets were winning every day. Mays' home run had propelled the Mets to their 3rd consecutive victory.

Mays went back to the bench for the next 3 games, but the Mets won all three to run their winning streak to 6.

Mays got his next start on May 18th at Shea against the Montreal Expos.

Mays led off the bottom of the 1st with a walk and scored a moment later on a Teddy Martinez triple. The Mets went on to win the game 2 - 1 and extend the streak to 7 games.

On May 19th, the Mets were in Philadelphia and Mays sat again and watched the Mets win their 8th in a row in an 8 - 3 rout.

On May 20th, Mays started the 1st game of a doubleheader at first base and drove in the first run of the game on a double against Phillies lefty Woodie Fryman. Mays also walked and scored in the 8th inning, thus producing 2 of the Mets 3 runs in a 3 - 1 victory. It was the Mets 9th consecutive win.

The Mets went on to win the nightcap 2 - 1 to make it 10 straight.

This set up a classic game yesterday, on Sunday, May 21st.

57,267 fans crammed into Veterans Stadium in Philadelphia on bat day to see Tom Seaver face off against Steve Carlton.

It was a record crowd for a baseball game in Philadelphia.

It was also the 2nd largest crowd ever to see a National League single day game.

Mays got the start against the big lefty. Carlton came into the game at 5 - 3 with a 1.99 ERA. He promptly struck out the side in the 1st inning including leadoff hitter Mays, who was caught looking at the third strike.

Seaver started the game with a 6 – 1 record and a 2.25 ERA, but he hadn't felt his mechanics were right all spring. ***"I'm making innumerable bad pitches,"*** Seaver sighed after the game. He let up a run in the 1st inning, allowing 2 hits and a walk. Then he gave up a 2-run homer in the 4th that put him in a 3 - 0 hole on the road.

Carlton meanwhile was mowing down the Mets.

When Willie Mays came to the plate in the top of the 6th inning, Carlton had already struck out 7 and had not given up a hit.

Mays promptly broke up the no-hitter with a drive into the gap in deep left center for a double. Two batters later Tommie Agee took a Carlton fastball and sent it over the wall in right center to cut the Phillies lead to 3 - 2.

The score remained 3 – 2 Phillies into the 8th inning when Jim Beauchamp pinch hit for Seaver and reached first base on a single.

The next batter up was leadoff man Willie Mays. The 'Say Hey Kid' turned on Carlton's first pitch and hit it off the top of the left field fence for the 648th home run of his career. The 2-run shot put the Mets in front to stay 4 - 3. It was the 2nd game winning home run for Mays in just over a week.

Willie Mays' game winning homer ran the Mets winning streak to 11 games.

After the game, Tom Seaver was asked if he saw Mays winning shot. *"Yes, I saw him hit the home run. He's fantastic. Isn't he? He just makes things happen. First, he comes up and gets the first hit. Then he comes up with the winning run at the plate, and boom, he puts it out."*

Willie himself was more modest. When asked about his key role in helping the Mets to victories in all four games he had played in he said, *"To me, I don't think I did anything exceptional. Sure, I was involved in the 4 wins, but everybody contributed."*

The May 22nd New York Times wasn't as humble as Mays. The headline at the top of the front page of the sports section read, *"Mets capture 11th Straight 4 – 3, on Mays's 2-run Homer in the 8th."*

The victory tied the franchise record winning streak that was first set by the Miracle Mets in 1969.

NOTE From The Sports Time Traveler™,

Upon returning to 2022, I have verified that the 11 straight wins remains the Mets franchise record to this day (although it has been tied several times, most recently in 2015).

Now back to 1972.

Willie Mays start with the Mets was the stuff of legends.

Multiple game winning home runs.

A franchise record winning streak.

Key runs scored in all four games in which he played.

Willie's stats were something else in those first 4 games. He batted .333 and had an on base percentage of .500.

After the games of May 21st the Mets held the best record in the National League:

25 – 7	New York Mets
19 – 12	Houston Astros
20 – 13	Los Angeles Dodgers
18 – 12	Pittsburgh Pirates
18 – 15	Cincinnati Reds
15 – 15	Chicago Cubs
15 – 16	Philadelphia Phillies
15 – 18	San Diego Padres
13 – 19	Montreal Expos
12 – 20	Atlanta Braves
12 – 21	St. Louis Cardinals
11 – 25	San Francisco Giants

And so, Sports Illustrated rightly put Willie Mays on the cover of the magazine on May 22, 1972.

You can see the cover via a simple internet search or at this link:

https://www.ebay.com/itm/125200034160

Or you can find it by searching on Google for, "Willie Mays cover of sports illustrated May 1972."

The Sports Time Traveler™ will continue to report on the 1972 Mets, 50 years ago to the day, whenever there is something so interesting that I just have to share it with you.

CHAPTER TWO

A Momentous Mid-Season Game

ATLANTA, GA - June 15, 1972

The Sports Time Traveler™ is in Atlanta, where the Mets concluded a 3-game set against the Braves last night, in what turned out to be a momentous mid-season game.

I'm here because I'm following the 1972 New York Mets day-by-day 50 years ago.

It's been an exciting spring so far. The Mets came to Atlanta 3 days ago, still in 1st place in the NL East. Quite unexpectedly the Mets seem like they're driving for another pennant just 3 years after the miracle of 1969, although they've hit a skid losing 12 of 20 games going into last night.

What is most surprising about the strong start to this season is that the Mets top two pitchers, Tom Seaver ("The Franchise") and Jerry Koosman, have been quite "off" throughout most of the spring. Seaver has an 8 - 3 record, but his E.R.A. is an uncharacteristic 3.09 at this time. And while Seaver completed 21 of the 35 games he started last season, he hasn't completed a single game in his last 9 starts.

Koosman hasn't completed a game all season and he was demoted to the bullpen for a month.

The Mets have been carried at the plate by an off season move to bolster their weak hitting line up. Trading 3 young players to the Montreal Expos for "Le

Grande Orange," Rusty Staub, the Mets acquired a legitimate slugger for the clean-up spot. Staub is the only Mets full-time player batting over .300 and his line of 9 HRs / 35 RBIs / .307 BA is respectable among the big hitters in the league at this stage.

The Hackensack Record sports section contained a profile of Staub in Sunday's paper, and flatly stated, *"The only constant is Rusty Staub, the main reason the Mets are in first place."* Staub is the only Mets player who is not platooned by manager Yogi Berra based on whether the starting pitcher is lefty or righty.

Two other bright spots on the 1972 Mets so far are rookie starter Jon Matlack and relief ace Tug McGraw. Matlack won his first 5 starts and was 6 - 0 with a 1.95 ERA at the end of May. McGraw has 10 saves and an E.R.A. of just 1.45. His E.R.A. had been as low as 0.35 one month into the season.

Dave Anderson of the New York Times wrote an interesting piece about Tug in his column in the Sunday New York Times.

Anderson's story told of several amusing anecdotes about life in the bullpen in Shea Stadium. Tug McGraw revealed that, *"in the early innings I fall asleep down here a lot."* One of his favorite napping spots is, *"the golf cart with the big Mets cap for a roof."* He also described how the pitchers park their cars just beyond the green wooden fence at the back of the bullpen and he sometimes goes out to his car for a snack of barbecued spare ribs.

However, don't get Tug wrong. He's a true competitor. *"By the 6th or 7th inning I'm always awake. I start sniffing out the saves. It wakes me up right away."*

And Tug described his general excitement about being the Mets number one reliever. *"I love relieving. Driving here, when I see big, beautiful Shea, I tell myself, 'there's a ballgame there today and I've got a chance to be in it.'"*

These 1972 Mets also have a part-time player on the bench named Willie Mays. It's kind of magical just to see his name on the Mets roster. Fans in New York love Willie Mays, and many remember when he roamed centerfield in the Polo

Grounds a generation ago when he led the Giants to their last World Series title in 1954.

And Mays is performing beyond anyone's expectations. In his first month on the Mets, he has started 12 games and is batting .333 and has an OBP (on base percentage) of .500 in his first 56 plate appearances.

Of course, no one else here in 1972 knows he has a fantastic OBP of .500 because virtually no one in 1972 has ever heard of that statistic. But it reveals the hidden value that Willie May is providing to the Mets.

For most of Mays' career his value on the field was never hidden. He was the most prolific performer of his generation and was the all-time leader in the National League in home runs until last week when Hank Aaron of the Braves passed him.

Going into last night's game the major league career home run list looked like this:

714 – Babe Ruth

650 – Hank Aaron

648 – Willie Mays

38-year-old Aaron is being used almost exclusively as a first baseman this season for the first time in his career after playing more than 2,000 games in right field.

41-year-old Willie Mays was the leadoff hitter for the Mets yesterday, the first time he was in the lineup in this 3-game series.

In the top of the 1st inning Willie Mays singled to left field to open the game.

This set up one of the rarest occasions in baseball history.

For what must be the first time it had ever occurred, Hank Aaron was covering Willie Mays at first base. The two legends were standing next to each other during live action in a game. A picture of the two greats standing next to each other on field appeared in today's Hackensack Record.

And when Mays had to dart back to first base on a pickoff attempt from Braves' pitcher Jim Nash, it created a situation in which Hank Aaron tagged Willie Mays. This was almost certainly the first time Aaron had ever tagged Mays.

A photo just a moment prior to the tag appeared in today's New York Daily News on page 129. In the photo, Mays is hustling back to first base while Aaron waits to receive the throw from Nash and apply the tag.

One reason Nash was holding Mays closely on first base was that Willie Mays was still a legitimate steal threat past the age of 40. The year before, in 1971, Willie had stolen 23 bases in 26 attempts.

Mays didn't try to steal second this time, but he did eventually make it there when Mets second baseman Ken Boswell walked. Then Mays tagged up and took third base after John Milner flied out to center. And when clean-up hitter, Rusty Staub, lofted a sacrifice fly to right field, Mays tagged up again and scored the Mets first run.

At 41, Willie Mays could still run and could still impact a game and the Mets took the early lead 1 – 0.

Yet Willie Mays was not even supposed to play on this date. The lineup was shuffled before the start of the game when Mets centerfielder Tommie Agee asked manager Yogi Berra if he could sit out.

Red Foley in the New York Daily News wrote a story about Agee's request to sit out last night's game. He quoted Agee saying, ***"I've been going lousy lately and maybe it'd be better if I stayed out tonight."***

Agee was reeling from the sting of being the cause of the Mets losses to the Braves in each of the previous 2 games. Those losses had knocked the Mets out of 1st place and put the Pittsburgh Pirates on top of the NL East.

Agee had inexplicably dropped 3 fly balls, and made a throwing error, allowing key runs to score that led to the 2 Mets losses.

In the 1st game of the series, the Met had led 7 – 4 in the 8th when the Braves scored 4 runs. One of the runs came in when Agee's throw from center, trying to cut down Dusty Baker at third base, ended up in the Mets dugout.

In the game 2 nights ago, the Mets again had a 3 run lead in the next to last inning. Tom Seaver had the Mets up 5 - 2 with 2 outs in the 8th when a dropped fly ball by Agee led to 3 unearned runs. The Mets then lost the game in the 10th when Hank Aaron hit a walk off home run, the 650th of his career.

An interesting twist was revealed when Agee described why he had dropped the balls. In the June 14, 1972, New York Times, Agee put the blame in part on Willie Mays. The article quotes Agee saying, *"I've been using a bigger glove for about three weeks. It's one of the gloves Willie brought with him. But it's too big and I don't have the feel of the whole glove. I'm going to have to go back to using my old one."*

Back to last night's game, Mets rookie Jon Matlack retired 9 of the Braves first 10 batters and the Mets led 2 - 0 when Willie Mays came up again in the 4th. With runners on first and second, Mays breezed past Aaron at first base this time, hitting a double. Mays collected an RBI on the hit when Teddy Martinez scored, putting the Mets up 3 - 0.

In the bottom of the 4th, Hank Aaron got 1 run back. He put the Braves on the board with his 651st home run of his career. It was also his 3,311th hit putting him into 5th place all-time.

But the Braves never caught the Mets. With Matlack pitching brilliantly, scattering 6 more hits, and Tug McGraw earning a save in the 9th, the Mets won it 8 - 3.

The win put the Mets back in 1st place in the NL East ahead of the Pittsburgh Pirates (the prior year's World Series champions).

As a Mets fan, we haven't had too much to celebrate in our franchise history, aside from the Miracle of 1969, so we take pleasure in the high moments when they come, and this was one of them.

The Daily News sportswriter, Red Foley declared, *"No club ever clinched the pennant on this date, but the very fact the Mets chose Flag Day to regain first place via tonight's slump snapping 8 - 3 romp over the Braves, might indicate they have more than a sense of timing or a flare for the dramatic."*

Here are the standings in the National League following last night's game:

34 - 19 New York Mets

34 - 19 Cincinnati Reds

32 - 18 Pittsburgh Pirates

34 - 22 Los Angeles Dodgers

31 - 23 Houston Astros

28 - 22 Chicago Cubs

25 - 27 Atlanta Braves

23 - 30 St. Louis Cardinals

21 - 30 Montreal Expos

20 - 33 Philadelphia Phillies

18 - 35 San Diego Padres

19 - 39 San Francisco Giants

CHAPTER THREE

Wondrous Willie!

CINCINNATI RIVERFRONT STADIUM - June 17, 1972

The New York Mets came to Cincinnati last night in 2nd place in the NL East, a half-game behind the Pirates. Facing the NL West leading Reds they had no easy task.

Fortunately, the Mets had Willie Mays leading off their lineup as he got the start in centerfield.

For the 41 year old Mays it was his 13th start and 14th game he had played in since he came to the Mets in mid-May as a part-time player.

He led off the game with a single, but was doubled up on a fly ball and the Mets went scoreless in the 1st.

However, with that single, Mays extended his streak of getting on base in every one of the first 14 games he has played for the Mets.

In the bottom of the 1st inning, Mets pitcher Jerry Koosman took the mound and showed he was back on his game. He got the Big Red Machine out in order.

The game continued on as a pitcher's duel. Going into the 7th inning the Reds led 1 – 0. Then the Mets Duffy Dyer led off with a single and made it to third base with 2 outs.

Up came Willie Mays and he delivered a run scoring single to tie the game.

The game remained 1 – 1 into the 9th inning.

With 1 out in the top of the 9th, Mets shortstop Bud Harrelson tripled. Willie Mays then came up facing Reds starter Gary Nolan. Mays had already been on base 3 times in 4 trips to the plate.

According to Red Foley in The New York Daily News, Willie Mays, ***"provoked Gary Nolan into wild pitching the winning run across."***

In the bottom of the 9th, Tug McGraw came in to close out the game. When Willie Mays caught a fly ball by Denis Menke, Tug had the save and the Mets had the victory.

In his 14 games with the Mets, Willie is nothing short of wonderous. He has a batting average of .348 and an OBP (on-base percentage) of .508.

Despite the win, the Mets remain in 2nd place at 35 – 19, a half-game behind the Pirates who have a record of 35 – 18.

Chapter Four

Meet Tom Terrific!

CINCINNATI RIVERFRONT STADIUM - June 18, 1972

The New York Mets, who had dropped out of 1st place in the NL East 2 days ago are back in 1st thanks solely to The Franchise - Tom Seaver.

Seaver pitched masterfully yesterday against the NL West leading Cincinnati Reds allowing 5 hits, all singles, in a complete game victory, to improve his record to 9 – 3.

But it was Seaver's bat that won the game. Coming to the plate in the top of the 7th, with the score tied 1 - 1, Seaver got the count to 3 - 2. Ross Grimsley then tried to get Seaver out on a fastball. But instead, Seaver drilled it for a home run to give the Mets a 2 - 1 lead.

It was Seaver's 2nd homer in his last 4 at bats!

Seaver took care of the remainder of the game by himself, retiring the last 6 Reds batters in a row including Joe Morgan, Johnny Bench and Tony Perez.

This was the first complete game for Seaver in nearly 2 months.

Seaver told Bob Hertzel of the Cincinnati Enquirer, *"This past month the ball has been feeling heavy, like it was taking a long time to get off the fingers. Today, even in the first inning, it was jumping off my fingers."*

Two weeks ago Seaver faced Cincinnati at Shea and the Reds hitters said he wasn't challenging them. Seaver allowed 4 runs in 6 innings in that game.

Yesterday was different. In the 8th inning when Seaver got 2 strikes on Bench he came back with a high inside fastball for a strikeout.

In the 9th inning, Seaver got Perez to hit a pop fly for the first out.

Perez told Earl Lawson of the Cincinnati Post, *"He must have known I was up there looking for breaking pitches. Why else would he throw me three straight fast balls. I can't figure out why he threw me the fast balls. I say to myself he must feel so good that he wants me to hit a home run so he can keep on pitching. Seaver beat us all by himself."*

The win improved the Mets record to 36 – 20 and gave them a half game lead over the Pittsburgh Pirates.

Unfortunately, the Mets also got some bad news. Right fielder Rusty Staub sprained his wrist as he fouled off a pitch and had to be removed from the game. Staub had not missed an inning all season up to this point according to Murray Chass writing in the New York Times.

CHAPTER FIVE

Pirates are Plundering NL Pitching

THE METS ARE FINDING IT TOUGH TO KEEP PACE WITH THE POWERFUL PITTSBURGH PIRATES

HOUSTON ASTRODOME, TX - June 20, 1972

The Mets are here in Houston for a 3-game series against the Astros. They lost the opening game of the series last night. But that's not the extent of the bad news. It was announced today that Rusty Staub, who injured his right wrist while batting in the 6th inning in Cincinnati 2 days ago, is going to miss an extended period of time as his wrist has been placed in a cast.

Without Staub in the lineup, the Mets managed just 1 hit in a 3 – 0 loss.

The Mets (36 – 22) are now 1 game behind the Pittsburgh Pirates (36 – 20) in the NL East.

But the gap between the Mets and Pirates is greater than it looks in the standings.

The Pirates as a team are batting .285, 40 points ahead of the Mets.

It's going to be very difficult for the Mets to keep pace with the Pirates if Pittsburgh continues to hit at their present pace.

Even more striking is a look at the league leaders in batting average as posted 2 days ago in the Sunday edition of The New York Times.

The top 3 batters, and 6 of the top 12, in the NL are Pirates.

The poorest average among those six comes from Willie Stargell who has a line of 14 HRs / 46 RBIs / .314 BA.

Here's the top 12 batters in the NL:

.363 Vic Davalillo, Pirates

.352 Rennie Stennett, Pirates

.342 Manny Sanguillen, Pirates

.331 Rico Carty, Braves

.328 Matty Alou, Cardinals

.322 Joe Torre, Cardinals

.320 Bill Buckner, Dodgers

.319 Roberto Clemente, Pirates

.319 Cesar Cedeno, Astros

.318 Al Oliver, Pirates

.316 Bobby Tolan, Reds

.314 Willie Stargell, Pirates

The Mets have just one batter, Rusty Staub, hitting over .300, and he is just barely above that threshold at .302. Staub would be the 7th best hitter on the Pirates.

And now Staub is out injured for an undetermined amount of time.

The Sports Time Traveler™ will be continuing to follow the 1972 Mets and reporting to you when there is something so compelling I just have to share it.

CHAPTER SIX

Duffy Who?

LONG TIME BACK UP CATCHER DYER PROVES THAT EVERY DUFFY EVENTUALLY HAS ITS DAY

HOUSTON ASTRODOME - June 21, 1972

The Sports Time Traveler™ is following the 1972 Mets who are playing at the Houston Astrodome tonight. Yesterday the National League office selected the player of the week. There are a lot of legendary names having big seasons "this year" including Johnny Bench, Willie Stargell and Steve Carlton. That's make it even more absurd that the NL Player of the Week for June 12 - 18 was announced to be Duffy Dyer.

Duffy who?

Long time Mets fans probably will recognize the name. Dyer has worn the catcher's mask as the Mets back up to Jerry Grote since 1968. The key phrase there is "back up." Dyer seldom gets to play because Jerry Grote is one of the best defensive catchers in baseball and was the starting catcher in the 1968 All-Star game. Dyer only starts when Grote needs a rest. Dyer appeared in just 53 games in 1971.

But this year is different. Grote has some nagging injuries, and Dyer has a hot bat. Although he only started 10 games through June 8th, he was batting over .300. That was enough for manager Yogi Berra to make the switch. Beginning on June 10th, Duffy Dyer took over as the Mets starting catcher.

All Duffy has done since then is hit the ball regularly. He went 11 for 28 from June 10 - 18 (.393 average) along with 3 home runs and 8 RBIs. And he's had some great defensive plays. In Cincinnati last week, he gunned down Joe Morgan attempting to steal second. And 2 nights ago he tagged out Houston's Tommy Helms at the plate in the Astrodome.

Dyer told reporter Bob Hertzel, of the Cincinnati Enquirer, that he credits the late Gil Hodges and Mets broadcaster Ralph Kiner (7-time NL home run champion) for his hitting surge. *"Gil was always trying to get a little movement in my hands before I swung,"* said Duffy. But he never actually tried it until this past winter when he was working with Kiner in the instructional league.

Despite Dyer's run saving play at the plate, the Mets lost the game 3 - 0. Larry Dierker of the Astros pitched a complete game one-hitter. The one hit was by none other than Duffy Dyer!

The Mets are now one game behind the Pirates who unleashed a ferocious 16 hit attack 2 nights ago in defeating the Dodgers 13 - 3 behind 2 doubles and a home run from Roberto Clemente, yet another legend who Dyer beat out for the Player of the Week honors.

CHAPTER SEVEN

Battling Pirates

THE TOP TWO TEAMS IN THE NL EAST, THE METS AND PIRATES, CLASH AT SHEA.

NEW YORK - SHEA STADIUM - June 28, 1972

The World Champion and NL East leading Pittsburgh Pirates came to New York this week for 2 games against the 2nd place New York Mets. The Mets entered the short series 3 games back, but with a Jerry Koosman victory in the first game, the Mets were just 2 games out going into yesterday afternoon's game.

The skies were sunny for the day game, but the outfield was like a swamp due to rain over the past week.

It's been a rollercoaster season for the Mets so far. After they acquired Willie Mays in mid-May, the team went on a franchise record 11 game winning streak. They built their record to 25 - 7 and held a 6 game lead over Pittsburgh.

But the Mets have now cooled off the past few weeks, they've lost 18 of their last 31 games coming into today's game against the Pirates.

The problem with battling the Pirates is that they're brandishing the best bats in baseball. Mets coach Rube Walker discussed the Pirates before the game as he looked at their batting averages. *"This is the damndest thing to look at. They're hitting .283 as a team and that includes pitchers! They've got 636 hits already. We've got 494."*

Writing in the New York Daily News, Phil Pepe said, *"The way the Pirates are going they might end up with 10 .300 hitters... Gene Clines couldn't*

get in the game and he's hitting .351. Neither could Rennie Stennet, .345.
Who says there is no hitting in baseball anymore. It's all on the Pirates
bench."

Jerry Koosman, who beat the Pirates 2 nights ago by spreading 7 hits over 8 and
2/3 innings, provided some insights about what it's like to face them, *"You're*
under constant pressure. You have to go hard all the time. There's nobody
in that lineup you can ease up on."

It was no surprise then that in yesterday's game, the Pirates chased Mets starter
Jim McAndrew in just 4 innings and built a 4 - 2 lead.

But in the bottom of the 6th the Mets manufactured 2 runs, on a combination
of 3 walks, 2 singles and a passed ball, to tie the game.

Then in bottom of the 8th, Mets magic took over. With one out, John Milner
hit a fly to center, but Al Oliver slipped on the wet grass and Milner's ball fell for
a triple.

The Pirates then elected to intentionally walk Cleon Jones to bring up Mets
third baseman Jim Fregosi. Fregosi, the man who had been traded for Nolan
Ryan, has been in the midst of an abysmal slump with 13 hits in his last 68 at
bats and just 2 RBIs in his past 26 games.

With stats like that, Fregosi guessed that Pirates pitcher Bob Miller would try
to blow a fastball by him on the 1st pitch. Fregosi guessed correctly and smashed
the ball over the wall in left for a 3-run homer.

Then Mets pitchers Ray Sadecki and Danny Frisella held the Pirates to 2 hits
in the last 5 innings to secure the 7 - 4 victory.

Now the Mets (39 – 25) are just one game back of the Pirates (39 – 23).

But while the standings look hopeful, the situation in the clubhouse is somewhat grim.

The Mets are ravaged by injuries. Rusty Staub, the team's leading slugger, is
out with a hand injury.

Centerfielder Tommie Agee pulled a groin muscle as he slid on the outfield
grass in the middle of the game and had to be replaced by Willie Mays, who
himself is battling a hamstring issue.

And Cleon Jones has been ineffective lately (4 for 27) due to an elbow injury.

The Sports Time Traveler™ is a big Mets fan and will keep an eye on them for the remainder of the 1972 season.

CHAPTER EIGHT

The Seavers Put the Mets in First

THE 1972 METS ARE BACK IN A FIRST PLACE TIE THANKS TO NANCY SEAVER AND HER HUSBAND TOM.

VETERANS STADIUM, PHILADELPHIA - June 29, 1972

The Mets played a doubleheader here in Philadelphia yesterday.

It wasn't a typical doubleheader. The first game was a 2 inning softball exhibition with the Phillies wives taking on the Mets wives.

Nancy Seaver batted 2 for 2 and led the Mets wives to a 9 - 0 victory. *"The blond former model played shortstop gorgeously,"* according to Bruce Kredan in the Philadelphia Inquirer.

The Inquirer also featured a giant picture of Nancy Seaver as she was batting on the front page of today's sports section.

In the nightcap, Seaver's husband Tom was on the mound and had a shaky start giving up 5 hits and 2 runs in the first 2 innings. He told the Inquirer, *"I wasn't in the game mentally or physically in the first couple of innings. I was throwing lousy."*

Bruce Kredan speculated on the obvious reason for the Mets pitcher's problem, *"If Seaver shared anything in common with the other post-pubescent males among the audience of 26,545, what he had to be thinking about when he took the mound was Nancy Seaver."*

Tom Terrific eventually got his focus back and he retired 20 out of the next 21 batters, throwing 10 strikeouts in a complete game performance.

Meanwhile the Mets had a ragtag team of position players on the field supporting Seaver. The Mets were playing without their entire starting outfield (Cleon Jones, Tommie Agee and Rusty Staub), all of whom are injured.

Willie Mays, who is also injured, had to play centerfield, where he mishandled the first 3 balls hit to him and never managed to get on base.

Teddy Martinez, a utility infielder, had to play left field.

The Mets scrapped for 3 runs though, and that was just enough to give Seaver a 3 - 2 win.

Seaver improved his record to 10 - 4.

More importantly the Mets (40 – 25) pulled even with the Pirates (39 – 24) on top of the NL East.

Chapter Nine

Dependents Day

SHEA STADIUM - July 5, 1972

The Sports Time Traveler™ was at Shea Stadium on Independence Day yesterday in 1972 to see the Mets take on the San Diego Padres.

It was 77 degrees and cloudy with a light northwest breeze – a great day to be at the ballpark for a doubleheader.

Sadly, for the Mets outfield, it was more like dependents day than Independence Day. The Mets were completely dependent on their reserves as all three regular outfield starters, Cleon Jones, Tommie Agee and Rusty Staub, were out with injuries.

Back up outfielder Dave Marshall was also out.

Infielder Teddy Martinez had to start the 1st game in right field and moved to centerfield for the 2nd game.

Regular first baseman, John Milner, who also has a pulled muscle started in left in game 1 and moved to right for game 2, while little used Jim Beauchamp played left in game 2.

And Willie Mays, who is battling a pulled muscle, started in centerfield in the 1st game, and at age 41 did double duty playing first base in the 2nd game. It was the first time all season that Mays had played both ends of a doubleheader.

Mays played remarkably well getting on base 4 times in 7 plate appearances, and also executing a bunt sacrifice.

In the 1st game Tom Seaver started for the Mets.

Without their regular outfield sluggers, the Mets only managed 2 runs through the first 8 innings.

The Mets were dependent on their pitcher Tom Seaver to shut down the Padres, and he did.

Through the first 8 innings, Tom Seaver struck out 11 Padres, walked 4 and did not allow a hit.

Seaver was so good that no baseball thrown by Seaver had even left the infield, until the Padres' Leron Lee flied out to center in the 7th inning.

Seaver needed 3 more outs in the 9th to record the Mets first ever no-hitter.

You can listen to the 9th inning at this YouTube link:

https://youtu.be/zf6Afv5CGCs?t=9250

At 2:35:05 on the video you can hear Ralph Kiner making the call as Seaver gets the leadoff batter Dave Roberts to ground out.

Seaver now needs just 2 more outs for the Mets first ever no-hitter.

The next batter is LeRon Lee. At 2:35:35 on the first pitch to Lee, he breaks his bat, but the ball manages to bloop out to centerfield and drops in for a hit. The no-hitter had been broken.

A moment later Seaver got Nate Colbert to ground into a double play and the ball game was over. Seaver had a 1 hit shutout and improved his record to 11 – 4 on the season.

In game 2, the Mets remained anemic at the plate and lost 4 – 2.

They ended the day 1 game back of the Pirates.

Here were the standings in the NL East after the July 4th games:

43 – 26 Pittsburgh Pirates

43 – 28 New York Mets

37 – 33 Chicago Cubs

38 – 34 St. Louis Cardinals

31 – 39 Montreal Expos

25 – 46 Philadelphia Phillies

CHAPTER TEN

1972 Mets 0 – 0 Game Goes Into the 14th

THE 1972 METS HAVE STELLAR PITCHING, BUT INJURIES HAVE DECIMATED THE METS OFFENSE AND SHORTSTOP BUD HARRELSON CAN'T CATCH A BREAK WITH THE UMPIRES

FLUSHING MEADOWS - July 7, 1972

The Sports Time Traveler™ is interested in following the 1972 Mets for several reasons.

First and foremost, I was an 8-year-old Mets fan in the summer of 1972.

Second, the Mets acquired Willie Mays in 1972 and even though it was the end of his great career, it was a special thing to have a living legend on "my team."

Third, the Mets had their best start in franchise history in 1972, winning 25 of their first 32 games and were in first place for most of the spring.

However, "now" in early July, the Mets are coming back down to Earth as epitomized by the game last night against the last place San Diego Padres at Shea stadium on July 6, 1972.

Jerry Koosman pitched his best game of the season. He went 10 full innings. He struck out 12. He only gave up 5 hits and 1 walk. And no runners scored.

Unfortunately, he literally got no run support. In fact, he got almost no hit support either. In those 10 innings, the Mets managed 1 hit, a single by seldom used outfielder Dave Marshall.

In the top of the 11th, Mets manager Yogi Berra brought in his top relief pitcher Tug McGraw. Tug came into the game with an ERA of 1.54. In the 11th, 12th and 13th innings Tug allowed no runs, 2 hits and no walks. It was a great relief effort.

Unfortunately, the Mets could only manage 1 single in the 11th - 13th innings.

The Mets offense is crippled as they are missing their best hitter, RF Rusty Staub as well as regular starting LF Cleon Jones and CF Tommie Agee. Infielder Teddy Martinez had to start in centerfield because Willie Mays is injured as well.

So, the game was still tied at 0 - 0 going into the 14th. McGraw in his 4th inning of relief had to face the top of the Padres batting order. Derrel Thomas led off with a single to right. Dave Roberts then laid down a bunt right in front of home plate. Mets catcher Duffy Dyer whipped the ball to second base to try and catch the lead runner Thomas. Bud Harrelson applied the tag, but umpire Lee Weyer called Thomas safe.

Gabe Buonaro of the Hackensack Record was covering the game and wrote, *"Harrelson immediately started jumping up and down and screaming at Weyer. Manager Yogi Berra joined the argument."* But it was to no avail.

With 2 on and no one out, Leron Lee singled to load the bases for the Padres. Next up was Padres' clean-up hitter Nate Colbert. Colbert hit a grounder to 2nd and the Mets Ken Boswell threw to home. Umpire Dick Stello called the runner Thomas safe. But then changed his call to out. Now with bases loaded and 1 out, McGraw struck out Cito Gaston.

Now the bases were loaded with 2 outs as Jerry Morales came up. Tug got behind on the count 3 - 0. Then he threw a strike. The next pitch was ball 4. The first run of the entire game was the result of a walk. McGraw then got the next batter, Pat Corrales, to pop up to end the inning. Padres 1 Mets 0.

In the bottom of the 14th the Mets needed a run to tie and 2 runs to win.

Bud Harrelson led off with a walk and moved to second on a wild pitch. The tying run was now on second with no outs. Ken Boswell bunted Harrelson over to third. Weak hitting Dave Marshall then grounded out.

Now there were 2 outs and Harrelson, the tying run, was on third.

John Milner came to the plate and the first pitch got passed the catcher, Pat Corrales. Gabe Buonaro wrote that *"Harrelson hesitated until the batter, John Milner, signaled him home. The slight delay made the difference. (Padres' pitcher) Ross and Harrelson both slid into the plate, the pitcher got there a second sooner to take Corrales' throw and came down hard with his glove just to the right of the plate."* Umpire Dick Stello called Harrelson out. Game over. Mets lose 1 - 0.

Gabe Buonaro wrote, *"Harrelson was stunned at first by umpire Dick Stello's out call, jumped up and threw his helmet in the air."* Some reports say the helmet went at least 30 feet up. Harrelson was enraged. And he couldn't cool down after the game. He ranted to Joe Donnelly of Newsday about the umpires, *"They let some of them get so fat, they can't even move around."*

However, Leonard Koppett writing in the New York Times indicated that slow motion instant replay revealed that Harrelson was out at the plate.

It was a gut-wrenching loss and dropped the Mets to 2.5 games behind the Pirates in the NL East at 43 - 29.

CHAPTER ELEVEN

I Asked for Gary Gentry

CALIFORNIA ANGELS GM HARRY DALTON MAKES A STUNNING REVELATION ABOUT THE NOLAN RYAN TRADE

NOTE From The Sports Time Traveler™

I opened the July 12, 1972, New York Times this morning and nearly fell out of my chair. Let's go back to 1972 and see what happened.

ANAHEIM - July 12, 1972

Joseph Durso, one of the long-time baseball writers for the New York Times interviewed California Angels general manager Harry Dalton last night in Anaheim. Durso asked Dalton about the Jim Fregosi - Nolan Ryan trade. The trade didn't raise a lot of eyebrows when it was made last December 10th. But in hindsight it's starting to look like the Frank Robinson deal that Harry Dalton masterminded back in December, 1965.

In November 1965, Harry Dalton was hired as the GM of the Baltimore Orioles. Just one month into the new job, Dalton made one of the great trades in major league history when he quite literally "stole" Frank Robinson from the Cincinnati Reds for Milt Pappas. Playing for Baltimore in 1966, Robinson won the triple crown, was the American League MVP, and led the Orioles to a four-game sweep in the World Series over the defending champion Dodgers.

With Dalton still the GM, the Orioles had the best record in baseball over the past three seasons from 1969 -1971, appearing in the World Series each year and adding another World Series victory in 1970.

Last season the Orioles made history with four 20 game winners on the same pitching staff. That was made possible when Dalton traded for Pat Dobson in December, 1970, to be the 4th starter to go along with Jim Palmer, Dave McNally and Mike Cuellar in what became the 20 game winner quartet.

After last season, Dalton was hired by the California Angels as their new GM. And it was Dalton that negotiated the trade for Nolan Ryan on December 10, 1971. Dalton's goal was to get rid of Jim Fregosi. He wanted to sever ties with the Angels' past and unload the former 6 time all-star who had missed 55 games due to injury in 1971, and was thought to be on the back side of his career. Fregosi batted just .233 for the 1971 season. At the time of the trade last December, Fregosi himself said he couldn't blame Dalton for making the deal and he suspected the Angels wanted a "complete renovation."

On the Mets side of the negotiating table was GM Bob Scheffing. The day after the trade, Scheffing told the New York Daily News, *"I expect criticism. That goes with the job. But if I think in my mind I'm doing the right thing, I do it."*

The late Mets manager Gil Hodges wasn't quite sure it was the right thing at the time the deal was made when he said, *"You always hate to give up on an arm like Ryan's. He could put together things overnight, but he hasn't done it for us, and the Angels wanted him."*

But now it turns out that Ryan wasn't the guy Dalton even wanted.

In the interview with Durso yesterday, Dalton said, *"When I asked for Gary Gentry last winter the Mets said no. So, I asked about Nolan Ryan, and they said yes."*

The Sports Time Traveler™ has to interrupt this article to SCREAM!

OMG! The Angels wanted Gary Gentry and the Mets said NO!

The Mets could have kept Nolan Ryan by just saying yes to trading Gary Gentry!

This is unbelievable. I can't even breathe!

Breathe in.

Breathe out.

It's going to be okay.

Let's go back to 1972.

It's not a surprise that Dalton should have been interested in Gary Gentry. He was a solid starter for the Mets from his rookie year in 1969 through the end of last season. He started 95 games in those three seasons. He had 8 shutouts while compiling a record of 34 - 32.

Most notably Gentry pitched 6 and 2/3 scoreless innings to win game 3 of the 1969 World Series.

But Gentry has been very disappointing this season with a 4 - 5 record and 3.95 ERA.

It's also not a surprise that Dalton was interested in Ryan as his second choice. Ryan had shown great promise despite compiling a 29 - 38 record for the Mets.

Ryan had also been one of the heroes of 1969. He won the decisive game 3 of the NL Pennant when he relieved Gentry in the 3rd inning, and then pitched the final 7 innings allowing just 2 runs.

Then in the World Series, Ryan saved Gentry's game 3 win, allowing 1 hit and no runs in 2 and 1/3 innings.

On the day the Fregosi – Ryan trade was made Dalton had told Durso, *"We picked up one of baseball's best arms in Ryan."*

Now in mid-July the trade is looking like another one of Dalton's dazzling deals.

Ryan is 11 - 5 with a 2.34 ERA. And it seems like he's still warming up. Ryan's last 2 starts have been shutouts giving him 5 for the season (after posting just 2 in his whole Mets career).

And in Ryan's last game on Sunday he retired the last 26 batters of the game in posting a one-hitter. He also struck out 16 in that game. And that's the 2nd time in 8 days he's struck out 16.

Ryan did one more thing on Sunday that's never been done in baseball history. He became the first pitcher to strike out the side on 9 pitches in each league.

He also became only the 3rd pitcher in history to perform the 9 pitch / 3 strikeout inning more than once. The other two are Lefty Grove and Sandy Koufax. Grove is in the Hall of Fame and Koufax will be inducted next month.

Think about that. Ryan, Grove and Koufax in the same sentence. And this was the Angels' 2nd choice after Gary Gentry.

Some people have said Ryan needed a change in scenery or a new pitching coach and that he was never going to reach his potential with the Mets. But talking to Durso yesterday, Ryan said, *"I definitely feel I could have achieved this for the Mets."*

That doesn't make the trade easier to swallow for Mets fans. It's starting to look like a debacle, especially when you consider the other side of the deal.

Jim Fregosi just isn't working out so great for the Mets. He's batting just .249 and has been fighting off injuries. He's also playing out of position. He was an All-Star shortstop in the American League. But the Mets have All-Star Bud Harrelson at short. So, Fregosi is learning to play third base.

The Mets meanwhile are badly in need of hitters. The Mets have dropped 6 of their last 7 games and have fallen to 4.5 games out of first.

The Mets outfield injuries are also continuing to mount. Last night John Milner collided with Bud Harrelson on a pop fly to short left and Milner had to be carted off the field on a stretcher. After that the Mets only outfielder left on the roster was 41 year old Willie Mays, who is playing with a pulled muscle. Infield utility man Ted Martinez had started the game in right field and backup catcher Duffy Dyer had to go out and play left field after Milner went down.

It's starting to look like it will be a long summer at Shea for the Mets.

The Sports Time Traveler™ will keep touching base on the 1972 Mets when there are compelling stories to share.

CHAPTER TWELVE

A Fortuitous Trade

50 YEARS AGO, UTILITY INFIELDER TED KUBIAK MAY HAVE RECEIVED THE MOST PUBLICITY OF HIS LIFE WHEN HE WAS TRADED TO THE OAKLAND A'S.

NOTE FROM THE SPORTS TIME TRAVELER™ - I'm diverging from Mets coverage to share somewhat of a personal story. It's also relevant to the Mets as the featured player in today's article, Ted Kubiak, will play a key role in a big game against the Mets in 1973.

As I was reading the Los Angeles Times from 50 years ago today, July 20, 1972, I came across this headline in the middle of page 3 of the sports section:

"Mincher, Kubiak Traded to A's"

A similar headline ran in most newspaper sports sections across the country that day.

"Kubiak," in that headline, was Ted Kubiak, a utility infielder who was traded, along with Don Mincher, from the Texas Rangers to the Oakland A's.

Ted Kubiak was not the most famous player in baseball and any type of headlines in the newspapers was a real anomaly for him.

Ted Kubiak spent 10 years in the majors for 6 different teams. He appeared in nearly 1,000 games and had nearly 3,000 plate appearances. But he never batted higher than .252 or hit more than 4 home runs in a single season. He never made an All-Star game and he had only one year, 1970, where he was an everyday player when he started 156 games for a Milwaukee Brewers team that lost 97 games.

However, I was excited to see Kubiak's name in the headline because I have a special connection to Ted Kubiak.

Ted Kubiak grew up in Highland Park, NJ, where my family lived before I was born. One of Ted Kubiak's best friends in high school was my cousin Alan and they stayed in touch when Ted became a major league baseball player.

When I was 10 years old in the summer of 1974, and my cousin Alan lived in the Boston area, we traveled to New England to visit. Alan took us to Fenway Park to see the Oakland A's play the Red Sox. And I got to meet Ted Kubiak on the field. He gave me a baseball signed baseball by all the World Champion A's. What a thrill this was.

The Oakland A's were the team of the decade in the 1970s. They won 3 consecutive World Series titles with famous players like Reggie Jackson, Catfish Hunter and Sal Bando.

And Ted Kubiak was on each of the three A's World Series teams as a utility infielder. He played in 256 games and started 125 games for the A's in those 3 seasons.

Ted had actually started his career in the A's organization and played with Jackson, Hunter and Bando for several years before he was traded to the expansion Seattle Pilots. The trade back to the A's was like a homecoming for Ted.

The A's brought Ted Kubiak back in July 1972, because their regular 2nd baseman at the time, Tim Cullen, was injured and they needed help immediately.

Kubiak got action right away as he started both games of a doubleheader against the Red Sox 50 years ago tonight on July 20, 1972.

The next day a wire photo made it into newspapers around the country showing Kubiak as he made an athletic throw to first base trying to complete a double play.

Two days in a row, Ted Kubiak was featured prominently on the sports pages across America!

After Ted's playing career was finished, he went on to a long career in baseball in various functions including managing several minor league teams. In 2019, he wrote a sensational book that chronicles his life in baseball called *"Old School - The Evolution of America's Pastime."* You can find it on Amazon.

Here is the picture of Ted Kubiak and The Sports Time Traveler™ at Fenway Park in August, 1974.

Chapter Thirteen

Willie Mays' San Francisco Homecoming Game

On July 21, 1972, Willie Mays returned home to Candlestick Park in San Francisco for the first time since his trade to the New York Mets

CANDLESTICK PARK - July 22, 1972

Last night Willie Mays returned to one of his former home towns for the 2nd time this season. As previously reported by The Sports Time Traveler™, the first time Mays returned home was back on May 14, when he took the field for his new team, the New York Mets. Mays had become a legend playing in New York for the Giants from 1951 to 1957. He then spent 14 years with the Giants after the team moved to San Francisco before being traded on May 11th to the New York Mets.

In that May 14 game, his first in New York with the Mets, Mays hit the game winning home run. And he hit another game winning home run a few days later as he helped fuel a Mets franchise record 11 game winning streak. It was a fairy tale return to the Big Apple for Mays. As a result, Mays was featured on the cover of Sports Illustrated on May 22, 1972:

https://vault.si.com/vault/1972/05/22/how-sweet-it-is

This brings us to last night, July 21, 1972, for Mays' 2nd homecoming of the season. This time Mays was returning with the Mets to San Francisco's Candlestick Park where Mays roamed centerfield for 14 years.

Mays was originally not scheduled to play last night because the Giants were pitching a right hander. In addition, Mays was due for a rest as he has played a lot recently due to the Mets injury depleted roster. And Mays himself had been playing through a pulled muscle injury for the past month.

But realizing the magnitude of the return appearance in San Francisco, Mays asked Mets' manager Yogi Berra if he could play. Mays told reporter Murray Chass of the New York Times, *"I think I have to play... so many people are going to pay their money to come out especially to see me play. If you pay $4.50 to see a person play and he doesn't, I think you're going to be pretty mad."*

Berra relented and Mays was penciled in as the starting center fielder.

Unfortunately for San Francisco fans the size of the crowd, 18,117, was smaller than would have been expected for Mays' homecoming precisely because Berra had previously remarked in the press that Mays wouldn't play the first game of the series.

Mays received a standing ovation when he came to the plate in the top of the 1st inning. In that first at bat he grounded out.

He received another ovation when he came up in the 3rd inning, although he popped out.

Once again, the crowd cheered when Mays stepped into the batter's box in the 5th inning and this time he didn't disappoint the crowd. He slammed the first pitch 400 feet. The ball cleared the wall in centerfield for a 2-run homer. The 2 runs turned out to be decisive in the Mets 3 - 1 victory, giving Mays yet another game winning hit (his 2nd of the week).

Writing in the Oakland Tribune, Pat Frizzell said, *"Willie Mays rising to another exciting occasion in typical phenomenal fashion beat the team he served for 20 years by pounding a ball across the centerfield fence last night."*

Willie himself said, *"I got more satisfaction out of that than out of the home run in New York."*

NOTE FROM THE SPORTS TIME TRAVELER™ - Willie Mays season in 1972 for the Mets was highly underrated. In addition to several game winning hits, at this point in the season, on July 22, Mays had a .412 On Base Percentage. This stat was never reported in 1972 when only batting averages were considered important (Mays was hitting .258 for the Mets at that time).

Another interesting stat is that in games that Willie Mays started for the Mets up to this point, the team was 20 - 13. In games he had not started they were 15 - 16.

Overall, the Mets are now 49 - 36 and 4.5 games behind NL East leaving Pittsburgh.

THE SPORTS TIME TRAVELER™ will continue covering the 1972 Mets when there are interesting stories to share.

Chapter Fourteen

You Don't Have to Live in New York to Like The Mets

50 YEARS AGO THIS WEEK THE METS PLAYED A DOUBLE-HEADER AGAINST THE PHILLIES ON BANNER NIGHT AT SHEA STADIUM

SHEA STADIUM - August 2, 1972

The 1972 New York Mets are sliding fast. They're not sliding into bases. They're sliding in the National League East standings.

The beginning of the season looked so promising. They had the fastest start in franchise history racing out to a record of 25 - 7 and a 6 game lead on May 21st. They won a franchise record 11 consecutive games in mid-May. And while they cooled off in June, they ended that month tied for 1st place with the Pirates at 41 - 26.

July, however, was another story. Injuries decimated the Mets outfield and their top batters. The Mets went 11 - 15 in July to drop to 7 games behind the Pirates.

The team batted an anemic .188 for the month of July, 1972, with just 8 home runs.

If not for spectacular pitching, the hallmark of the Mets, things could have been much worse. Mets pitchers had a collective ERA of just 2.42 for the month.

NOTE FROM THE SPORTS TIME TRAVELER™ – I interrupt the gloomy beginning of this article to let you know that there is a heart-warming human-interest story coming up.

Now back to August 2, 1972.

Hope Renewed for the Mets on Banner Night

What a relief it was for the Mets to start the month of August facing the worst team in baseball. The Philadelphia Phillies have lost nearly twice as many games as they've won. And the Mets got to face them twice last night in a double-header at Shea on banner night.

Banner night was a brilliant idea that the Mets started in 1963, to give fans something to get excited about when the team on the field was the laughingstock of baseball history. The early Mets set records in futility that might stand for a century.

On banner night, any fan that created a banner could line up to march onto the field in between a double-header to share their creation and perhaps win the prize for the best Mets banner.

The First Game - Before the Banner Night Festivities

The first game of the double-header started at 5:35pm with Jon Matlack on the mound for the Mets. Matlack, a rookie, has been stellar all season. He has a record of 10 - 5 with a 2.08 ERA and he just keeps getting better. In July, he had 2 shutouts and an ERA of just 0.86 in 5 starts.

Matlack looked sensational again yesterday retiring the first 10 Phillies batters. He allowed no runs until there were 2 outs in the 7th when he let up a home run to the Phillies' Bill Robinson. As usual the Mets weren't doing much scoring either, but they had forged a 2 -1 lead going into the 9th inning.

Banner Night Fans Line-Up

As early as the 7th inning, fans with banners began the process of lining up outside the centerfield fence. As soon as the 1st game ended the fans would have the thrill of walking into the stadium outfield to wave their banner to the Shea Stadium crowd.

Unfortunately, they had to wait longer than expected.

Much longer.

In the top of the 9th inning, the 1st Phillies batter was Don Money. He drove a Matlack pitch into the Phillies bullpen for a home run to tie the game. Matlack got the next 2 batters out. But when Bill Robinson came up, manager Yogi Berra thought it was best to take Matlack out for relief pitcher Tug McGraw.

McGraw is another Mets pitcher having a great season. His ERA stands at just 2.02. Tug got the Mets out of the inning. But with the score tied it was on to the 10th inning. And this meant the fans outside of the centerfield fence would have to hold on to their banners a little longer.

The Game Goes Into Extra Innings - Banner Night Fans Must Wait

In the 10th inning both teams sent 3 men to the plate and recorded 3 outs.

The 1st extra innings base runner was Ken Boswell who managed a walk in the bottom of the 11th. But he was stranded on first base, when Duffy Dyer popped out.

The score remained tied through the 12th, 13th, and 14th innings.

In the bottom of the 15th, the Mets finally mounted an offensive attack. Ted Martinez walked. Bud Harrelson moved him over to second on a bunt. Tommie Agee was intentionally walked putting men on first and second. Willie Mays was sent up next as a pinch hitter. But Mays stuck out as did the Mets next batter, Dave Schneck and it was on to the 16th inning.

McGraw who had pitched 6 shutout innings, his longest relief stint so far this season, was replaced by Ray Sadecki in the top of the 16th. Sadecki had an easy time with the Phillies in the 16th and 17th, but the Mets batters still couldn't get the job done.

Meanwhile the fans with the banners continued to wait.

The 18th inning brought some excitement. Sadecki got into a jam in the top of the 18th with a runner reaching third base on a single and a wild pitch with just 1 out. But Ray was able to get the side retired.

In the bottom of the 18th, Tommie Agee, in his 8th trip to the plate, hit a double and scored on a Cleon Jones single. The Mets were, at last, winners by a score of 3 - 2.

The Banner Night Parade Finally Begins

It was after 10pm, and it was finally time for the fans to march onto the field in between games. These hardy Mets fans had waited over two-and-a-half hours, some standing beyond the fence, some lined up further back under the stands, all out of viewing sight of the game, and they did it happily for this rare opportunity to walk onto the outfield grass under the bright lights and gaze up at the multi-tiered stadium seats holding 30,000 fans as they proudly held their banners high for them.

The first fan onto the field was a boy named Herbert whose banner read, *"The best banner is a Mets pennant."*

Another boy named Bob held a banner with the line, *"The Mets R Grand, we must admit, but they need a basketball to get a hit!"*

For 30 minutes about 4,000 fans marched across the field and a panel of 4 judges made notes about their choices for the best banner.

When the announcement of the winners was made, Herbert's father thought that his son had won the grand prize which was a trip for two to California. But Herbert informed his dad that he had come in 5th place and won a radio and 2 free tickets.

The Grand Prize Winner

The grand prize winner was a 3-year-old by the name of Drew Mowat. Writing in Newsday, Joe Gergen said, *"The little fellow wore a green martian costume complete with antennae and he sat inside a silver space ship."* His banner fittingly declared, *"You don't have to live in New York to like the Mets."*

Drew had no comments about his victory. When the announcement was made he was fast asleep in his mother's arms.

Wait - There's still another game!

When the banner parade was over it was time for the 2nd game of the double-header. This game featured the Mets Jerry Koosman against the Phillies Steve Carlton.

It was 11pm when the 1st pitch was thrown. Fortunately for everyone this game had the makings of a pitcher's duel.

Koosman has been one of the mainstays of the Met's starting rotation since winning 19 games in his rookie season in 1968. While the big lefty, Carlton, was a 20-game winner last year, and is having a career year this season.

Entering the game, Carlton had a record of 15 – 6, including victories in his last 10 decisions. In July, Carlton was 6 - 0 with a 1.48 ERA.

The game started as expected. In the first 8 innings Kooz allowed just 3 singles and 1 run. Carlton allowed just 5 singles and no earned runs. But the Mets did manage an unearned run when Willie Mays singled, moved to second on a passed ball and then scored on a Cleon Jones single to tie the game in the bottom of the 4th.

The score was tied in the top of the 9th when Koosman got the first 2 batters out. But then he loaded the bases on 2 singles and a walk. The next batter, Bill Robinson, doubled to drive in all 3 baserunners. The Phillies led 4 - 1.

When Carlton retired the side in order in the bottom of the 9th, the double-header finally came to an end. Carlton had his 11th straight win.

It was like a Triple-Header

Mets fans had essentially witnessed a triple-header as the two games lasted a combined 27 innings. It was 12:45am when the 2nd game concluded. With 2 veteran pitchers posting complete games, the 2nd game was like a sprint as it lasted just 1 hour and 45 minutes. But the entire 2 game affair, plus the parade, consumed a total of 7 hours and 10 minutes.

CHAPTER FIFTEEN

A Chance at a Record

50 YEARS AGO LAST NIGHT, ON AUGUST 8, 1972, WILLIE MAYS HAD AN OPPORTUNITY TO SET A CAREER RECORD

ST. LOUIS - August 9, 1972

The Mets reached a season low last night. In a year that started out with so much promise, they are now 9.5 games behind the 1st place Pirates. That marks the farthest out of first they've been in 1972.

The Mets spotted the Cardinals 4 runs last night in the 1st inning. Gary Gentry started the game and only got 2 men out before Yogi Berra had to remove him from the game.

The Same Gary Gentry

This is the same Gary Gentry who the California Angels wanted in the Jim Fregosi trade last winter. When the Mets balked at Gentry the Angels asked for and received Nolan Ryan. Ryan is now 12 - 9 with a 2.81 ERA, while Gentry is 5 - 8 with a 3.83 ERA.

Jim Fregosi, who the Mets received for Ryan, is injured and is batting .227 which puts him 7th from the bottom of all National League batters per the New York Times listing of player batting averages last Sunday.

SPECIAL NOTE FROM THE SPORTS TIME TRAVELER™

I interrupt this article for a couple of reasons. First, as you can see from the last 2 paragraphs, I'm still venting about the Nolan Ryan trade.

But more importantly, this is about to become a feel-good article about Willie Mays. I was 8 years old when the Mets acquired Mays early in the 1972 season. I felt it was a special thing to have Willie Mays on "my team." I keep finding out just how special it really was the more I learn about the Say Hey Kid.

Recently my great friend Mark told me to read the new autobiography by Willie Mays written with John Shea. It's a sensational and easy read. The book is titled, "24." It also includes an introduction by Bob Costas.

Here is the link to the book on Amazon: https://www.amazon.com/2 4-Life-Stories-Lessons-Say/dp/125023042X

I also found another special gem about Willie Mays when I read the newspapers today about the Mets game from 50 years ago last night. I'm about to share it with you in a moment.

First, let's go back to the recap of the game played on August 8, 1972, in St. Louis.

The Mets clawed their way back and took a 5 - 4 lead in the 6th inning. The Mets were still ahead last night 5 - 4 in the 8th inning, when the Cardinals Luis Melendez hit a 2 run homer that proved to be the game winner in a 6 - 5 Mets loss.

Willie Mays Sets a Career Fielding Mark

There was some consolation for Mets fans in this game. Willie Mays started the game in centerfield with 7,152 career chances, just 3 behind Tris Speaker's career record for outfielders. In the 2nd inning, Mays caught 2 fly balls to give him 7,154 chances. Mays caught another fly ball in the 3rd inning to tie Speaker at 7,155.

Going into the 6th inning, Mays had not had another chance. Up to the plate came Luis Melendez (who hit the game winner 2 innings later). Melendez hit a line shot to deep center that sent Mays running. Near the fence Mays speared the ball for the out.

It was also the new major league record 7,156th chance by an outfielder. Fittingly, Willie Mays had set the record in style.

A Record That Stood for 44 Years

Tris Speaker retired in 1928, so his career record for chances by an outfielder had stood for 44 years.

POSTSCRIPT

Willie Mays finished his career in 1973 with 7,284 chances in the outfield. In the 49 years since he retired no one has approached his career record.

Mays also has the record for putouts by an outfielder.

Willie Mays is the only man to ever catch more than 7,000 fly balls in the outfield.

He finished with 7,024. And no one will break that record for quite a long time.

The career leader among active players is Andrew McCutchen, who is 61st all-time with 2,959.

Chapter Sixteen

A Classic Game for a Couple of 41's

On August 12, 1972, there was a game to remember for Mets fans as they battled for 2nd place in the NL East at Wrigley Field

WRIGLEY FIELD - August 12, 1972

Number 41 on the Mets is "The Franchise" - pitcher Tom Seaver. And Willie Mays is 41 years old but still playing centerfield like the Say Hey Kid... sometimes.

Both of them were in classic form yesterday afternoon at Wrigley Field in Chicago. And so were other Mets stars Tommie Agee and Tug McGraw.

Dick Young was at the game for the New York Daily News. He wrote that, *"the only thing that prevented this contest from being a memorable game is that the two teams are fighting for 2nd place, not 1st."*

George Langford of the Chicago Tribune wrote, *"For pure entertainment, baseball will seldom put on a better show than the Mets and Cubs staged yesterday for 32,229 customers at Wrigley Field. Even the umpires contributed to the suspense."*

NOTE From The Sports Time Traveler™

I made the virtual trip back to experience yesterday's 1972 Mets vs. Cubs game just because I'm following the '72 Mets every day. I wasn't expecting something this special.

Now let's find out just what made this such a memorable game 50 years ago at Wrigley.

A Game for Second Place

The Mets and Cubs entered the game separated by just 1 game. Unfortunately, they're both about 10 games behind the NL East leading Pittsburgh Pirates who have the best record in baseball at 66 - 39.

The Mets were 9.5 games out at 56 - 48 and the Cubs were 10.5 back at 57 - 51 entering the afternoon contest. A Cubs win would put them in a tie for 2nd with the Mets just percentage points ahead.

Hooton Starts Strong for the Cubs

The Cubs had pitcher Burt Hooton on the mound. The 22-year-old rookie throws a knuckle curve ball. And while his record is just 7 - 9, his ERA of 2.71 demonstrates just how hard he is to hit against.

Hooton must have been baffling to Mets hitters in the top of the 1st. He struck out leadoff batter Tommie Agee, then struck out the number 2 hitter Wayne Garrett.

Mays - 1st Plate Appearance

Next up was Willie Mays who drew a walk. But clean-up batter Cleon Jones also struck out and so after half an inning it was Tom Seaver's turn to take the mound.

Seaver Matches Hooton

Seaver also started out strong. He struck out the leadoff hitter Don Kessinger, walked Jose Cardenal and got Billy Williams to ground into an inning ending double play.

Williams, by the way, is a triple crown threat. With a line of 24 HRs / 76 RBIs / .340 average, he's near the NL lead in all three categories.

Mays - 2nd Plate Appearance

Hooton and Seaver continued their pitching duel, and the score was 0 - 0 when Willie Mays came to the plate with 2 outs in the top of the 3rd and Wayne Garrett on 2nd.

Mays hit a long drive towards the centerfield fence. But according to Dick Young the wind was coming straight in and held the ball up. Cubs centerfielder, 6'3", Rick Monday, made a leaping catch at the wall for the out.

Mays later said, *"That was the best ball I hit all day."*

Seaver Gets Into a Jam

In the bottom of the 3rd inning, Seaver got into his first jam. After getting the first 2 batters out he gave up consecutive singles to Kessinger and Jose Cardenal and then walked Billy Williams to load the bases. But then he got clean-up hitter Jim Hickman to strike out to retire the side.

Seaver described the 3rd strike after the game, *"That pitch to Hickman was probably the best pitch I've thrown all year. It was a fastball that just exploded."*

NOTE From The Sports Time Traveler™

I interrupt this article for a moment to ponder Seaver's comment. Imagine what that pitch must have been like for a perennial all-star, Tom Seaver, to say it was the best pitch he's thrown all year.

Now back to the game in 1972.

Mays - 3rd Plate Appearance

The Mets *"were doing nothing against Hooton,"* according to Alan Solomon, a Newsday special correspondent. The Mets had *"scattered four harmless singles,"* and the score was still 0 - 0 when Willie Mays made his 3rd trip to the plate in the top of the 6th.

Here's how Alan Solomon described the play, *"(Willie Mays) lined a knuckle curve, that neither curved nor knuckled, over the right field wall. It was home run No. 6 for Mays this year and No. 652 lifetime."*

Mays home run put the Mets in the lead. Mets 1, Cubs 0.

Seaver Finally Yields a Run

The Cubs got on the board in the bottom of the 6th. Jose Cardenal led off with a fly ball to left. Cleon Jones dove for the ball and caught it, but it jarred loose when he hit the ground, according to Dick Young, and Cardenal was on second with a double.

Then with 2 outs Ron Santo hit a liner to left and Jones dove again but could not catch it. Santo's double scored Cardenal to tie the game 1 - 1 after 6 innings.

Umps Rob the Mets

In the top of the 7th, Duffy Dyer was on second with 2 outs when Tommie Agee hit a little *"squibber,"* towards first base, according to Dick Young. The ball went through Jim Hickman's legs and second baseman Glenn Beckert got it and threw to Hooton who ran over to cover first, but was not in time to beat Agee.

Meanwhile Dyer raced for home and Hooton, alerted by the screams from the crowd, fired the ball to the plate. The throw was high and catcher J.C. Martin had to leap for it. He then made *"a sweeping attempt to tag Dyer,"* as he was sliding into the plate, according to Al Harvin in the New York Times.

Umpire Ed Vargo yelled *"safe!"* But then he immediately changed his mind and yelled, *"out!"*

Manager Yogi Berra tore out of the dugout screaming. Vargo insisted Martin had tagged Dyer on the shoulder.

Dick Young wrote, *"The TV showed he missed by a foot."*

Incredibly, George Langford of the Chicago Tribune noted that, *"A couple of the Cubs even indicated that Duffy Dyer of the Mets had been safe at home plate."*

The game remained tied 1 - 1 in the 7th.

Mays - 4th Plate Appearance

Mays came up again in the top of the 8th. There are varying accounts about exactly what happened.

Harvin said, *"Mays hit a shot over the ivy in left."*

Solomon said Mays, *"hit another ball that looked like it would go out. The ball appeared to land in a screened in portion atop the bleacher wall, then bounced out."*

Dick Young reported, *"It hit behind the net said a man in the nearby Cubs bullpen."*

According to Langford of the Chicago Tribune if the ball lands in the basket above the left field wall it's a home run. And Langford said that is what happened.

Umps Rob the Mets Again

But umpires Harry Wendlestedt and Jerry Dale saw it differently. They ruled the ball hit off Rick Monday's glove.

And Mays was robbed of his 2nd homer of the game (3rd homer if you count the shot to center in the 3rd inning that was caught at the wall after the wind drove it in).

There was even a dispute as to what the umpires' actual ruling was. Harvin in the New York Times said the umpires ruled the ball had hit the wall.

The outcome, however, didn't change. Mays was on second with a double, not a home run, and the Mets couldn't drive Mays home.

The game remained tied 1 - 1 in the middle of the 8th.

The Games Goes to Extra Innings

Both Seaver and Hooton remained strong, and the score was still tied after 9.

In the top of the 10th, Tommie Agee, the first batter, hit a 2 – 1 Hooton pitch into the 2nd row of the left field bleachers.

This was a clear home run, and the Mets were up 2 - 1.

Mays - 5th Plate Appearance

Mays came up two batters later. He hit a ground ball single into centerfield, but showing his incredible speed and baserunning savvy he managed to turn it into a double.

Hooton was finally taken out of the game and 2 different Cubs relief pitchers got the final 2 outs.

The Bottom of the 10th

Tom Seaver came out to the mound to start the 10th inning to try and close out his 13th win of the season. But the 1st batter, Paul Popovich, hit a triple.

With the winning run coming to the plate, Berra went to the mound and asked Seaver how he felt. Seaver said, *"tired,"* according to Solomon in Newsday. That was all Berra needed to hear. Seaver had pitched a strong game, going 9 innings and allowing just 1 run and striking out 9.

Berra decided to bring in his ace reliever, lefty, Tug McGraw, even though the Cubs were sending 3 right-handed batters to the plate. McGraw is in the midst of a great season with an ERA of just 1.86 entering the game.

McGraw got Tommie Davis out on a foul pop fly.

McGraw got Don Kessinger on a grounder to 3rd.

Then McGraw got Jose Cardenal to hit a weak fly to center.

Willie Mays grabbed the ball, and the game was over.

Mets win 2 - 1. And boost their lead on 2nd place over the Cubs to 2 games.

What a game for Willie Mays!

Mays was inches away from having a 3 home run game plus a double. He hit home run worthy balls to all fields - right, center and left. He had reached base 4 out of 5 trips to the plate and the one time he didn't, was his hardest hit ball of the day.

5 times Mays had come to the plate and each time he had entertained the crowd. This was a classic game for Willie Mays at age 41.

POSTSCRIPT

At this point in the season, Mays was batting .283 for the Mets with a .430 OBP in 193 plate appearances. He's also been setback by nagging muscle strains.

Mets fans at the time might not have realized how well he was hitting because the New York Times only reported Mays season totals in their daily Mets statistics.

Since Mays had gotten off to a horrid start with the Giants before the trade, when he was batting just .184, his total numbers for the season didn't look so good.

Is this the high point for Willie Mays on the Mets? I don't remember and I won't look ahead.

By the way, Wrigley Field was very good to Willie Mays during his career. He had 691 at bats in Wrigley in 179 games (a little more than one season's worth of games) and his line there was 54 HRs / 146 RBIs. / .342 average.

The Sports Time Traveler™ is going to continue following the Mets each day, 50 years ago, and will report to you again when there is something compelling to share.

CHAPTER SEVENTEEN

Seaver Plunders the Pirates' Champagne

THE PITTSBURGH PIRATES NEED ONE WIN TO TAKE THE 1972 NL EAST DIVISION TITLE, BUT TOM SEAVER KEPT THEIR CHAMPAGNE ON ICE.

SHEA STADIUM - September 21, 1972 -

The Mets are out of the pennant race earlier than any time since 1968. They're in 3rd place in the NL East with a 74 - 68 record, 15.5 games behind the division leading Pirates.

The Pirates have the best record in baseball at 90 - 53 and enjoy an 11.5 game lead over the Cubs with 12 games to go in this strike shortened season.

It's a foregone conclusion that the Pirates will win their 3rd straight East Division crown. It's just a matter of when and where they will do it.

Last night, the Pirates had 4 cases of champagne waiting in the visiting team locker room in Shea Stadium for their division title celebration.

Tom Seaver made sure that the Pirates didn't taste a drop.

Seaver pitched one of his best games of the season, which was somewhat surprising given his last start was one of the worst of his 6 year career. In Chicago last Saturday afternoon, Seaver gave up 8 earned runs in just 2 and 1/3 innings in the Mets 18 - 5 loss.

That was the largest margin of defeat in Mets history.

Against the Pirates last night, Seaver started out shaky again. The Pirates lineup is the best in baseball. The first 7 batters are collectively hitting over .300. The 1st batter in the game, Vic Davillilo, hit a shot to centerfield for a triple. The 2nd batter, Rennie Stennett, hit a single. The Pirates led 1 - 0, with nobody out and the next 2 batters were Roberto Clemente and Willie Stargell. Things didn't look good for Seaver.

Tom Seaver then demonstrated why he is one of the elite players in the game and why he is deserving of the nickname - "The Franchise." He struck out Clemente. Then he struck out Stargell. And after the Stargell strikeout, Stennett was caught stealing at second.

Tom Terrific was out of the first inning with just 1 run scored.

After that Seaver was basically untouchable. In the next 7 innings he allowed only 3 hits and struck out another 10 batters.

Then in the 9th inning Seaver got even better. He struck out the 1st batter, Roberto Clemente. He struck out the 2nd batter, Willie Stargell. And finally, he struck out the 3rd batter, Richie Zisk to end the game.

Seaver notched his 18th win with a 5 hit, 15 strikeout masterpiece.

Bob Smizik, writing for the Pittsburgh Press said, *"The Pirates were ready to uncork the champagne. Unfortunately for them, Tom Seaver was ready to uncork his lethal right arm."*

Seaver is disappointed with the Mets finish this year, and his own inconsistent pitching, but he voiced an optimistic tone about the impact of his performance last night. *"I'm supposed to be the #1 pitcher. It's good for the team if the players know over the winter that I'm still the kind of pitcher I'm supposed to be."*

CHAPTER EIGHTEEN

1972 SEASON WRAP UP

The Pirates clinching of the NL East was inevitable as they held an 11.5 game lead over the Cubs and 15.5 game over the Mets after the September 20, 1972, game in which Seaver mowed down the Pirates great lineup.

The next day, Gary Gentry allowed 4 earned runs in just 2 innings of work and the Pirates beat the Mets 6 – 2 to clinch the division.

Here were the final standings in the NL East in 1972

96 – 59 Pirates

85 – 70 Cubs

83 – 73 Mets

75 – 81 Cardinals

70 – 86 Expos

59 – 97 Phillies

The Pirates finished with the best record in baseball, but lost a tough 5 game NL Championship Series to the Reds.

The American League division winners were Oakland and Detroit. They played in a tight AL Championship Series.

In the next series of articles, I followed The A's Ted Kubiak, a Highland Park, NJ native, and a friend of my family, through his key moments in the 1972 American League Championship Series and the 1972 World Series.

The Mets 1972 season which had started out so magically, with the acquisition of Willie May and a 25 – 7 record in late May, were beset by injuries and a lack of hitting. The Mets finished last in batting in the NL at .225.

Willie Mays cooled off after his sensational start with the Mets. In his first 5 weeks with the Mets he batted .325 and had an OBP of .508. For the entire season with the Mets his batting average leveled off to .267. But that was good for 3rd best on the team for all players with more than 200 plate appearances.

And Mays led the team with an OBP of .402, which was actually the 2nd best in the National League.

May was also 2nd on the Mets in HRs per at bat, behind only John Milner.

Mays was much more productive at the plate than regular center fielder Tommie Agee, who batted just .227 for the season.

I mention all of this because the narrative on Willie Mays for the past 50 years has been that he was washed up when he came to the Mets.

Although Mays was a fraction of the player he had been in his prime, on the Mets he was a very productive team member.

CHAPTER NINETEEN

Kubiak's Biggest Little Hit

WITH THE METS DONE FOR THE YEAR IN 1972, THE SPORTS TIME TRAVELER™ IS FOLLOWING TED KUBIAK OF THE OAKLAND A'S IN THE POST SEASON

NOTE From The Sports Time Traveler™

A few months ago I wrote an article about Ted Kubiak, a utility infielder who played 10 years in the major leagues and was a close friend growing up of my cousin Alan in Highland Park, NJ.

Now I've traveled back in time to Detroit in 1972, to watch Ted play in game 4 of the 1972 American League Championship series pitting the Oakland A's against the Detroit Tigers. The A's lead the series 2 games to 1 in this best of 5.

A win today would put the A's in the World Series for the first time in 41 years.

Now let's go back to Detroit on October 11, 1972.

DETROIT - October 11, 1972

Ted Kubiak was not the starting shortstop for game 4 of the ALCS championship today. Dal Maxvill, a veteran shortstop, who was the starter on the Cardinals World Series championship team from 1967, got the start when the injured Bert Campaneris, the regular shortstop, could not play today.

The game was a pitcher's duel between Jim "Catfish" Hunter and Mickey Lolich. Through 7 innings the score was tied at 1 – 1. As manager Dick Williams often does, he brought in Kubiak late in the game for defensive purposes.

After 9 innings the score remained tied at one.

In the top of the 10th, Tigers relief pitcher Chuck Seelbach gave up a 1 out single to pinch hitter Gonzalo Marquez and that brought up the top of the order for the A's. Leadoff man, Matty Alou, promptly hit a double driving in Marquez and giving the A's a slim 2 - 1 lead, and he took third base on the throw to home plate.

Now up to the plate came Ted Kubiak for his 1st at bat of the game. Here was a golden opportunity to give the A's an insurance run that would put them in prime position to close out the Tigers and head to the World Series.

All of northern California must have been on the edge of their seats as they watched the TV broadcast of Ted Kubiak's turn at bat in the 10th inning.

Let's see what happened next. Go to the 2:30 mark of the video to watch Ted Kubiak at the plate:

https://www.youtube.com/watch?v=-ZU9CF6pMUs&t=150s

Kubiak's fly ball to shallow right could not be caught by hall of famer Al Kaline, and was good for a single. The hit drove in Matty Alou from 3rd base and put the Oakland A's up 3 - 1. The team was now just 3 outs away from going to the 1972 World Series.

That had to be one of the biggest little hits of Ted Kubiak's career.

Unfortunately, in the bottom of the 10th inning the Tigers pulled off a minor miracle as they scored 3 runs and won the game 4 - 3. The victory tied the series at 2 games apiece. You can see the finish of the game by watching the end of the above video.

Tomorrow at Tiger Stadium will be the winner-takes-all game to go to the World Series. The Sports Time Traveler™ will be staying here in Detroit, in 1972, for 1 more day to see what happens and to see if Ted Kubiak gets another chance to play in the late innings.

CHAPTER TWENTY

Kubiak Cuts Down Rose and the Reds

50 YEARS AGO LAST WEEKEND, TED KUBIAK'S INFIELD PLAY ON PETE ROSE WRAPPED UP GAME 1 OF THE 1972 WORLD SERIES FOR THE OAKLAND A'S

CINCINNATI - October 15, 1972

The 1972 Oakland A's have a special character about them that is readily apparent when you look at the players. Most of them are adorned with mustaches. It's the result of an idea from A's owner, Charles O. Finley, who offered every player $300 who grew a mustache.

The Cincinnati Reds on the other hand, are a more conventional group. Reds manager Sparky Anderson recently said, *"Millions of kids see our ball club on television, I want them to see neat, well-disciplined men."*

Newspapers have billed the series as the mods vs. the squares.

Series Oddsmakers Favor the Reds

Prior to game 1 of the 1972 World Series, Jimmy the Greek had the squares (the Reds) as the 7 - 5 favorite. The Big Red Machine had just knocked off the team with the best record in baseball, the defending champion Pittsburgh Pirates in the NLCS. And A's superstar Reggie Jackson is out for the World Series, having sustained a torn hamstring in the ALCS victory over the Detroit Tigers.

While missing Jackson's bat is an enormous blow, the A's strength is pitching and defense. They allowed just 2.95 runs per game, 2nd lowest in the major leagues behind the Baltimore Orioles. And every A's starting pitcher posted an ERA under 3 this season, including game 1 starter Ken Holtzman who sported 19 wins to go along with a 2.51 ERA. Holtzman also no-hit the Reds last season when he was pitching for the Cubs.

Pete Rose yelled to Holtzman before the start of yesterday's game, *"Don't pitch no more no-hitters at us."*

NOTE From The Sports Time Traveler™

Watching at home when I was 9 years old in the Fall of 1972, I couldn't help but wonder what it would be like to see "my team," The New York Mets in the World Series. It felt like a fantasy that would never happen. I knew the World Series was reserved for the power house teams like Pittsburgh, Cincinnati, Baltimore and Oakland.

The 1972 World Series Begins

Game 1 was a low scoring affair.

The Reds manufactured 2 runs in the first 4 innings, with both runs scoring on ground outs.

The A's got 3 runs in the first 5 innings, all of them driven in by the surprise slugger of the day, catcher Gene Tenace. Tenace had hit just 5 home runs all season, but he went deep twice in just the first 5 innings off Reds starting pitcher Gary Nolan. His 1st was a 2 run shot in the 2nd. And his 2nd homer was a solo shot in the 5th that put the A's up 3 - 2.

And that's how the score remained until the bottom of the 9th inning.

The A's brought in Vida Blue as a relief pitcher in the bottom 7th. Blue, the dominant pitcher in baseball in 1971, had not saved a game in the entire regular season, but manager Dick Williams had brought him in to save the decisive game 5 of the ALCS. Now Williams was banking on Blue again to close out game 1 of the World Series.

Williams also brought in Ted Kubiak to play 2nd base in the 8th inning.

Bottom of the 9th - A's lead the Reds 3 - 2

Hal McRae led off the last of the 9th for the Reds with a single. George Foster was brought in as a pinch runner.

The next batter, Dave Concepcion, bunted Foster over to 2nd base.

Now there was 1 out in the bottom of the 9th and the tying run was on 2nd base.

The next batter, Julian Javier, hit a grounder to Ted Kubiak at 2nd base. Ted tossed it to 1st base for the out. Foster moved to 3rd base on the play.

Bottom of the 9th - 2 Outs. A runner on 3rd. Pete Rose at the Plate

The next batter was Pete Rose. George Foster stood on 3rd base as the potential tying run.

NOTE from The Sports Time Traveler™

I interrupt this article to put Rose's at bat in the bottom of the 9th in context.

Rose is perhaps the fiercest competitor in the game. And this is arguably the most important at bat of his career-to-date. The two-time batting champ is in his prime at age 31, having just completed his 8th consecutive year batting over .300.

But Rose is hitless in 4 earlier trips to the plate today.

He has the opportunity to tie or win the game. And if he doesn't come through the Reds lose game 1 of the World Series on their home field, giving away their home field advantage. It's an unusually large home field advantage because the Reds, a National League team, play on astroturf, which is common in the NL but a rarity in the American League (only the White Sox infield is made of astroturf in the AL).

In 10 seasons, Rose's Reds teams have NEVER won a World Series game at home, and in fact they have won just a single World Series game. That was 2 years ago when, down 3 games to none, the Reds won the 4th game of the 1970 World Series in Baltimore, on their way to losing the series to the Orioles 4 games to 1.

This is a climactic moment for Pete Rose.

Now back to October 14, 1972, in the bottom of the 9th with two outs, George Foster on 3rd base and the A's leading the Reds 3 - 2.

A's manager Dick Williams called for Sal Bando to play in to guard for a bunt. And Rose did try to bunt on the 1st pitch and punched it foul.

The unusual move in this critical situation prompted the radio announcers to comment that Rose won one of his batting titles on a bunt hit in the last game of the season.

Now Bando signaled to catcher Gene Tenace that if the ball comes to him, he's going to throw to the plate.

Here's the radio call of the next play:

"One strike, the count on Rose. Vida Blue winds, here's the pitch. High hopping ball on the infield, they're going to have to hurry, Kubiak has got it! Throws to first. He got him! And the Oakland A's have won the 1st game of the 1972 World Series. The final score of an exciting ball game, Oakland 3 and Cincinnati 2!"

You can hear that and the radio call of the entire game by searching on YouTube for, "1972 World Series Game 1."

The Central Jersey Home News, near Ted Kubiak's home town of Highland Park, NJ wrote about the exciting finish to the game:

"Kubiak, the only graduate of Highland Park High School to make the major leagues, was a key factor in Oakland's opening victory. With the tying run on 3rd base, Kubiak charged a slow roller and threw to 1st baseman Mike Epstein for the final out of the game.

Kubiak said, "The play probably would have been harder on regular turf because I would have had to play a short or in-between hop. On the Astro turf, the ball just took a high hop."

POSTSCRIPT From The Sports Time Traveler™

The next day the New York Daily News ran a story about the last play of the game from Pete Rose's perspective which read, *"Pete Rose believes Ted Kubiak's inexperience playing Astroturf cost the Reds a chance to tie in the ninth. With two out and a runner on third, Rose hit a hopper to second and was thrown out by Kubiak."*

"'If he had played in the National League all year,' Rose said, 'he'd have known you have to play deeper on Astroturf to keep the ball from going through. And if he had played deeper, I would have beat the ball out. If the ball takes one more hop, I beat the ball out and we have a tie game.'"

A couple of days later the San Francisco Examiner gave Ted Kubiak an opportunity to respond to Pete Rose about the final play of game one. Kubiak defended any notion that he was playing out of position when he fielded the final out to win game one, *"Horsefeathers. We know that in a situation like that Rose is apt to bunt for a hit and the second baseman has to be prepared to cover the bag at first."*

The Sports Time Traveler™ Discusses the Final Play with Ted Kubiak 50 years later

I had incredible opportunity to discuss the final play of game 1 of the 1972 World Series with Ted Kubiak on the 50th anniversary weekend via telephone.

Here's what Ted recalls:

"I made it a point to always position myself in the center of the total area I needed to cover depending on what I knew of the hitter, our pitcher, the field, the inning, the possibilities that could occur, etc.

The ball Rose hit was a high bouncing ball, I don't know how he thought it might be a hit. Unlike today's infielders who play back on the edge of the outfield grass because of how the game has changed, I never wanted any hitter to beat out a slow roller or a bunt...I had pretty good success.

Our scouting report on the Reds that season was extensive, plus our pitchers had such great control, positioning the opposition was easy."

Maybe he thought he should have beaten it out. I thought his comment was ridiculous but that's Pete. He is a different kind of guy. I played against him my first year in the minors when he hit 30 triples in the big ballparks in The Florida State League. He was an opposite field gap hitter. I marveled the first time I saw him sprint to first on a walk."

Ted Kubiak's Baseball Books Now Available on Amazon

FYI - Ted Kubiak has written two excellent books on baseball and has another coming out soon.

"Old School: The Evolution of America's Pastime," is a fascinating account of how the game has changed from the perspective of a man who has been involved in professional baseball as a player, manager and instructional consultant for 60 years.

You can order the book on Amazon by searching "Old School Ted Kubiak."

Ted's 2nd book is an instructional book for infielders titled, **"How to Field a Ground Ball: An Ultimate Guide for Infielders".** It should be required reading for anyone playing the infield positions.

You can also order "How to Field a Ground Ball," on Amazon.

CHAPTER TWENTY-ONE

Tommie Agee: "They Didn't Want Me Anymore"

THE NEW YORK METS TRADE ONE OF THE HEROES FROM THE MIRACLE 1969 TEAM

NOTE from The Sports Time Traveler™

At the time this article was written the current Mets news was that Jacob DeGrom was signing with Texas. The Mets brass let their franchise pitcher go away. It was a gut punch to Mets fans.

50 years ago this week there was a similar sorrow among Mets fans, when it was announced that one of the main heroes from the Miracle of 1969, Tommie Agee, had been traded.

Here is my report from my virtual trip back to the winter baseball meetings in 1972.

HONOLULU, HI - December 2, 1972 -

The Sports Time Traveler™ is in Hawaii, virtually, at the 1972 baseball winter meetings to unravel a shocking story for Mets fans. The Mets management have quit on Tommie Agee, giving him away for a pittance.

THE COLD FACTS

Tommie Agee was traded to the Houston Astros on November 27th for two minor league players, outfielder Rich Chiles and pitcher Buddy Harris, both of whom played AAA ball in Oklahoma City last year.

Both players had a whiff of major league experience in the past.

In 1971, Chiles played 67 games for the Astros and batted .227.

In 1970 and 1971, Harris pitched 37 innings for the Astros and had an ERA of 6.32.

Meanwhile Agee spent the last 5 seasons playing 661 games for the Mets, mostly as their starting center fielder and often as the leadoff hitter. In the recently concluded 1972 season, Agee was the club leader in hits, doubles and extra base hits despite starting only 108 games due to injuries.

SO HOW DID THIS HAPPEN?

The short story is that the Mets felt the 30 year old Agee could no longer play centerfield at a high level, and it was time to move on. And apparently no other team was willing to trade a big league player for him.

There is much more to this unraveling story that we'll dive into in a little bit, but first let's celebrate the man, because Tommie Agee will forever be right up there with Tom Seaver, Jerry Koosman, Tug McGraw, Bud Harrelson and Cleon Jones as one of the heroes of the 1969 Miracle Mets.

TOMMIE AGEE - AN EPIC HERO FROM 1969

In 1969, Agee was the team leader in home runs, runs scored and runs batted in, as the Mets won 100 games and captured the National League East crown.

He was 6th in the MVP voting in the National League. The only Mets player ahead of him was Seaver (who narrowly lost the MVP award to Willie McCovey).

In the NLCS, Agee batted .357 and hit 2 home runs as the Mets swept the Braves in 3 games to win the pennant and move on to the World Series against the Orioles.

GAME 3 OF THE 1969 WORLD SERIES

Then came the big game of Agee's life - game 3 of the 1969 World Series. The game that made him a legend in New York. With the series tied 1 - 1, game 3 was pivotal.

Take a look at what Tommie Agee did in game three of the 1969 World Series in this YouTube highlight video:

https://www.youtube.com/watch?v=EtgL-GX6pE8

You can easily find the video on YouTube via this search, "1969 WS Gm3: Agee homers and makes two great catches"

NOTE from The Sports Time Traveler™. I interrupt this article to let you know this 90 second highlight film is definitely worth watching - several times.

Agee almost single handedly won game 3 for the Mets. His leadoff home run in the bottom of the 1st against Jim Palmer gave the Mets an instant 1 - 0 lead.

And his 2 spectacular catches in centerfield (I never get tired of watching them) are not only all-time World Series highlights, they saved 5 runs according to the legendary announcer Curt Gowdy (listen to Gowdy say this at the 1:10 mark of the video).

The Mets won the game 5 - 0.

It's hard to understate the importance of Agee's heroics. Winning game 3 put the Mets in the driver's seat in the World Series as they went up 2 games to 1 with Seaver and Koosman slated to start games 4 and 5 at Shea.

On the other hand, if the Mets would have lost game 3, not only would they have been behind by a game to the 109-win Orioles team, but they would have needed to win 3 of the last 4 games to win the series. And they would have had to return to Baltimore and win at least one game there.

Seaver and Kooz did go on to win games 4 and 5 to complete the Miracle.

The Mets became World Series Champions in decisive fashion, 4 games to 1, over one of the most formidable teams in baseball history.

Tommie Agee was a key part of that.

And now he's gone from the Mets.

WHY THE METS TRADED TOMMIE AGEE

The man responsible for making the trade was Mets GM Bob Scheffing. The only quote Scheffing offered was one sentence to Mets beat writer Joseph Durso in the New York Times:

"I guess you'd have to say we were dissatisfied with Agee's playing."

The fact that the Mets couldn't even get a major league player in return for Agee indicates that GM's from the other 23 major league teams weren't thrilled with Agee either.

Dick Young wrote in Daily News, *"The Mets offered Tommie to just about every team in the bigs. There just was no market. His value had slipped beyond belief."*

There appears to be several factors that led to Agee's sudden demise:

He Became Erratic at the Plate and in the Field

After hitting consistently well from 1969 - 1971, Agee had wild swings in 1972. He was batting .311 on May 29th. But then hit just .153 during the month of June. He batted only .206 for the entire 2nd half of the season, including a horrific September slump in which he went 6 for 63.

He was also dropping balls in centerfield. Dick Young wrote, ***"One night in Atlanta, he muffed two or three balls... out of sheer shame he asked Yogi to take him out of the lineup."*** It should be noted that Dick Young had a shockingly harsh assessment of Agee in his final article about the former hero's trade.

He Was Slowing Down

In 1970, Agee stole 31 bases. In 1971, he stole 28 bases and was only caught six times. But in 1972, he stole just eight bases and was caught nine times.

And at least one reporter noted that Agee was putting on weight. Dick Young wrote in the Daily News, ***"From the looks of Tommie, at times, he qualified for the fatman's ballgame. He was atrociously out of shape."***

He Had Chronic Leg Ailments

Agee struggled with injuries in the past 2 seasons. After starting a team high 141 and 146 games in 1969 and 1970, Agee only started 106 and 108 games in 1971 and 1972. It was reported that prior to some games in 1972, he had to have his knee drained.

His Friendship With High School Chum Cleon Jones Had Grown Toxic

This one is a little less clear. When Scheffing was asked by Joseph Durso if he was trying to separate Agee and Jones, his reply was, ***"Draw your own conclusions."***

Agee and Mets left fielder, Cleon Jones, were born 5 days apart and knew each other well growing up in Mobile, Alabama. When the Mets were traveling they were roommates. And when the Mets were home, they were business partners in a restaurant.

Steve Jacobson writing in Newsday asserted, ***"There was a feeling in the front office that Agee and Cleon Jones, partners in the Outfielder's Lounge in Elmhurst Queens, were too close. That they'd do better without each other."***

Jacobson was able to reach Agee on the phone and asked him about whether Jones would play better without Agee on the team. Agee strongly disagreed, ***"I can't see that. I know when I do good, Cleon tries to do better. If I have a good year Cleon doesn't want me to outdo him. I think I'm going to have a good year."***

He Couldn't Handle The Crowd's Adoration of Willie Mays

This one is the most complex. Agee's woes at the plate began shortly after Mays was acquired in mid-May.

Mays, of course, played Agee's position - centerfield. And Mays played it better than anyone in his generation (and maybe better than anyone in history).

But at 41 years old, Mays was not brought in to replace Agee. He was traded from the Giants to the Mets in a benevolent baseball move by the two teams' owners to help ensure Willie would be taken care of financially after all he had contributed to the game.

Mays was also a hero of mythic proportions in New York from his playing days in the Polo Grounds in the 1950s.

When Mays arrived at Shea, the fans wanted to see Willie. And Agee, just like the fans, worshiped his fellow Alabama native.

But then an incident occurred one day at Shea that shook Agee. The crowd booed the announcement that Agee was starting in centerfield.

Agee took it personally.

Dick Young reported that Agee told GM Bob Scheffing that he found it very difficult to play with Mays on the bench. Scheffing took this to mean that Agee wanted out. However, Agee assured him he wanted to stay in New York.

But the Team was Better With Agee than Without in 1972

Despite all of the above, the fact is that in games Agee started in 1972, the Mets had a record of 61 - 47. And in games he didn't start they were 22 - 26. The Mets didn't come close to winning the division, but they were a winning ball club with Agee playing centerfield.

Agee summed it up this way in his phone call with Jacobson:

"I gave it all I had for five years. I'm very disappointed they thought so lowly of me to make that trade. It seems like they didn't want me anymore."

POSTCRIPT from The Sports Time Traveler™

Looking back now from 2022, the Mets GM and the other AL and NL GMs were right about Tommie Agee. He was finished as a ballplayer. He batted just .235 for the Astros in 1973.

In August of that year, the Cardinals, seeking extra hitting down the stretch of a pennant race, traded for Agee. But Agee couldn't deliver hitting just .177 in 26 games.

In 1974, the Dodgers brought in Agee to spring training. Agee was upbeat about the team and told his wife to move to Southern California. But before the end of March, the Dodgers cut Agee.

And he never played again.

The Los Angeles Times announced the end of Agee's career this way:

"Tommie Lee Agee, 31, has had highlights and lowlights during his 12 years in the major leagues, but the biggest blow came Tuesday when he drew his unconditional release from the Dodgers."

Neither player the Mets received for Agee was any factor for the team. Rich Chiles played 8 games for the Mets. Buddy Harris never played any.

After his playing career ended in the spring of 1974. Agee returned to New York where he owned his restaurant, The Outfielder's Lounge, not far from Shea Stadium. He was also active in youth programs and worked in the insurance industry in Manhattan.

In 1999, Agee appeared in the TV show "Everybody Loves Raymond" (season 3 episode 19) along with several other teammates from the Miracle Mets of 1969.

Sadly, Agee passed away at just 58 from a heart attack as he was walking out of a Manhattan office building on January 22, 2001.

Chapter Twenty-Two

Remembering Roberto Clemente

The Pirate from Puerto Rico perished on New Year's Eve in 1972 as he was embarking on a humanitarian mission

NOTE From The Sports Time Traveler™

Most sports fans have had at least one moment of pure ecstasy when their team pulled off the impossible. For Pittsburgh fans in December 1972, that moment was The Immaculate Reception – running back Franco Harris' miraculous touchdown to win a playoff game. Last week, I made the virtual trip back in time to cover the story.

Tragically, just one week later, Pittsburgh fans experienced the worst moment in their city's sports history, when they learned of the loss of another hero - Roberto Clemente.

Now, I'm headed back 50 years ago to Pittsburgh again, where an entire city is grieving.

PITTSBURGH, PA - January 2, 1973

Roberto Clemente of the Pittsburgh Pirates, the greatest right fielder in National League history and the MVP of the 1971 World Series, was killed in an airplane crash late on New Year's Eve while embarking on a humanitarian relief mission. Although the accident happened 2 nights ago in Puerto Rico, word did not reach Pittsburgh until yesterday.

Three Days of Mourning Declared

In Puerto Rico, where Clemente is a hero of mythical proportions, 3 days of official mourning were declared throughout the island, and the inauguration of the new governor was canceled.

Clemente - An All Time Assist Man

While most people were making party plans on the evening of December 31st, Roberto Clemente was focused on delivering aid to earthquake ravaged Nicaragua.

He wasn't a native of Nicaragua. He was the pride of Puerto Rico. But he felt a kinship with the earthquake victims 1,300 miles away who he had visited just several weeks ago.

A front-page article in the Pittsburgh Post Gazette, by Gabriel Ireton, quoted a Clemente friend, *"Clemente had devoted himself to making aid available... he was putting in 14 hours a day... when I brought him some food to eat, he wouldn't stop to eat it."*

The Mission Becomes Personal

Clemente felt that the only way to ensure the aid would get to those who needed it was to deliver it personally.

Another Clemente, friend quoted in the Post Gazette, said, *"He had received reports that some of the food and clothing he had sent earlier had fallen into the hands of profiteers."*

As a result, Clemente took over as head of the Puerto Rico relief effort and made television appeals to donate food, water, medication and clothing. He then was determined to go to Nicaragua with the plane full of supplies to guarantee its receipt.

The DC- 7 plane he boarded was known to have had mechanical problems. It took off in the late afternoon and returned immediately to San Juan International for repairs. Then hours later, it took off again, this time diving into the sea just over a mile away. The rescue team found no survivors.

The man, who is the National League career leader in assists by a right fielder, died while trying to make the biggest assist of his life.

The Great One

The headline on the editorial page of the Post Gazette today read, *"Roberto Clemente, the Great One."* The tribute to Clemente started out with his baseball accomplishments in which they called him, *"The best player who ever wore a Pirate uniform."* The editors then went on to write about the man as much more than just a baseball player:

It was not those skills alone that won Roberto an enduring place in the hearts of Pittsburgh fans. They knew that he reciprocated their admiration with a very special affinity for this city, his second home. We remember him telling a Dapper Dan banquet audience one winter a few years ago that he would never play for any team but Pittsburgh."

"The handsome young Puerto Rican was also a good family man and a humanitarian, always ready to help the needy."

"He was truly the Great One both as an athlete and a fine human being."

Reaction From the Pittsburgh Pirates

On the front page of the sports section in the Post Gazette, Pittsburgh Pirates GM Joe Brown was quoted saying about Clemente, *"He died caring. I'm sorry about baseball last. The big thing is losing Roberto Clemente, the man."*

Several Pirates players went to Brown's home and *"sat in disbelief."* Pitcher Dave Giusti said, *"I still can't believe it. I've been around other superstars. I never saw any of them have as much compassion for his teammates like Clemente did. He would treat a rookie like he was Willie Stargell."*

Brown later flew to Puerto Rico to be with Clemente's wife Vera and the 3 young Clemente boys.

Former manager, Danny Murtaugh, who guided the Pirates to 2 World Series Championship teams with Clemente on the field had this to say, *"He was the best player I've ever seen. It was typical of Clemente going out to help someone else when he had the unfortunate accident. He was an unselfish person. He always was doing things for others and never expected anything in return."*

Pirate teammate Willie Stargell echoed Murtaugh's comments, *"Clemente's work with the relief effort was typical. Roberto was always trying to help someone."*

The Best They Ever Had

In the Pittsburgh Press, Mayor Pete Flaherty was quoted saying, *"The tragic death of Roberto Clemente has saddened Pittsburgh and the entire nation."*

It was also reported that the Pittsburgh Jaycees established a Clemente-Nicaragua Memorial Fund. Karl Ohrman, the president of the Jaycees, said, *"Here's something we can do rather than gnash our teeth and wring our hands. We can help continue his work."*

The Pittsburgh Press also quoted several Pirates fans. One of them said, *"I feel Pittsburgh lost the best they ever had or will ever get."*

POSTCRIPT from The Sports Time Traveler™

When I was seven years old in 1971, I opened a pack of baseball cards one day and found myself in possession of a Roberto Clemente card. I was so excited that I ran out of my house to my friend Jerry's home to show him the card. I couldn't quite pronounce Clemente's name right and Jerry corrected me. He was also in awe of the card as well. Even though we weren't Pirates fans, we both appreciated great players. And a little over a year later we were crushed the day we found out he had died.

Roberto Clemente, for those who don't remember him, was something special on the ball field. His numbers include:

- 15 All-Star games

- 12 Gold Gloves

- The 1966 National League MVP

- Four batting titles

- 3,000 hits

He also hit safely in all 14 world series games he played in - the only man to ever do that.

But it was his arm in right field that was the most gifted part of his game. He could throw people out from right field like perhaps no one ever before or since.

Here's a one-minute video that provides a glimpse of what Clemente could do in right field:

https://www.youtube.com/watch?v=enjypJWXVQs

You can also find the video by searching in YouTube for, "Roberto Clemente Making Unbelievable Throws From the Outfield."

In March 1973, the Baseball Hall of Fame voted to make a special exception to the 5 year waiting period after a player's career, and immediately voted to induct Roberto Clemente into the Hall of Fame.

CHAPTER TWENTY-THREE

1973 Spring Training Delayed

FOR THE 2ND YEAR IN A ROW A LABOR DISPUTE IS THREATENING TO DELAY THE START OF BASEBALL SEASON

ST. PETERSBURG, FL - February 23, 1973

Last season the first ever players strike delayed the start of baseball season to mid-April.

A year later we're faced with another possible delay as the owners and players' association only agreed on a one year deal and they remain far apart in negotiations on a new contract.

Training camps cannot open without a deal and The New York Mets yesterday announced the first 2 spring training games on March 3rd and 4th have been canceled.

Meanwhile, Tom Seaver has taken the initiative to start an "underground" training camp for New York Mets players. So I have traveled here virtually to watch some of my favorite Mets players performing at the Northwest Youth Center in St. Petersburg. It's on north 22nd avenue and it's a public playground with a muddy field.

"I organized this because I wanted to workout," Seaver told Joseph Durso of the New York Times. Seaver has rounded up 10 players at this training camp including pitchers Jerry Koosman, Jon Matlack and Tug McGraw as well as first baseman Ed Kranepool and Seaver's road games roommate, shortstop Bud Harrelson.

Talking about Harrelson, Seaver told Durso, *"as soon as we're done he's under orders to get a haircut."* Harrelson indicated there was fat chance of that.

Seaver did stop by the Mets official training camp location late yesterday to pick up his mail. He told Durso, *"They said I could use the club's whirlpool bath if I brought my own water."*

POSTSCRIPT from The Sports Time Traveler™

Next month I will be in St. Pete and I'm going to go visit the playground where Tom Seaver's spring training camp took place 50 years ago.

Regarding what happens next in 1973, I know the regular season will play a full schedule. But exactly when spring training will start I have no idea. I will be keeping you posted.

CHAPTER TWENTY-FOUR

1973 METS: Re-Living the Magic

HERE'S WHY I'M GOING TO FOLLOW THE 1973 METS, 50 YEARS AGO EACH DAY. ALSO, 50 YEARS AGO TODAY: FIRST SPRING TRAINING UPDATE.

I'm embarking on an ambitious project I've been planning for several years.

I wish to re-live the New York Mets iconic 1973 "Ya Gotta' Believe" season.

I will be going back in time virtually every day from now until sometime in October to experience that season again.

I was 9 years old at the start of the season in 1973 and I was already a lifer as a Mets fan. It was prime time for a little boy to be attached to a sports team. The Mets meant everything to me in 1973.

Although the Miracle Mets had won the World Series in 1969, that was like reading about ancient history to me in 1973. It might as well have happened in Roman times. I was not yet aware of baseball in 1969. I went to my first Mets game in 1970. So, I completely missed out on the glory of the miracle.

My personal memories of the Mets began in 1970 and all I knew was that from 1970 - 1972, "we" had a very mediocre team. Great pitching. No hitting.

In the summer of 1972, when I really understood baseball completely, the Mets were mired in futility.

They did have a sensational start to the 1972 season, in which the Mets raced out to a 25 - 7 record and reached a peak of 19 games over .500 at 32 - 13.

But when school let out and I could spend time watching baseball games they went on a 34 - 50 malaise, making them one of the worst teams in the National League during that long summer (and summer seemed really, really long when I was 9 years old).

In July 1972, the Mets were barely scoring any runs. In their 26 games that month, Mets runners crossed home plate just 57 times, a little more than 2 per game.

A final surge of 17 - 10 after September 7th (when I was back in school starting 4th grade) was meaningless and made their record of 83 - 73 look a lot better than it felt. And it didn't feel good at all to finish in 3rd place, 13.5 games behind the Pirates.

None of this dampened my passion for the Mets. In fact, it only increased it. We were the underdogs. We would have to earn every victory. And maybe one day, miraculously, like the baseball history books showed me in 1969, I could watch the Mets play in the World Series. But 50 years ago on this day, that seemed like a fantasy.

At the beginning of the 1973 season, in my 9 year old mind, the World Series was only played on hallowed grounds in places like Oakland, Cincinnati and Pittsburgh. Those cities had the super teams. And, they had superstars like Reggie Jackson, Johnny Bench and even a man who was such a great star that he had "star" in his name - Willie Stargell. Boy did I wish we had a player like Willie Stargell.

We didn't have any superstars at the plate. Our top home run hitter was John Milner, a rookie in 1972, who hit just 17 home runs and batted a lowly .238.

Yes, we did have Willie Mays. It was hard to believe. He had been acquired by the Mets in May 1972, a month into the season. And I still couldn't believe Willie Mays was on "my" team.

I used to stare at Willie Mays' 1972 baseball card, showing him on the San Francisco Giants. The statistics on the back of the card were eye popping. Oh, how I wished TOPPS would reissue the 1972 card so it could show that Willie Mays was on the Mets. It didn't seem completely real, that Mays was a Met, until the 1973 cards came out. Boy, that was a tough wait at 9 years old.

I knew unfortunately that we would never again see statistics from Willie Mays like those on the back of his baseball card. This was the soon to be 42 year old Willie Mays, who had hit only 8 home runs last year, and was hanging on because he loved baseball and because New York, and especially Mets owner Joan Payson, loved him.

Mays had primarily come to the Mets, not because he had designs on playing in the World Series one more time (this surely was not the place for that), but rather because owner Joan Payson could help ensure his financial future in a way that the Giants ownership could not.

SPECIAL NOTE from The Sports Time Traveler™

I wish to share an important anecdote about Willie Mays. Back in the 1970s, we never heard of On Base Percentage (OBP). It was never reported as a statistic. It is quite astonishing to now find out, 50 years later, that in 1972, Willie Mays, on the New York Mets, was actually 2nd in the National League in OBP at .400. Only Joe Morgan of the Reds at .417 was higher. Mays only batted .250 for the season (.267 on the Mets), so you couldn't readily see that he was providing real value to the team.

Now back to the introduction.

Although the Mets had terrible hitting, we did have outstanding pitching. That was the identity of the team. I was a pitcher in little league, so it was my identity as well.

Our ace pitcher was one of the top pitchers and hardest throwers in baseball, Tom Seaver. He had performed so spectacularly in his first 6 seasons with the Mets that his nickname was The Franchise.

And we had the 1972 NL Rookie of the Year, Jon Matlack, as well as a solid 3rd starter in Jerry Koosman. Kooz battled injuries in 1972, but was still highly regarded. People with longer memories than me, stuck by Kooz because he was one of the heroes of 1969, winning 2 of the 5 games in the World Series.

Yet a question hung over the pitching staff coming into spring training. In 1972, the Mets vaunted pitching staff had only managed the 5th best E.R.A. in the National League after being 1st in 1971. Could the rest of the staff return to form?

As a result, when spring training opened in 1973, it did not appear that the Mets would do anything magical. The oddsmakers had Pittsburgh as the 6-5 favorite to capture the NL East Division title, despite the tragic loss of Roberto Clemente in an airplane accident on his way to personally deliver humanitarian aid to earthquake ravaged Nicaragua on New Year's Eve.

The powerful Pirates, who were the best hitting team in the majors in 1972, were also a 5 - 2 favorite to win the NL pennant.

The Reds were favored to win the NL West and were a 3 - 1 favorite to return to the World Series where they had lost in 7 games just 5 months earlier.

The favorite to win the World Series was last year's champs, the Oakland A's.

The Mets were not in the discussion.

And now the virtual journey back in time to follow the 1973 Mets begins...

CHAPTER TWENTY-FIVE

The Hole in Center

AS THE 1973 METS PLAYED THEIR FIRST EXHIBITION GAME, THE BIG QUESTION WAS WHO IS GOING TO PLAY CENTERFIELD?

INTRODUCTION from The Sports Time Traveler™

This is the 2nd article in my project to follow the New York Mets iconic 1973, "Ya Gotta' Believe," season day-by-day 50 years ago. I'm very excited about this endeavor and hope you enjoy the ride with me.

Below is my report on the opening game of the preseason, which took place a little way up I-275 and I-4 from St. Pete, at the spring training home of the Detroit Tigers in Lakeland, Florida.

LAKELAND, FL - March 9, 1973

The Mets defeated the Tigers in the first exhibition game of the 1973 season yesterday 4 - 3 in 10 innings.

Mets pitchers performed well against the 1972 AL Central Division champs. Jim McAndrew started and gave up no earned runs in 3 innings.

Tug McGraw followed with just 1 earned run in 3 innings. And that was without pitching any screwballs - his signature pitch. ***"We don't let McGraw throw screwballs this early,"*** explained manager, Yogi Berra.

The winning run was driven in by Don Hahn, one of a large cast of candidates for the Mets wide open centerfield position. And this brings us to the main topic of today's story.

The Conundrum in Center

Mets manager Yogi Berra said, ***"We're weak in centerfield. The job is open."***

Weak is an understatement.

The Mets have a conundrum in centerfield.

On paper it doesn't look so bad. The Mets have Willie Mays, arguably the greatest center fielder in the history of the game.

Of course, this is 41 years and 10 months old Willie Mays who has chronically sore knees and is a fraction of the legendary player he used to be.

Willie Mays - Will He Play?

Mays is in training camp, but he didn't make the short trip to Lakeland. His knees are already swollen and puffy after just a few days of working out.

Mets doctor Pete LaMotte said this about Mays' knees. ***"There is nothing to be alarmed about at this stage. It's puffed up from running after a long layoff. We'll just watch him."***

Willie isn't even certain he will play this year. He has said he's going to train for a few weeks and make a decision.

However, Mays has a big financial incentive to play. He will make $165,000 this year as a player, the highest salary on the team. If he retires, the Mets are only obligated to pay him $50,000 as a coach.

And while he may need to wear braces on his bum knees, the rest of his body looks perfect according to the New York Times columnist Arthur Daly who has known Willie since he first came up with the Giants in 1951.

Daly had this to say about Mays, *"The body is beyond belief. Almost as if he got it in Shangri-La. When he strips he shows the body of a 25 year old. His muscles are tightly drawn. He has no flab. No fat. Unless my memory was playing me false, he seemed little changed physically from what he was when I first got to know him 22 years ago."*

And as reported last week in The Sports Time Traveler™, Mays actually led the Mets in OBP last season at .400, but no one around here knows that because OBP is not a statistic anyone tracks here in 1973.

If Mays does play it will only be as a part-time player. Willie has made this clear, *"If they want somebody to play every day, then it will have to be one of the kids."*

Who Will Play Centerfield?

So, who will play centerfield for the other half of the season or more?

The question became very complicated when the Mets traded their regular centerfielder of the past 5 seasons, Tommie Agee, over the winter. Agee, one of the heroes of 1969, dropped off in performance so dramatically in the 2nd half of the 1972 season that the Mets couldn't even get a full-time big league player in return for him. Agee simply is done at age 30.

Here's the long list of candidates that will be auditioning for the position:

- Dave Schneck

- Don Hahn

- Rich Chiles

- Teddy Martinez

- George Theodore

Dave Schneck is the leading candidate on Berra's list right now. But Dick Young in the New York Daily News wasn't too enthusiastic about this 23-year-old who batted .187 in 37 games for the Mets in 1972.

"He doesn't sound like a centerfielder. A centerfielder's name has a ring to it. Willie Mays, Mickey Mantle, Duke Snider, Cesar Cedeno. Dave Schneck?

He doesn't look like a centerfielder. There are classic lines to a centerfielder. Tall. Lithe. Long striding grace. Dave Schneck is built very close to the ground. Squat. Small steps, lots of them."

Schneck however is a brave man. He spent 14 months in Vietnam. *"Eight of them shooting it out in the rice paddies of Xuan Loc,"* according to Young. And he did hit 58 HRs in the minors in the past 2 years.

But strong doubt about Schneck's value at the plate in the big leagues was raised by Mets coach Eddie Yost who said, *"He doesn't adjust to the slow stuff."* Dick Young further advanced that idea writing, *"The word got around and he took the slow boat to Tidewater."*

The Other Guys

The other candidates are perhaps even less appealing than Schneck.

Don Hahn, 24, batted .162 in 17 games for the Mets in 1972.

Rich Chiles, 23, batted .231 in 76 games for the Astros over the past 2 seasons. Chiles started in centerfield in the exhibition game yesterday and went 0 for 3.

Teddy Martinez, 25, is a utility infielder who was sent out to centerfield for 5 games last year when the Mets simply needed a body in the outfield. He batted .224 for the season.

Finally, there is George Theodore, 26, who has never played a big league game. He did have a big year in single A ball in 1971 at Visalia in the California League with a line of 28 HRs / 113 RBIs / .333 avg. But last year in AAA ball at Tidewater his production was down considerably.

Needless to say, manager Yogi Berra has a big hole to fill in centerfield.

Chapter Twenty-Six

Where's Willie?

For one day the Mets couldn't find Willie Mays

ST. PETERSBURG, FL - March 12, 1973

When Willie Mays left practice on Thursday, he didn't tell anyone where he was going. Friday was a day off for the team. On Saturday at 8am, Mays didn't show up for a full team practice. A 2nd practice was scheduled for 11:30am for Mets players that were not playing in Saturday's exhibition game. Mays was scheduled to be at that practice. He missed that one too.

Mets officials became concerned.

The team sent a search party, consisting of Mets traveling secretary, Lou Niss and clubhouse man Herb Norman, to check Willie's apartment at Broadmoor Country Club.

The 2 men knocked on the door.

No answer.

They checked the parking lot for Mays' car, easily identifiable with his "Say Hey" license plates.

They couldn't find the car.

Later that afternoon, the Mets lost to the St. Louis Cardinals 4 - 0. Mets hitters could only manage 3 hits (2 by new second baseman Felix Millan). It seems the team was out of sorts with Willie missing.

After the game, Mets manager Yogi Berra said, *"I'm starting to worry. He could be in some ditch."*

Finding Mays

Later that evening, Niss and Norman went back to Willie's apartment and breathed a sigh of relief.

Mays had just arrived back.

It turns out that Willie had flown on a 10pm flight from Tampa to San Francisco on Thursday to be with his wife Mae who is ill and lonely. He hadn't told anyone on the team he was leaving Florida.

He planned to be back in time for the Mets 8am practice on Saturday morning.

The Best Laid Plans of Mays and Men

But the best laid plans of Mays and men often go astray. Willie's late Friday return flight from San Francisco to Tampa was canceled. He caught another plane to Atlanta, but that one had a 5 hour layover. Mays didn't arrive back in Tampa until late afternoon on Saturday.

After Mets Officials Couldn't Find Mays, Berra Fined Mays

On Sunday at 8:30am Mays was at the Mets spring training facility early as usual. Berra called Mays into his office.

Later Berra said, *"I told him he was fined for two things. Leaving the club without permission and missing the workout on Saturday. He seemed down and said he was sorry."*

Mays Apologizes

Mays was quick to apologize for alarming Berra and the team. After the meeting with the manager, Mays said, *"He made his point, and he was right. I should have told him. Mostly my wife is lonesome, but she'll join me here next week.*

Later Mays reiterated his poor handling of the situation, *"It was my fault. When I'm wrong. I'm wrong. I'm not going to cop out on that."*

When asked why he didn't call the Mets, he said he didn't know the phone number and he thought he would be back before anyone knew he was gone.

Neither Mays nor Berra would comment on the amount of the fine. It is estimated to be either $500 or $1,000.

Mets GM Bob Scheffing indicated that it was Yogi's decision alone to assess the fine. Scheffing also said, *"I was really worried that something happened to him. Willie isn't the type to miss a ballgame or a workout. A banquet or personal appearance, yes, but not baseball."*

Managing a Legend

Berra seems to be in a quandary about how to manage Willie Mays. Mays has chronic knee problems and can't workout or play every day. But Berra is loathe to have 2 sets of rules, one for the team and one for Mays.

However, Berra's dilemma seems unfounded when talking to Mets relief ace, Tug McGraw. *"I don't hear grumbling from the other players. They don't resent him. They appreciate him."*

Mays still hasn't decided if he is going to play this year. He's not sure if his knees can hold up. He indicated that he is going to play his first exhibition game tomorrow and that he will make his decision in a few weeks.

NOTE from The Sports Time Traveler™

The Sports Time Traveler™ is having a great time covering the 1973 Mets spring training in St. Petersburg. I will be here the rest of the month virtually and will continue to report when there is something really compelling to share.

Chapter Twenty-Seven

Say Hey! Willie's Playing Wonderfully!

HAVING PLAYED SPRING TRAINING IN ARIZONA HIS ENTIRE CAREER WITH THE GIANTS, WILLIE MAYS PLAYS IN FLORIDA WITH THE METS FOR THE FIRST TIME

ST. PETERSBURG, FL - March 23, 1973

It makes for a quirky bit of trivia. Willie Mays never played in a major league baseball game in Florida until this year, at nearly 42 years old. His old team, the Giants, played spring training in Arizona every year that Willie was on the team from 1951 - 1972.

On March 13th, Mays was ready to play his first spring training game for the New York Mets, his first game ever in the state of Florida. And against who else - his long time nemesis the Dodgers.

Before the game, sports columnist Frank Dolson heard Dodgers long time manager Walt Alston yelling out to Willie, *"You going to play this year?"*

Willie shot back, *"Everybody asks me that. You trying to get me to quit?"*

Dolson commented about this exchange, *"The smile indicated he was kidding. But the eyes said something else. It isn't easy for a future hall of famer, a man who has spent two decades in the major leagues, to acknowledge that the fun and games are about to end."*

But perhaps not just yet.

Mays is beginning his test to see if he can still play.

If he decides he can play, he will be the part-time center fielder for the Mets.

If he decides he can't, he will retire and take up a coaching job with the club.

The Mets are leaving the decision up to Mays himself.

Dolson commented further, *"Hasn't Willie Mays earned the right to decide for himself if he can still play the game?"*

Willie started in centerfield for the Mets on this day.

Pitching for the Dodgers was Claude Osteen, a 20-game winner in 1972.

Mays First Spring Training Trip to the Plate in Florida

In his 1st at bat in the bottom of the 1st, at the Mets home in St. Pete, Al Lang Field, Mays hit Osteen's 2nd pitch deep into left field. The ball sailed over the head of left fielder Steve Garvey. On one hop the ball smacked against the fence.

Frank Dolson wrote, *"20 feet from 2nd base Mays ran out from under his batting helmet. See. Same old Willie."*

In the 3rd inning May struck out. But in the 5th he hit, *"a vicious line drive into the 3rd baseman's* (Ron Cey) *glove"*, according to Dolson.

In the field, Mays got one chance. Dolson described the play, *"Osteen lifted a soft, routine fly to center. Instantly the crowd came to life. There was a cheer when the ball left the bat. A murmur swept through the stands as Mays coasted under it. 'Watch him,' the older timers were telling the kids. 'Watch how he catches it.' Mays caught it easily, his hands cupped at his waist, and the people reacted as if he had done something very special."*

It was a classic Willie Mays basket catch.

After 5 innings Mays was done for the day. And it was a special day for Willie Mays. He had passed his first test of whether he could still play.

In those 5 innings, the fans got to see Mays exhibit 4 of the 5 tools (hitting, hitting for power, running the bases and fielding) that made Willie Mays one of the game's only complete 5 tool players. The only tool they didn't see that day was his sensational throwing arm.

Willie Mays Batting after Game 1: 1 for 3 (.333)

Mays took the day off on March 14th, but on March 15th he started in centerfield and went 1 for 3 again against the Dodgers in an away game at Vero Beach. Mays' hit came in the 1st inning against Andy Messersmith who had a 2.81 ERA in 21 starts for the Angels in 1972.

Willie Mays Batting after Game 2: 2 for 6 (.333)

The next day Berra started Mays again, his 3rd start in 4 days. The game was against the Braves in West Palm Beach.

This marked the 1st time that Willie Mays and Hank Aaron played on the same field in Florida.

In the 1st inning Mays faced Pat Dobson, a winner of 36 games in the past 2 seasons with an ERA under 2.80. Mays drilled the 1st pitch into center for a single.

In the 5th inning he faced Craig Morton, the former ace of the Expos staff, and hit his first pitch for a single.

Mays had 2 of the Mets 7 hits as they won the game 2 - 1.

Even better, Mays played without his knee braces for the 2nd straight day, *"because the knees feel good,"* Mays told the New York Daily News.

Willie Mays Batting after Game 3: 4 for 9 (.444)

After a day off, the next game was on March 18th back in St. Pete, and it was the 1st Mets spring training game Willie played that was televised in New York.

Playing against the 1972 pennant winners, the Cincinnati Reds, Mays again started in centerfield, batting 3rd.

In the 4th inning, Mays faced right hander Pedro Borbon, a relief pitcher who had appeared in 62 games in 1972 with an 8 - 3 record. He had also pitched in 6 of the 7 games in the World Series.

With the count 0 and 1, New York Times writer Joseph Durso described the next play, *"(Mays)* **lifted the 0 and 1 pitch from Pedro Borbon over the left field screen. He received a standing ovation from the 4,703 customers in Al Lang field."**

That was all for Mays on this day.

Jon Matlack was beat up by the Reds machine and lasted just 3 of a planned 5 innings enroute to an 8 - 3 Mets loss.

After the game, Mets manager Yogi Berra had this to say about Mays, *"If his knees hurt with all this work he would tell me. It was my own idea to play him 3 out of 4. You've got to find out about him, and he's got to see the pitching,"*

Willie Mays Batting after Game 4: 5 for 11 (.455)

After a couple of days off, Mays was out in centerfield again on March 21st against the Yankees at the Mets spring training home in Al Lang field.

On the mound for the Yankees was Fritz Peterson, a 17 game winner in 1972 and more recently the man involved in the most bizarre trade in baseball history.

Two weeks earlier Peterson announced that he and a fellow Yankees pitcher, Mike Kekich, were trading wives. Each of the pitchers was divorcing his wife to marry the other's wife.

In the 3rd inning, Mays came to bat against Peterson and hit his 2nd home run in 2 games. Mays also hit 2 hard outs against Peterson in his other at bats.

Willie Mays Batting after Game 5: 6 for 14 (.429) with two HRs and a double

After 5 games the question of whether Willie Mays can still play has been answered. Dick Young, writing yesterday in the New York Daily News said, *"the answer of the moment seems to be yes. Yes, Willie Mays will play. Yes, he will open in center against Steve Carlton on April 6. Willie is stinging the ball. The knees have held up. The braces have been discarded by Mays."*

POSTSCRIPT from The Sports Time Traveler™

Back here in 2023, Al Lang field is no longer the Mets spring training home. They have a beautiful facility, a shrine to the Mets team history, in Port St. Lucie, a little north of West Palm Beach now.

But Al Lang field still stands in St. Pete. It's presently the home of the Tampa Bay Rowdies soccer team that plays in the United Soccer League.

I recently made a pilgrimage to Al Lang field to honor the 50 years since Willie Mays played his only spring training in Florida with the Mets back in 1973.

Chapter Twenty-Eight

Mays Homers Again!

Willie Mays is batting .350 and leads the Mets with 3 homers in spring training

ST. PETERSBURG, FL - March 27, 1973

An amazing thing is happening in St. Petersburg. Joseph Durso reported in the New York Times today about Willie Mays and the Mets, *"For the first time they need him more than he needs them."*

In the Mets spring training camp, Willie Mays is currently the best hitter the Mets have, batting .350 (7 for 20) with 3 home runs.

Yesterday he hit a 2-run shot in the 7th inning to lead the Mets to a 5 - 2 victory over the Braves. Augie Borgi, in the New York Daily News, described Mays homer as a *"vicious shot over the left field fence."*

Mays told reporters recently he is having his best spring ever.

Think about that. This is Willie Mays, who has been playing in the majors since 1951, and he says that this is his best spring ever!

Meanwhile Jerry Koosman and Tug McGraw kept Hank Aaron hitless and allowed no earned runs and only 4 hits.

The regular season opens in 10 days on April 6th against the Phillies and Steve Carlton. Mets manager Yogi Berra expects 41 year old Willie Mays to be his starting center fielder.

CHAPTER TWENTY-NINE

Goodbye St. Pete

WILLIE MAYS FINISHES HIS FINAL SPRING TRAINING WITH A FLOURISH

FT. LAUDERDALE, FL - April 1, 1973

The Sports Time Traveler™ has really been thrilled this past month in my virtual trip to Florida following the New York Mets. While the Mets finished their Florida spring training games with a mediocre record of 9 - 11, it has been quite amazing to follow the resurgence of the "Say Hey Kid," 41-year-old Willie Mays.

Just 3 weeks ago all the talk about Willie was whether or not he would even play this season.

Now on April 1st, he stands above all Mets as the best hitter on the team and Mays is slated to start in centerfield in the opening game of the season at Shea on April 6th.

All Mays has done is bat .357 with a team leading 3 HRs and 3 doubles.

CONTENDERS OR PRETENDERS?

"Contenders or pretenders?" is the question Mets beat writer Augie Borgi posed today in the New York Daily News.

When your best hitter is 41 years old that's a problem. And Mays has made it clear he is not going to be a full-time player this year. His knees simply won't hold up for more than about 80 games. Going into yesterday's game against the Yankees, here in Ft. Lauderdale, the rest of the Mets team was batting under .230.

Rusty Staub, who got off to a great start in 1972, before he broke a bone in his right hand and missed nearly the entire remainder of the year, is a big question mark. Manager Yogi Berra said, **"I know Rusty hasn't hit much this spring. But I know Rusty has always hit when it's counted. If Rusty can't hit, we might as well forget it."**

Fortunately, Rusty claims his hand is perfectly healed. His problem is that he doesn't like spring training. **"I hate spring training. It's all work without fun. But it's necessary and I'm pleased with my progress."**

PITCHING LOOKS STRONG

The good news is the pitching staff looks ready. Tom Seaver, who was ill the first couple of weeks in March, looked sharp in his last outing and has not let up an earned run in his 2 starts against big league clubs.

The Mets are hopeful Jon Matlack, the 1972 Rookie of the Year, will be a solid number 2 starter again. Matlack went 7 innings without allowing a run in his last start.

And Yogi is very upbeat about the number 3 and number 4 starters. **"McAndrew is throwing better than he ever has. He's in midseason form already and Koosman is throwing better than he has in two years."**

Yesterday, Koosman pitched 7 innings and allowed just 2 earned runs. He was followed by the new righty relief pitcher, Phil Hennigan, who finished off the Yankees allowing no runs in the last two innings for a 7 - 2 Mets win.

Hennigan, who had a 2.67 ERA in 38 appearances last year for the Indians, is a 26 year old Vietnam veteran that the Mets acquired for 2 minor league pitchers during the offseason. He once rescued 17 Americans and 21 South Vietnamese after a mortar attack. He figures to be the top righty relief pitcher in the Mets bullpen.

There's also a promising rookie pitcher in Harry Parker. In 14 innings of spring training, he let up just one earned run. That earned him a spot on the 25-man roster, and it was good enough to win a wrist watch for outstanding rookie in the Mets spring training camp. Of course there wasn't much competition. 2nd place in the voting was out fielder / first baseman George Theodore who batted .176 this spring.

FOUR MORE EXHIBITION GAMES

The Mets now go on a barnstorming tour as they make their way up north to start the season. They will play 2 games against the Yankees in New Orleans, one in Kinston, NC and one in Norfolk, VA.

PREDICTIONS

So, are the Mets contenders or pretenders? Borgi and the other New York Daily News writers don't think they're contenders. They all pick the Mets to come in 3rd in the East. Borgi sees Pittsburgh, with their mighty lineup, despite the loss of Roberto Clemente, as the NL East champions.

CHAPTER THIRTY

1973 METS – Opening Day at Shea

TOM SEAVER FACED OFF AGAINST STEVE CARLTON IN THE OPENING GAME OF THE 1973 MLB SEASON

INTRODUCTION from The Sports Time Traveler™

Today is a big day for which I've been eagerly waiting for several years.

It's exactly 50 years since the 1973 baseball season opened. 4 years ago, after I watched the entire 1969 World Series on YouTube, I came up with a vague idea that I wanted to "re-live" the 1973 Mets experience I had as a little boy. I was 9 years old on opening day in 1973. And the Mets were nearly as important to me as my family and my dog. The 1973 Mets were a foundational part of my childhood.

I wasn't quite sure how I would accomplish this attempt at time travel when I first conceived of the idea. But I since have developed a methodology of following sports in the newspaper archives each day, exactly 50 years ago. And I never read ahead. That's a cardinal rule of sports time travel.

By following this routine, I get into a zone. I have the feeling of what it was like 50 years ago. It's the closest thing you can do in the 21st century to experience actual time travel.

50 years ago, I mostly followed the Mets in the newspapers every morning. I probably watched a couple of games a week on TV. But every morning I read about the Mets in the New York Times.

So, when I read the New York Times archive this morning about the Mets opening game on April 6, 1973, it was the exact same experience I had 50 years ago. Luckily, on a day-by-day basis, I don't remember what happened. So as part of my virtual time travels, I get the thrill (or anguish) of the game's outcome all over again.

Here's my report from my virtual trip back to the New York Mets opening day in 1973.

SHEA STADIUM, FLUSHING MEADOW, QUEENS, NY - April 7, 1973

It was 61 degrees, at 2:05pm, under mostly sunny skies, when Tom Seaver, making his 6th opening day start for the Mets, threw the 1st pitch of the New York Mets 1973 season yesterday afternoon. A crowd of 27,326 at Shea Stadium came to see the Mets face 27 game winner Steve Carlton and the Philadelphia Phillies.

Minutes earlier the ceremonial first ball was thrown out, not by one man, but by 11 men simultaneously. They were all former Vietnam War POWs.

The 1st batter, shortstop Larry Bowa, popped out to Mets shortstop Bud Harrelson. The Mets were off to a good start.

The next batter, center fielder Del Unser, hit a grounder back to Seaver, who threw to first. Two outs.

Seaver then walked Willie Montanez. He got out of the inning when Tom Hutton grounded out to John Milner at first base.

In the bottom of the 1st, Carlton issued a walk to leadoff batter Harrelson. But then got Felix Millan to hit a grounder to second, that the Phillies turned for a double play.

Carlton then got Willie Mays to hit a pop fly to first. And that was the inning.

Mets 0 Phillies 0 - End of 1st inning

In the top of the 2nd Seaver got his 1st strikeout of the season and pitched a 1-2-3-inning.

In the bottom of the inning, Cleon Jones, who struggled at the plate in 1972, got a single, marking the 1st hit for the Mets in 1973.

But Carlton retired the rest of the side.

Mets 0 Phillies 0 - End of 2nd inning

The 3rd inning went quickly as both teams went out 1-2-3.

In the top of the 4th, Seaver allowed his 1st hit, a single to Montanez. Catcher Duffy Dyer promptly threw Montanez out trying to steal second. And Seaver retired the rest of the side.

In the bottom of the inning, Felix Millan led off with a double, and Cleon Jones put the Mets on the board when he hit a fastball over the 371 foot sign in left field for a 2 run HR off Carlton.

Mets 2 Phillies 0 - End of 4th inning

In the top of the 5th, Seaver let up his 2nd hit, a double to Jose Pagan. But he struck out the other 3 Phillies he faced, giving him 6 K's through 5 innings.

The Mets went down quietly in their half of the 5th.

And the 6th inning was quiet for both teams.

Mets 2 Phillies 0 - End of 6th inning

Seaver recorded 2 more strikeouts in the top of the 7th and didn't allow a runner past first.

Seaver and the Mets did have a scare in the inning when Willie Montanez hit a 2 out line drive. Here's how Joseph Durso described the play in The New York Times, *"**Montanez hit a long drive to right center where (Rusty) Staub made a sparkling catch while crashing into the fence. Staub lay on the ground briefly, reminding the Mets of their casualties last summer, but was not hurt.**"*

In the bottom of the inning, Cleon Jones led off against Carlton. On a 2 and 2 pitch, he drilled a ball deep into center. It cleared the fence for Jones' 2nd home run of the game.

This is great news for the Mets, as Jones, one of their top hitters from 1969 - 1971, had only 5 HRs all of last season. And he's now 3 for 3 to start the season against the best pitcher in baseball in 1972 - Steve Carlton.

Mets 3 Phillies 0 - End of 7th inning

In the top of the 8th, Seaver gave up a double and a walk. With men on first and third and 2 outs, Yogi Berra decided to bring in his ace reliever, Tug McGraw.

Seaver left the game having recorded 8 strikeouts while giving up just 5 hits, 2 walks and no runs in 7 and 2/3 innings.

Tug McGraw got the 1st batter he faced, Deron Johnson, to pop up for the 3rd out.

The Mets went down on 3 straight groundouts in the bottom of the inning.

In the 9th inning Tug McGraw got 3 fast outs and the game was over.

Mets 3 Phillies 0 - FINAL SCORE

The game took just 1 hour and 56 minutes.

POST GAME INTERVIEWS WITH CLEON JONES

After the game, Cleon Jones, who went 3 for 3 and drove in every run in the game, spoke to Augie Borgi of the New York Daily News, *"There are a lot of people talking about me and I want to do something about it. I really worked my butt off to get in shape, get ready. I know I'm not going to hit 40 or 50 homers, but I'm going to bat. 300, prove something to these people and myself."*

Jones, who only hit .245 last year, had a simpler explanation for his great opening game to Joseph Durso in the New York Times, *"I'm trying harder."*

I will continue to follow the 1973 Mets day-by-day and report to you when there is something compelling to share.

CHAPTER THIRTY-ONE

Willie Mays' First Big at Bat

IN THE 2ND GAME OF THE SEASON, WILLIE MAYS HAD HIS FIRST BIG OPPORTUNITY

SHEA STADIUM, NY - April 8, 1973

I'm here in New York in 1973, virtually, covering the Mets as part of my season long project.

Yesterday afternoon was the 2nd game of the season and in his first 3 at bats Willie Mays did not get a hit. This put him at 0 for 6 for the season so far.

Mays next came to the plate in the bottom of the 7th with the bases loaded and no outs in a 2 - 2 ball game against the Phillies.

This would have been a good time to break out and return to stinging the ball all over the park as he did in the preseason in Florida.

Starting pitcher Jon Matlack was standing on third base. He had fouled off 5 pitches before drawing a walk to open the inning. Matlack was still in the game because the 2nd year starter had given up only 4 hits through 7 innings.

Bud Harrelson was standing on second base. He had laid down a perfect bunt along the first base line for a single. And Felix Millan was on first base. Millan had reached base on a comical play. He had bunted to the third base side of the mound. The ball was fielded by Phillies starter Jim Lonborg. Lonborg looked up to throw to third base for the force out, and found that third baseman Jose Pagan was right near him trying to field the ball too.

Without a ball leaving the infield the Mets had bases loaded and no outs in the 7th inning of a tie game.

Now 41 year old Willie Mays stepped in with an opportunity to do some real damage.

Mays hit a pop fly foul ball right next to the box seats. As the ball came down both catcher Bob Boone and a fan tried to grab it and the ball hit the ground.

The Phillies protested but umpire Doug Harvey refused to call fan interference.

The "Say Hey kid" had another chance to be a hero.

This time Mays hit a bouncer to third base. Pagan grabbed the ball and threw home to Boone. Boone got the force out at the plate, then whirled and threw to first base where he got Willie out. It was a double play for the Phillies.

2 - 2 Bottom of the 7th. 2 outs. Mets Runners on 2nd and 3rd.

Now Rusty Staub came to the plate. Staub had doubled and scored on a Cleon Jones single in the 3rd inning. This time the Phillies gave an intentional walk to load the bases for Jones. But Jones hit a hopper to second base to end the threat.

Matlack continued to pitch strong getting the side out on 3 straight grounders to Harrelson in the top of the 8th, and working through the heart of the Phillies line up without allowing a hit in the top of the 9th.

2 - 2 entering the bottom of the 9th

Now the Mets could win this tight game with a run.

Ed Kranepool pinch hit for Matlack and drew a walk.

Teddy Martinez replaced Kranepool as a pinch runner.

Harrelson fouled out trying to bunt Martinez over to 2nd.

Felix Millan grounded out to 2nd, but succeeded in moving Martinez over to 2nd base.

2 - 2 bottom of the 9th with 2 outs and the winning run on second

Next up was Willie Mays again with a chance to redeem himself.

Mays was now 0 for 7 for the first 2 games of the season.

Pitching now was Phillies reliefer Dick Selma. Selma had heat and averaged over 10 strikeouts per nine innings back in 1970.

With the count at 1 - 2 on Willie, Selma threw a slider outside, and Mays lunged for it. He punched it over the infield for a hit. Martinez raced around third and reached home safely.

The Mets had won the game!

Willie Mays had the winning hit!

For the first time in franchise history the Mets are 2 - 0.

GAME NOTES

First baseman John Milner got the Mets on the scoreboard in the 2nd with a solo home run. Milner, a 2nd year player, was 3rd in Rookie of the Year balloting in 1972 and led the Mets with 17 home runs. Last year he played mostly in the outfield, but this year he is going to be the primary first baseman.

Cleon Jones is now 4 for 7 with 4 RBIs in the first 2 games.

The Sports Time Traveler™ is staying right here in New York in 1973. I can't wait for game 3 of the 162 game season.

Chapter Thirty-Two

The Cards vs. KOOZ in Frozen St. Louis

IN THEIR 3RD GAME OF THE SEASON THE METS BRAVED THE COLD IN THE CARDINALS HOME OPENER

ST. LOUIS, MO - April 12, 1973

Due to scheduling quirks and snowy, freezing Midwest weather, the Mets had three days off after winning their first two games at Shea "last week."

The Mets were 2 - 0 after Seaver and Matlack won the opening 2 games of the season in New York.

But it took 4 days until the Mets 3rd game of the season could be played. The Mets had a travel day, then it snowed and finally St. Louis called off the game 2 nights ago because of cold.

Mets manager Yogi Berra, a native of the area, said he had never seen cold like that in April.

NOTE from The Sports Time Traveler™

I interrupt this article to explain just how cold it was. The temperature reached a low of 24 on the night of April 10, 1973, in St. Louis when the game was canceled due to cold.

Yogi was right. He had never seen cold like this in April. The 24 degree night remains the coldest temperature in the month of April in the history of St. Louis.

Now back to 1973.

Even last night, when the Cardinals home opener finally took place, the temperature was still in the low 40s. But that was warm enough to play ball.

However it was not warm enough to risk playing Willie Mays. Berra decided to keep the 41 year old Mays on the bench and start his new back up centerfielder, Rich Chiles.

Here was the Mets starting lineup:

1 Bud Harrelson SS

2 Felix Millan 2B

3 John Milner 1B

4 Rusty Staub RF

5 Cleon Jones LF

6 Jim Fregosi 3B

7 Rich Chiles CF

8 Duffy Dyer C

9 Jerry Koosman P

For Jerry Koosman this was a big game. It was an opportunity for Koosman to begin to reclaim his position as one of the Mets top starters, which was in doubt after 3 mediocre seasons.

JERRY KOOSMAN

Kooz was one of the big heroes of 1969, winning 2 games in the World Series, including the series ending game 5 that sealed the miracle.

In his first 2 seasons in 1968 and 1969, he was a combined 36 - 21 with a 2.20 ERA and 13 shutouts.

But in the past 3 seasons, Koosman has struggled. He's gone 29 - 30 with an ERA over 3 and just 2 shutouts. At 30 years old, there is some doubt by Mets brass over whether Koosman can still be an effective starter.

METS BATS START STRONG

As soon as the game got underway in the cold, the Mets bats were hot. The first 4 batters all singled and the Mets jumped out to a 2 - 0 lead.

In the bottom of the 1st, Koosman gave up a leadoff single to Lou Brock, but he got speedy Lou off the bases when a Ted Sizemore grounder led to a force out of Brock at second. Kooz then got out of the inning when Sizemore was caught stealing and Luis Melendez flied out. It was a good start for Kooz.

METS 2 CARDINALS 0 after 1 inning

In the top of the 3rd, Mets 1st baseman John Milner hit his 2nd HR of the season to put the Mets up 3 - 0.

In the bottom of the 3rd, Kooz gave up an unearned run due to an error by Mets 3rd baseman Jim Fregosi. The Mets still led 3 - 1.

METS 3 CARDINALS 1 after 3 innings

Koosman didn't face any real trouble until the bottom of the 4th when he gave up 2 singles and a double leading to a run which cut the Mets lead to 3 - 2.

The Mets padded Koosman's lead in the 5th when Felix Millan's triple scored Duffy Dyer, and then Millan scored on a passed ball. Mets 5 Cardinals 2.

Koosman gave up one more run in the bottom of the 6th when the Cardinals manufactured a run on a walk, a single and a groundout.

In the bottom of the 7th, Kooz gave up a leadoff double and then got the next three Cardinals out.

That was all for Koosman - seven innings and just 2 earned runs. It was a quality start.

METS 5 CARDINALS 3 after 7 innings

Berra brought in his ace reliever, lefty Tug McGraw to pitch the 8th inning. McGraw gave up a leadoff walk to Ted Sizemore. After striking out Luis Melendez, he gave up a single to Joe Torre. This put the tying run on base with Ted Simmons at the plate. Tug got Simmons to hit a grounder and the next batter to hit a flyball and he got out of the inning.

METS 5 CARDINALS 3 after 8 innings

The Mets had the bottom of the order up in the top of the 9th. Centerfielder Rich Chiles hit a pop fly. He finished the game 0 for 4. Duffy Dyer and Tug McGraw went quietly.

Now Tug was back on the mound for the bottom of the 9th, trying to close out his 1st save of the season. But Tug got into trouble. He gave up a walk and a single and had runners on first and third and 2 outs when Ted Sizemore came up. Sizemore singled to drive in a run and make it a 5 - 4 game.

Now Yogi Berra called in the Mets new right-handed reliever, Phil Hennigan, to pitch to the right handed batter Bernie Carbo. This was Hennigan's 1st appearance for the Mets and his 1st in the National League. He had played four seasons in Cleveland and had a 2.67 ERA in 38 games in 1972. Berra was hoping Hennigan could be his right-handed relief ace.

Hennigan got off to a good start in his Mets debut. He got Carbo to hit a flyball to centerfield for the final out.

FINAL SCORE: METS 5 CARDINALS 4

The Mets are now 3 - 0 and tied for 1st place with the Pirates.

The top three starters - Seaver, Matlack and Koosman all won their 1st start of the season.

1973 is off to a good start for the Mets, actually it's the best start in franchise history. No prior Mets team had ever started the season 3 - 0.

The Sports Time Traveler™ will continue following the 1973 Mets and filing stories when there is something compelling to share.

Chapter Thirty-Three

Seaver vs. Gibson

Two of the highest paid pitchers in baseball clashed in St. Louis 50 years ago last night

NOTE from The Sports Time Traveler™

I promise that I will not be writing 162 articles about the 1973 Mets. But so far this is the 4th article in 4 games. The storylines are so compelling I have to share them with you.

Here's a little gem.

ST. LOUIS, MO - April 14, 1973

Last night I dialed the sports time machine back exactly 50 years to experience a classic match up - Tom Seaver vs. Bob Gibson. They're 2 of the highest paid players in baseball. Gibson, in his 14th season, will earn $160,000 this year. Seaver in his 7th season, will earn $140,000.

In the top of the 1st, the 37 year old Gibson may have been showing his age or the effects of the cold weather, as the Mets first 3 batters reached base for the 2nd game in a row. Shortstop Bud Harrelson led off the game with a double. Second baseman Felix Millan bunted Harrelson over to third, and made it safely to first on an error. Then first baseman John Milner singled to score Harrelson and give the Mets a quick 1 - 0 lead.

After getting Rusty Staub to ground out, Gibson yielded a sacrifice fly to Cleon Jones. Mets third baseman, Wayne Garrett, then flied out to end the top of the 1st. But the Mets were already ahead 2 - 0.

In the bottom of the 1st Seaver put down the Cards 1-2-3.

METS 2 CARDINALS 0 after 1 inning

In the top of the 2nd Seaver got a single off Gibson, but this time Gibson got out of the inning without further damage.

Seaver continued to pitch strong. He didn't allow his 1st hit until Ted Sizemore led off with a bloop double to right in the 4th. Seaver stranded him there and after 4 innings it was still Mets 2 Cards 0.

The 5th inning was routine for both pitchers. Harrelson got his 2nd hit of the game to lead off, but Gibson got the next 3 batters out. And Seaver had another 1-2-3 inning in the bottom of the 5th.

METS 2 CARDINALS 0 after 5 innings

In the 6th inning there were some fireworks between the fireballers. Gibson was batting against Seaver, when Seaver threw a pitch that Gibson had to duck away from to avoid getting hit in the head. A heated exchange ensued between the 2 pitchers:

GIBSON: *"You got better control than that Tommy!"*

SEAVER: *"Remember when you threw under my helmet last year."*

After the game, Seaver told Dick Young of the New York Daily News, *"He (Gibson) also threw at Milner twice this spring and hit him the 2nd time. No matter how long he has been in the league, you can't let an opposing pitcher run you off the field or intimidate your teammates. Ask our guys who swing a stick for a living. I feel like we're even now."*

Seaver eventually struck out Gibson on his way to his 4th 1-2-3 inning. Through 6 innings Seaver had allowed just the one bloop hit.

FIREWORKS CONTINUE

But if Seaver thought he and Gibson were even, it didn't appear to be the case. In the top of the 7th, Seaver came up to bat against Gibson. Gibson threw one pitch that was over the heads of the catcher, the umpire and Seaver and hit the screen behind home plate. Another Gibson pitch made Seaver back off the plate. The other 3 pitches were down the middle and Seaver struck out.

After the game, Gibson refused to discuss the battle with Tom Seaver to the New York reporters or even the Cardinals beat writers. Speaking to Dick Kaegel of the St. Louis Dispatch, Gibson's comments were terse, **"You can say anything you want. But I won't talk about it."**

In the bottom of the 7th, Seaver began to tire. He gave up a leadoff homer to Jose Cruz. This was just the 2nd hit off Seaver and the first solid one. He struck out Joe Torre but then gave up a double to Ted Simmons. Seaver got the next 2 batters out and got out of the inning giving up just 1 run.

METS 2 CARDINALS 1 after 7 innings

In the bottom of the 8th, Seaver gave up a leadoff single to pinch hitter Tim McCarver, and this brought up Gibson again. This time there were no brush backs or bean balls. Seaver struck out Gibson as he attempted to bunt.

Seaver got Lou Brock to fly to center for out number 2. But when he walked Ted Sizemore to put men on first and second, Yogi Berra decided it was time to bring in his right-handed reliever Phil Hennigan.

Hennigan did his job. He got Jose Cruz to pop up to end the 8th and he put down the Cards quickly in the 9th.

FINAL SCORE: METS 2 CARDINALS 1

The Mets are now 4 - 0. The first 4 - 0 start in franchise history.

Seaver is now 2 - 0 with a 0.59 ERA.

CHAPTER THIRTY-FOUR

Willie Mays Injures Shoulder

MAYS, PLAYING IN JUST HIS 3RD GAME OF THE SEASON, HAD TO EXIT WITH A SHOULDER INJURY

INTRODUCTION from The Sports Time Traveler™

I previously reported to you about Willie Mays' fantastic spring training in 1973.

And last week I reported on Mays' game winning hit in the 2nd game of the season. Things looked promising for the Mets soon to be 42-year-old centerfielder.

Mays then sat out the next 3 games. He didn't play in the 2 games in St. Louis because of the extreme cold weather that hindered his ability to warm up his aching knees.

And he missed the next game in Philadelphia because of a severe dental problem for which he was being treated in New York.

We now pick-up the 1973 Mets for their 6th game of the season which took place in Philadelphia on the night of April 14, 1973.

PHILADELPHIA - APRIL 15, 1973

Willie Mays started in centerfield last night for the first time in a week as the Mets faced Steve Carlton for 2nd time this season.

The Mets got off to a good start when Bud Harrelson, the first batter of the game, drew a walk. Harrelson has now reached base leading off the game in 5 of the Mets 6 outings. But Carlton next got Felix Millan to fly out. And then he struck out Willie Mays and Rusty Staub to end the top of the 1st.

In the 2nd inning, the Mets began by tagging Carlton for 3 straight hits. The last of the 3 was a double by Jim Fregosi that scored 2 runs. Fregosi was then caught stealing 3rd and Carlton got out of the inning quickly after that.

METS 2 PHILLIES 0 - Middle of the 2nd

The Mets sent Jim McAndrew to the mound for the 1st time this season. McAndrew pitched well last year compiling an 11 - 8 record and a 2.80 ERA in 23 starts. The Mets hope McAndrew can be a solid starter in the rotation this season.

McAndrew had a good first run through the Phillies order retiring 8 of the 9 batters. Then he ran into trouble with the top of the order the 2nd time around. He gave up consecutive singles to Larry Bowa and Cesar Tovar, followed by a triple to Willie Montanez that tied the game before he got the last out.

METS 2 PHILLIES 2 - end of the 3rd

In the top of the 5th, the Phillies Denny Doyle led off with a double. The next batter was Carlton and he singled to center. Willie Mays fielded the ball. Dick Young described the play, which turned out to be the most important one of the game, in the New York Daily News:

"Mays, playing short center, winged it home, giving it all he had. Ironically, it was a terrible waste. Doyle had tripped over 3rd and stayed there. He scored on the next play, a healthy sacrifice fly.

When it came time for Mays to go to center in the next inning, George Theodore was announced instead."

Mays had hurt his shoulder on that throw from center trying to save a run.

After the game Mays told Dick Young, *"It's been bothering me off and on for a couple of years."*

Young reported that Mays has been *"trying to minimize it, hide it, so that runners won't take advantage. It can no longer be hidden... In reality it is worse than his aching knees, and could, more than the knees, cause a sudden end to his playing career."*

Before Mays came out of the game, he came to bat in the bottom of the 6th and showed why he can contribute in so many ways. He drew a walk. Then he went from first to third on Rusty Staub's single. And he scored on the next play when Cleon Jones hit a grounder. The game was tied at 3. But Mays was done for the day.

METS 3 PHILLIES 3 - middle of the 6th

In the bottom of the 6th, the Phillies erupted for 4 runs, knocking McAndrew out of the game.

Meanwhile Carlton finished the game in dominant fashion taking down the Mets last 11 batters of the game after Mays scored. The Phillies won it 7 - 3.

PHILLIES 7 METS 3 - FINAL SCORE

NL EAST STANDINGS

4 – 1 Pittsburgh
4 – 2 New York
3 – 3 Chicago
3 – 3 Montreal
3 – 3 Philadelphia
1 – 6 St. Louis

CHAPTER THIRTY-FIVE

Tom Seaver vs. Ferguson Jenkins

SEAVER PITCHES IN HIS 3RD STRAIGHT DUEL AGAINST A LEGENDARY STARTER.

SHEA STADIUM - April 18, 1973

Yesterday afternoon at Shea Stadium, the Mets sent Tom Seaver to the mound for his 3rd start of the season.

And for the 3rd time, Seaver was facing one of the top pitchers in baseball over the past decade. In the 1st game of the season, it was Steve Carlton. In Seaver's 2nd start it was Bob Gibson. He beat both of them.

In yesterday's game it was Ferguson Jenkins of the Chicago Cubs. Jenkins has had 20+ win years in each of the past 6 seasons. In those 6 seasons he's won 127 games, including 24 shutouts.

During the same period, Seaver has been nearly as prodigious, winning 116 games with 21 shutouts.

Seaver threw the 1st pitch at 2:05pm and he was sharp. It was a 1-2-3 inning. He closed it out by getting 1972 NL MVP Billy Williams to look at a called 3rd strike.

Jenkins, who was rocked for 5 runs in Pittsburgh last week, got off to a shaky start. Bud Harrelson singled to left field to lead off. Felix Millan bunted Harrelson over to second. And John Milner walked. That put men on first and second with 1 out for the clean-up hitter, Rusty Staub.

But Jenkins got Staub to flyout to left and then got Cleon Jones to hit a grounder to short and he was out of the inning.

METS 0 CUBS 0 - end of 1st inning

In the top of the 2nd, Seaver got the 4-5-6 hitters all to fly out.

Jenkins matched him in the bottom of the inning.

METS 0 CUBS 0 - end of 2nd

Seaver had another 1-2-3 in the top of the 3rd, finishing it off by striking out Jenkins. It was 9 up and 9 down for Seaver. Perfect through 3.

Jenkins returned serve again! 1-2-3 including striking out Seaver.

METS 0 CUBS 0 - end of 3rd

Seaver's dream of a perfect game ended with the 1st batter of the 4th inning. Leading off and playing centerfield for the Cubs, Rick Monday drilled one deep to right field. It cleared the fence for a home run.

After the game, Seaver told Joseph Durso of the New York Times, ***"When I threw it, I thought it was a decent pitch. But I guess it got over the plate."***

Seaver then gave up 2 walks with 2 outs before getting out of the inning.

In the bottom of the inning, John Milner, the Mets leading batter so far this season at .320, started things off with a single. Staub moved him over to second on a grounder. And Milner reached third on a passed ball.

But with 1 out and a man on third, neither Cleon Jones nor Jim Fregosi could get the run in, and Jenkins maintained his shutout.

CUBS 1 METS 0 - end of 4th

In the 5th both pitchers had 1-2-3 innings.

Seaver gave up a single and nothing else in the top of the 6th.

Jenkins went 1-2-3 again in the bottom frame.

CUBS 1 METS 0 - end of 6th

Seaver gave up 2 singles in the top of the 7th and then struck out Jenkins to end the inning.

Jenkins cruised through the Mets again 1-2-3 in the bottom of the inning.

In the top of the 8th, Seaver got the Cubs in order.

Then in the bottom of the 8th, with 2 outs and Seaver due up, Berra elected to let Tom Terrific go to bat, even though the Mets were still down a run.

Following the game Berra told Durso, *"If Seaver had led off the inning, I'd have pinch hit for him. But I told Seaver when the inning started that he'd bat if there were two down and he did."*

Seaver flew out to center giving Jenkins yet another 1-2-3 inning.

CUBS 1 METS 0 - end of 8th

Seaver gave up a single and nothing else in the top of the 9th.

Now the Mets were down to their last 3 outs with the top of the order coming up.

Harrelson hit a grounder to short for out number 1.

Millan hit a grounder to 3rd for out number 2.

That brought up 2nd year player John Milner.

Milner worked the count to 3 and 2.

A walk would put the winning run at the plate with Rusty Staub coming to bat.

On the next pitch Milner checked his swing and the ball was clearly outside the strike zone, so the Hammer, as he is called by the Mets, started trotting to first.

But while Milner was on his way to first, catcher Randy Hundley turned and had words with home plate umpire Augie Donatelli.

Suddenly, Donatelli yelled that Milner was out! He motioned with his hands that Milner had tipped the ball on his check swing which was caught by Hundley for out number 3.

Durso wrote, *"Berra shot out of the dugout to argue."*

It was for naught. The game was over.

The Mets, however, were sure there was no foul tip. They immediately went to look at the videotape in the clubhouse. The game was not televised, but the Mets tape all their games.

Red Foley of the New York Daily News wrote, *"the picture from behind home plate failed to show anything conclusive."*

Milner told Foley, *"If I tip it, I don't run to first."*

But Donatelli stuck by his decision when interviewed after the game.

CUBS 1 METS 0 - FINAL SCORE

The game took just 1 hour and 45 minutes.

Seaver had thrown 110 pitches, and gave up 5 hits, 2 walks and 1 earned run on the Rick Monday homer.

Jenkins had thrown a 113 pitch shutout. He gave up just 2 hits and 1 walk.

Jenkins also retired the Mets last 18 batters in a row.

The Mets are now 5 - 3 but are batting just .181.

Seaver, who had pitched a brilliant game sounded a little frustrated when he told Red Foley of the New York Daily News, *"You just don't like to waste those kind of games."*

Seaver (2-1) has now pitched 24 innings and given up just 2 runs. In those 3 games the Mets have only scored 5 runs.

CHAPTER THIRTY-SIX

Tormenting Tom Terrific

THE METS ARE IN AN OFFENSIVE STALL, ESPECIALLY WHEN TOM SEAVER IS ON THE MOUND.

SHEA STADIUM, NY - April 23, 1973

Tom Seaver took the mound at Shea at 1:05pm for the 1st game of a double-header on a sunny day against the Montreal Expos. It doesn't get better than this.

Seaver came into the game with a 2 - 1 record and a 0.74 ERA in his 3 starts this season. His loss was a 1 - 0 game.

Seaver is frustrated with the lack of run support he's receiving.

The Mets as a team are batting just .188, over 100 points below the MLB leading Pirates who are batting .298.

No National League team in history has ever batted below .200.

It seems that Seaver has to be brilliant just to have a chance to win a game. And he started out sensational in this game.

He put down 19 of the first 20 Expos batters.

Unfortunately, the 1 batter he didn't get out was Ron Fairly who led off the 2nd inning with a home run.

Seaver explained what happened against Fairly to Augie Borgi in the New York Daily News, *"It was a fastball that didn't move away. It was right over the plate, straight."*

That was the only run Seaver gave up. He pitched a 9 inning four hitter. His ERA after 4 games now stands at 0.81.

But going into the bottom of the 9th inning Seaver was losing 1 - 0 as the Mets only supported Seaver with 2 hits and no runs in the first 8 innings.

In the last of the 9th, Jim Fregosi led off with a walk and moved to second on a wild pitch. Jerry Grote bunted Fregosi over to third. And now Berra took Seaver out of the game for a pinch hitter. With the tying run on third and 1 out, Ken Boswell singled to center bringing in the tying run.

But that's all the Mets could do, and the game went into the 10th.

Seaver now officially had a no decision for his brilliant effort.

In the 10th, reliever Phil Hennigan immediately got into trouble and let up a run.

Down 2 - 1 in the bottom of the 10th, the Mets had their 3, 4 and 5 hitters up. Willie Mays was up first. Mays is batting just .045, after a fantastic spring training at the plate in which he hit around .350.

Mays struck out.

Rusty Staub, batting not much better at .119, flew out.

Next up was John Milner. Milner is leading the Mets in all 3 main offensive categories with 5 HRs / 9 RBIs / .341 average. But he flew out to end the game.

Mets lose 2 - 1.

Hennigan took the loss.

Tom Seaver has now started 4 games and only allowed 3 runs. But the Mets have only scored 6 in those 4 games.

After the game Seaver spoke with Murray Chass of the New York Times, *"You can't let it get you down. There's nothing I can do now. Those games are gone. You can't have a defeatist attitude. You can't be pessimistic."*

GAME 2

In the 2nd game of the doubleheader the Mets bats suddenly came alive.

After scoring just 28 runs in their first 13 games of the season, the Mets won the back end of the doubleheader in a 13 - 3 rout.

Jim McAndrew had a great start for the Mets going 7 innings and allowing just 3 hits and 2 runs to pick up his 1st win of the season.

The Mets piled up 16 hits including 3 from Ed Kranepool who got a single, double and triple and drove in 4 runs.

Even Willie Mays back up in centerfield, Rich Chiles, managed 2 hits to raise his average to .136.

The Mets are now 8 - 6 and in 3rd place 2 games behind the NL East leading Pirates who have started the season 8 - 2.

CHAPTER THIRTY-SEVEN

Ted Kubiak's Chance to be the A's Hero

THE 1973 OAKLAND A'S UTILITY INFIELDER GOT HIS CHANCE TO WIN A GAME 50 YEARS AGO THIS WEEKEND

INTRODUCTION from The Sports Time Traveler™

The Sports Time Traveler™ is following the colorful 1973 Oakland A's for several reasons, one of which is because they have a backup utility infielder named Ted Kubiak.

I previously shared the story that one of Ted Kubiak's best friends in high school was my cousin Alan and they stayed in touch when Ted spent 10 years in the major leagues.

When I was 10 years old, Alan took me to Fenway Park to see the Oakland A's play the Red Sox. And I got to meet Ted Kubiak on the field. He gave me a baseball signed by all the World Champion A's. What a thrill that was.

The Oakland A's were the team of the decade in the 1970s, with players who became household names like Reggie Jackson and Catfish Hunter.

And Ted Kubiak was on all of their World Series championship teams.

I've been loosely following the A's as the 1973 season has gotten underway 50 years ago. And over the weekend I came across a very special game for Ted Kubiak that I just have to share.

OAKLAND, CA - April 23, 1973

This past Sunday afternoon in Oakland a small crowd of 7,442 in the vast Oakland-Almeda County Coliseum came out to see their 1972 World Series Champions take on the California Angels.

The A's have not started the season like champs however. They began the day in 5th place in the AL West at 4 - 8.

They needed a hero to help them avoid falling 5 games under .500.

To make matters worse, the Kansas City Royals with several young rising stars such as former Mets player, Amos Otis, are threatening to run off with the division after starting 10 - 5.

Two of the top pitchers in the American League were facing off against each other. The Angels Nolan Ryan (also a former Mets player) and the A's Jim "Catfish" Hunter.

Ryan came into the game with a 3 - 0 record and a 1.67 ERA. He had struck out 37 batters in his 1st three games.

The duel delivered, and after 7 innings it was a tight game that the A's led 2 - 1.

A's 2 Angels 1 - End of 7th inning

In the top of the 8th, Catfish got the first 2 Angels out and then gave up a single, just his 4th hit allowed. But A's manager Dick Williams decided it was time to go to the bullpen.

As Hunter handed the ball to his manager, he also relinquished his opportunity to be the hero of the game for the A's.

Relief pitcher Darold Knowles now had that opportunity to be the hero if he could get 4 more outs to save the game.

But Knowles promptly yielded a single, putting runners on 1st and 3rd with 2 outs and the legendary Frank Robinson coming to the plate.

Out came Dick Williams again to bring another relief pitcher, Horacio Pina.

Now Pina had the opportunity to be the hero. First, he needed to get Frank Robinson out.

Robinson himself now had an opportunity to be the hero of the game for the Angels. An extra base hit or home run would give the Angels the lead.

Coming into this game Frank Robinson had 524 career home runs. He had been in countless situations like this.

NOTE from The Sports Time Traveler

I interrupt this article to let you know that before the 1973 season would end, Robinson would pass Mickey Mantle and Jimmy Foxx on the all-time list and move into 5th place). Robinson was the 1st player to win MVP awards in both the American and National league.

Now back to 1973.

But Pina struck out Robinson to retire the side. Pina's hero hopes were very much alive.

In the bottom half of the 8th Nolan Ryan got the A's out in order.

A's 2 Angels 1 - End of 8th inning

Now Pina needed 3 outs to save the win.

The 1st batter he faced was Tommy McCraw. Pina had the count at 1 - 2 and threw the next pitch over the plate trying to strike out the light hitting McCraw. Instead McCraw belted it for a home run to tie the game.

Although Pina didn't allow another run, he had blown the save opportunity.

A's 2 Angels 2 - Bottom of the 9th

Ryan took the mound for the bottom of the 9th. With 1 out, Dick Williams decided to pinch hit for starting 2nd baseman Dick Green. The pinch hitter, Rich McKinney walked.

Williams then inserted Ted Kubiak into the game as a pinch runner. Kubiak could then play second base if the game went into extra innings.

Kubiak now represented the winning run. He would have an opportunity to be the hero of the game.

With 1 out and Kubiak on 1st, Bert Campaneris hit a single. Kubiak tried to go from first to third on the play. The throw came into third base and Kubiak was safe. Campaneris went to second base on the play.

Now the A's had runners on second and third and just 1 out.

Kubiak was 90 feet away from winning the game.

The next batter, Bill North, was intentionally walked to load the bases.

This brought up Joe Rudi, one of the stars of the 1972 World Series. Ryan got Rudi to strikeout for out number 2.

With left-handed batter Reggie Jackson coming up, Angel's manager Bobby Winkles decided to bring in a lefty pitcher, Ron Perranoski.

Jackson was one of the most dangerous hitters in the American League and was off to a hot start to the season batting .349. A single would drive in Kubiak for the win.

The 37 year old Perranoski *"broke 2 jug-handle curves to Reggie Jackson that Jackson missed violently,"* according to Ron Bergman writing in the Oakland Tribune. With the count 0 and 2 to Jackson, Perranoski threw 2 more breaking balls that went wide.

On the 2 - 2 pitch to Jackson, Bergman described the action, *"Reggie slammed a rising liner to right. Right fielder Lee Stanton (yet another former Mets player) fighting sunlight directly in his eyes went back, stumbled and jumped up for a leaping catch. Jackson set the American League record for the helmet throw."*

Stanton had made a spectacular game-saving catch that cost Reggie a grand slam and the chance to be the game's hero.

Stanton told Ron Bergman after the game, ***"When it hit my glove, my hand was all the way over the fence. I had to look in my glove to make sure I had it."***

Newspapers carried a photo of the catch in which Lee Stanton robbed Reggie Jackson of a grand slam in the bottom of the 9th that would have made Jackson the hero of the day for the A's.

The catch not only took a grand slam away from Jackson, but it stranded Ted Kubiak on 3rd base and sent the game to extra innings.

A's 2 Angels 2 - End of 9th inning

Dick Williams sent Pina back out to pitch the top of the 10th.

He gave up a single to Sandy Alomar and then got Bobby Valentine and Jeff Torborg out.

This brought up Frank Robinson again.

And Pina struck out Robinson again to retire the side.

A's 2 Angels 2 - Bottom of the 10th

Ron Perranoski pitched the 10th inning for the Angels. He quickly got 2 outs as both Sal Bando and Billy Conigliaro grounded to short.

Next up was Angel Manguel who drew a walk.

Ray Fosse then singled to put runners on first and second with 2 outs.

Ted Kubiak came up next. It was his first at bat of the game. The switch-hitting Kubiak had to bat right handed against the lefty Perranoski, which is not his better side.

With the count 0 and 1, Kubiak hit a line drive to left field for a base hit.

The hit was deep enough that Angels left fielder, Tommy McCraw didn't even bother to throw home.

Thus, Angel Manguel came around to score uncontested and the A's won the game 3 - 2.

A's 3 Angels 2 - FINAL SCORE

Ted Kubiak was the hero of the game. Not Reggie Jackson. Not Catfish Hunter. But switching hitting, utility infielder, Ted Kubiak, who had not even entered the game until the bottom of the 9th.

The next day the front page of the sports section in the San Francisco Examiner had a headline that read, *"A's Handy Fill-In Kubiak to Rescue."*

Glenn Schwarz of the Examiner interviewed Kubiak and asked him when was the last time he was the subject of an interview. Kubiak jokingly replied, *"Oh, I was interviewed on the radio once before. I think it was to fill in time during a rain delay."*

Dick Williams wasn't joking however when he praised Kubiak's play and assessed his value to the team in his interview with Schwarz, *"He grows on me. And not just because of his hit today. He can switch-hit. He's a good fielder. He can do so many things well."*

POSTSCRIPT from The Sports Time Traveler™

Long after their baseball careers ended, Tony La Russa, the hall of famer manager, and a former A's player, once said this about Ted Kubiak:

"I always thought Kubiak was the most valuable player on that team (Oakland A's) *because he could fill in for Dick Green at second, or Campy Campaneris at short, or Sal Bando at third, and the team would go on winning."*

After he retired as a player, Ted Kubiak remained involved professionally in baseball as a minor league manager and as an instructor for major league teams.

And he is still active today as a baseball author and consultant.

You can visit his website and learn about the baseball books he has published at this link: https://www.oldschoolmvp.com/

CHAPTER THIRTY-EIGHT

Seaver Faces the Big Red Machine

TOM IS ON THE MOUND FOR THE FIRST TIME IN MAY

SHEA STADIUM - May 3, 1973

The Sports Time Traveler™ hopes to be camping out virtually in Shea Stadium for nearly every game of the 1973 season, and especially when Tom Seaver takes the mound as he did yesterday.

SEAVER'S STRANGE SEASON

Seaver has had a strange season so far and yesterday was no exception.

Coming into the game Seaver had started 5 games and given up just 5 runs, all of them on home runs. Despite his "Gibsonian" 1.12 ERA, Seaver had a record of just 2 - 2. That's because in those 5 games, the Mets had only scored 6 runs, including 2 games where the Mets gave Seaver no run support at all. He lost those 2 games by scores of 1 - 0 and 2 - 0.

Yesterday, against Cincinnati's Big Red Machine, Seaver was stellar again.

SEAVER ALLOWS NO HITS THROUGH THE FIRST 15 BATTERS

Seaver got through the Reds first 15 batters without giving up a hit (although he had given up 3 walks). Then Dave Concepcion hit a double that scored Tony Perez and put the Reds up 1 - 0 in the 4th inning.

On that play, Willie Mays narrowly missed making a spectacular leaping catch in deep right center. Mays had the ball in his glove, but it popped out when he hit the wall.

Concepcion, the Reds shortstop, is batting .365 and leads the team with 18 RBIs. It's a difficult lineup when the shortstop hits like that.

Seaver responded to the run by striking out the next 5 Reds batters in a row including the top of the Reds order: Pete Rose, Joe Morgan and Bobby Tolan.

Then came the clean-up hitter Johnny Bench. Bench was the NL MVP in 1970 and 1972 when he hit 45 and 40 HRs.

With the count 1 and 0 to Bench, Seaver threw a slider which he thought was a strike, but was called a ball.

Bench said to The Cincinnati Enquirer's Bob Hertzel after the game, *"It could have been called a strike."*

Instead of a 1 - 1 count it was now 2 and 0.

A moment later the count went to 3 and 0.

Seaver's next pitch was a fastball right down the middle.

It was power against power.

Joe Trimble in the New York Daily News wrote, *"Bench rocketed one into the left field bullpen."*

It was the 1st home run Bench had ever hit off Tom Seaver.

"I'm hitting something (like) .150 off of him," Bench said to The Cincinnati Enquirer's Bob Hertzel after the game. *"He doesn't make too many mistakes. When you get a chance you've got to do it."*

SEAVER STRIKES OUT 8 OF 9 REDS

Seaver then struck out Tony Perez and Joe Hague to retire the Reds in the 6th. And he struck out Concepcion leading off the top of the 7th.

Seaver had now struck out 8 of the last 9 Reds batters.

He then got Denis Menke to groundout.

That brought up Reds pitcher, Ross Grimsley, with two outs.

Grimsley had no hits in 15 at bats on the season. Trimble described Grimsley's at bat, *"Grimsley caught Tom in a mistake and looped a single over second baseman Felix Millan's head."*

With 2 outs and a man on first, next up was leadoff batter Pete Rose. Rose described to Joe Trimble, after the game, what happened on Seaver's 1 - 1 pitch, *"It was a slider which Tom intended to be low but broke high."* Rose smashed it for his 1st home run of the season, just missing the scoreboard in right center field.

Seaver got out of the inning when he got Joe Morgan to fly out. But the Mets were now down 4 - 1.

Seaver was lifted for a pinch hitter in the bottom of the 7th. And reliever Ray Sadecki gave up 2 more runs.

The Mets lost 6 - 1.

SEAVER WAS WELL... TERRIFIC

Bob Hertzel started his article in The Cincinnati Enquirer this way, *"Tommy (terrific) Seaver was well... terrific. He was fantastic, great and overpowering. He was also a loser."*

Seaver had given up just 4 hits in 7 innings and struck out a season high of 13, while facing one of the toughest lineups in baseball, the defending NL champions. But those 4 hits yielded 4 runs and the Mets only gave him 1 run in support. The Mets actually out hit the Reds for the game 9 - 7. But they left 10 men on base.

"Everytime I make a mistake they hit it hard," Seaver lamented to the New York Times' Joseph Durso in the locker room.

Mets pitching coach Rube Walker described to Joe Trimble what happened to Seaver, *"Great pitchers are hurt by their few mistakes because the hitters lay back and hope for that one pitch they can take advantage of. That's what's been happening to him. All the hitters who have homered off of him are good hitters who should hit homers. They waited and got the pitch they wanted."*

METS IN FIRST PLACE

Despite the loss, the Mets are actually in 1st place!

Here are the National League East standing as of the morning of May 3, 1973

12 – 9 Mets

12 – 9 Cubs

9 – 7   Pirates

9 – 11 Phillies

9 – 11 Expos

4 – 16 Cardinals

The Pirates notably have lost 5 of their last 6 after jumping out to an 8 - 2 start.

METS INJURIES

The Mets are already plagued by injuries. Left fielder Cleon Jones is out. Willie Mays is playing part-time with an assortment of ailments. And first baseman John Milner, is on the disabled list with a pulled hamstring.

Milner was off to a great start in his 2nd season with 5 HRs / 13 RBIs / .327 Avg. in April.

METS BATTING UNDER .200 NOT COUNTING MILNER

Not counting John Milner, the rest of the Mets are batting under .200.

With Milner the team average is just .207 - good for last place in the major leagues.

The Mets 2, 3 and 4 batters are hitting miserably:

2 - Felix Millan .173

3 - Willie Mays. 108

4 - Rusty Staub .164

PITCHING IS CARRYING THE METS

The Mets pitching staff combined for a 2.29 ERA in April.

Leading the way is Jerry Koosman. Here are the records of the Mets starters and top relievers:

STARTERS

Jerry Koosman 4 - 0 1.06 ERA

Tom Seaver 2 - 3 1.71 ERA

Jon Matlack 2 - 3 3.86 ERA (He was 15 - 10 with a 2.32 ERA and won the NL Rookie of the Year in 1972)

Jim McAndrew 2 - 2 5.40 ERA (He was 11 - 8 with a 2.80 ERA in 1972 in 23 starts)

Harry Parker 2 - 0 0.61 ERA

The 25 year old Parker has had just 2 starts so far for the Mets. In 13 innings he's let up just 1 run. Last year he showed strong promise in AAA going 14 - 9 with a 2.61 ERA and 5 shutouts.

RELIEVERS

Lefty Tug McGraw 1.35 ERA and 5 saves

Righty Phil Hennigan 2.35 ERA and 2 saves

CHAPTER THIRTY-NINE

Will Willie Retire?

WILLIE MAYS GOES ON THE DISABLED LIST FOR THE 1ST TIME IN HIS CAREER AND THERE IS SPECULATION HE MIGHT NOT BE COMING BACK

PITTSBURGH - May 14, 1973

The Sports Time Traveler™ is in Pittsburgh, virtually, to catch the Mets 3 game series against the Pirates at Three Rivers Stadium.

It was a turbulent weekend for the Mets filled with ups and downs and speculation about the future of the legendary Willie Mays.

The Mets came into the series tied with the Pirates with a .500 record, the Mets at 14 - 14 and the Pirates at 12 - 12. Both teams trailed the 1st place Cubs by 2 games.

A New 5th Starter Emerges

On Friday, May 11th, the Mets sent 25-year-old Harry Parker to the mound. Parker, who only had started 4 games in his career prior to joining the Mets this year, has been very promising so far. In his 4th start for the Mets this season, he held the Pirates, the NL's best hitting team, to 3 runs in 6 innings. Tug McGraw held them scoreless in the last 3 and the Mets won it 4 - 3, beating Dock Ellis, who has a record of 34 - 16 over the past 2 seasons.

Harry Parker is now 3 - 0 with an ERA of 2.30.

A Costly Win on Friday Night

But the good news was tempered by the fact that 3 Mets were injured in the game.

The 3 Mets were all hit by pitches: Cleon Jones, Rusty Staub and Jerry Grote.

Jones was able to brush off the hit and continue playing, but he would feel the bruise the rest of the weekend.

Staub, who had missed 90 games last season when he broke a bone getting hit by a pitch, had to be taken out of the game and sent to the hospital for X-rays. Fortunately, they came back negative.

Starting catcher Jerry Grote was not so lucky. He was also sent to the hospital for X-rays which revealed a broken wrist. He will be in a cast for 6 weeks.

Willie Mays Didn't Make the Trip

In addition to the 3 injuries in last night's game, Willie Mays, remains sidelined and was advised by the team physician, Dr. Peter LaMotte, to not even make the week-long road trip, in which the Mets will stop in Chicago and Montreal after this weekend.

Mays injured his shoulder playing last Sunday on his 42nd birthday. And that's in addition to his 2 aching knees.

Seaver Takes the Mound on Saturday Afternoon

On Saturday, Tom Seaver made his 7th start of the season. Seaver came into the game with a record of just 3 - 3, but with a stellar 1.60 ERA. Two of Seaver's 3 losses were in games in which the Mets gave him no run support. He lost those games 1 - 0 and 2 - 0. In 5 of the 7 games Seaver has started coming into today, the Mets had given Seaver 2 runs or less of support.

When the Mets got a run off Pirates starter Bob Moose in the top of the 1st inning, Dick Young wrote facetiously in the New York Daily News, that it gave Seaver, *"the strangest feeling that he was in the wrong place."*

Seaver then got the Pirates first 8 batters out in a row before giving up a single to the pitcher, Bob Moose, in the bottom of the 3rd.

Seaver then retired the next 9 Pirates batters in a row.

That adds up to 17 of the first 18 batters retired by Seaver against the NL's best hitting team.

Yet going into the 8th inning it was still just a 1 - 0 lead for Seaver.

Then the Mets finally decided to support their franchise pitcher (not that he needed it) with 2 runs in the 8th and 3 in the 9th.

Seaver's Gem

Seaver went the distance for a 6 - 0 shutout. He gave up just 2 hits and 1 walk. Pitching in Pittsburgh, against the team that won more games than any other team in baseball in the past 2 years, this had to be one of the finest starts of Seaver's career.

And Yet Another Toll

The victory proved costly again. Backup catcher Duffy Dyer was hit by a ball, but shrugged it off. However, Felix Millan twisted an ankle and was done for the weekend. And Jim Gosger, a replacement outfielder for the depleted Mets, hurt his back when he crashed into the centerfield fence. He too missed Sunday's game.

A Song for the Outfield

After Saturday's game, Joseph Durso of the New York Times wrote about singer Jerry Vale's surprise visit to the Mets locker room. *"(Vale) saw Yogi poring over medical reports and asked in some shock, 'what's going on with you guys?' To which Yogi quickly replied, 'Can you play the outfield?'"*

Mays on the Disabled List

Before Sunday's game, which was another day game, Willie Mays was placed on the 15-day disabled list for the first time in his 22 year MLB career.

Immediately there was speculation that Willie might retire. He's only batting .105 for the season with just 4 hits, although one of those hits was a game winner.

Mets GM Bob Scheffing was asked if Willie is going to retire and he said to the New York Times, *"I hope he'll play again."*

Mets manager Yogi Berra, when asked about Mays possibly retiring said, *"He didn't tell me he'd retire. He's discouraged because he's not hitting and his shoulder hurts. But will he retire now? Not that I know."*

Dick Young wrote in The New York Daily News, *"Has the countdown started on Willie Mays' great career?"*

NOTE From The Sports Time Traveler™

I interrupt this article to tell you how much I'm shocked at this discussion 50 years ago.

I wish to remind you that just 2 months prior, in the warmth of St. Petersburg, Florida, Willie Mays led the team in spring training, batting about .350, for what Willie called the best spring training of his career.

It shocks me to learn how quick everyone was in May 1973 to speculate that Willie Mays was never coming back.

Now back to 1973.

Not Writing Mays Off for Good

GM Bob Scheffing walked back his earlier remarks, and any implications that Mays was set to announce his retirement, when he said, *"Willie still believes he can play when the weather gets warm. And it's likely he can."*

Matlack Misses a Start on Sunday

Jon Matlack missed his starting turn on Sunday because he was recently released from Roosevelt Hospital with a hairline skull fracture suffered when a line drive hit him in the head last week.

Yet another injured Met.

Starting in his place was Jim McAndrew. McAndrew, who pitched to an 11 - 8 record with a 2.80 ERA last year has been shaky this year with a 4.91 ERA coming into this game.

Today, he was a little shaky again against the hard hitting Pirates. He gave up 10 hits and 3 walks in just 6 innings. But he only allowed 3 runs to score. And with Tug McGraw allowing just one run in the last 3 innings, the Pirates only scored 4 runs.

Meanwhile Mets back up first baseman, Jim Beauchamp, playing because regular first baseman John Milner was also out with an injury, came up big today with 4 RBIs and the Mets beat the Pirates 6 - 4.

That gave the New York Mets a 3 game sweep in Pittsburgh against a Pirates team that won the past 3 NL East Division titles.

The 2nd Place New York Mets

As the weekend closed, the Mets were beat up, but they were now in sole possession of 2nd place in the NL East.

Here were the NL East standings on Sunday, May 13th, 1973:

21 – 13 Cubs

17 – 14 Mets

13 – 15 Expos

12 – 15 Pirates

11 – 19 Phillies

8 – 22 Cardinals

CHAPTER FORTY

Seaver's Slender Support

CANDLESTICK PARK, SAN FRANCISCO - May 30, 1973

In prior articles this spring I've been informing you of the paucity of run support for Tom Seaver by Mets batters here in the spring of 1973.

Seaver routinely has had to get by with just a couple of runs from his own team.

Meanwhile, Seaver has been stellar on the mound. When he arrived in San Francisco this week he sported an ERA of 1.68.

Last night Tom Seaver looked brilliant in the early going again as he faced the team with the best record in the National League - the Giants. It was the epitome of why Seaver is called "Tom Terrific."

Through 5 innings he had allowed just one hit and already had accumulated 10 strikeouts.

Not only that, Seaver had hit a home run himself. It came in the top of the 5th and it gave him a 1 - 0 lead.

METS 1 GIANTS 0 - middle of the 5th inning

Sadly, none of the other Mets scored any runs in the first 8 innings.

Seaver had made just one mistake in the first 8 innings. It came when he faced Willie McCovey in the bottom of the 6th.

McCovey came to the plate with 2 outs and Tito Fuentes on 2nd base. McCovey had struck out in his first 2 times up against Seaver.

Seaver faces McCovey in the bottom of the 6th

This was a classic confrontation. It pitted the 2 men who had finished 1st (McCovey) and 2nd (Seaver) in the close NL MVP vote just 4 years ago in 1969.

Red Foley, writing in the New York Daily News described what happened in McCovery's at bat, *"Seaver, after making McCovey swing and miss at an up pitch, challenged the Giants longballer again. This time Seaver's serve was down into the uppercutting McCovey's groove. The result was a whistling rocket that became Willie's 10th home run."*

It was the 394th home run in the great career of Willie McCovey, who is at this time, in 1973, the 14th leading home run hitter of all time.

After the game, Tom Seaver told Pat Frizzell of the Oakland Tribune what happened on the pitch, *"McCovey's still an awesome slugger. I was throwing the best I had this season though, so I went after him instead of pitching around him. I had struck him out twice. I had to do it again, and I didn't. I got a fastball in the wrong place."*

The home run by McCovey put the Giants ahead 2 - 1 and that remained the score after the 6th, 7th and 8th innings.

GIANTS 2 METS 1 - end of 8 innings

Going into the top of the 9th, the Mets were down to their last 3 outs and coming to the plate was the bottom of the order.

That meant Tom Seaver could potentially be the Mets final batter of the game. If Mets batters wouldn't help Seaver avoid losing another one run game, at least Seaver would have a chance to do it himself.

Leading off the top of the 9th was Ken Boswell, who was pinch hitting for catcher, Duffy Dyer. Boswell drew a walk from Giants starting pitcher Jim Barr.

This prompted a change of pitchers as the Giants brought in Randy Moffitt, who is the brother of tennis star Billie Jean King.

Next up was the 8th hitter, shortstop Bud Harrelson, who singled to right field to put runners on first and second.

Now Mets manager Yogi Berra let Seaver take his turn at bat with instructions to bunt. Seaver's bunt went to the pitcher Moffitt, who looked toward third base and made his throw too late to first. Seaver was safe.

The leadoff hitter, 3rd baseman Wayne Garrett now stepped in with no one out and the bases loaded.

Mets Load the Bases in the 9th

Moffitt promptly walked Wayne Garrett on 5 pitches. That brought Boswell in to score.

The game was tied. The bases were still loaded. And there were still no outs.

Next was the number 2 batter, second baseman Felix Millan. Millan hit a grounder that shot past the Giants third baseman and brought home Harrelson and Seaver. The Mets now led 4 - 2.

That was all for Moffitt.

The Giants brought in fireballer Sam McDowell. He allowed one more run, on a sacrifice fly by George Theodore, before retiring the side. The Mets had scored 4 times in the 9th and now led 5 - 2.

METS 5 GIANTS 2 - middle of the 9th

Seaver took the mound in the bottom of the 9th with an uncharacteristic 3 run lead. Mets batters had finally supported their sensational starter.

Seaver had to face the heart of the Giants order in his attempt to seal the game.

1st up was the number 3 batter Garry Maddox. Seaver struck him out for "K" number 15.

Next up was the clean-up hitter, McCovey.

Seaver struck out Big Mac for the 3rd time in the game.

It must have felt like sweet redemption after giving up the homer in the 6th.

It was also Seaver's 16th strikeout of the game. He had struck out at least one of the San Francisco Giants in each of the 9 innings.

The next batter was Ed Goodson. He grounded to first baseman John Milner. Milner flipped the ball to Seaver who dashed to cover first base.

Seaver fittingly made the final put out himself.

The game was over. Tom Seaver had beaten the Giants.

Seaver's record is now 6 - 3.

Seaver told a UPI reporter after the game, ***"The strikeouts were nice, and so was the homer. But the biggest thing was winning the game."***

The Mets are now in 2nd place in the NL East, 5 games behind the Chicago Cubs. Here are the standings:

28 – 18 Cubs

21 – 21 Mets

19 – 20 Pirates

18 – 21 Expos

18 – 24 Cardinals

19 – 26 Phillies

CHAPTER FORTY-ONE

Tom Seaver is the Mets OVP

TOM SEAVER IS SINGLE HANDEDLY KEEPING THE 1973 METS FROM FALLING INTO AN ABYSS

SAN DIEGO - June 4, 1973

Coming into yesterday's afternoon's game in San Diego, the Mets had not scored a run in 21 innings.

Tom Seaver, the Mets starting pitcher, was likely mentally preparing himself for another game in which he gets almost no run support.

A good sign occurred in batting practice that things might go differently. Mets pitching coach Rube Walker decided to step into the cage, and he blasted a home run.

Walker must have inspired the Mets batters as they surprised Seaver with a rare scoring binge.

Teddy Martinez led off for the Mets. Martinez, a utility infielder, started in center due to the decimated state of the Mets outfield. Cleon Jones has just been put on the 15-day disabled list and Willie Mays is just coming off of it, but is not quite ready to play. In addition, the Mets have given up on Rich Chiles, the minor league player whom they traded Tommie Agee for in the off season.

Teddy drew a walk to open the game.

Then second baseman Felix Millan singled.

A couple of batters later, first baseman John Milner singled home Martinez and Millan and Seaver suddenly had a 2 - 0 lead before he had thrown a pitch.

The Mets manufactured 3 more runs in the 3rd, 4th and 6th to take a 5 - 0 lead.

That was more than Seaver needed.

In the first 4 innings Seaver was once again dominant. He gave up just one hit and then in the bottom of the 5th he struck out the side.

The Padres put up 2 runs on 3 singles in the 6th. But Seaver came back with 1 - 2 - 3 innings in the 7th and the 8th.

The Mets cruised to a 9 - 2 victory.

Seaver, who gave up just 6 hits, all of them singles, is now 7 - 3 with a 1.74 ERA.

Seaver is not just the MVP for the Mets, he is the OVP – Only Valuable Player.

In the Mets last 14 games, Tom Seaver has started 4 times and the Mets have won all 4 games.

In the other 10 games, when Seaver was not pitching, the Mets went 0 - 10.

Seaver was recognized for his efforts. He won the NL Player of the Week award.

The Mets are now 22 - 24, tied for 3rd place in the NL East and 6.5 games behind the Cubs.

CHAPTER FORTY-TWO

The Comeback in Queens

JUNE 9, 1973, WAS A SPECIAL DAY IN NEW YORK WITH OLD TIMERS DAY, THE RETURN OF WILLIE MAYS AND THE BELMONT STAKES

INTRO From The Sports Time Traveler™

June 9, 1973, was a great day in New York. It was sunny and warm. At Shea Stadium the Mets hosted the Dodgers at 1:30pm on Old Timers Day. One "Old Timer" would play in the real game. Willie Mays was back on the field for the Mets, starting in centerfield at Shea for the first time in a month.

Shortly after the baseball game ended, and 10 miles to the east, 2 horses, Secretariat and Sham, would meet for their final epic battle in the Belmont Stakes. Secretariat would have a chance to win the coveted Triple Crown, a feat that had not been accomplished in 25 years, and some said might never be done again.

This was a must see day in sports for which The Sports Time Traveler™ just had to travel virtually back to New York and catch both of these events.

Here is the article on the ballgame.

NEW YORK - June 10, 1973

There may be nothing better than traveling virtually in time back to Shea Stadium. When I arrived here yesterday, 50 years ago, there was a buzz in the air and the sun was shining. It was a dream-like scene as Willie Mays trotted out to centerfield to play against the Dodgers.

For Willie it must have seemed like one of the many days he had done this in New York in the 1950s at the Polo Grounds and Ebbets Field. Now he was in his first game at Shea Stadium since turning 42 years old. He would get to play centerfield in New York against the Dodgers once more.

Mays, who had his best ever spring training this year in the Florida warmth (it was the only spring training he ever played in Florida), started the regular season poorly when he had to play in the cold northeast. He was batting an abysmal .105 with no home runs when he hurt his shoulder in the first week of May. He missed an entire month of action.

Willie is not 100% yet, but the Mets outfield is depleted by injuries, so he is making a go of it. He got a chance to play an exhibition game earlier this week when the Mets took on their AAA farm club, Tidewater, in Virginia. Mays led off the game with a home run in his only at bat and the Mets beat their top minor league team in a wild 17 - 11 game.

Now Mays is set to play his 2,953rd major league game in front of a near capacity crowd of just under 48,000 fans.

Old Timers Day

Prior to the start of the game, it was Old Timers Day at Shea.

A group of retired Mets players, mostly from the early 1960s, played a group of retired Dodgers and Yankees from the 1940s and 1950s.

Some of the Mets "Old Timers" are only in their 30s since the franchise didn't start play until 1962. Former Mets pitcher Jay Hook, 36, said to New York Times writer Leonard Koppett, *"why can't they call us alumni?"*

Casey Stengel, the Mets first ever manager, took the reins of the club for the 2 inning game and he changed pitchers after every batter.

Former Dodger Jim Gilliam opened the game with a single off the Mets Roger Craig, who lost 24 games in the Mets first season. Gilliam then stole second and moved to third base on a grounder.

That brought up the great Joe DiMaggio with just 1 out and a man on third. Stengel brought in Al Jackson, another 20 game loser on the 1962 squad, to face Joltin' Joe. DiMaggio hit 2 foul balls to deep left field, and then hit a grounder to short that resulted in a double play.

In the bottom of the 1st, Richie Ashburn reached first on an error, stole second and came home when Yogi Berra, the Mets current manager, singled to center.

That turned out to be the only run of the 2 inning game. The Mets won it 1 - 0.

The Retiring of Gil Hodges #14

After the Old Timers Game came a somber ceremony. The Mets used the occasion to retire #14 for Gil Hodges, the first Met to ever have a number retired in the 11 year history of the franchise.

Gil Hodges was the Mets manager from 1968 until he dropped dead from a heart attack at age 47 just prior to the start of the 1972 season. The tragic passing of one of the most gracious men to ever take part in major league baseball was a shock to the city.

Hodges had been one of the key players on the Brooklyn Dodgers "Boys of Summer" teams in the 1950s. In 1960, he became the National League's all-time home run leader for right-handed batters. His record was broken in 1963 by none other than Willie Mays.

Gil actually finished his career with the New York Mets 10 years ago in 1963. But the reason his number is being retired today has nothing to do with his play in Brooklyn or with the Mets or his home run record.

The Mastermind of the Miracle

Gil Hodges number is being retired because he was the mastermind behind "The Miracle of 1969."

Gil Hodges quite literally authored what is arguably the greatest fairy tale in the history of sports - the World Series victory by the New York Mets in 1969. He led the Mets, the laughingstock of baseball, a team that had never finished better than 16 games under .500, to a 100 win season in 1969.

He then guided them to sweep Hank Aaron's Atlanta Braves in the first ever National League Championship Series.

Then he capped off the most unlikely story in the annals of sports by piloting the Mets to a decisive 4 games to 1 defeat of one of the great teams in history, the 109 win Baltimore Orioles.

NOTE from The Sports Time Traveler™

I interrupt this article to inform you that the Baltimore Orioles won 109 games in 1969 and followed that up with 108 wins in 1970.

Their 217 wins across 2 seasons remains the MLB record.

They were a near perfect team led by hall of famers Frank Robinson, Brooks Robinson and Jim Palmer.

The Orioles also crushed the Cincinnati "Big Red Machine" four games to one in the 1970 World Series, thus adding even more of an aura of incredulity to the Mets victory over the Orioles in 1969.

Gil's Wife Speaks to the Crowd

Joan Hodges spoke to the crowd during the number retirement ceremony. *"You are the greatest fans in the world. I want to thank you for your loyalty, devotion and love for Gil. We're very happy that he had the opportunity to bring you a world championship."*

Mets 1969 3rd baseman Ed Charles, also spoke about his former manager, *"Gil instilled a whole different attitude. He made us believe in ourselves."*

Former Dodger teammate, Roy Campanella, who is confined to a wheelchair after the automobile accident that ended his career after the 1957 season penned a statement that was read aloud by Dodgers broadcaster Vin Scully, *"Gil Hodges was the greatest guy I ever had the pleasure to play with."*

Willie Mays Takes the Field

Now it was time for the regular season game to begin. Willie Mays at 42 is 4 years younger than the Mets starting centerfielder from the Old-Timers Game, Richie Ashburn. And he is older than 12 of the players from the game.

In the top of the 3rd inning with the game tied at 2, the Dodgers Willie Davis hit a fly ball to deep straightaway centerfield. Joseph Durso of the New York Times described the play in the field by Willie Mays, *"Mays misjudged it, finally drew a bead on the ball, backpedaled and made a remarkable catch over his head. It became even more remarkable, though, when he fell backward and rolled twice across the dirt at the base of the wall."*

Joe Trimble of the Daily News called it, *"a diving catch on the warning track in front of the 410 foot marker."*

Mays at the Plate

After saving a possible run in the top of the inning, Willie Mays came to bat on the bottom of the 3rd. He drove an Al Downing pitch over the 371 foot sign in left field for his first home run of the season giving the Mets a 3 - 2 lead.

The home run vaulted Mays past the 6,000 mark in total bases. With 6,003 total bases he became only the 3rd player in history to reach that mark.

Matlack Dominates

After giving up 2 early runs, starter Jon Matlack shut down the Dodgers the rest of the way, allowing just 3 hits and no runs in the last 6 innings. The Mets won it 4 - 2.

For Matlack, it was his best game since he suffered a hairline fracture on his head when he was hit by a batted ball on May 8th.

The Sports Time Traveler™ will continue following the Mets throughout the 1973 season. "Tomorrow" Jerry Koosman will get the start.

CHAPTER FORTY-THREE

Tom Seaver is Back

Special Thanks to Readers of The Sports Time Traveler™

I'd like to thank all of you who have come on this journey with me.

Most of all, I'd like to thank my gorgeous bride Heather.

We just celebrated our 35th anniversary and this incredible experience I'm having as The Sports Time Traveler™ would not have happened without her encouragement and support.

Heather's passion for the Outlander series of novels about an English woman who is transported back in time, "through the stones," in the Scottish Highlands to the 18th century, was one of the primary inspirations for my "invention" of sports time travel.

And now here's the background on today's article on the 1973 New York Mets.

I set the dial on the virtual sports time travel machine to take me back exactly 50 years to Pittsburgh on June 25, 1973. The Mets had just finished up a disastrous Pennsylvania road trip in which they lost 5 of the first 6 games to the Phillies and the Pirates.

They had one more game to play before heading back to New York. It was a Sunday afternoon affair in Pittsburgh's Three Rivers Stadium. And

Tom Seaver was pitching again after a brief injury scare had forced him to miss a start.

THREE RIVERS STADIUM - June 25, 1973

Tom Seaver was back on the mound in Pittsburgh yesterday after an 11 day layoff. He missed a start last week after he had strained his back lifting boxes in his house.

Boy did the Mets miss him.

Jim McAndrew started in Seaver's place last week and gave up 4 runs in 1 and 1/3 innings and the Mets lost 9 - 6.

In the top of the 1st inning yesterday, the Mets did something highly unusual. The worst hitting team in the NL, at .238, provided Seaver with 2 early runs as Ed Kranepool doubled home Felix Millan and John Milner.

Seaver, rusty from his time off perhaps, had a rocky time in the bottom of the 1st as he gave up a 2 run blast to Willie Stargell. It was Stargell's 22nd HR which leads the majors.

But after that, Seaver was stellar. From the 2nd inning on the Pirates never got a runner past first base.

Meanwhile the Mets provided Seaver with a few insurance runs. Kranepool doubled home another run in the 3rd. And they scored 2 more runs in the 5th on 3 singles and a fielder's choice.

With the victory, Seaver is now 9 - 4 with a 1.97 ERA. The Mets are 10 - 5 in games Seaver has started. The Mets are 20 - 29 in games when Seaver has not started.

The case for the MVP is in the making.

Meet The Newest Met

One of the Mets runs in the 5th was driven in by catcher Ron Hodges. Hodges, who is no relation to the Mets former manager Gil Hodges, is experiencing a bit of a Cinderella story.

Two weeks ago he was playing AA ball at the Mets affiliate in Memphis. He was batting just .170, and not exactly looking like major league material.

The Mets, however, were suddenly in need of a catcher as their 1st string and 3rd string catchers were injured.

Coincidentally, the Mets had an exhibition game against their AAA minor league team Tidewater. They called Hodges up from Memphis to play in the exhibition. Mets manager Yogi Berra liked what he saw and told Hodges he was not going back to Memphis.

Hodges told Vinnie Di Trani, of the Hackensack Record, *"Yogi told me I was on the big club's roster, and I could hardly believe him."*

In Hodges first big league game on June 13th his pitcher was Tom Seaver. After that game Hodges told Di Trani what it was like catching Tom Seaver, *"He threw some fast balls that were un-Godly. He's some kind of pitcher. I've never caught anything like him before."*

Seaver had some very positive things to say about Hodges after that game. He shared a great little story with Di Trani, *"I threw a high change up to Goodson and he hit a long fly ball on it. I look up and there's the kid telling me to 'get the ball down baby.' I had to laugh. I've had about 15 different catchers in seven years and every one of them has told me to keep my change up down. It didn't take him long... he kept his composure throughout and handled himself well."*

Hodges is even hitting the ball well so far. He has hit in 7 of his 8 games and is batting .375.

Mets Avoid Slipping Into Last Place

The Mets victory helped them avoid exchanging places with the Pirates for last in the NL East.

The Pirates, winners of the NL East the last 3 seasons, are in a totally understandable malaise as the team clearly misses Roberto Clemente.

A couple of days ago New York Daily News sports columnist, Dick Young, wrote a great piece about the impact the tragic loss of Roberto Clemente has had on the 1973 Pirates. Young explained how Clemente had a major impact on the pitching staff in prior years, *"It believed in itself beyond it's true ability, and a large part of that belief flowed from Roberto Clemente. When things would go badly there was always that strident sing-song voice ringing across the locker room."*

National League East Standings

Here are the standings in the NL East as of this morning. The Cubs are still solidly in front:

41 – 30 Cubs
32 – 31 Expos
33 – 34 Cardinals
30 – 34 Mets
31 – 36 Phillies
29 – 36 Pirates

The Hot Red Birds

The Cardinals, who had reached .500 the day before, are actually the hottest team in the NL East. They had started an abysmal 5 - 20 and have gone 28 - 14 since.

The Cardinals are doing it with good pitching and the ability to manufacture runs. They have 3 starting pitchers with ERA's under 3 in Bob Gibson, Rick Wise and Alan Foster.

Yet they are last in the majors in home runs with just 27 in 67 games. Their leading hitter, Joe Torre is batting .335, but has just 4 homers. Their leader in that department is Jose Cruz with just 6.

And of course, with Lou Brock they have a man who is batting .296 and turns every single into a potential double with his base stealing ability.

The Bronx Bombers are the Hottest AL Team

Across the East River from the Mets home in Queens, the Yankees are the surprise team in the AL this season. After starting 6 - 10, the Yankees have gone 34 - 20. They now have the best record in the American League at 40 - 30.

Yesterday, in front of 62,107 fans at Yankee Stadium, they swept a doubleheader over the 1972 AL East champion Detroit Tigers. In the 2nd game they beat The Tiger's top pitcher, Mickey Lolich, who has won 47 games in the past 2 seasons.

One more thing to watch with the Yankees is DH/first baseman Ron Blomberg, who is batting .410 to lead the majors.

The Best Record in Baseball

The hottest team in all of baseball right now is on the west coast. The Los Angeles Dodgers, who have not won a pennant or division title since Sandy Koufax's last season in 1966, have a record of 46 - 26, the best in baseball. The Dodgers also started out shaky at 7 - 11. Since then, they are 35 - 11.

The Dodgers are doing it with both pitching and hitting. They have 5 solid starters with Don Sutton, Tommy John, Claude O'Steen, Andy Messersmith and Al Downing. And they have 2 relief pitchers in Pete Richert and Jim Brewer with ERAs of 1.54 and 1.36.

They are also the best hitting team in baseball, batting .277, and have 4 players hitting above .300 in Manny Mota, Willie Crawford, Ron Cey and Davey Lopes.

CHAPTER FORTY-FOUR

The Wrong Garrett

THE METS SENT TOM SEAVER TO THE MOUND IN CHICAGO HOPING TO TURN THINGS AROUND AGAINST THE 1ST PLACE CUBS

WRIGLEY FIELD - June 30, 1973

I've traveled back virtually to the end of June 1973, to the Windy City, where it's a great time to be a Chicago baseball fan.

The White Sox and the Cubs are both in first place in their divisions.

The Mets arrived here yesterday trying to get a grip on their sinking season.

Five weeks ago the Mets were in 2nd place, just 2 games behind the Cubs.

Coming into yesterday's game they had dropped 9 of their last 12 and stood 10.5 games behind the Cubs.

Fortunately, Tom Savior, I mean Seaver, was on the mound for the Mets.

But just as in his last start, Seaver was a bit shaky at the start. He walked the leadoff batter Rick Monday, who proceeded to steal 2nd and score on a single.

Then Seaver got down to business and shut down the Cubs in the 2nd through the 6th innings.

The Mets manufactured their first run in the 6th when Rusty Staub singled home Mets centerfielder Don Hahn.

Cubs 1 Mets 1 - Middle of the 7th

Prior to yesterday's game, the Cubs manager Whitey Lockman did something former manager Leo Durocher would have never done. He decided to rest his best hitter, Billy Williams, one of the most feared sluggers in the NL, due to Williams ailing back.

Playing left field in Williams' place was Adrian Garrett. He is the older brother of Mets third baseman Wayne Garrett.

Adrian Garrett came into the game with a career batting average of .083 in 62 at bats in the big leagues going back to 1966. Lockman threw some extra batting practice at 10am to get Garrett ready for just his 5th start of the season.

In his first 2 at bats against Tom Terrific, Garrett grounded out and struck out.

Now he led off the bottom of the 7th against Seaver.

What happened next was summed up by George Langford of the Chicago Tribune, *"(Garrett) rifled a Tom Seaver fastball into the right field seats in the 7th to snap a 1 - 1 deadlock."*

Seaver retired the side in order after the home run.

But the damage was done.

Adrian Garrett's home run was the key play of the game.

Seaver had to be lifted for a pinch hitter in the top of the 8th, and even though Ken Boswell, batting for Tom, delivered a game tying home run, Seaver was not there to pitch the rest of the game.

Without Seaver as their savior, the Mets lost in 10 innings 4 - 3 when Adrian Garrett's kid brother, Mets 3rd baseman Wayne Garrett, was stranded at second base after a leadoff walk.

So now it's the last day of June and the Mets are all alone in last.

Here are the NL East Standings as of this morning:

46 – 31 Cubs

36 – 37 Cardinals   8 games back

34 – 36 Expos   8.5 games back

35 – 39 Phillies   9.5 games back

33 – 38 Pirates   10 games back

31 – 39 Mets   11.5 games back

Even though the Mets are in last place, The Sports Time Traveler™ will continue following the 1973 Mets.

It's what Mets fans do.

CHAPTER FORTY-FIVE

All Eyes On Chicago

THE WINDY CITY HOSTS 3 MAJOR SPORTING EVENTS, THAT INCLUDED 3 OF THE GREATEST ATHLETES IN THEIR SPORTS, ON THE SAME DAY IN 1973

NOTE From The Sports Time Traveler™

I can't recall 3 sporting events ever being held in one city on the same day that featured 3 athletes that were among the greatest ever in their respective sports.

So, when I saw the stars aligning over Chicago on June 30, 1973, I knew I had to hop into the sports time travel machine and race back to witness this.

The 3 events in Chicago 50 years ago yesterday were:

• Secretariat in his first race since winning the Triple Crown

• Arnold Palmer competing in The Western Open Golf Championship, just 2 weeks after Arnie lost the U.S. Open when Johnny Miller caught and passed "The King" on the back 9 enroute to his record round of 63

• Willie Mays starting in centerfield against the Cubs at Wrigley, playing in the visiting field in which he has hit the most home runs (54) in his career

Naturally, I went to Wrigley Field on my virtual trip.

The byline date for this story is July 1st, because that's when I read the newspaper accounts of the game.

WRIGLEY FIELD – July 1, 1973

The first place Cubs hosted the New York Mets yesterday afternoon. Both Chicago area teams, the Cubs and the White Sox entered the day in 1st place in their divisions.

The Cubs sent knuckle ball pitcher Burt Hooten to the mound while the Mets countered with 1972 Rookie of the Year, Jon Matlack. Matlack is having a tough season. He comes into the game with a record of 4 - 10 and an ERA of 4.06. Part of the problem is that he was hit on the head by a line drive in May and suffered a hairline fracture of his skull. Matlack, however, missed only a few starts after the mishap.

Matlack started strong yesterday. He retired the Cubs in order in the 1st and didn't allow a hit until the 3rd.

Willie Mays, starting in centerfield and leading off, doubled home the 1st run of the game in the top of the 3rd. For the 42-year-old Mays it was his 103rd extra base hit of his career that he had hit in Wrigley.

The Mets added another run, and Matlack held a 2 - 0 lead going into the bottom of the 6th, when he finally gave up a run.

Still leading 2 - 1 in the 7th, Matlack had another 1-2-3 inning.

In the 8th, Matlack got into trouble. The Cubs put runners on first and third and Ron Santo came to the plate with 2 outs. Santo with 43 RBIs and a .305 batting average is the best hitter on the Cubs at this time.

Phil Pepe in the New York Daily News wrote, *"It was to be the crucial situation of the game... Matlack got two quick strikes on fouls, then blew his best fastball. It was up and away. 'Too up and too away,' said Santo."*

But the umpire, Ed Sudol, disagreed. He called strike 3.

Matlack was out of the inning.

In the 9th, Matlack had one last challenge. Billy Williams, who nearly won the triple crown in 1972, with 37 HRs / 122 RBIs / .333 average, came up with 2 outs and no one on. Williams connected on a deep fly to right field.

But it stayed in the park and Rusty Staub caught it for the final out.

George Langford wrote in the Chicago Tribune, ***"Billy Williams held his thumb and forefinger apart about the width of a half dozen razor blades, 'I just got under it that much. Another centimeter and it's gone.'"***

The Mets came away with a 2 - 1 win.

For Matlack it was his 3rd complete game victory of the month, improving his record to 5 - 10.

However, the game didn't make a dent in the standings. The Cubs are still in 1st place, 7 games ahead of the Cardinals.

And the Mets are still in last.

CHAPTER FORTY-SIX

The Sure Thing

THE 1973 METS COUNT ON TOM SEAVER MORE THAN ANY OTHER PLAYER

MONTREAL - July 5, 1973

I've traveled back virtually exactly 50 years and ventured far north of New York to follow the last place 1973 Mets. Why do I do this?

Because it's what you do when you're a Mets fan.

Three nights ago the Mets lost a typical game. It was 1 - 1 in the 10th and Buzz Capra, a young pitcher with potential, gave up a game winning home run to Boots Day that made the Expos fans very happy.

I stuck around for another game.

Two nights ago the Mets had a rare offensive breakthrough, scoring 8 runs, including a 3 run homer by John Milner, his 12th of the season.

They ended up losing by 11.

That's right.

The Expos scored 19 runs against the Mets.

Think about that.

The Montreal Expos are a team that didn't exist until 4 years ago. They traded their greatest player, Rusty Staub, a.k.a. Le Grande Orange, to the Mets for 3 emerging players last year.

This team scored 19 runs against the vaunted Mets pitching staff?

That's the most runs ever scored against the Mets in their 11 year history.

Not even when they lost 231 games in their first 2 seasons (1962 and 1963) did they allow an opponent to cross home plate 19 times in 9 innings.

I had to stick around for one more game.

This time I knew I was assured to see the Mets win.

Tom Seaver was on the mound for a July 4th game.

It was a sure thing

In an 8 week stretch earlier this season from, May 2 - June 28, the Mets went 8 - 1 when Seaver started. In the games Seaver did not start they were 11 - 28.

That gives you an idea why Seaver is referred to as "The Franchise."

And yesterday Seaver started out like he was a man on a mission. A mission to finally get the no-hitter that tantalized him in the past. The no-hitter he desperately wants on his resume to go along with World Series Champion and Cy Young Award winner.

Seaver can never forget the day, 4 years ago this week, when Jimmy Qualls of the Cubs, a lifetime .223 hitter, broke up his no-hitter in the middle of the 9th inning.

In the 6th inning last night, with one out, Seaver faced Mike Jorgensen, one of the former Mets who was traded for Staub. John Robertson described the action in today's Montreal Star as Jorgensen slapped a ball back towards Seaver, *"off the pitching rubber, scant inches under Tom Terrific's glove."*

Officially it was a single for Jorgensen.

And the no-hit bid was broken.

Seaver quickly got out of the inning and had a one-hitter through 6.

Meanwhile the Mets had already provided enough fireworks for Seaver, 5 runs, all via homers.

Most notably Willie Mays had hit the 657th homer of his career to lead off the 3rd inning.

Seaver was ahead 5 - 0 with 3 innings to play and he was working on a one-hitter against the Expos.

It was a sure thing.

In the 7th, Seaver got the first 2 batters out. Then he let up a single to Tim Foli (another one of the other former Mets in the Staub trade) and another single to John Boccabella.

Okay, so Seaver gave up 2 more singles.

Who doesn't want to see John Boccabella get a hit?

Sorry, I just had to say John Boccabella one more time. It's the most fun name in baseball.

Seaver then got back to business and got Hal Breeden to fly out to the end the inning.

Mets 5 Expos 0 - End of 7 innings

Six outs to go. Seaver is working on a 3-hit shutout.

In the bottom of the 8th, Seaver issued a walk to Ron Hunt and Jorgensen got a clean single. With men on first and second and no outs, Seaver got Ron Fairly to fly out. This brought up Ken Singleton, the 3rd former Met in the Staub deal last year.

Singleton hit a *"perfect double play ball to shortstop Teddy Martinez,"* according to Robertson in the Montreal Star.

Seaver told Robertson after the game, *"The ball Singleton hit did exactly what I wanted it to do."*

Robertson described the rest of the play, *"(the ball) even led him (Martinez) towards second, so all he'd have to do was just flip it to Millan for one and then over to first to end the inning, shutout intact."*

It was a sure thing.

There was one problem about the double play ball

Seaver's roommate, perhaps the best fielding shortstop in the National League, Bud Harrelson, was on the disabled list and was not there to field the ball.

And the shortstop who was there, Teddy Martinez, bobbled it according to the New York Times. He booted it according to the New York Daily News. Whatever he did to it, he didn't handle it like Bud.

Not only was everyone safe, but Hunt even scored from second.

The next batter, Boots Day, of recent fame, promptly doubled, no doubt off a stunned Seaver, and suddenly the score was 5 - 2.

Then Bob Bailey hit a single up the middle for 2 more runs.

Seaver, who should have been out of the inning, was now pulled out of the game by manager Yogi Berra.

Buzz to the Rescue

Berra decided to send Seaver to the showers in favor of Buzz Capra.

This is the same Buzz Capra who made a hero out of Boots Day 2 nights earlier.

This is Buzz Capra who has pitched in a total of 24 games in his career.

Buzz Capra is going to get Tom Terrific out of a jam and save the game?

Yogi Berra told Robertson, *"I figured he could get us out of the inning and then I'd have Sadecki to pitch to their left-handed hitters in the 9th."*

I actually expected to find a better Yogi-ism than that in the newspapers, something like, *"When you're stuck between 2 pitchers pick one."*

Capra gave up a single to the first batter he faced to put runners on first and second and then 2 batters later he served up a 3 run bomb to Ron Woods.

The New York Times Murray Chass wrote, *"The Expos fans roared. The Expos sprung from their dugout seats with glee. And Woods jumped on home plate before his teammates jumped on him."*

Buzz Capra has been a sure thing for the Expos this week.

It was a bitter loss for the Mets.

Expos 7 Mets 5 - Final Score

Phil Pepe wrote in the New York Daily News, *"The Mets... did what seemed impossible. They lost a game in which Tom Seaver went into the 8th with a 5 - 0 lead. It could make a man bet against Secretariat the next time he runs."*

NOTE from The Sports Time Traveler

I've come back to 2023 to let you know that Secretariat actually did lose his next race! Now back to 1973.

Despite my tone of sarcasm today, don't worry, I'm not giving up on the 1973 Mets.

But they're making it very difficult.

Here's the National League East standings after last night's loss:

48 – 34 Cubs

41 – 38 Cardinals (5.5 games back)

37 – 39 Expos   (8 games back)

37 – 42 Phillies   (9.5 games back)

36 – 41 Pirates   (9.5 games back)

33 – 43 Mets   (12 games back)

The Case for the Cubs

Realistically, it's starting to look like the Cubs year is finally here. This is essentially the same Cubs team that blew the division in 1969.

They have the nucleus of a contender with power hitters Billy Williams, last year's near triple crown winner, and Ron Santo, having a career type year in this campaign (11 / 47 / .319).

They're sensational up the middle with Don Kessinger at short, Glenn Beckert at second and Rick Monday in centerfield, who leads the team with 20 home runs.

And they've got tough starting pitchers in Ferguson Jenkins, Burt Hooton and Rich Reuschel (1.95 ERA).

And the Cubs are older and wiser since 1969. Manager Whitey Lockman is strategically resting his players, unlike Leo Durocher, who exhausted his pitching staff 4 years ago.

And notice the number of games the Cubs have played, 82, more than anyone else in the division, six more than the Mets and Expos. That means the Mets have nearly a week's more games to play than the Cubs, but in the same amount of time left in the season. The Cubs will get more rest during the 2nd half of the season than any other team.

Advantage Cubs.

The Case for the Cards

If the Cubs do somehow falter again, look out for the St. Louis Cardinals. The Redbirds have come on like a raging flock in the last 2 months. After starting out a horrendous 5 - 20, since May 8th they have a record of 36 - 18, best in the division by far.

They have veteran leadership in the field in Joe Torre (.309) and Lou Brock (.302) and on the mound in Bob Gibson (103 strikeouts) and Rick Wise (2.87 ERA). And the Cardinals have been to the World Series 3 times in the last 9 years.

Advantage Cardinals.

The Case for the Mets

What is the case for the Mets? If they can't win a sure thing with a 5 - 0 lead for Tom Seaver, it's getting awfully tough to make the case.

Nevertheless, The Sports Time Traveler™ will continue to follow the 1973 Mets.

CHAPTER FORTY-SEVEN

Willie Mays Say Hey, New York Never Saw This

50 YEARS AGO WILLIE MAYS IS MAKING A SUMMER SURGE

INTRODUCTION From The Sports Time Traveler™

Today's article involves a bit of Sports Time Travel archeology, for in my virtual travels back in time, I've uncovered something never seen by most Mets fans in New York. It involves some of the great last on field moments from Willie Mays.

The prospect of making these types of monumental "discoveries" is what keeps me so excited in my daily sports time travels. I just have to share this one with you.

BACKGROUND

I'm a big Willie Mays fan. When I was a 9 year old kid, in the summer of 1973, I cherished the moments that I got to see 42 year old Willie Mays playing for "my Mets."

It was surreal to have the greatest legend in the game on "my team."

And so, I've always taken offense to the narrative that Willie should have hung it up before he came to the Mets in 1972. It was popular in the press, at that time, to bash Mays, saying he was embarrassing himself and tarnishing his legacy with mediocre play.

I took the opposite view.

I felt Mays had earned the opportunity to come back and play in New York at the end of his career, and to contribute in any way he could, whether it was on the field or in the clubhouse.

I loved having Willie Mays on the Mets.

50 years later I still find it surreal that Willie was on "our team."

And here's the sad thing. The analytics of the time didn't reveal the great value he brought to the Mets.

For example, in 1972, Willie Mays led the Mets in on base percentage at .402.

By comparison to 2023, Brandon Nimmo leads the Mets presently in on base percentage at just .359.

How great was Mays .402 on base percentage in 1972? It was good for 2nd in the National League behind Joe Morgan.

But no fan had even heard of on base percentage in 1972.

Then in spring training of 1973, as I previously reported, Mays was sensational, spraying the ball to all fields.

The warm Florida weather suited Willie well. It was the only spring training he ever had in the Sunshine State, because the Giants played spring training in Arizona.

Mays said 1973 was his best spring training ever. He led the Mets batting .350 and led the team with 3 home runs.

But when he hit the cold weather in New York, in April 1973, to begin the season, he couldn't get untracked. He got off to a horrid start and was quickly beset with injuries. In one game, his shoulder was so bad that he couldn't make a throw from centerfield. He tossed the ball to a stunned rookie left fielder George Theodore to throw it.

Mays had to go on the disabled list and missed nearly the entire month of May and early June. When he went hitless in his first couple of games back, Mays' average dipped to a humiliating .095 on June 11th.

And then for one last run, Willie Mays became the Say Hey Kid once again.

In the first half of July, Willie was batting over .300 for the month.

The resurgence of Mays was on display in Atlanta on the nights of Monday, July 16 and Tuesday, July 17, 1973, with 2 special moments that only Willie Mays could ever produce.

Naturally I had to go back in time virtually to see this.

ATLANTA, GA - July 18, 1973

On Monday, 2 days ago, the Mets arrived in Atlanta for a night game that few people saw.

The game was not broadcast on television, not in Atlanta, not in New York, not anywhere.

Here in 1973, the nationally televised NBC Monday Night Game of the Week takes precedence on TV, and that game featured St. Louis vs. San Francisco.

And there were hardly any people in the stadium either. It was a sparse crowd in Atlanta Stadium of just 7,688 fans.

The Last Games for Aaron and Mays on the Same Field

It was a shame that almost no one saw this game, because it was the 1st of a 3 game series that will almost certainly mark the last time that Hank Aaron and Willie Mays play on a ball field at the same time.

Both legends were there on the field, on Monday night, starting in the outfield. Aaron was in left field for the Braves. And Mays was in centerfield for the Mets.

Here were the 2 men who stand at 1st and 2nd place in career home runs in the National League.

Only Babe Ruth, who played in the American league, is ahead of them on the all-time home run list.

Coming into Monday's game the all-time home run list looked like this:

1. Babe Ruth 714

2. Hank Aaron 697

3. Willie Mays 658

4. Harmon Killibrew 544

5T. Mickey Mantle 536

5T. Frank Robinson 536

7. Jimmie Foxx 534

8. Ted Williams 521

9T. Ernie Banks 512

9T. Eddie Mathews 512

11. Met Ott 511

12. Lou Gehrig 493

It is interesting to note that a 3rd player on the above list was in uniform in the stadium. Eddie Mathews is the current manager of the Braves.

Roger Maris is in the House

And one more home run legend was in the stadium. Roger Maris, who broke the Babe's single season home run mark 12 years ago, with 61 in 1961, was on hand to watch the game with his 4 sons, the youngest of whom is a 9 year old Mets fan.

With Aaron closing in on Ruth's all-time home run record, Maris is suddenly in demand in baseball as the only other man who knows what it's like to chase the Babe. He was given box seats right behind the Braves dugout.

A picture of Maris shaking Aaron's hand appeared on the front page of the sports section of the Atlanta Constitution on Tuesday.

Aaron comes into this series among the league leaders in home runs this season with 24.

He seems almost certain to catch Babe Ruth and become the all-time home run leader by late September.

Willie Mays Resurgence

Willie Mays meanwhile is in the middle of what certainly appears to be the final season of his career. But after a poor and injury riddled start to the year, he has hit the ball well for over a month now. And coming into this game he has raised his batting average over 100 points from its horrific early season depths.

Sadly, the national press doesn't seem to recognize the resurgence and has been vilifying Mays. A UPI story keeps appearing in newspapers across the country with the headline, *"Mays Washed Up."*

Monday and Tuesday's games in Atlanta proved that Mays can still play ball and that he is giving it 100%.

On Monday, in the top of the 1st he reached base when he was hit by a Phil Niekro pitch, as the knuckleballer was likely trying to pitch around Mays with Felix Millan on 1st.

Dialing Back to 1954

Then in the 3rd inning Mays made a play in centerfield that was nearly as great as any in his storied career.

With 2 outs, Mets starter Jerry Koosman was facing Braves shortstop Marty Perez. Perez possesses little power, so it is likely that Mays was playing shallow in center.

Unexpectedly, Perez hit a deep fly to straightaway center.

Willie Mays turned around and ran at full speed towards the centerfield fence.

Red Foley of the New York Daily News wrote, *"he tried to emulate the famed going away, over-the-head catch he made against Vic Wertz in the 1954 World Series."*

Wayne Minshew of the Atlanta Constitution wrote similarly that Mays sprint to reach the ball was, *"reminiscent of Willie's back-to-the-infield grab of Vic Wertz' drive in the 1954 World Series."*

SPECIAL NOTE:

For anyone who has never seen, "The Catch," from the 1954 World Series, the catch that turned Mays from a great player into a legend of almost mythical stature, you can see it in this YouTube link:

   https://www.youtube.com/watch?v=7bLt2xKaNH0

   Or simply type, "Willie Mays the Catch," in a YouTube search.

   Now back to Atlanta in 1973.

Mays gets to the ball and catches it

Michael Strauss wrote in the New York Times, *"Mays and the ball arrived at the barrier simultaneously. The outfielder courageously reached for the ball."*

The batter, Marty Perez, told Wayne Minshew of the Atlanta Constitution, *"He caught it for a second."*

Minshew himself wrote in his article, *"Mays had the ball for an instant."*

ANOTHER SPECIAL NOTE:

I interrupt this article for another special note. There is an important difference between the outfield where Willie Mays made, "The Catch," in 1954 and the outfield in Atlanta on July 16, 1973.

Centerfield in the Polo Grounds, in 1954, had the longest stretch of room of any baseball stadium in the 2nd half of the 20th century. It was nearly 500 feet to the wall.

Atlanta Stadium, in 1973, conversely had a wire mesh fence at just 400 feet in dead center.

Mays had much less running room on July 16, 1973, to track down the ball than he had in 1954.

Now back to 1973.

The Crash

And then Willie crashed full speed into the wire screen outfield fence.

Red Foley of the New York Daily News described how Mays then hit the fence, *"Just as the 42-year-old center-fielder appeared to snare the ball, he ricocheted off the screen and fell heavily to the ground. Mays whack... (was) incurred by ramming the screen with his forehead."*

And the ball popped out of his glove.

Michael Strauss wrote in the New York Times, *"Mays... succeeded in gloving it, only to have it pop out as he started falling."*

Minshew wrote, *"(Mays) hit the fence, and had it fall out of his glove."*

The Braves Marty Perez told Minshew, *"I almost stopped running. I thought he had it."*

Mays was knocked onto his back by the force of his crash into the fence. But he still managed to try and throw the ball while he was lying on the ground.

Strauss described it this way, *"Mays picked up the ball and threw it backward over his head toward the plate."*

Minshew wrote, *"He gamely flipped the ball over his shoulder, but Perez was in to score by then."*

Marty Perez had an inside-the-park home run. It was just the 8th of his entire career.

But for one instant, Mays had nearly a completed carbon copy of his greatest catch.

Minshew wrote, *"Perez blast was almost turned into a sensational play by Mets' center fielder Willie Mays."*

*I call it, **"The Catch II,"** since he did have the ball in his glove momentarily and perhaps an umpire in the outfield might have called it an out.*

Mays is Down But Not Out

After the play Willie Mays lay motionless on his back in deep centerfield.

Strauss described it, *"With Mays lying on the grass, out rushed Berra, trainer Tom McKenna, most of the Mets players and all of the tenants of the nearby Braves bullpen. Mays moved his legs about slowly and then his arms to make sure there were no injuries. Then he announced he was ready to continue."*

Mays stayed in the game.

When play resumed Darrell Evans grounded out to end the 3rd inning with the Braves ahead 2 - 0.

Back in Action

And then Willie Mays was right back in action, leading off the top of the 4th inning with a double to deep left and then he scored the Mets 1st run of the game, racing from second to home, when Cleon Jones hit a single. The Mets scored another run later in the inning and tied the game at 2.

Mays played the entire game and got another hit in the 9th when he hit a single to center. He finished the game 2 for 4.

Willie Mays, however, could not help the hapless Mets defeat the Braves. The Braves scored 5 times in the 7th and the Mets lost the game 8 - 6.

It was their 50th loss of the year to go with just 38 wins. And the Mets are still in last place.

It's beginning to look hopeless.

Pictures of the Catch and Crash

The pictures of the catch and crash incredibly did NOT appear in any Atlanta or New York area newspapers.

It sounded so fantastic that I thought pictures just might have made it into another newspaper via one of the wire services.

After a concerted effort I found it!

I found it in the July 17, 1973, Tampa Times.

I was so excited!

And it wasn't just one photo, but a four-photo sequence of **"The Catch II."**

In photo number one, Mays is about to make the sensational back-to-the-infield catch. You can see the ball just as it is about to land in his glove.

It's an amazing picture that looks very similar to still pictures of the "The Catch," from 1954.

In photo number two, Mays has smashed into the fence, and is about to land on his back. The ball can be seen in the air above him, having been dislodged when Mays careened into the fence.

In photo number three, Mays has grabbed the ball on the ground and is trying to fling it backwards, as Mets left fielder Cleon Jones nears Mays.

Finally, in photo number four, Mays lies motionless on his back after the play.

TUESDAY's GAME - July 17, 1973

The 2nd game of the series was played "last night."

This time it was on TV on WOR channel 9 in New York. But there were again well under 10,000 people in the stands.

Aaron started in left field. But Mays was on the bench, feeling "stiff" from his crash into the fence on Monday night.

Yogi Berra made an odd move and started his ace reliever Tug McGraw. McGraw responded by giving up a home run to the Braves 1st batter of the game, Ralph Garr.

In the 6th, McGraw also gave up a home run to Marty Perez, his 2nd in two games, and another home run, number 698 to Hank Aaron. Aaron told Ed Shearer of the AP, *"I felt like when I hit it, it was just icing on the cake."* It was the 6th run of the game for Atlanta.

The move to start McGraw had backfired. The Braves led the game 7 - 1 going into the 9th.

Braves 7 Mets 1 - Top of the 9th inning

The Mets opened the 9th with a single by Wayne Garrett.

After Felix Millan lined out, Rusty Staub belted a home run to cut the deficit to 7 - 3.

Next up was Cleon Jones who singled to center.

John Milner followed with a home run, and suddenly the Mets were down by just 2 runs at 7 - 5, and still had only 1 out.

The next batter, catcher Ron Hodges, grounded out, and now the Mets were down to their last out.

Don Hahn, who started in center for Mays, singled to keep the game alive.

Then Ed Kranepool walked, and Teddy Martinez was brought in as a pinch runner.

The next batter, Jim Beauchamp singled to right, scoring Hahn and sending Martinez to third. Now the Mets were down by just 1 run with the tying run on third base.

The scheduled next batter was lefty Wayne Garrett. Braves manager Eddie Mathews brought in a left-handed pitcher, Tom House.

Yogi Berra countered by bringing up a right-handed pinch hitter for Garrett - Willie Mays.

Willie Mays Pinch Hits

Mays stepped in with runners on first and third and 2 outs in the bottom of the 9th and the Mets down a run.

House got ahead of the count on Mays at 1 - 2. The Mets who had come valiantly back were now down to their last strike.

Red Foley in the New York Daily News describes what happened on the next pitch, *"**Willie, despite a sore back from Monday night's collision with the**"* *center field fence, responded in the way that always set him apart from other ballplayers. House had Willie 1- 2 but, Willie punched the next pitch into right center to plate Martinez from third."*

Then, Willie Mays cleverly took a wide turn at first base to draw the attention of the relay thrower, Braves second baseman, Davey Johnson.

Mays told Wayne Minshew of the Atlanta Constitution, *"I made the big turn at first, figuring that they were looking at me."*

That proved to make the difference for Mets runner Jim Beauchamp as Johnson's throw to the plate was high.

Michael Strauss in the New York Times wrote, *"Mays hit was so long that Beauchamp, who does not have the reputation of being fleet, hoofed it all the way from first, just beating the throw to the plate."*

The Mets now led 8 - 7.

When Mets pitcher Harry Parker, normally a starter, retired the Braves in order in the bottom of the 9th it sealed one of the most improbable victories in franchise history.

And the hero was none other than the Say Hey Kid - Willie Mays, coming off the bench, shaking off a bruised head and body from smashing into the fence the night before, to sock the game winner when the Mets were down to their last strike.

Ed Shearer of the AP opened his article about the game with this, *"Willie Mays, aging superstar of the New York Mets, upstaged Hank Aaron again Tuesday night."*

For Willie's part he brushed off the game winning hit. He told the UPI, *"That's what I'm supposed to do."*

Mays is a .300 hitter again

Willie Mays is now enjoying a summer resurgence. With 3 hits in his last 5 at bats, Mays is now hitting .317 since June 27th, going 19 for 60 in that stretch with 9 extra-base hits.

But even with the win last night, the Mets are still in last place.

POSTSCRIPT

On Thursday, July 19, 1973, Wayne Minshew of the Atlanta Constitution, one of the few people to see Monday's game, wrote this about Willie Mays, *"Like Willie Mays or not, it was a good feeling to watch him cavort all about the place as he did Monday night in that 8 - 6 Atlanta victory. For the truly great ones come few and far between."*

"Willie hit, he ran the bases, and he rendered a brief glimpse into the past when he almost picked off Marty Perez' drive with his back to the infield. It looked for all the world like that nationally wire service-distributed photo of Mays robbing Vic Wertz in the Polo Grounds during the 1954 World Series."

It was also the last complete game that Hank Aaron and Willie Mays ever played against each other.

SPECIAL DEDICATION From The Sports Time Traveler™

This article is dedicated to my good friend, John Keselica, who was also my 1st supervisor when I started working full time in 1988.

John is a huge Willie Mays fan. He grew up watching the Say Hey Kid play for the New York Giants in the Polo Grounds.

John is also a Mets fan. He once took our work team on a required field trip to Philadelphia to watch the Mets play, and, of course, get cheesesteaks at Pat's.

Thanks so much John for all the great years we had working together! I'm looking forward to going with you to see a Mets spring training game in Port St. Lucie next March just like we did before Covid. Maybe we'll run into Steve Mix again.

CHAPTER FORTY-EIGHT

Seaver's Squeeze

THE METS PLAYED THEIR LAST GAME BEFORE THE 1973 ALL-STAR BREAK 50 YEARS AGO LAST WEEKEND

KANSAS CITY - Tuesday, July 24, 1973

I'm here virtually in Kansas City, exactly 50 years ago, where at 7:15pm CT tonight they're playing the All-Star game.

I've been following the New York Mets day-by-day here in 1973.

Two Mets players will be on the National League team tonight - Tom Seaver and Willie Mays.

Seaver will be here because he earned his spot based on his play this year. He just might be the best starting pitcher in baseball.

Willie Mays will be here because he has earned his spot over the last 20 years. He just might be the greatest living baseball player.

Mays was not actually selected by National League manager Sparky Anderson, who picked all the reserve players. Major league baseball commissioner Bowie Kuhn added Mays to the roster, and Sparky and millions of baseball fans were okay with that. After all, Mays holds most of the All-Star game batting records and has been in every game since 1954.

Last Game Before the All-Star Break

A couple of nights ago the Mets finished up a series against Houston in the Astrodome. This was the last game before the All-Star break. So, manager Yogi Berra decided to squeeze in another start for Tom Seaver, on just 3 days rest.

I'm always excited to go back in time and experience Tom Seaver's starts, so I was particularly interested in this game in the Astrodome.

Things began well for the Mets. After Astros starter Jerry Reuss got Willie Mays to strike out to open the game, the Mets got 4 consecutive hits. Felix Millan got things going with a double to right. Then Rusty Staub followed with another double to right, scoring Millan. Cleon Jones then singled to center, scoring Staub. And John Milner singled to left.

Then Reuss, the Astros 2nd best starter, got out of the inning when Jerry Grote hit a double play ball. Grote is still not back to 100% from the hand injury that had him out for 2 months.

Seaver, with a 10 - 5 record, took the mound in the bottom of the 1st with an unusual 2 - 0 lead. Sometimes Seaver must think he's got to do it all by himself to win a game. In his 5 losses this year the Mets have scored a total of 5 runs.

But Seaver promptly gave away half of his 2 - 0 lead in the bottom of the 1st. After giving up a single to Tommy Helms, Seaver's pick-off throw to first base was wild and Helms moved safely to second. Then Cesar Cedeno doubled to left and scored Helms. Seaver got the next 2 batters out, but his lead was down to 1 run.

METS 2 ASTROS 1 - end of 1 inning

Over the next 4 innings the game became a pitcher's duel. Both Reuss and Seaver gave up just 2 hits and allowed no runs in the 2nd through 5th innings. The score was still 2 - 1 going into the 6th inning.

Reuss got the heart of the Mets order, Staub, Jones and Milner to go 1 - 2 - 3 in the top of the 6th.

In the bottom of the inning, Seaver had to face the Astros power hitters. He got Cedeno to fly out to center. Then, he had Bob Watson on a 2 - 2 count. Watson blasted Seaver's next pitch into the outfield seats for a home run. The game was now tied at 2.

Seaver got Doug Radar and Lee May out, but the damage was done.

Tom Seaver had lost his lead.

METS 2 ASTROS 2 - end of 6 innings

The Mets had the bottom of the order coming up in the top of the 7th. Jerry Grote popped out to first. Then Wayne Garrett singled to left. And Bud Harrelson walked.

This brought up Seaver with 1 out and men on first and second.

With the count at 1 - 1, Seaver was given the order to bunt.

The idea was to move up the runners for Willie Mays, the next batter.

But Seaver missed on his bunt attempt. And Wayne Garret was caught too far off second base. Astros catcher Johnny Edwards, a 2-time gold glove award winner, threw the ball to second to catch Garrett. But instead of trying to get back safely into second, Garrett took off for third. The throw from second to third was not in time and Garrett was safe. And Harrelson moved up to second on the play.

Seaver's muffed bunt attempt moved up the runners, and Seaver was still at bat with a 1 - 2 count.

Leonard Koppett, covering the game for the New York Times, wrote, ***"So the missed bunt became a double steal."***

Now Seaver got the bunt sign again. This time he hit a perfect squeeze bunt to first baseman Lee May. Garrett came running home on the bunt and beat the throw to the plate.

Tom Seaver had gotten his lead back by himself.

Reuss then got Willie Mays to strike out for the 3rd consecutive time.

Thus, the original idea of the bunt, to move the runners up for Mays, likely would not have worked.

METS 3 ASTROS 2 - middle of the 7th inning

Now that he had the lead, Seaver went into lock down mode. He gave up a 1 out single in the 7th, and then struck out the next 2 batters to get out of the inning.

In the 8th, he gave up a leadoff single to Helms, and then erased the runner when he got Cedeno to hit a double play ball. Seaver quickly ended the inning by getting Watson to also hit a grounder.

In the 9th Seaver had a slight scare. On a pitch to leadoff hitter Doug Radar, Seaver felt a twinge on his right side. But he stayed in the game and got 3 ground outs to close it out.

No runner reached second base on Seaver after Watson's homer in the 6th.

METS 3 ASTROS 2 - FINAL SCORE

The win raised Seaver's record to 11 - 5 and maintained his league leading ERA at 2.02.

Being both the victor on mound and the man with the game winning hit prompted Red Foley in the New York Daily News to start his article on the game with this, *"When they refer to Tom Seaver as the Mets' franchise, baseball people ain't just whistlin' Dixie. That Tom Seaver can do it all was displayed again Sunday when he not only struck out nine Astros but squeezed home the winning run."*

The squeeze bunt by Seaver sounded even more impressive when pitcher Jerry Reuss spoke to the press about it after the game. He told Red Foley, *"The pitch was high and outside, probably the toughest one for a batter to bunt."*

TEAM STANDINGS AT THE ALL-STAR BREAK

Here are the National League East standings at the All-Star break:

51 – 45 St. Louis Cardinals

51 – 46 Chicago Cubs 51 - 46 0.5 games back

46 – 38 Pittsburgh Pirates 46 - 48 4 games back

46 – 51 Philadelphia Phillies 46 - 51 5.5 games back

44 – 51 Montreal Expos 44 - 51 6.5 games back

42 – 51 New York Mets 42 - 51 7.5 games back

The Mets are in last, and have been in last since June 29th. The Mets had started well this season. At the end of April, they were 12 - 8 and tied for 1st. Then they went 22 - 38 as they dropped from 1st to last.

Their lowest point was two weeks ago, on July 8th, when their record stood at 34 - 46 and they were 12.5 games back.

Since then they are 8 - 5 and have moved up to just 7.5 games back.

The Mets improvement to just 7.5 games back has a lot to do with Cubs collapse. The Cubs high point was June 29th when they were 47 - 31. Since then, the Cubs have gone 5 - 16 and have lost 1st place to the Cardinals.

The Cards have had a real merry-go-round season. They started with a horrific 5 - 20 record. Even the 1962 Mets started with a better record after 25 games. But since then, the Cards have gone 46 - 25 and are now at the top of the division.

If the Cardinals continue at this pace they could run away with the division. The Cardinals went to the World Series 3 times in the past 9 years, in 1964, 1967 and 1968, winning 2 of those 3 World Series', so they are formidable opponents. Team leaders Lou Brock and Bob Gibson were on all 3 of those World Series teams and are playing well again this year.

Chapter Forty-Nine

1973 METS – Midseason Grades

It's the 1973 All-Star break and time to assess the top Mets players

INTRO From The Sports Time Traveler™

I've been following the 1973 Mets day-by-day since the start of spring training. I do this by reading newspaper archives each day exactly 50 years ago. My stories are all based on the factual accounts of the Mets games.

Today's post is different. No newspaper that I have seen in 1973 had a midseason report card on the Mets like those we're used to seeing in online articles for sports teams in 2023.

So, I decided to create my own grading of the key Mets personnel based on everything I've experienced in covering the team. I support my assessments with statistics from the newspapers in 1973 and www.base ballreference.com.

Now I'm very excited to share The Sports Time Traveler's™ midseason report card for the 1973 New York Mets.

1973 METS - MIDSEASON GRADES

NEW YORK - July 25, 1973

We're now at the All-Star break at this time in 1973. The All-Star game was played 50 years ago last night. So, it's officially the midseason break. And that means it's time to step back and assess how the Mets are doing as a team and individually.

GRADE: A

Tom Seaver, SP

Only one Mets player deserves this status and that's "The Franchise" - Tom Seaver.

Seaver is arguably the best starting pitcher in major league baseball. While he hasn't won 15+ games like several other starters, none of those 15+ game winners has an ERA even close to Seaver's 2.02. And his positive impact on the Mets is unquestionable. The Mets are 13 - 8 when Seaver has started and just 29 - 43 when he doesn't.

GRADE: B

Rusty Staub, RF

Felix Millan, 2B

John Milner, 1B

Bud Harrelson, SS

George Stone, SP

Jon Matlack, SP

The Mets are pretty solid on the right side of the field with quality players at first, second and in right field. They're also good at shortstop when their man is healthy. And 2 starting pitchers besides Seaver are proving dependable.

Let's take a deep dive on each of these 6 players.

Rusty Staub, RF

Rusty Staub got off to a terrible start and was batting under .200 as late as May 13th. In the last 2 months he has become a reliable power hitter. He has hit 10 HRs, has a team leading 47 RBIs and he's batting .280. He has also hit .417 with 9 RBIs in his last 10 games. The Mets seem to be set in right field.

Felix Millan, 2B

Millan, like Staub, started out miserably at the plate. He was batting under .200 in early May. Since then he has been a reliable number 2 hitter in the batting order. He is now batting .302. And he is an excellent defensive player. The Mets are solid at second.

John Milner, 1B

23-year-old Milner was 3rd in the Rookie of the Year voting last season. He got off to a hot start batting .327 with 5 home runs in the first 16 games of the season. Then he got hurt and missed 3 weeks. And when he came back his average dipped all the way to .206 in early July. But he has continued to hit homers and drive in runs. He leads the team with 14 HRs and is 2nd to Staub with 43 RBIs - impressive stats for a 2nd year player. And in his last 10 games, Milner is hitting .417.

Bud Harrelson, SS

Harrelson is one of the best defensive shortstops in baseball. He won a gold glove in 1971 and he was 20th and 22nd in NL MVP voting in 1970 and 1971.

His value on the field was proven recently when he missed a month with an injury. His back up, Teddy Martinez, was simply not reliable to make the plays Bud does routinely.

When Harrelson can hit a little bit it's a big plus. And this year he's doing alright. While he's only batting .254, his on base percentage is nearly a 100 points higher at .345. That's 13 points higher than the Mets leading hitter, Felix Millan, whose OBP is just .332.

Of course, in 1973 no one knows what OBP is, so they don't realize how valuable Bud is at the plate.

Harrelson has another intangible value he brings to the team. He is Tom Seaver's roommate on the road. And while Harrelson was out the Mets lost both games that Seaver started on the road.

In addition, the Mets recent surge, in which they've won 8 of their last 13, started the day Bud came back into the starting lineup. Overall, the Mets are 30 - 30 with Harrelson and 12 - 21 without him this season.

The Mets need Bud to stay healthy.

George Stone, SP

George Stone was a so-so starter for the Braves for the past 4 seasons. The Mets acquired him, and Millan, in the Gary Gentry trade, which is starting to look like a brilliant move. Gentry is out for the season, while Stone is pitching well. Stone started the season in the Mets bullpen, but after he allowed only 1 earned run in 7 appearances in April and May, he took away Harry Parker's starting job and became part of the Mets rotation. As a starter he has pitched into the 6th inning every time and he's gone 4 - 3. His ERA stands at 2.74.

Jon Matlack, SP

Matlack has been on a roller coaster ride this year. He was the Rookie of the Year in 1972 in which he was sensational with a 15 - 10 record and 2.32 ERA. He appeared to be the solid number 2 starter behind Seaver when he won on a 4-hitter in the 2nd game of the season. Then in the next game he gave up 6 runs in 4 innings. The Mets lost 5 of the next 6 games in which he started, and his ERA almost cracked 5.

Then Matlack literally had his head cracked when he was hit on the forehead by a line drive on May 8th. He was diagnosed with a fractured skull. Amazingly, he came back just 11 days later and pitched 6 innings without allowing a run. But he performed poorly in his next 3 starts, only to then pitch a gem against the Dodgers, one of the best hitting teams in baseball. That game started a stretch in which he has gone 5 - 4 and dropped his ERA from 4.63 to its current 3.45. If he can continue to pitch this way, the Mets have a solid 2nd starter.

GRADE: C

Jerry Koosman, SP

Willie Mays, CF

Wayne Garrett, 3B

Ed Kranepool, LF/1B

Ray Sadecki, RP

These players have had highs and lows, and the Mets need more consistent strong play from them.

Jerry Koosman, SP

Koosman has been frustrating Mets fans this entire decade. After a brilliant rookie season in 1968 and then being a major part of the miracle in 1969, Kooz has not been able to be the lock down number 2 starter behind Seaver that it appeared he would be.

This season he appeared to finally be ready be that man when he opened the season with a 1.06 ERA in April, and won his first 5 starts. Since then, he has gone 3 - 9 and his ERA has gone up to 3.40.

The Mets need Kooz to be better than this.

Willie Mays, CF

It is perhaps unfair to grade 42-year-old Willie Mays. The legend is obviously well past his prime, but he is a beloved figure in New York, so he is being given the opportunity to play. And besides, the Mets literally have no one better to play centerfield.

Mays started out hot in spring training, batting .350 and leading the team with 3 HRs. Then the cold New York weather and nagging injuries led him to a horrific start to the season. Things got worse for Willie when he injured his shoulder and missed a month. When he came back he still couldn't get untracked, and his batting average got as low as .094 on June 11th.

Since that time Willie has improved dramatically. His batting average reached .220 last weekend. And since June 27th he is batting .294.

Wayne Garrett, 3B

Third base has been a sore spot for the Mets in their 11 year franchise history. More than 50 players have put in time at third for the Mets.

Wayne Garrett won the 3B job from the banished Jim Fregosi early in the season (Fregosi was sold to the Texas Rangers). But Garrett has been a liability at the plate for much of the year. His average dropped to .217 in late June. Since then he has batted .333 in his last 90 at bats. If he can keep doing that the Mets may finally have the third baseman they have always lacked.

Ed Kranepool, LF/1B

It's hard to rate Ed Kranepool. He's the only player that has been in a Mets uniform for all 12 seasons of the Mets existence. He does what is asked of him. He plays where they need him. This season he has started 47 of the Mets 93 games filling in for Jones in left field when he was out and for Milner at first when he was injured.

Kranepool started the season nicely and was hitting .300 in late May. And he is still the Mets 4th leading RBI man with 27. But he has hit just one homer all season and even worse he has gone into a terrible slump. He has just 7 hits in his last 49 at bats for a .142 average. The Mets need more from Kranepool.

Ray Sadecki, RP

Sadecki is another one who is hard to rate. He's envisioned as the Mets 2nd best relief pitcher, even though he is a lefty just like relief ace Tug McGraw. Sadecki is a veteran who used to be a starter and won 20 games for the World Champion St. Louis Cardinals in 1964. He beat Whitey Ford to win game 1 of the World Series that year.

Now Sadecki is called up whenever Yogi needs him. Sometimes he finishes games, sometimes he takes over when a starter bombs. More recently he has been inserted in the rotation for a couple of starts.

The problem with Sadecki is he's only great against the Cubs. He's pitched 52 innings this year. 15 of those innings have been against the Cubs, and he has yet to allow them a single run. In the other 37 innings he's given up 18 earned runs.

So, while his overall ERA stands at a respectable 3.14, it's highly subsidized by the city of Chicago.

The Mets need Sadecki to apply that same Magic to his other appearances.

GRADE: D

Tug McGraw, RP

Jim McAndrew, SP

Duffy Dyer, C

These players have been bitter disappointments so far this season and the Mets need them to dramatically improve.

Tug McGraw, RP

McGraw is another puzzle on the 1973 Mets. He has been one of the top relief pitchers in baseball since Gil Hodges moved him to the bullpen before the 1969 season. And this season he started out as the old reliable Tug. He saved 5 games in April and his ERA got down to 1.32.

Since then, Tug has had several disastrous appearances, and his ERA currently is 6.17 and he has had more blown saves and losses than saves.

The Mets need McGraw to return to form as the trusted lefty closer.

Jim McAndrew, SP

McAndrew is one of the big disappointments on the pitching staff. He earned a spot in the rotation after his 11 - 8 2.80 ERA performance last year in 23 starts. But his first start of the season went badly and in his 2nd start he couldn't get out of the 1st inning, giving up 5 runs. After a couple of quality starts his ERA recovered to 5.40 at the end of April and it looked like he was getting on track.

But since then McAndrew has not had a start in which he lasted past the 6th inning. His ERA is up to 5.65. The Mets have lost the last 4 games he started and his record stands at 3 - 7. He officially lost his spot in the rotation after a July 3rd game in which the Expos scored 19 runs. That's the all-time record for runs scored against the Mets in their 12 seasons in the National League.

Duffy Dyer, C

In fairness to Duffy Dyer, he is a backup catcher. He was thrust into a starting role when Jerry Grote went down early in the year and missed 2 months. But Dyer has simply not been able to give the Mets anything at the plate. When Grote came back 2 weeks ago Dyer was hitting just .183.

UNGRADED

Jerry Grote, C

Cleon Jones, LF

These players have been injured for much of the season, but were expected to be the starters at their positions this year. The Mets need them to get healthy and begin to contribute.

Jerry Grote, C

Grote is back, but he is still not 100%. He has missed most of the season. It is too early to grade Grote, who is regarded as one of the best defensive catchers in baseball and has been a reliable, but never prolific player at the plate.

Cleon Jones, LF

Jones was another hero of 1969 when he batted .340 for the season. He has been a staple in left field ever since. This year he couldn't have started much better. He smashed 2 home runs in the opening day victory. And he was batting .300 going into a doubleheader against the Cubs on April 19th. That day he got hurt and missed the next 3 weeks. When he came back, he hit in 6 straight games and then got hurt again and missed another 6 weeks. Since his return he has had 8 RBIs in 10 games. It's possible that if Jones can remain healthy, he will have a big 2nd half of the season.

MANAGER YOGI BERRA - GRADE: C

Yogi Berra has had a difficult season so far. The expectations were high for the Mets this season. Although they have not won more than 83 games since winning 100 in the Miracle year of 1969, they have not had a losing record since 1968.

And after going 83 - 73 in 1972, even though Rusty Staub missed half the season, there was some thought that the Mets might be able to build on that record, especially since they had 2 of the top 3 rookies in the National League from last year in Matlack and Milner.

But after a solid start in which the team was 12 - 8 at the end of April, they floundered for the next 60 games going 22 - 38 to fall from a tie for 1st all the way to last and 12.5 games back.

Now the team has shown some life in the last 2 weeks going 8 - 5. But they are still in last place in the NL East.

Last place at midseason is a position the Mets have not been in since the 1967 season in which they lost 101 games.

The team, despite the injuries, has significantly under-performed up to this point.

It's going to be up to Berra to keep the little bit of momentum going and make smart choices with his personnel. However, one recent situation in which he pulled Tom Seaver in a close game for young Buzz Capra stands out as a questionable move, especially because it didn't work. And the Mets need Berra to make things work.

METS OUTLOOK

The Mets are in last place and have been stuck there since June 29th.

All their regular starters that were injured have now returned to the line up and the team has won 8 of their last 13 games.

And while they are in last they are only 7.5 games back.

In the last 10 games the Mets regular number 2 through number 5 batters are hitting well:

Felix Millan .391

Rusty Staub .417 with 9 RBIs

John Milner .417 with 8 RBIs

Cleon Jones .256 with 8 RBIs

Leonard Koppett of the New York Times wrote on Monday, *"The direction of those figures is whatever hope the Mets have along with Seaver's normal excellence."*

But Koppett is not predicting a pennant for the Mets.

There is, however, one sportswriter in America who thinks the Mets might have a chance to win the NL East.

Toby Beckham, a sportswriter for the Rock Hill, SC Evening Herald wrote this about the New York Mets in the July 19th edition of the newspaper, *"For the first time in quite a while they have some of their regulars back in the lineup... with a solid club New York now has a chance at a divisional title."*

That seems like a pretty outlandish forecast for a last place team. But I'll take it.

1973 ALL-STAR GAME

Before I close, I'd like to share the results of the 1973 All-Star game which was played last night, July 24, 1973, in Kansas City.

The National League continued their dominance, winning for 10th time in 11 years by a 7 - 1 score.

Willie Mays came up in the top of the 8th and drew a standing ovation.

Hank Aaron and Willie Mays were the only two players last night that received standing ovations.

You can watch Willie Mays only at bat in the game at the 24:35 mark of the YouTube video.

https://www.youtube.com/watch?v=pAZigqxG164&t=1476s

Or, type, "1973 MLB ASG @ Kansas City MLB Film," in the YouTube search bar.

CHAPTER FIFTY

Grading the Mets' Trades

FOLLOWING UP ON YESTERDAY'S MIDSEASON GRADES, TODAY I'M GRADING THE METS GM

INTRO From The Sports Time Traveler™

In yesterday's article, I provided midseason grades on the 1973 Mets key players and their manager as we are in the middle of the All-Star break.

Today, I'm following up with a grade for the 1973 Mets General Manager Bob Scheffing.

Before beginning the article, I'd like to share something I read in the New York Daily News from 50 years ago today. There was an interesting article in which Red Foley summarized a conversation he had with Willie Mays.

The article underscores the value that Willie's experience and optimism provides to the team.

Here's what Foley wrote:

"Willie Mays is very big on momentum. He thinks winning is like a virus, it's infectious, and right now, according to Mays, the Mets have all the symptoms of a winning virus."

Foley then quoted Willie directly saying, *"We're still last, but we're only six games back on the losing side. And I think those wins we had in Atlanta and Houston gave us some momentum... If everyone plays up to his capabilities, it'll make a difference."*

Foley summed up Willie's comments, *"May's isn't predicting any miracles, but he thinks the Mets schedule for the next two weeks can go a long way towards indicating what the club might do the rest of the season."*

The Mets are in last place in the NL East, 7.5 games back, but just six behind in the loss column as Mays pointed out.

Tonight, in 1973, they start the 2nd half of the season with a doubleheader against the 1st place Cardinals. Jon Matlack faces Bob Gibson in game 1 and Jerry Koosman faces Alan Foster in game 2.

Seaver pitches tomorrow.

I can't wait!

And now today's article.

1973 METS - Grading the Mets Trades

NEW YORK - July 26, 1973

It's time to rate the performance of Mets General Manager, Bob Scheffing.

General managers need to be graded over a longer horizon than just this season. Bob Scheffing took over the job of GM prior to the 1970 season. I would contend that all his major moves since 1970 need to be considered for this assessment.

I'm going to focus on the four biggest moves:

1. The Gary Gentry for Felix Millan Trade - DEAL GRADE: A

2. The Dumping of Tommie Agee - DEAL GRADE: D

3. The Nolan Ryan for Jim Fregosi Debacle - DEAL GRADE: F

4. The Acquisition of Rusty Staub for 3 Young Mets - DEAL GRADE: B

A notable move that I have left off this list is the trade for Willie Mays. That deal was not masterminded by Bob Scheffing. Rather, Mets owner Joan Payson made a backroom deal with the San Francisco Giants to enable Willie Mays to come back to New York and have financial security after his playing career. Payson was a huge Willie Mays fan going back to the 1950s and had coveted the idea of putting Willie in a Mets uniform since the start of the franchise in 1962.

Let's now look at each of the four above named deals.

The Gary Gentry for Felix Millan Trade – DEAL GRADE: A

A year after Gentry was deemed untouchable, Bob Scheffing parted with him to get a steady second baseman, Felix Millan.

Millan has proved his value as a .300 hitter this season, and through his stellar play as part of a great double play combination with Bud Harrelson.

Meanwhile Gentry started poorly for the Braves and is now out for the season.

As a throw in, the Mets got George Stone, who has now cracked the Mets starting rotation.

This has turned out to be a great deal for the Mets.

The Dumping of Tommie Agee - DEAL GRADE: D

This was a bewildering move.

Tommie Agee was one of players most associated with the Miracle of 1969. He almost single handedly won game 3 of the 1969 World Series as documented in an earlier article I posted last year when he was inexplicably traded.

As previously reported, it is hard to explain this deal. And it looks even worse now.

Rich Chiles, the minor league center fielder the Mets got in return, was a bust and the Mets gave him away early in the season. This created a huge hole in center field for the 1973 Mets.

Meanwhile Agee, although well past his prime, has been somewhat productive for the Houston Astros with 7 HRs and a .253 average in 65 games. There is however a telltale sign lurking in Agee's stats. He has stolen only 1 base and has been caught stealing 5 times. Agee clearly doesn't have the legs he had just 2 years ago when he stole 28 bases and was caught just 6 times.

Even if Agee is aging the Mets still could have benefited from keeping him. Given that Willie Mays is not able to play every day anymore and the Mets have no true major league center fielder on the roster besides Mays, this has put Yogi Berra in a bind all season to find players to fill the gap in center that was unnecessarily created when Scheffing dumped Agee. Berra has on occasion even resorted to starting utility infielder Teddy Martinez in center.

If the Mets had kept Agee, he could have at least platooned with Mays in centerfield.

The Nolan Ryan for Jim Fregosi Debacle – GRADE F

This is the worst trade in Mets history to date.

Here's how it happened.

After the 1971 season, Bob Scheffing decided he needed to solve the problem at third base where the Mets had never had a steady player.

He had brought in veteran third baseman Bob Aspromonte to play the position prior to the 1971 season and that didn't work out. Aspromonte hit just .225 in 104 games.

Wayne Garrett, who looked promising, platooning at second and third base in 1970 with 12 HRs / 45 RBIs / .254, missed much of the 1971 season on active military duty. He finished the season in a 0 for 29 slump that left him with an ugly looking .213 average in 56 games. Apparently, Scheffing figured Garrett would never pan out at third.

This prompted Scheffing to become enamored with the idea of trading for the California Angels' Jim Fregosi.

NOTE From The Sports Time Traveler™

I interrupt this article to let you know that die hard Mets fans over age 50, including myself, are now shuddering just from the mention of that name, Jim Fre...

I can't say his whole name again.

I need to pause for a moment to try and collect myself.

Breathe in. Breathe out. It's going to be okay.

Alright let's continue.

Fregosi had been a steady player, in the top 30 in the American League MVP voting for 8 straight seasons from 1963 to 1970.

But in 1971, his production on the Angels dropped off a cliff. He had a line of 5 HRs / 33 RBIs / .233 average and played in just 107 games after having missed only about 20 games in the prior 6 seasons.

That should have been a red flag for Mets GM Bob Scheffing.

The other red flag was that Fregosi had spent 100% of his time in his All-Star years at shortstop.

I don't mean figuratively 100%. It's a fact that Jim Fregosi NEVER played a single game at third base in his 11 year major league career before coming to the Mets.

But Scheffing decided Jim Fregosi was his man and that he could be the Mets savior at third base.

Initially the Angels asked Scheffing for Mets starting pitcher Gary Gentry.

But Scheffing balked at that.

He countered with Nolan Ryan. Scheffing had soured on Ryan who could throw the ball faster than anyone in baseball, but had a 29 - 38 record with the Mets in 74 starts over 5 seasons as a spot starter.

And on December 10, 1971, the deal was made.

NOTE from The Sports Time Traveler™

I previously wrote about Scheffing balking at Gentry and offering Ryan in an earlier chapter titled, "I Asked for Gary Gentry."

As a veteran player, the move to third base for Fregosi, and being in a new league, must have not phased him one little bit, because his stats remained remarkably consistent from 1971 to 1972.

He hit the same number of home runs - five.

He drove in just one less run - 32 instead of 33.

And he lost just one point on his batting average dipping from .233 to .232.

There was no sign of him returning to form as a top 30 player.

And this year he didn't start any better.

Fregosi was dumped for cash to the Texas Rangers 2 weeks ago.

Meanwhile Nolan Ryan turned into... well... Nolan Ryan.

With a rotation spot secure on the Angels from day one, something he never had on the Mets, and perhaps a less stressful environment in Anaheim as opposed to the Big Apple, Ryan became one of the best pitchers in baseball overnight.

In 1972, he won 19 games, on a team with a sub. 500 record, and he posted a 2.28 ERA. He also threw 9 shutouts. The entire Mets pitching staff only threw 8 shutouts in 1972.

And Nolan Ryan also led the major leagues with 329 strikeouts.

This season Ryan has tossed 2 no-hitters, and last week, he nearly had a 3rd no hitter, giving up one bloop single in 9 innings.

The Acquisition of Rusty Staub for 3 Young Mets – GRADE B

In a move made just prior to the 1972 season, Scheffing shipped out 3 young Mets players:

- Tim Foli (age 20)

- Mike Jorgensen (age 22)

- Ken Singleton (age 24)

These were not prospects. They were part-time players on the Mets throughout the 1971 season. They collectively had more than 10% of all the Mets at bats in 1971.

Foli was a capable utility infielder. While Singleton showed some power potential, hitting 13 HRs (just one less than team leaders Cleon Jones and Tommie Agee). And he did that with less than 300 at bats.

In return the Mets got Rusty Staub, an established star in the prime of his career.

Staub was a beloved figure in Montreal where he earned the nickname, " Le Grand Orange," because of his red hair and power hitting.

Staub was coming off a strong season for the Expos in 1971, when he was 27 years old. He had 19 HRs / 97 RBIs / .311.

The Mets simply didn't have a slugger like that on the team and they needed one.

Staub, however, broke a bone in his hand when he was hit by a pitch early in the 1972 season and missed most of the year.

This season he had some early injury troubles, but he is now gaining his stride. In his last 10 games he's batting .417. And he leads the Mets with 10 HRs / 47 RBIs and is batting .280.

It appears the Mets have the man they wanted.

On the Expos, the three former Mets all became full time starters in 1972, though none of them had a break out year. This year Singleton's stat line is similar to Staub's. While Foli and Jorgensen are full-time players with mediocre production.

This is a tougher one to grade. Staub is clearly a club leader, a cleanup batter, and a fan favorite. So, it's hard to say the Mets should have stuck with the home-grown talent.

OVERALL GRADE FOR GM BOB SCHEFFING: C

I know some Mets fans will want to give Scheffing an F overall just because of the mega failure of the Ryan trade. But I don't think it's fair to make that one trade the only criteria for judging his performance.

In the four trades I focused on, the grades were A, B, D and F. So I'm going to go with the average and give Bob Scheffing a C.

C by the way is not acceptable. Scheffing needs to do better to make the Mets into a competitive, World Series contending team again.

I will be continuing to follow the 1973 Mets day-by-day and reporting to you when there is something so exciting I just have to share it.

CHAPTER FIFTY-ONE

It's in the Cards... New York may be a World Series Team Again

THE FIRST GAMES AFTER THE ALL-STAR BREAK PORTENDED GREAT THINGS FOR TWO STORIED FRANCHISES

NEW YORK - July 27, 1973

Last night, here in 1973, every team was back in action after the All-Star break.

The last place Mets were in St. Louis for a big doubleheader against the 1st place Cardinals.

The Mets were starting the 2nd half of the season with reason to believe. Even though they're in the cellar, they're just 6 games back in the loss column. And they've won 8 of their last 13. Most importantly, the entire starting lineup is playing again after several had missed protracted time with injuries.

And 2 of the Mets best pitchers were starting in the doubleheader - Jon Matlack and Jerry Koosman.

This evening had all the makings of something big for the Mets.

In the 1st game things started out well for the Mets as they faced Cardinals ace Bob Gibson. The Mets manufactured a run in the top of the 2nd inning on a 3 base error and Ed Kranepool's sacrifice fly.

But in the bottom of the 2nd, Matlack allowed 7 base runners and 5 of them scored.

CARDINALS 5 METS 1 - end of two innings

Three more singles in the 4th gave the Cardinals a 6 - 1 lead.

Yogi Berra then sent in Don Hahn to pinch hit for Matlack in the top of the 5th and he brought in John Strohmayer, a reliever picked up on waivers a couple of weeks ago, to take the mound in the bottom of the inning.

Stohmayer loaded the bases on 2 singles and a walk before facing Cardinals ace pitcher Bob Gibson. Gibson then launched the 24th home run of his career, a grand slam, giving him a 10 - 1 lead.

The Mets were playing like little leaguers and this game should have been called over at this point.

Gibson completed the game, which ended 13 - 1. It was the 236th win of his career moving him one win ahead of Juan Marichal for the winningest active pitcher in baseball. It was also the 245th complete game of his career. On the season the 37-year-old Gibson was now 11 - 9 with a 2.82 ERA.

GAME 2

The 2nd game pitted Koosman against Alan Foster. This one settled into a pitcher's duel. Kooz was "on", giving up just 3 hits and 1 run in seven innings before he was taken out for a pinch hitter in the 8th because the Mets had given no support. Literally none. The Mets had not scored.

In the bottom of the 8th, relief pitcher Harry Parker got the first 2 batters out. Next up was Joe Torre. He put the Cardinals in front 2 - 0 with a solo home run.

The Mets were down to their final at bat in the top of the 9th. Here was a chance to make a comeback, salvage this game and split the doubleheader. That would at least keep them 6 games back in the loss column with Tom Seaver on the mound tomorrow night.

Cleon Jones led off with a single. And John Milner followed with another. Jim Beauchamp grounded out, but moved the runners over to second and third. Then a Jerry Grote grounder scored Jones.

The Mets were down 2 - 1 with 2 outs in the 9th.

Now Berra pinch hit for Bud Harrelson and sent Willie Mays to the plate. Mays had batted in the tying and winning runs in a game last week. Now he had a chance to do it again.

Relief pitcher Diego Segui was brought in. The count was 2 - 1 and Neal Russo of the St. Louis Dispatch described the next play, *"Mays had taken a wicked cut at a fastball that he fouled off."*

After the game, Segui told Russo, *"3 years ago I don't get that fastball by Willie."*

Segui, with a 2 - 2 count on Mays, then threw a forkball. Neal Russo wrote, *"Mays, obviously fooled, took a half-baked swing."*

Willie Mays struck out.

The game was over. The Cardinals had won it 2 - 1

Sadly, they had wasted Jerry Koosman's best outing since May 9th, when he won his 5th straight start to go 5 - 0 on the season. Now Kooz' record dropped to 8 - 10.

And the Mets had lost a doubleheader by a combined score of 15 - 2.

They are now 8 games back in the loss column in last place with a record of 42 - 53.

The Cardinals are in 1st place, 1.5 games up and surging. After a 5 - 20 start to the season, St. Louis has gone 48 - 25.

One of the storied franchises in baseball history look like they could be headed to the World Series.

Back in New York at Yankee Stadium

Meanwhile, back in New York, the 1st place New York Yankees, who sport the best record in the American League, were at home against the Milwaukee Brewers.

This game was also a pitcher's duel between Jim Colborn, the Brewers' ace and Pat Dobson, a 20-game winner with the Orioles in 1971, who was having a so-so season with the Yankees. Dobson entered the game with a 9 - 10 record and a 4.23 ERA.

But Dobson had looked good in his last 2 starts before the All-Star break, and he was in his 1971 form last night. Through 9 innings, Dobson had allowed no runs and just 2 hits.

There was one problem. Colborn was nearly as sharp. He had given up no runs and 7 hits through 9 innings.

The game went into the 10th and so did the 2 starters. No runs were scored and both starters stayed in the game for the 11th inning. Again no runs were scored.

YANKEES 0 BREWERS 0 - End of 11 innings

Dobson came back out on the mound to start the 12th inning at Yankee stadium. He gave up a single to Dave May and that prompted Yankees manager Ralph Houk to take Dobson out for his closer, Sparky Lyle.

Murray Chass of the New York Times wrote, ***"Dobson received a well-deserved standing ovation... If there was a disappointing note for the Yankees it was that they couldn't get a run for Dobson."***

It was the finest pitching performance of Pat Dobson's career, and he had nothing to show for it.

Lyle then proceeded to get the Brewers out of the 12th quickly.

In the bottom of the 12th, Bobby Murcer led off with his 3rd walk of the game. Ron Blomberg tried to bunt Murcer over to second. He did and he beat out the throw to first.

The Yankees now had men on first and second and no outs.

Graig Nettles lined out, bringing up catcher Thurman Munson. Munson already had 3 of the 8 hits that Colborn have given up in the game. On a 2 - 1 count Munson hit a line drive single to right field and Murcer scored to win the game.

With the win the Yankees are now 58 - 44 and have a 2 game lead in the AL East over the Orioles. Their record is 1 game better than the AL West leading Oakland A's.

The Yankees are looking like they are a legitimate World Series team. It looks like the World Series could be a repeat of 1964, the last time the Yankees were in the Fall Classic, when they faced the St. Louis Cardinals. Or perhaps a repeat of 1963, when the Yankees last faced the Dodgers. The Dodgers are running away with the NL West this year.

And there is strong reason to believe in this Yankees team. They have 5 solid starting pitchers in Mel Stottlemyre, Fritz Peterson, Pat Dobson, Doc Medich and the recently acquired Sam McDowell. They have a top closer in Sparky Lyle. And Bobby Murcer is playing like the true heir apparent to Ruth, DiMaggio and Mantle. He's following up his 33 HR / 96 RBI 1972 season with 18 HRs / 68 RBIs so far this season. Ron Blomberg is batting .347. Thurman Munson is batting .305. And several other players are hitting well.

The Sports Time Traveler™ is keeping an eye on all the division races as we enter the last couple of months.

Chapter Fifty-Two

The Pennant Races Begin in 1973

August 1 is the traditional date when pennant races kick into high gear and fairy tale finishes are dreamed about

It's August 1st. This is the traditional date that pennant races start in baseball.

There have been some rare cases in which a team has come from way back on August 1st.

The Giants were in 2nd place, 9.5 games behind the Dodgers, in 1951 and we all know what happened. Russ Hodges repeated screams of, *"The Giants Win the Pennant!"* became the greatest radio call in baseball history.

The 1914 Braves were 8 games back, and in 4th place, with just a .500 record, on August 1st. And they won the pennant and became known as the Miracle Braves in a bygone era.

There have been some great comebacks in baseball history after August 1st.

But to the best of my knowledge there has never been a team that won the pennant when they were in last place or next to last place on August 1st.

The 1973 New York Mets are in last place in the NL East this morning 50 years ago.

And they are in 2nd to last place if you combine both divisions and look at the standings for the entire National League.

On August 1, 1973, I was a 9 year old boy who lived for the New York Mets. I had a baseball jacket with the New York Mets logo. I had my "Property of the New York Mets" t-shirts. I dreamed about pitching for the Mets when I grew up.

I most likely read the New York Times that morning while I ate a bowl of Life cereal. That was my morning routine in those days. It was a Wednesday, and I was getting ready to catch the bus to Lake-Vu Day Camp in East Brunswick, NJ.

Here's the standings I would have seen in the New York Times at about 8am:

56 – 48 St. Louis Cardinals

55 – 51 Chicago Cubs 2 games back

51 – 51 Pittsburgh Pirates 4 games back

50 – 53 Montreal Expos 5.5 games back

49 – 57 Philadelphia Phillies 8 games back

44 – 57 New York Mets 10.5 games back

The Mets were solidly in last. They had occupied last place almost since school had let out in June.

Oh, how I wished the Mets could be a division leader or be like one of the powerhouse teams - The Pittsburgh Pirates or the Cincinnati Reds.

Oh, how I wished we could have some big bats on our team like Johnny Bench or Willie Stargell. Or a league leading hitter like Pete Rose or Joe Torre.

I did take pride in the fact that we did have good pitching. In fact, we had one of the best in Tom Seaver.

But besides Tom Terrific, our other pitchers were just not getting it done this year.

Last year's Rookie of the Year, Jon Matlack, had a 7 - 13 record on August 1. The New York Times was speculating this morning that Matlack could become the 5th 20 game loser in Mets history. All of those other 20 game losers came in the Mets laughingstock years in the early 1960s when they were a brand-new expansion team.

Tug McGraw, the closer, was pitching so poorly in the bullpen, with an ERA over 6, that Yogi Berra decided to start him for a game on July 30th to break him out of his slump. Mets pitching coach Joe Pignatano told the New York Times, *"If he does well tonight, we'll send him back to the bullpen."*

McGraw did pitch well that night, allowing just one run in 6 innings (but the Mets still lost), so perhaps that bodes well and will kickstart his upcoming relief performances.

On this morning in 1973, I'm sure I was a little down as I read the story of the Mets loss to the Pirates "last night," their 4th in a row after showing some signs of life prior to the All-Star break.

Murray Chass had this to say about the game, *"The Pirates, although still in 3rd place, played like a team very much in a pennant race; The Mets looked like a team very much in last place."*

"The Mets were outpitched, outhit and outfielded by the Pirates, who after a lethargic 1st half of the season have stormed back into contention for their 4th straight Eastern Division title with 14 victories in their last 21 games."

The Pirates won the game 4 - 1. To make matters worse, they beat Jerry Koosman, a man who used to be a reliable starter, almost as good as Seaver in 1968 and 1969. Kooz was a lefty who pitched 6 no-hit innings against the Orioles and won 2 of the 4 games in the 1969 World Series. Now Koosman had a record of 8 - 11.

On the morning of August 1, 1973, I'm pretty certain that I was about as depressed about my Mets as I had ever been. But they were my Mets. I was sticking with them. They were a part of my identity. They were as close to me as our family dog.

The pennant races were getting underway in earnest on August 1st, as they do every season. The Cardinals were in front with the Cubs and Pirates lurking close behind in the East. And the Dodgers were on top of the West, but the Reds were moving up.

And my Mets were nowhere. They were buried in last.

The idea of the Mets challenging for the pennant... well that didn't cross my mind as I ate another spoonful of Life cereal on the morning of August 1st.

It would have been like entertaining a fairy tale.

It just doesn't happen.

It had never happened.

SPOILER ALERT

Skip to the next chapter if you don't want to know any further hints about what will come about in the next 10 weeks in 1973.

THE ARC OF THE STORY TO COME

For those who really want to know, I'm going to share with you the arc of the story to come.

It's a story that 50 years later I still can't quite believe. It sounds like such a tall tale that in the couple of decades afterwards, before the internet, when it wasn't so easy to research things, I wasn't sure it actually happened as I recalled it. It was so stunning that I didn't trust my memory of things when I was 9, soon to turn 10 before the end of the 1973 season.

All I'm going to tell you at this point is that magical things are going to happen.

A team leader will emerge who will maniacally chant an iconic mantra that will enter the American lexicon.

The team will rally.

They will contend for the pennant.

5th grade boys at Warnsdorfer elementary school in New Jersey will cheer wildly in my classroom on more than one occasion.

And fans will storm the field at Shea.

I actually don't know much more than that.

Yes, I do know the final score of the final game.

But how did the Mets get there? What happened day-by-day? I don't remember.

The Genesis of The Sports Time Traveler™

It was my desire to re-live the experience of the next 10 weeks in 1973, exactly 50 years to the day as it happened, that was one of the initial sparks that started me on the path to develop The Sports Time Traveler™.

This was the foundational story of my entire childhood.

Now that time is upon us.

I'm so excited to begin the journey. I hope you enjoy it as well.

The Sports Time Traveler™ will continue posting updates on the 1973 Mets, exactly 50 years ago, whenever there is something so compelling that I just have to share it with you.

CHAPTER FIFTY-THREE

The Savior of the Cellar Dwellers

THE LAST PLACE 1973 METS SEND TOM SEAVER TO THE MOUND

SHEA STADIUM - August 2, 1973

When I opened the New York Times this morning, here in 1973, I found a story too good to spare you from it. This is a quick read you won't want to miss.

Last night, the last place Mets, with a record of 44 - 57, had a twi-night doubleheader against the Pirates. This was the Mets 2nd twi-night doubleheader in 3 days.

The 1st didn't go so well when the Expos beat the Mets twice.

But last night was different because the Mets had Tom Seaver pitching the 1st game.

Seaver got 3 strikeouts in the top of the 1st. That's our Tom Terrific at work when we need him.

In the bottom of the 1st the Mets did something weird. They scored a run.

The Mets don't usually score runs in the 1st inning for Seaver. But that wasn't the weird part. It was that they scored it without a hit. A leadoff walk to Wayne

Garrett, a bunt by Felix Millan to move Garrett to second, a wild pitch by Pirates 1971 and 1972 ace, Steve Blass, and a sacrifice fly by Rusty Staub gave the Mets a 1 - 0 lead.

In the top of the 2nd Seaver notched 2 more strikeouts.

In the bottom of the inning it got even weirder. The Mets scored 2 more runs. Here's how they did it:

- Walk to John Milner

- Walk to Bud Harrelson

- Walk to Tom Seaver

- Walk to Wayne Garrett (Milner scores)

- Felix Millan gets hit by Blass (Harrelson scores)

The Mets scored 3 runs in 2 innings without getting a hit.

METS 3 PIRATES 0 - end of 2 innings

The Mets only threatened to score one more time. In the 4th inning the Mets got their 1st hit when Bud Harrelson singled. Seaver then followed with a single. And Felix Millan singled but Harrelson was thrown out at the plate to end the inning.

Those were the only 3 hits the Mets had in the entire game.

Meanwhile after the 2nd inning, Seaver let just one runner get to second base when MVP candidate Willie Stargell doubled with 2 outs in the 9th.

The Mets won it 3 - 0.

Seaver had pitched an 11 strikeout, 4 hit shutout.

His league leading ERA is now 1.97. He has a record of 13 – 5.

Seaver was so efficient in putting away the Pirates, one of the best hitting teams in baseball, that the game took just 1 hour and 44 minutes to play.

The Mets are now 15 - 8 when Seaver has started and just 30 - 49 when someone else has started.

The 2nd game was started by George Stone, the surprise pitcher of the season for the Mets.

He was the "other guy" in the Gary Gentry for Felix Millan trade and Stone has been the only other bright spot on the staff this season.

Last night he pitched 8 scoreless innings before giving up 2 runs in the 9th. But the Mets supported Stone with an uncharacteristic 10 hits including 2 homers by John Milner and they won the game 5 - 2.

Stone is now 7 - 3 with a 2.60 ERA.

Despite the sweep, the Mets are still in last place 10.5 games behind the 1st place Cardinals who also swept a doubleheader last night against the Expos in convincing fashion 9 - 3 and 2 - 0.

The Cards are now 53 - 28 since they turned around their season in early May. That's a 106 win pace for the Cards if they could have thrown out their absurd 5 - 20 start.

It doesn't look like anyone is catching the Cards.

The Sports Time Traveler™ will continue posting updates on the 1973 Mets, exactly 50 years ago, whenever there is something so compelling that I just have to share it with you.

CHAPTER FIFTY-FOUR

The Little Hits that Could

WILLIE MAYS PROVES HE CAN STILL PLAY

SHEA STADIUM - August 3, 1973

I have another quick article today with a story that just was too good to pass up.

Willie Mays has suffered from criticism, here in 1973, that he should retire.

On May 10th a UPI article ran nationwide with the headline, *"Mays washed up but won't admit it."*

Meanwhile the idea of Mays retiring is a little absurd since the Mets don't have another true major league center fielder on the roster.

And Mays is making valuable contributions to the team.

As previously reported in The Sports Time Traveler™, Mays had a great spring training, and after a poor start to the season, in which he was injured, he had a surge in July batting around .300 over a 5 week stretch and coming up with at least one dramatic game winning hit, and a play in centerfield that nearly rivaled his famous catch in the 1954 World Series.

Then, last night Willie Mays single handedly took down the Pittsburgh Pirates.

In the 3rd inning of a nothing-nothing game, Mays came to the plate with 1 out and Felix Millan on first and Don Hahn on third. Murray Chass of the New York Times wrote, *"Mays hit a chopper high into the air near the third base line not far from home plate. But as Hahn raced home all Rooker (the pitcher) could do was wait for the ball to descend. When it finally did, falling slowly as if attached to a parachute, Rooker threw it past first trying to get Mays. Millan scampered all the way home."*

The Mets were up 2 - 0.

Mays then scored when Cleon Jones doubled to become the 1st player in Mets history to reach 1,000 hits.

There was no more scoring until the bottom of the 8th. With Felix Millan on first and no one out, Mays surprised the Pirates when he tried to bunt for a single to the left side of the infield. The panicking Pirates didn't cover first base. Yet the pitcher, John Lamb, threw in that direction. Mays wound up on second and Millan raced all the way home.

A few minutes later Mays scored on a suicide squeeze bunt by Jerry Grote.

Willie Mays had accounted for all 5 of the Mets runs in the game.

Meanwhile Mets starter, the veteran Ray Sadecki, was pitching one of his finest games of the year and went into the 9th inning with a shutout. But when he gave up a walk and a single, putting 2 men on with no one out, Yogi Berra decided it was time to bring in his closer - Tug McGraw.

There was just one problem. Tug hadn't been pitching like Tug for the past few months. He came into the game with an ERA of 5.77.

Yogi had this to say to Phil Pepe, of the New York Daily News, about the situation, *"If you ain't got a bullpen, you ain't got nothing. I've got to die with him. He's still the best I've got."*

The 1st batter McGraw faced, Richie Zisk, singled scoring Al Oliver to make it a 5 - 1 game.

Now the powerful Pirates had one run in and runners still on first and second and no outs.

It was a critical situation.

Richie Hebner stepped up to face Tug McGraw. He crushed a drive toward first base where Willie Mays was stationed for just the third game this year.

Phil Pepe in the New York Daily News described how Mays, *"backhanded Richie Hebner's smash and made the unassisted putout."*

The Pittsburgh Press wrote, *"Willie Mays, playing at first base, made a fine play on Hebner's hard smash in the 9th to take the heart out of a late Pirates rally."*

Tug McGraw said about Mays' play, *"I knew that was my break and I had to take advantage of it."*

McGraw finished off the Pirates. The Mets were 5 - 1 victors.

The Mets have now won 3 straight and improved their record to 47 - 57.

Yet they are still in last place in the NL East, 9.5 games behind the Cardinals.

Phil Pepe though saw some hope for the cellar dwellers, *"They are still 10 games under. 500, but they think they may have something going. If they can stay hot over the next few days, they could make some noise in the NL East race yet."*

The St. Louis Cardinals are coming to Shea Stadium tonight for the 1st of a very rare 6 game series. Tonight, they will send their ace Bob Gibson to the mound against 1972 Rookie of the Year Jon Matlack.

I can't wait!

CHAPTER FIFTY-FIVE

Say Hey One More Time

WILLIE MAYS AND THE METS ENTERTAINED THE 1ST PLACE CARDINALS AT SHEA LAST NIGHT IN 1973

SHEA STADIUM - August 4, 1973

Yet again when I opened the August 4, 1973, New York Times and New York Daily News, the accounts of the Mets game last night was so gripping I just had to share it with you.

The Mets were off to what looked like a great start in the 1st inning when John Milner smashed a ball off the right field fence to drive in 2 runs. But Milner racing for a triple, had his helmet and cap fly off and then the throw to third slammed into the back of his unprotected head.

Milner was on the ground face down for several minutes and was removed from the game.

Later it was reported that Milner, the team's leading HR hitter with 18, only had a bruise and would be able to play today.

Milner was replaced by Rusty Staub who is also injured. Staub is suffering from a flare up in his right hand that he broke last year. Rusty had been on the bench for a doctor ordered 2-day rest when he was summoned by Yogi Berra to replace Milner.

To make matters even worse on the injury front, the Mets learned before the game that shortstop Bud Harrelson has a fractured sternum and is going to miss at least two weeks. The Mets have gone 33 - 33 with Harrelson and 14 - 24 without him this season.

On the mound Jon Matlack was struggling for the Mets. Through 7 innings Matlack had allowed 11 base runners, but he had struck out 10 and had managed to only let 3 Cardinals score.

The Mets were clinging to a 4 - 3 lead.

In the bottom of the 7th, Yogi Berra let Matlack bat for himself with one out and he drew a walk. Leadoff batter Don Hahn popped out and the Mets had 2 outs. Hot hitting Felix Millan who batted .386 in July, got a single moving Matlack to second.

This brought up Willie Mays with 2 outs and 2 on. It was a crucial situation in the game. Matlack looked like he needed at least 1 or 2 insurance runs.

Diego Segui was pitching for the Cardinals. Last week I reported that Segui had said he got a fastball by Willie that he wouldn't have been able to 3 years ago. Perhaps Segui was thinking about that when he threw Willie a fastball on a 3 - 2 count trying to strike out the 42-year-old Mays and end the inning.

Mays crushed the fastball, and it sailed over the left centerfield fence for a 3 run shot.

It was the 659th home run of his amazing career. Mays is 42 behind Hank Aaron who hit number 701 this week. Mays led Aaron his whole career until Aaron passed him last spring. Willie Mays is not going to catch Babe Ruth at 714, but he can still win a ball game.

With a 7 - 3 lead, Yogi Berra let Matlack finish the game. He allowed a couple of more baserunners, but no more runs and the Mets won the game.

Willie Mays 3 run homer was not technically the game winning hit, but it certainly was a game icing hit.

Phil Pepe of the New York Daily News started his article with this, *"The people keep coming to see Willie Mays as if he were a museum piece, hoping he'll hit one for them... Friday night, Willie hit one... his last? Nobody knows, but it made a lot of people happy."*

After the game, Mays told Ken Rappaport of the Bridgewater (NJ) Courier News, *"I was just looking for something fast... and there it was."*

Despite the win, the Mets are still in last place at 48 - 57. But now they're only 8.5 games behind the division leading Cardinals. And the Mets have 5 more home games in this series against St. Louis.

The Mets face the Cardinals again at 2:15pm this afternoon (in 1973). Cardinals ace Bob Gibson, who had his start against the Mets moved out a day due to the flu, will face Jerry Koosman.

I can't wait!

CHAPTER FIFTY-SIX

Upstate, Down State

2 LEGENDS OF THEIR SPORTS PERFORMED "YESTERDAY" IN 1973 IN NEW YORK; THE OUTCOMES WERE STARTLING

NEW YORK - August 5, 1973

Upstate in Saratoga Springs and down state in the Flushing Meadows section of Queens, 2 of the biggest names in sports were on display in New York yesterday in 1973.

In Shea Stadium, Bob Gibson, the National League career leader in strikeouts, was set to pitch against the Mets.

Shortly after that, Secretariat was racing at the Saratoga Race Course.

Bob Gibson vs. the Mets

Channel 9, WOR in New York, had the action as Jerry Koosman threw the opening pitch to Lou Brock of the St. Louis Cardinals at 2:20pm.

Brock is on his way to leading the National League in steals for the 7th time in eight seasons. But Kooz got him to groundout to John Milner, who thankfully was back in the lineup a day after being struck on the head by the thrown ball.

Bob Gibson Takes the Mound at Shea

Kooz got out of the 1st inning easily. And Bob Gibson took the mound. He gave up a single to the Mets hottest hitter, Felix Millan, but got the other 3 batters to hit flyballs for outs, making it an easy inning for both pitchers.

In the 2nd Kooz retired the Cards in order.

The Mets managed a run in the bottom of the 2nd on an error to take a 1 - 0 lead, but otherwise Gibson looked strong as he got Jerry Koosman to look at a called 3rd strike to end the inning.

Gibson comes to bat

Bob Gibson is an exceptional hitter for a pitcher, with 24 home runs in his career.

In the top of the 3rd, Gibson got a single off Koosman. Then leadoff hitter, Ted Sizemore came up for the Cardinals with 1 out.

He hit a line drive that was caught by Mets third baseman Ken Boswell. Gibson who had been running on the play, had to pivot quickly to get back to first base to avoid the double play.

He didn't make it.

His sudden pivot motion resulted in a sharp pain in his knee. Gibson went down and he laid on the infield dirt for a few minutes. It appeared a stretcher would need to be brought out.

But Gibson managed to get up.

Since the top of the inning was over, he walked over to take his place at the pitcher's mound to face the Mets in the bottom of the inning.

He told Murray Chass, of the New York Times, *"It stopped hurting; there was no pain then."*

It was just a temporary reprieve.

What happened next was shocking. Gibson explained, *"When I started pushing off it collapsed."*

Bob Gibson, *"fell flat on the mound,"* according to Chass, *"and had to be helped to the dugout."*

Cardinals team physician, Dr. Stan London, is concerned that Gibson has torn cartilage, and will be out for the rest of the season.

If that is the case, it will be a huge blow for the 1st place Cardinals, who are tied with the Dodgers for the best record in all baseball since their 5 - 20 start.

The Cardinals veteran core group of players, Gibson, Brock, Tim McCarver and Joe Torre, all between 32 and 37 years old, had never panicked at the beginning of the season. This great lesson is described in a feature article in Sports Illustrated's August 6th issue, which is already on newsstands here in 1973.

The Cardinals went on to win the game 4 - 3. But it will be a hollow win, if Gibson can't pitch again.

Secretariat in Saratoga

7 minutes after the Mets game ended, WCBS in New York, and the CBS television network nationwide, aired the Whitney Stakes from Saratoga Race Course in upstate New York.

This was a heavily anticipated horse race for which a record crowd of 30,119 had come out. They were here to see Secretariat run in the 1 and 1/8 mile $50,000 Whitney Stakes. This would be the 1st running of Secretariat since he had captured the Triple Crown 2 months ago by annihilating the field in a record time at the Belmont Stakes.

Secretariat was such a prohibitive favorite yesterday that the betting reached the absurdly low odds of 1 - 20 before settling back to 1 - 10 before post time. This also marked the 1st time Secretariat would run against horses older than age 3.

Only 4 other horses entered the race. Here were the post positions and odds:

1. West Coast Scout 22 to 1

2. Rule By Reason 26 to 1

3. Secretariat 1 to 10

4. Onion 6 to 1

5. True Knight 8 to 1

Onion took the lead on the 1st turn and Secretariat settled into 4th. Onion came through the 1/4 mile in a brisk 22.4 seconds.

Onion maintained the lead through the half mile in 45.6 seconds, with Secretariat moving up to 3rd on the inside.

On the far turn things got tight. Onion was still ahead but the 4 horses were all within 2 lengths.

Coming out of the turn West Coast Scout and Rule By Reason dropped back and it became a 2 horse race.

Secretariat pulled up next to Onion on the inside as they moved into the final stretch. He even seemed to nose ahead just before the 3/4 mile pole which they reached in 1:11.

But as they passed the mile pole, Secretariat seemed to be boxed in between Onion and the rail. Onion, with more freedom to move, accelerated and left Secretariat behind to win by a length in a shocking upset.

What Happened to Secretariat?

Ron Turcotte, the jockey who rode Secretariat to all three Triple Crown races, tried to explain to the Daily News what happened yesterday to Big Red, *"When I set him down in the stretch, he just wasn't the same horse. Certainly not the same horse that won the Triple Crown and the Belmont by a record 31 lengths. I really can't explain what happened to him. Maybe the fact that he tried to break through the gate at the start and hit his head affected him. But he seemed to be running all right."*

Secretariat's trainer, Lucien Laurin, was stunned by the result. The Daily News reported that Laurin was, *"numb and befuddled."* All he could mutter to the press was, *"I think he was better outside,"* referring to his disadvantageous position along the rail down the stretch.

That's all for today.

The Mets still have 3 more games against the Cardinals in this series. And Secretariat is expected to race again next month at the Marlboro Cup.

A Tribute to Anthony Boni

ALSO, AN UPDATE ON THE 1973 NEW YORK METS FROM DODGER STADIUM

SPECIAL EDITION of The Sports Time Traveler™

This is a special edition of The Sports Time Traveler™ in which I start out reporting from the present.

I have two items I'd like to share with you today:

    1. A brief tribute to my father-in-law Anthony "Tony" Boni

    2. A report on the 1st game of the 1973 Mets west coast trip

SPECIAL TRIBUTE TO ANTHONY BONI

Last weekend we lost my father-in-law, Anthony "Tony" Boni at the age of 81.

The circumstances by which I came to know Tony are a small miracle.

The man my wife Heather called "dad," had passed away over 30 years ago.

In 2017, Heather took a 23andMe DNA test purely to learn about her medical history.

When Heather received the results she got the surprise of her life.

23andMe informed her that a man named Anthony Boni was in fact her biological father.

Heather made contact with Tony, who never knew that she existed, and he was amazed to learn that he had a daughter.

Tony, and his wife Lourdes, welcomed Heather's outreach. And what ensued was a beautiful relationship in which Tony and Heather became great friends.

Tony was also a supporter of my efforts to develop The Sports Time Traveler™. He offered me constant encouragement and often commented on my articles.

Tony, the last 6 years since we met you were like a special gift from heaven, a real-life fairy tale.

We will miss you forever.

THE 1973 NEW YORK METS VISIT DODGER STADIUM

Join me now back in 1973, exactly 50 years ago in Los Angeles, to hear the story.

DODGER STADIUM - August 9, 1973

I'm back here in Los Angeles where last night the NL East's last place team, the Mets, opened a series against the NL West's first place team, the Dodgers.

Don Hahn started again in centerfield for the ailing Willie Mays. Hahn drew a walk against the Dodgers' Andy Messersmith. But Hahn was out quickly when Felix Millan grounded into a double play. Rusty Staub also hit a grounder and Messersmith was out of the top of the 1st very easily.

NOTE: Don Hahn went 0 for 3 in his other 3 trips to the plate to extend his hitting slump in which he is 3 for 23 (.130 average).

In the bottom of the 1st, Jon Matlack, who has been pitching well of late, retired the Dodgers with similar ease allowing just a single to Willie Davis, who didn't make it past 1st base.

In the top of the 2nd the Mets got on the board when Jerry Grote singled home John Milner. Grote then was thrown out at the plate for the final out of the inning, laying waste to a Ted Martinez double. But the Mets led 1 - 0.

Now Matlack really went to work. He struck out the side in the bottom of the 2nd.

Matlack registered 2 more strikeouts in a 1-2-3 third inning.

In the 4th, Matlack gave up a leadoff single to Manny Mota, who has led the NL in batting for most of the season until Pete Rose passed him at the end of July. Matlack then struck out Willie Davis, got Steve Garvey to pop up and Joe Ferguson to ground out.

Mets 1 Dodgers 0 - end of 4 innings

Matlack struck out Ron Cey leading off the 5th on the way to another 1 - 2 - 3 inning.

He had yet another 1 - 2 - 3 inning in the 6th.

In the 7th Matlack allowed a walk, and that was all.

Meanwhile the Mets were not mounting any scoring threats against Messersmith.

Mets 1 Dodgers 0 - end of 7 innings

To start the 8th inning, Matlack struck out both Willie Crawford and Bill Russell. Then Dodgers manager Walt Alston pinch hit for Andy Messersmith and sent Ken McMullen to the plate. He hit a foul pop finishing another easy inning for Matlack, who was now pitching like his 1972 Rookie of the Year form.

The Mets gave Matlack no insurance runs as they went down in order in the top of the 9th against relief pitcher Pete Richert.

Now Matlack had the opportunity to close out a shutout against major league baseball's best hitting team. To do it he would have to shut down the top of the Dodgers batting order.

1st up was Davey Lopes who is batting .278. Lopes flew out to Rusty Staub in right.

2nd up was Manny Mota, batting .331. He hit a grounder to Felix Millan at 2nd.

3rd up was Willie Davis, the 14 year veteran who is in the middle of a solid season, batting .296. He is arguably the best center fielder in baseball having won the gold glove in each of the past 2 seasons.

Matlack got Davis to pop up towards 3rd base. Wayne Garrett caught it to end the game.

Jon Matlack had shut out the Los Angeles Dodgers 1 - 0 on just 2 hits. He also struck out 9 and only walked 2. He improves his record to 9 - 14 and lowers his ERA to 3.30. At one point, early in the season, Matlack's ERA had stood as high as 4.96.

Matlack told the Los Angeles Times Ron Rappaport that he was nervous before the game, *"It was a good kind of nervous. An excited kind of feeling, almost anticipation, not fear or apprehension. You just want to go out and go to work."*

And go to work he did.

But the Mets are still in last place, although they've won 3 in a row, and are still 8.5 games back.

Mets manager, Yogi Berra, told Joe Trimble of the New York Daily News, *"We're going to bother somebody before this is over."*

Trimble also wrote this in his article, *"Now that the Mets are reasonably healthy, they aren't the mess they were in June. They've won 15 of their last 28, including four of seven from division leaders."* Trimble is referring to the fact that the Mets last 7 games have been played against the NL East leading Cards and NL West leading Dodgers and the Mets have won 4 of those 7 games.

Here are the NL East Standings:

61 – 53 CARDS

55 – 56 PIRATES   4.5 games back

56 – 58 CUBS   5 games back

55 – 57 EXPOS   5 games back

52 – 61 PHILLIES   8.5 games back

51 – 60 METS   8.5 games back

CHAPTER FIFTY-EIGHT

Seaver is Serious

TOM SEAVER BATTLED JUAN MARICHAL AT CANDLESTICK LAST NIGHT IN 1973

CANDLESTICK PARK - August 11, 1973

I'm here 50 years ago in Candlestick Park in San Francisco, virtually, where there was an expected pitching duel last night between the Mets ace Tom Seaver, and one of the great pitchers of this era Juan Marichal of the Giants.

Although, at 34, Marichal is not as dominant as he once was, he sports an all-time record of 26 - 6 against the Mets and he beat the Mets here back on May 28th when the Mets were a 2nd place .500 team.

Now, the Mets come into this game as a last place team, 10 games under .500.

Marichal disposed of the Mets easily in the 1st.

And Seaver got the Giants 1-2-3 in the bottom of the inning.

The pitcher's duel was on.

In the top of the 2nd, Cleon Jones opened with a single off Marichal. After Marichal got Wayne Garrett and Jerry Grote out it looked like he might get out of the inning with .224 hitter Teddy Martinez coming up. But Teddy singled putting runners at first and third for Tom Seaver.

Perhaps Seaver sensed that to win this game he would have to do it all by himself. The Mets rarely give him much run support. Seaver promptly whacked a double to left field that scored both runners and the Mets had a 2 - 0 lead.

Seaver told Bucky Walter of the San Francisco Examiner after the game, *"I really crushed the ball."*

In the bottom of the 2nd, Seaver allowed 2 singles to the first 3 batters but then got Chris Speier to pop out and he struck out Dave Radar to end the inning.

METS 2 GIANTS 0 - End of 2 innings

Both pitchers had easy innings in the 3rd.

In the top of the 4th, third baseman Wayne Garrett opened the inning with a double for the Mets. But he was out at third on a fielder's choice and Marichal got the next 2 batters.

In the bottom of the inning, Seaver again found himself with runners on first and second, this time with no one out, but he got the next 3 batters out to retain his slim 2 - 0 lead.

The 5th started out easily for Marichal. He got the leadoff hitter, Don Hahn to pop out. Hahn ended up 1 for 5 for the game extending his slump to 4 for 31 as he fills in for the injured Willie Mays in centerfield. Marichal also got Felix Millan to fly out.

Marichal appeared to be out of the inning when Rusty Staub hit a choppy grounder to shortstop Tito Fuentes. But Fuentes had trouble fielding the ball and Staub was safe with an infield hit. That turned out to be a haunting play.

The next batter, first baseman John Milner singled. And then left fielder Cleon Jones also singled, driving in Staub to increase the Mets lead to 3 - 0.

This brought up Wayne Garrett. "Red", as some call him, was 1 for 15 against Marichal going back to 1971 coming into this game. But today was different. He followed up his 4th inning double with a 3-run homer, his 8th of the year. Suddenly the Mets were up 6 - 0 and Juan Marichal was knocked out of the game.

Seaver with a 6 run lead is golden. Giants manager Charlie Fox told Bucky Walter, *"Seaver's tough once he gets ahead. I've yet to see him fall apart."*

Although Seaver let up a run in the bottom of the 5th and allowed the Giants to get 2 runners on in the 6th, he got 10 of the last 11 Giants out to win the game 7 - 1.

METS 7 GIANTS 1 - Final Score

Wayne Garrett told Joe Trimble of the New York Daily News, *"It is easier to play behind Seaver than any other pitcher. There is less pressure. You know he's going to pour it on every inning. And if we get him ahead, we're pretty sure to win."*

After the game, Seaver was ecstatic about his 2 run blast off Marichal in the 2nd which turned out to be all he needed to beat the Giants. He said to a group of reporters rhetorically after the game, *"Who got the winning hit?"*

However, Tom Terrific was in no self-congratulatory mode about his pitching effort. He told Joe Trimble, *"It was the ugliest eight hitter I ever saw. I was overstriding* (on the mound).*"*

Despite the victory the Mets are still in last place at 52 - 61.

But with the 1st place Cardinals losing their 5th straight game, the Mets moved up to just 7.5 games out.

When a reporter offered this news to Seaver he shot back, *"Forget it. We can't win one then lose one. We've got to get a winning streak going."*

Seaver is serious. And he's pitching incredible. His record is 14 - 6 and he leads the National League with a 1.75 ERA and 175 strikeouts. In addition, The Mets are now 16 - 9 when Seaver starts and just 36 - 52 when he doesn't start.

The Sports Time Traveler™ will continue posting updates on the 1973 Mets exactly 50 years ago.

CHAPTER FIFTY-NINE

A Whirlwind Tour of the NL East in 1973

I DECIDED TO TAKE A WHIRLWIND TOUR TO SEE THE TOP 4 TEAMS IN THE NL EAST

NORTH AMERICA - August 15, 1973

I've been following the 1973 Mets day-by-day. And it's getting really difficult as they've been in last place all summer.

So, I decided to take a lightning-fast virtual tour to visit the top 4 teams in the NL East to see what is going on with them.

It's whacky!

The Chicago Cubs

The Cubs are in the midst of a putrid 9 - 31 run after they had started the season 47 - 31. They've lost 9 straight games. And they're frustrated.

Yesterday, Ferguson Jenkins was knocked out of the game against the Braves in the 5th. He was so angry at the ump that he went into the dugout and started throwing every bat he could get his hands on out onto the field. Coach Ernie

Banks had to restrain him. Billy Williams said Jenkins tirade was good therapy. Ron Santo said, *"he needed that, as long as he didn't hurt anybody."*

NOTE: Hank Aaron did not get a home run for the 8th straight game. He is stuck on 701. I will be following Aaron's quest to catch Babe Ruth at 714.

The St. Louis Cardinals

The 1st place Cardinals broke their 8 game losing streak by beating the Astros 9 - 5. The Cardinals are all about staying calm. They didn't panic when they started the year 5 - 20. And they didn't get excited when they played nearly .700 baseball for 2 months to take the division lead.

Tim McCarver told the St. Louis Dispatch last night how he handled the losing streak, *"We're not a bunch of mopers... you can't be mopers and win."* The Cardinals also announced they're going to a 4 man rotation for the rest of the season now the Bob Gibson is out. Gibson had knee surgery for torn cartilage he suffered last week against the Mets.

The Montreal Expos

The Expos are the exact opposite of the Cards. They're young and emotional. And this is their first pennant race. They lost a tough game to the NL West leading Dodgers last night in Los Angeles. John Robertson of the Montreal Star wrote about the Expos locker room after the game, *"Everywhere you looked... players dressed in sullen silence... seldom raised their eyes."*

The Pittsburgh Pirates

In the Pittsburgh Press, Bob Smizik commented yesterday about this Pirates team that has owned the NL East every year in this decade so far. After their close loss to the surging Cincinnati Reds, Smizik wrote, *"But, alas, it's 1973 and the magic is mostly gone."*

The Pirates are just not the same without Roberto Clemente.

Here's the standings in the NL East as of this morning in 1973:

62 – 58 CARDS

57 – 59 PIRATES   3 games back

57 – 61 EXPOS   4 games back

56 – 62 CUBS   5 games back

55 – 63 PHILLIES 6 games back

52 – 65 METS   8.5 games back

By the way, Tom Seaver is pitching for the Mets tonight in San Diego in 1973.

I can't wait to read about the game in The New York Times archives tomorrow morning!

Please don't tell me anything in advance. A basic rule of Sports Time Travel is you can't look ahead. If you do you immediately lose the feeling of being back in time.

CHAPTER SIXTY

A Mets Summer Night's Dream

WHILE I WAS SLEEPING 50 YEARS AGO, TOM SEAVER WAS ON THE MOUND IN SAN DIEGO

SAN DIEGO - August 16, 1973

Last night in 1973, in real life, I was asleep by 9pm. I was 9 years old, and I was going to day camp the next morning. The Mets game in San Diego didn't start until 10:25pm. And it wasn't broadcast on WOR Channel 9 in New York. In the New York area you could only listen to the game on the radio.

Naturally, my present self in 2023, just had to get in the sports time travel machine to go back and experience this game that no one in the New York area saw.

So, I'm here in San Diego, 50 years ago, virtually, where last night the 2 last place teams in the National League battled it out in the 3rd game of this series. The Padres, who own the worst record in the NL had already taken the first 2 games of the series.

Now it was up to Tom Seaver, the Mets franchise player, to get at least one win for the Mets against the Padres in this last game of what is turning out to be a disappointing west coast trip at 2 - 4. That record actually sounds better than it feels because the Mets have lost their last 3 straight by a total score of 16 - 3. And that may have had some of the Mets looking ahead to the scheduled all night charter flight back to the Big Apple after the game.

Fortunately, there is something about this expansion Padres team that brings out the best in Tom Seaver. In the Padres' 5 year existence, Seaver has a record of 13 - 1 against them coming into the game.

Another good omen for this game was when the Mets leadoff batter, Wayne Garrett, swung at the game's first pitch from the Padres Steve Arlin, and smacked it over the fence in right for a home run. This gave Seaver a 1 - 0 lead before he even took the mound.

In the bottom of the 1st, Seaver disposed of the Padres in order.

In the 2nd, Seaver got the clean-up batter, Nate Colbert, one of the top home run hitters in baseball the past 5 seasons, to fly out. The next batter, Cito Gaston reached base on an error by the shortstop.

Playing shortstop for the Mets last night was Wayne Garrett. Garrett is normally the third baseman. He has also played a considerable amount of time at second base. But coming into last night's game he had only started at shortstop 8 times in his 5 year career. The only reason he was at shortstop was because Bud Harrelson is out with a fractured sternum and back up shortstop, Teddy Martinez, went down with a heel injury 3 days ago.

The error didn't matter much because Seaver got the next 2 batters to fly out.

In the top of the 3rd, Seaver, as seems often to be the case, tried to get himself an insurance run. He led off with a triple. But the top of the Mets order could not get Seaver the rest of the way home.

In the bottom of the 3rd, Seaver had another 1-2-3 inning.

METS 1 PADRES 0 - end of 3 innings

In the top of the 4th the Mets gave Seaver his insurance runs. They loaded the bases with no outs and then Steve Arlin walked John Milner to score a run.

The next batter was catcher Jerry Grote. Grote has missed 75 games this season already due to injuries, and has hit no home runs this year coming into the game. In fact, Grote had not hit a home run since May 19th of last year. But Grote snapped that drought by slugging a grand slam, the first of his career, to give Seaver a 6 - 0 cushion.

In the bottom of the 4th, Seaver had another 1-2-3 inning.

He had allowed no hits through 4 innings.

In the top of the 5th, Cleon Jones belted his 5th homer of the year and Seaver now had a 7 - 0 lead to work with. This was a real rarity for the Mets, 7 runs and all due to homers.

In the bottom of the 5th, Seaver got the first 2 batters out. The next hitter was the Padres shortstop Derrel Thomas, who came into the game batting .225.

Thomas bunted a Seaver pitch and both Seaver and catcher Jerry Grote tried to field the ball as it rolled down the 3rd base line. The Mets battery crashed into each other in a scary Mets moment while the ball drifted foul.

Joe Trimble wrote in the New York Daily News, *"Seaver and Grote collided, Tom collapsing like a kayoed fighter. He lay sprawled for about 30 seconds, then roused himself groggily and returned to the mound."*

Seaver had survived a near calamity... for a moment. On the next pitch, Thomas drilled the ball right back at Seaver. Seaver got his glove on it, but couldn't catch it. Trimble wrote, *"The ball caromed to Garrett at short, but he bobbled it."*

According to Leonard Koppett in the New York Times, *"Garrett had plenty of time, but dropped the ball and never did throw it."*

Thomas was safe at first.

Despite the two sportswriters' independent accounts that indicated the runner was safe due to the mishandling of the ball by the inexperienced shortstop, the official scorer indicated it was a hit.

The crowd booed in San Diego.

Tom Seaver had lost his no-hit bid.

Seaver struck out the next batter to end the inning.

In the bottom of the 6th, the 2nd Padres batter, Jerry Morales, hit a high bouncing ball to Garrett. This time Garrett made the play, but the throw was late, and Morales was awarded a hit.

Morales made it to third base after a walk and a passed ball. With 2 outs Seaver had to face the dangerous Nate Colbert. Seaver got him to fly out.

Colbert was the 1st of 10 consecutive Padres batters that Seaver set down to end the game.

Dreaming About a No-Hitter

Tom Seaver had pitched a gem of a game, a 7 - 0 shutout.

More importantly for posterity purposes, it was a 2-hitter. And both hits could easily have been ruled as errors by the shortstop Wayne Garrett.

No offense to Wayne Garrett, who was thrust into the shortstop role as the Mets were missing their 1st and 2nd string men. But if Bud Harrelson, the gold glove winner at the position in 1971, had been in the game, there is every chance that last night, in San Diego, Tom Seaver would have pitched his first no-hitter, and the first no-hitter in Mets franchise history.

For Seaver it was the 9th time in his career he has pitched a shutout on 1 or 2 hits. He now has four 1-hitters and five 2-hitters.

Seaver improved his record to 15 - 6. And lowered his major league leading ERA to 1.77.

The Mets are still in last place at 53 - 65. But with the Cards losing for the 9th time in 10 games, the 1973 Mets are just 7.5 games back.

The Mets are off tonight and then begin a 4 game home series against the surging Cincinnati Reds at Shea Stadium. The Big Red Machine is getting fired up. After a slow start to the season, they have the 2nd best record in baseball only trailing the Dodgers, who lead them by 2.5 games in the NL West.

CHAPTER SIXTY-ONE

Faith and Fear in Flushing

THE HEADLINE TODAY IS THE NAME OF THE METS BLOG THAT FEATURED THE SPORTS TIME TRAVELER™ THIS WEEK. IT WAS ALSO APPROPRIATE FOR "LAST NIGHT'S" GAME IN 1973.

SPECIAL NOTE to Readers and Listeners of The Sports Time Traveler™

This week I was honored with a call out in the Mets blog, "Faith and Fear in Flushing", which has been covering the Mets since 2005.

Faith and Fear in Flushing is a blog for Mets fans who like to read. They're now in their 19th season of exploring the agony and the ecstasy of Mets baseball, whether it's the game from last night or a moment from the last century.

In their August 16, 2023, post they wrote this about The Sports Time Traveler™:

"If you'd like to take a delightful baseball flight of your own back some fifty years, I suggest the handiwork of Len Ferman, who bills himself as The Sports Time Traveler™."

I extend a hearty thanks to Greg Prince and Jason Fry, founders of Faith and Fear in Flushing, for that flattering furtherance of my work.

INTRODUCTION From The Sports Time Traveler™

The 1973 Mets are back home after a 3 - 5 west coast trip. They're in last place, where they've been since June 29th and they're 12 games under. 500.

They are a depressed group according to Joe Trimble, the Mets beat writer for the New York Daily News, who was with the team for their eight game trip. Trimble wrote yesterday, *"The players, mostly, know they are beaten and have a 'so what' attitude."*

Trimble went on to write that manager Yogi Berra thinks they have a chance because after August 30th they only play NL East teams.

But so do all the other NL East teams!

So that almost qualifies as a new Yogi-ism.

Before we get to the blissful final month of the season against only NL East teams, the Mets have to play 13 consecutive games against NL West clubs - all at Shea Stadium.

The homestand began last night, the first of a 4 game set against the Big Red Machine - The Cincinnati Reds. After the Reds, there will be 3 games each against the Dodgers, Giants and Padres.

The Dodgers, Reds and Giants, in that order, have the three best records in the National League. The next 10 games against those 3 teams just might bury the 1973 Mets.

The Reds can make a strong claim that they are the dominant team in the National League this decade. They went to the World Series in 1970 and again last season in 1972, losing a close 7 game series to the Oakland A's.

This season the Reds started slowly. They were 11 games behind the NL West leading Dodgers on June 30.

Since then the machine has revved up. They've had one of the great stretches in franchise history going 35 - 11, and have pulled to within 2.5 games of the Dodgers.

Sports Illustrated's August 20, 1973 issue is out on the newsstands. The cover story is about the Dodgers, a team of young, up and coming players, like Davey Lopes, Ron Cey, Steve Garvey and Bill Russell. They sport the best record in baseball, but they're being referred to as *"The Little Blue Bicycle,"* by SI, and SI ends the story with an ominous speculation that they may be, *"run over by the Big Red Machine."*

Last night the Mets had to face the Machine and one of their best starters, Don Gullett, who came into the game with a record of 14 - 8.

The Mets sent George Stone, 7 - 3, to the mound. Stone is having a very good season with a 2.99 ERA, and he won a starting job in June, but his last outing was awful, getting rocked for 4 runs and getting knocked out with just 1 down in the 1st inning.

Now he would face one of the most fearsome lineups in baseball.

Here's the story of last night's game.

SHEA STADIUM - AUGUST 18, 1973

I was back in New York virtually "last night," precisely 50 years ago, along with 36,803 fans to see the Mets play the Reds in the 1st game of a 13 game homestand for the Amazins'.

Mets starter, George Stone, lasted longer than he had in his last start after just five minutes, as he retired the Reds in order in the 1st.

That's no small accomplishment since the leadoff batter, Pete Rose, leads the NL in batting at .342. The number two hitter, Joe Morgan, is hitting .294 and led the league in OBP last year, and the 3rd batter Dan Driessen is batting .322.

The Mets also went quietly in the bottom of the inning facing Don Gullett, and a pitching duel was on.

In the top of the 2nd, Stone gave up a single to Tony Perez (batting .311), and then got Johnny Bench (the league leader in RBIs) to ground into a double play. He got out of the inning without stress after that.

The Mets again were quiet in the 2nd.

Stone got the 8th hitter and the pitcher Gullett out quickly to start the 3rd and then faced Pete Rose for the 2nd time. He struck him out.

In the bottom of the 3rd, Teddy Martinez got a single. Teddy is healthy enough to play shortstop again after Wayne Garrett, filling in at short for the injured Martinez and Bud Harrelson, proved ineffective (costing Tom Seaver a no-hitter in the Mets last game).

Martinez was left stranded at first.

METS 0 REDS 0 - end of 3 innings

Facing the heart of the Reds order in the top of the 4th, Stone was superb, getting Morgan to ground out and then striking out Driessen and Perez.

In the bottom of the inning, Felix Millan flew out and then Willie Mays came to the plate. With the count 2 - 2, Mays hit a curving line drive that cleared the fence in right center for his 660th home run. Mays had put the Mets ahead 1 - 0.

In the 5th, Stone again got the Reds 1-2-3.

Gullett gave up a double to Martinez in the bottom of the inning, but stranded him on the bases again.

In the 6th, Stone recorded his 3rd straight 1-2-3 inning, getting Pete Rose to fly out to end the inning.

In the bottom 6th, the Mets got runners on first and third on singles by Felix Millan and John Milner, but failed to score.

METS 1 REDS 0 - end of 6 innings

Stone got into his first stressful situation when Joe Morgan led off with a walk and stole second. Stone now had to contend with the Reds power hitters.

He got Driessen and Perez out.

Next up was one of the league's best sluggers, Johnny Bench. Bench at 25, is already a 2-time MVP and has smacked 112 home runs in the past 3 seasons.

Bench was ahead in the count 3 - 1 when he hit a slow roller to the left of the pitching mound. Stone got to the ball, but had to hurry his throw to first base. His throw was off and drew Willie Mays into the path of the hard charging Bench. (Mays was playing first base because his ailing shoulder doesn't enable him to make throws from the outfield).

Bench knocked Mays flat to the ground. And in the process Bench landed flat on his back as well.

United Press International (UPI) caught a comical picture that ran in newspapers around the country of both men on the ground with their legs pointing up in the air.

The Cincinnati Enquirer reported that Bench said to Mays, *"You alright?"* To which Mays shot back, *"You trying to run me over man?"*

Players from both teams came out of the dugout and onto the field. But the 2 players were okay. And Mays still had the ball. Bench was out.

Stone had survived the inning.

The bottom of the Mets order went down quickly in the last of the 7th.

In the 8th, Stone got the Reds easily again, allowing just a 2 out walk.

In the bottom of the inning, Gullett got the Mets 1-2-3.

METS 1 REDS 0 - end of 8 innings

George Stone went into the 9th inning with an opportunity to close out the best game of his career.

Stone held a 1 – 0 lead thanks to Willie Mays' home run.

With 3 more outs he would have a shutout of the Big Red Machine.

The leadoff hitter, Pete Rose came to the plate. Joseph Durso described what happened in The New York Times, *"Pete Rose... hit a line drive to right, but it was speared by Felix Millan."*

Millan has been sensational covering second base all season.

Now Stone needed 2 more outs.

The next batter was the crafty Joe Morgan. Morgan hit a grounder to Millan that he tossed to Mays.

George Stone needed 1 more out.

If he could get it, he would have a terrific 2-hit shutout, just like Tom Terrific had done 2 nights ago in San Diego. But this one would be against the Big Red Machine, quite an accomplishment.

The next hitter was Driessen. He hit a bouncer that got through the middle for a single.

Still, Stone could have a 3 hit shutout if he could get just 1 more out. That would still be extremely impressive.

Tony Perez came to the plate. Perez had 1 of the 3 hits against Stone in the game. Perez came into the game Red hot, piling up 14 hits in his last 28 at bats.

Stone got 2 strikes on Perez.

He was now 1 strike away from the shutout.

If he could get Perez, then Willie Mays would have yet another game winning hit. Mays homer was still the only score of the game.

That was the vision.

Tony Perez, in broken English, described what happened on the 0 - 2 pitch after the game to the Cincinnati Enquirer, *"I was going for the gas the first two strikes, but he make me look bad. So, I just try to make contact."*

Bob Hertzel of the Enquirer wrote, *"That's about all Perez did, hitting a weak ground ball to the left side."*

Hertzel then quoted Reds manager Sparky Anderson saying, *"I said, there goes the game, but I remembered Wayne Garrett was guarding the line."*

Neither Garrett playing close to the bag at third or Martinez at short could get to the ball, and Driessen and Perez were safe at first and second.

In all likelihood, if Bud Harrelson had not been injured he would have made the play and Stone would have had his 3-hit gem of a shutout.

Now with 2 outs Johnny Bench came to the plate.

Berra came out to the mound. Stone told him he was not tired. And Yogi figured that the 2 hits in the inning were both weak. So, he left Stone in to pitch to Bench.

Stone got 2 strikes on Bench.

Again, Stone was yet again 1 strike away from sealing a shutout that would have given 42 year old Willie Mays credit for another game winning homer.

But Bench punched a grounder through the hole between shortstop and third for a single and Driessen came around to tie the game at one.

Once again, it is possible that the gold glove shortstop, Harrelson, could have made this play to end the game.

"We couldn't let a 42 year old man (Willie Mays) *beat us,"* said Perez after the game.

Now Yogi decided to take Stone out and bring in Harry Parker.

Parker promptly got Bobby Tolan to pop up.

Now the Mets had the opportunity to win the game in the bottom of the 9th.

But Reds relief pitcher Pedro Bourbon set down the Mets in order in the 9th and the game went into extra innings.

METS 1 REDS 1 - end of 9 innings

In the top of the 10th, pinch hitter Hal King led off. King has only 23 at bats this season, but he had hit 3 home runs in those 23 trips.

On a 1-1 count, Parker threw a curve ball low and away. Parker must have felt that was a safe pitch. King thought otherwise. He drove the ball 400 feet deep over the right field fence.

The Reds were ahead 2 - 1.

Now the Mets, who had been 1 strike away from winning two times in the 9th, needed a run to extend the game.

Bourbon got Don Hahn to fly out.

He got Ken Boswell on a grounder to 1st.

And then he struck out Jim Beauchamp to get the win.

The Reds won it 2 - 1. It was their 36th win in 47 games.

For the Mets it was another crusher.

It was the 2nd game this week they had lost when they were ahead going into the 9th inning on a strong pitching performance from a starter.

The Mets are now 53 - 66.

It certainly appears to be a lost season for the Mets after finishing above .500 every year since 1969.

But with the Cardinals losing for the 9th time in 10 games, the Mets remain just 7.5 games back.

QUICK UPDATES on Hank Aaron and the Chicago Cubs

After going homerless in the first half of August, Hank Aaron hit number 702 in Chicago 2 nights ago. It was a 3 run shot that helped the Braves beat the Cubs.

That was the Cubs 11th straight loss and 14th in 15 games.

The Cubs have gone 9 - 32 after starting the season 47 - 31 when they built an 8.5 game lead in the NL East.

Yogi Berra commented that it's a mystery since the Cubs haven't even had an injury to a key player.

Last night Hank Aaron and the Braves were in Montreal where Aaron hit number 703. That pulls him to within 11 of Babe Ruth's career mark of 714, the most hallowed record in baseball.

It was also Aaron's 30th of the season, which gives him 15 seasons in which he has hit 30 or more homers. That's more than any other player in history.

It was also Aaron's 1,377th extra base hit, which ties him for the career record with Stan Musial.

Last night the Cubs broke their 11 game losing streak by beating the team with the best record in baseball, the Dodgers, 5 - 1, allowing the Dodgers just 3 hits.

Go figure!

NOTE From The Sports Time Traveler™

Hank Aaron still holds the career record for extra-base hits. And he is tied for the career record of most seasons with 30+ home runs with Alex Rodriguez.

If you lower the threshold to most seasons with 29+ home runs, then Aaron is the career leader by himself with 16.

CHAPTER SIXTY-TWO

A New Set of Points and Plugs

THE METS ARE SUDDENLY PLAYING COMPETITIVELY AGAINST THE BEST TEAMS IN BASEBALL

INTRODUCTION From The Sports Time Traveler™

6 days ago the 1973 New York Mets returned from a west coast trip in which they went 3 - 5. They were in last place and 12 games under .500 at 53 - 65. Joe Trimble of the New York Daily News, who was with the team on the trip wrote, *"The players, mostly, know they are beaten and have a 'so what' attitude."*

They promptly lost the first of their 13 game homestand, blowing a lead in the 9th inning when they were 1 strike away from winning... twice.

But something about that loss, to the hottest team in baseball, the Cincinnati "Big Red Machine", seems to have lit a fire in the Mets. That game proved they could play toe-to-toe with the best.

They beat Cincinnati the next day 12 - 1. And then beat them again the following afternoon.

They lost the last game of the series, another tight one that lasted 16 innings.

But it was perhaps another confidence builder. They knew they could have just as easily swept the Reds instead of split.

Next into Shea came the Dodgers, the team that still holds the best record in baseball. The Mets promptly defeated them in the first game of the series behind a 4 hitter by the bottom starter in the rotation, veteran Ray Sadecki, and a game winning single by John Milner with 2 outs in the bottom of the 9th.

So the Mets had now won 3 of 4 against the 2 best baseball teams in the world.

That takes us to last night's game. Here's today's story.

SHEA STADIUM - August 23, 1973

George Stone took the mound for the Mets last night against the Dodgers. He was coming off the best start of his career, a game in which he had come 1 strike away, twice, from a shutout against the Reds. He never got the third strike, and the Machine came back to beat the Mets in an extra innings heartbreaker.

Now Stone had a chance to redeem himself. But he was shaky in the top of the 1st giving up a walk, 2 singles and a sacrifice fly. The Dodgers were off to a 1 - 0 lead.

In the 2nd inning, Bill Russell hit a deep fly to left field, but John Milner leaped up over the top of the face to rob him of a home run.

Stone then settled down and breezed through the Dodgers lineup in 3rd and 4th.

Then good fortune gave Stone the lead. In the bottom of the 4th, Dodgers pitcher Andy Messersmith called off everyone else in his stellar infield on a 2 out pop fly to the pitcher's mound. The bases were loaded, and the Mets were all running as everyone in the stadium waited for the pop up to come down. But just before the ball arrived back to Earth, Messersmith tripped on the pitching rubber... and he dropped the ball. 2 runs scored on the error and the Mets ended the 4th with a 2 - 1 lead.

METS 2 DODGERS 1 - end of 4 innings

Stone continued to pitch well until the top of the 6th, when he gave up a double to Joe Ferguson and then Steve Garvey singled in the tying run.

In the 7th, Stone gave up 2 more singles and Willie Davis' sacrifice fly gave the Dodgers the lead again at 3 - 2.

Stone was then replaced by Harry Parker.

Stone had pitched okay going into the 7th inning against the team with baseball's best record, only allowing 3 runs.

Meanwhile Messersmith got through 7 innings against the Mets without allowing an earned run before he was replaced for Jim Brewer.

DODGERS 3 METS 2 - end of 7 innings

To pitch the top of the 8th, Yogi Berra inserted Tug McGraw on the mound.

McGraw came into the game as a big question mark. From 1969 - 1972 he had been one of baseball's most reliable relievers. But this season he has a 0 - 6 record and a 5.45 ERA. He has just 13 saves, and he has 5 blown saves and 4 blown losses.

In his most recent outing, he gave up 5 earned runs in just 3 and 1/3 innings.

But last night McGraw was more like the pitcher from years past.

He got the Dodgers out 1-2-3 in the 8th and again in the 9th, striking out 3 of the 6 batters he faced.

Now the Mets came into the bottom of the 9th, down 3 - 2.

The 1st Mets batter, Cleon Jones, singled to left.

Then Tug McGraw put down a perfect bunt and moved Jones, the tying run, to second base with 1 out.

The next hitter, Wayne Garrett, hit a fly to center. That moved Cleon Jones to third, but now the Mets were down to their last out.

This brought up Felix Millan, the Mets leading hitter at .282. Millan slashed a ball down the third base line that was just fair, and it drove in Jones to tie the game.

Joe Trimble wrote in the New York Daily News, *"The crowd of 25,442 went wild as though this was 1969 all over again."*

Now Rusty Staub came to the plate. He nearly ended the game when he hit a long ball that went foul. But then he followed it up with a single to left, putting Felix Millan on second.

Next up was John Milner who had won the game last night for the Mets in the bottom of the 9th.

Alston took out Brewer and brought in Pete Richert.

On Richert's first pitch, Milner drove a shot to centerfield for a single.

Millan came flying around third base, and gold glove center fielder Willie Davis threw home. Millan crashed into catcher Steve Yeager, but he didn't have the ball, as the throw had gone wide.

The dizzy Millan then stepped on home plate to win the game.

METS 4 DODGERS 3 - Final Score

Tug McGraw was credited with his first victory of the season, and he deserved it as he pitched 2 perfect innings.

Tug was quoted by John Bruns in the Central Jersey Home News, it was a quote that didn't appear in any of the New York papers, *"Our ballclub has got a new set of points and plugs. We're all tuned up and we're on our way."*

The NL East leading St. Louis Cardinals also won last night. They beat the Braves in Atlanta 6 - 4.

In that game, Hank Aaron hit his 32nd home run of the season, which is number 705 for his career. He is now just 9 shy of Babe Ruth's hallowed mark of 714.

The Cardinals win leaves the Mets 6 games back.

But the Mets are still in last place.

CHAPTER SIXTY-THREE

Mets Fans are Fired Up!

IT WAS TOM VS THE GIANTS AT SHEA YESTERDAY IN 1973

INTRODUCTION From The Sports Time Traveler™

The 1973 Mets came into yesterday afternoon's game against the San Francisco Giants 10 games under .500 at 58 - 68 and they're in last place in the National League East.

In the newspapers, however, there has been wishful talk of a magical surge that would springboard them from last to first in the final month of the season. This hope is fueled by three facts:

- The Mets enter the day only 6.5 games back

- They've won 5 of their last 7, all against the 3 best teams in the National League

- Mets starting pitchers have allowed only 11 earned runs in those 7 games

And things looked even brighter for yesterday afternoon's game. Skies were sunny, the temperature was about 80 degrees, Tom Terrific was on the mound, and 38,221 Mets fanatics were in the stands.

Naturally, The Sports Time Traveler™ had to make the trip 50 years back in time, virtually, to Shea Stadium and make it 38,222 fans experiencing the game.

FLUSHING MEADOWS, QUEENS, NY - August 26, 1973

The Sports Time Traveler™ is here, virtually, 50 years ago, in Shea Stadium, on a gorgeous day to see the best pitcher in baseball this year, Tom Seaver, take the mound against the hard hitting San Francisco Giants.

The Giants have the 3rd best record in the National League at 70 - 56. But they're 4 games back of the Reds and 8 games back of the NL West leading Dodgers. The Giants need to go on a winning streak if they want to make a run at the division in the last month of the season.

They have the power to do it. They're led by MVP candidate Bobby Bonds who has 33 home runs and 33 steals, and is vying to become the first player to ever record a 40 - 40 season. They also have the dangerous veteran slugger, Willie McCovey. The 35-year-old has 23 home runs on the year and 407 for his career. And they have 3 other batters hitting over .300.

But, Tom Seaver has been a Giant killer this year. In 3 starts against them, he's had 3 complete game victories and allowed a total of 4 earned runs in 27 innings. Seaver entered the game with a 15 - 6 record and a 1.76 ERA. He is the only starting pitcher in the majors with an ERA under 2.20.

However, Seaver gave up a single to the 1st batter of the game, .308 hitter Gary Matthews. Giants second baseman Tito Fuentes then bunted Matthews over to second. Seaver then got Bobby Bonds to pop up to Teddy Martinez at short. Martinez is playing in place of the injured Bud Harrelson.

So Seaver had 2 outs and next up was big Willie McCovey. Berra decided to give the left-handed hitting McCovey a pass so that Seaver could pitch to the right handed batter Garry Maddox. Maddox, however, leads the team in batting at .314.

The move appeared to work though when Maddox hit a pop foul on a 0 - 2 pitch from Seaver. Mets catcher Jerry Grote drifted over towards the box seats on the right side of the field close to the Mets dugout. Grote was poised to catch the ball, which was coming down just inside the playing ground. But also lining up for the catch was 15-year-old Mark Johnson, a fan in the first row, who was over enthusiastically reaching out onto the field to make the play.

Johnson told Joe Trimble in the New York Daily News, *"I thought it was going to come into the stands and I reached out to get it."*

Unfortunately, a catch by Johnson would not count for the 3rd out, while it would count for Grote, an all-star catcher in 1968, and generally recognized as one of the best defensive catchers in the league.

So, Johnson wisely deferred to Grote. He said to Trimble, *"When I saw him (Grote) near me, I tried to pull back my hands. I didn't touch the ball."*

But he did obstruct Grote's view and neither of them ended up snaring the ball which fell to the ground.

A picture appeared this morning on the back cover of The New York Daily News, as well as newspapers across the country, in which you see Johnson and Grote, arms extended, both trying to catch Maddox's foul pop.

Grote then argued with home plate umpire Ed Vargo that Maddox should be out due to fan interference. Vargo, however, ruled against Grote and the Mets.

Even the San Francisco Examiner sportswriter Bucky Walter indicated in his article this morning it should have been ruled interference. Walter wrote, *"This scribe felt certain the ball was touched as did many others including Giants manager Charlie Fox."*

But Mets manager Yogi Berra took the opposite viewpoint. He told the New York Times, *"The only way they could have called interference was if a spectator touched the ball over the field. I asked the umpire, and he said the fan didn't touch it. So, it was just a tough break."*

And the instant replay on WOR channel 9 in New York was inconclusive as to whether Johnson had touched the ball.

The play turned out to be consequential as Maddox came back to the batter's box and 2 pitches later he drove a single to right field that scored Matthews and the Giants took a 1 - 0 lead.

Seaver then got Chris Speier to ground out to end the top of the 1st.

In the dugout between innings, Jerry Grote called the press box and requested the official scorer change the on field ruling from a missed foul ball to an error so that the run scored would not count as an earned run against Seaver.

The catcher was denied this request as well.

GIANTS 1 METS 0 - middle of the 1st inning

The Giants sent Tom Bradley to the mound to start the game against the Mets. The 26-year-old had 2 strong seasons in 1971 and 1972, winning 15 games each year and posting ERAs under 3. This season he hasn't been quite as steady, coming into the game at 10 - 11 with a 3.68 ERA. And in 3 starts against the Mets he's given up 10 runs in 19 innings of work.

But Bradley returned to last season's form yesterday. He got the Mets 1-2-3 in both the 1st and 2nd innings. And he didn't allow a runner to reach base until the 3rd inning when Tom Seaver hit a grounder to 3rd and was safe on an error.

How many times this season has Tom Seaver had to take the offense into his own hands?

But Bradley stranded Seaver and made it through 3 innings with no hits and no runs.

Seaver was nearly doing the same. He allowed one single in the 2nd and got the Giants in order in the 3rd and 4th.

The Mets entered the bottom of the 4th still down 1 - 0, and they had their best hitters coming up.

Felix Millan started off with a double. Then he moved to third on a fly ball by Rusty Staub. John Milner then hit a bouncing grounder to the pitcher's mound. Felix Millan hesitated to run but then decided to race home. The pitcher Bradley said after the game, ***"My momentum was toward the right when I fielded*** *the ball and I had to reverse myself to throw home."* Bradley made the throw and Millan was out at the plate. But Bradley indicated that Millan, *"would have made it if he had gone all the way."* Bradley got out of the inning holding on to his 1 - 0 lead.

In the 5th and 6th innings, Seaver pitched out of jams as he let runners get to third base, but he didn't let anyone score. The Mets went down easily in both innings. Bradley was aided by a diving grab by second baseman Fuentes that ended the 6th inning when the Mets had runners on first and second with 2 outs.

GIANTS 1 METS 0 - end of 6 innings

Seaver got the Giants down quickly in the top of the 7th. And in the bottom of the inning the Mets got a one out base runner when Grote walked. The next batter would have been the light hitting Don Hahn, the center fielder, but Berra had Willie Mays pinch hit with the Mets behind. Mays popped up to 2nd and Bradley got Ed Kranepool to strike out.

In the 8th, McCovey reached base on an error and then Seaver got the Giants next 3 batters in order.

Bradley had an easy time with the Mets in the bottom of the inning and the game went to the 9th with the Giants still ahead by the one run they had scored in the 1st.

GIANTS 1 METS 0 - end of 8 innings

Tug McGraw came in to pitch the top of the 9th for Seaver who came out for a pinch hitter in the 8th. McGraw did the job, allowing just a walk.

Seaver's game was done. He had given up 7 hits and one walk in 8 innings. And he had let up just the one earned run in the 1st inning.

Now the Mets batters had one last chance to come back in the bottom of the 9th.

The 1st hitter was John Milner. Milner, the Mets HR leader with 21, had already won 2 games this week with hits in the bottom of the 9th. But this time

Milner could only manage an innocent fly ball to right which was caught for out number 1.

Next up was Cleon Jones. He came through with a single to right. This brought up the catcher Jerry Grote. And Willie Mays was on deck.

But Mays never got to the plate. Bradley got Grote to strikeout on a hit and run play and the game ended when Cleon Jones was caught as he raced to second base.

The Giants had beaten Tom Seaver for the 1st time in 4 tries this year by a score of 1 - 0.

Giants pitcher Tom Bradley, who pitched a 4 hit shutout for his best game of the season, told the New York Daily News, *"I was fortunate to have good stuff, particularly good control of my curve. You don't get more than one run off Tom Seaver very often and I had to make it stand up."*

Over Heated Fans

Mark Johnson, the fan who caused the dropped foul ball in the 1st inning, was deeply apologetic after the game. He told Joe Trimble in the New York Daily News, *"I'm sorry I cost them the game."* He told Newsday, *"I didn't feel good about it. I was shaking for about 20 minutes after it happened."*

Tom Seaver was quick to accept Johnson's apology. In the locker room he told Newsday, *"You can't do anything about it. You can't blame a fan for going after a ball."*

But many Mets fans were not so quick to forgive the 15-year-old, who attends 10 - 12 games a year and saw his first Mets game in the Mets inaugural season in 1962 when he was just 4 years old. The fans were so hostile towards Johnson that he needed a police escort to safely depart the stadium. Even one of the Shea Stadium ushers told Johnson, *"You know you cost them the game."* And one policeman called Johnson an, *"S.O.B."*

The loss dropped the last place Mets to 58 - 69. It's especially crushing because they can usually count on a win when Seaver pitches.

But thanks to another loss by division leader St. Louis, the Mets are still just 6.5 games back. The Cardinals have now lost 13 times in their 17 games after going through a stretch in which they had been one of the hottest teams in baseball for most of the summer.

Here's the NL East Standings as of this morning (August 26, 1973):

65 – 63 CARDS

62 – 63 PIRATES   1.5 games back

62 – 66 CUBS   3 games back

60 – 67 EXPOS   4.5 games back

59 – 69 PHILLIES   6 games back

58 – 69 METS   6.5 games back

CHAPTER SIXTY-FOUR

The Mets are Out of the Cellar

A VISIT BY THE PADRES WAS JUST WHAT THE METS NEEDED

SHEA STADIUM - August 30, 1973

I was in Shea Stadium, virtually, last night to see the last of the Mets 13 game homestand against NL west teams. The Mets finished a 3 game sweep against the NL's worst team, the San Diego Padres, thus vaulting the Mets past the Phillies and into 5th place in the NL East.

The Mets won the game on a combined 3 - 0 shutout by Jerry Koosman and Buzz Capra.

This marks the first time since June 28th, over two months, that the Mets have been out of the NL East cellar.

SPECIAL NOTE From The Sports Time Traveler™

As I think back to when I was a 9 year old boy, who lived for the Mets, that summer in the cellar in 1973 seemed like it lasted forever. It endured for the entire camp season. It truly felt like it was years long.

I remember looking in awe at the super teams like the Reds, the Orioles and the A's, and I wished my Mets could contend for the World Series like those teams.

Now back to this short article.

MAYS STILL CONTRIBUTING

Willie Mays singled home one of the 3 Mets runs as he filled in at first base for the injured John Milner. Mays continues to be an important contributor to the ball club despite a torrent of articles circulating around the nation's newspapers that Willie is washed up.

But Willie Mays is hitting .275 and has an OBP of .370 this month. And he's batted .267 and has an OBP of .333 since June 21.

MEET ME IN ST. LOUIS

After last night's game the Mets flew to St. Louis. And I will be there virtually tonight to experience the first of the 4 games against the Cardinals. Tom Seaver will be pitching for the Mets.

CONTENDERS OR PRETENDERS?

With the Mets in 5th place and 6 games back of the division leading Cardinals, Jack Lang wrote a story in the Jersey Journal that he titled, *"Contenders or Pretenders?"*

Lang wrote, *"We'll have the answer to that by Sunday night - maybe sooner - after they complete what all Mets players regard as the most important series of the year."*

But the Mets are still riddled with injuries. Felix Millan and Cleon Jones are doubtful for the game, although John Milner is expected to be back in the lineup.

However, the Mets strength lately has been pitching. Tom Seaver told Lang, *"I sincerely believe if we continue to get this type of pitching the rest of the way we can make a real challenge."*

All 4 games against St. Louis will be televised on WOR channel 9 in New York. I can't wait!

CHAPTER SIXTY-FIVE

Seaver vs. St. Louis

THE 1973 METS ACE STARTED IN THE FIRST OF FOUR GAMES AGAINST THE DIVISION LEADING CARDS "LAST NIGHT"

ST. LOUIS - August 31, 1973

I'm here in St. Louis to virtually experience the Mets four games against the first place St. Louis Cardinals.

The Mets players believe this is the most important series of the season, according to Jack Lang of the Jersey Journal, as it provides them an opportunity to get back into contention even though they arrived here just a half game out of last place in the NL East.

If the Mets could win three of four from the Cardinals they would leave St. Louis just 3.5 games behind the Cards.

And with Tom Seaver (15 - 7, 1.76 ERA) pitching the first game, a win in the initial game was a reasonable expectation.

In the opening frame, Seaver pitched out of a jam. He put runners on 1st and 3rd with one out. But he got Ted Simmons and Joe Torre on grounders to end the inning.

In the 2nd, 3rd and 4th he allowed one runner to reach 1st base in each inning and that was it.

He retired the side in order in the 5th. And allowed just a walk in the next frame.

Through 6 innings Seaver had a 3 hit shutout going.

There was a problem, however. The Mets had not scored either. The Cards' Reggie Cleveland had also blanked the Mets on three hits after six.

METS 0 CARDINALS 0 - end of 6 innings

The Mets went quietly again in the top of the 7th with just one walk.

In the bottom of the inning Seaver gave up two singles that put runners on first and third with 1 out. The next batter was Lou Brock. The Mets pulled the infield in. Brock hit a grounder to Felix Millan at second base. He threw home and nailed Mike Tyson at the plate (no, not that Mike Tyson). Seaver then escaped the inning with his shutout intact when he struck out Ted Simmons.

An oddly coincidental play took place in the 8th inning. Cardinals' catcher, Tim McCarver, raced to the stands to catch a foul pop by Felix Millan who was leading off the inning. McCarver was interfered with by a fan and Millan was called out.

Nearly the same thing had happened in Tom Seaver's last start at Shea Stadium against the Giants, when a Mets fan interfered with catcher Jerry Grote. When Grote was unable to make the routine catch to end the inning, the batter, Garry Maddox, was not called out. Given a 2nd chance by the umpire, Maddox drove in the only run of the game. The Mets and Seaver went on to lose that game to the Giants by a score of 1 - 0.

Back in St. Louis, after Millan was called out, the Mets managed two walks, but no hits and the score remained 0 - 0.

In the bottom of the 8th, Seaver again retired the side 1-2-3.

METS 0 CARDINALS 0 - end of 8 innings

In the top of the 9th, the Mets got a one out single from Bud Harrelson. They moved him to second on Tom Seaver's bunt. With two outs the Mets had their leadoff hitter Wayne Garrett come to the plate and the Cardinals walked him.

Now with runners at first and second and 2 outs the Mets leading hitter, Felix Millan, came up. But Millan grounded out and now the Cards had an opportunity to win it in their last at bat.

Tim McCarver led off the bottom of the 9th which started with an even stranger play than the one McCarver had been involved with in the 8th.

McCarver hit a towering foul pop to the right side. Mets first baseman John Milner raced over towards the bullpen, which is on the playing field in foul territory in Busch Stadium. But before Milner could get to the ball he tripped on the pitching rubber. He did a perfect somersault. Then he caught the ball. And as he came back up to his feet, he dropped the ball.

The umpire ruled that it was not a catch because Milner had not had possession of the ball long enough.

Milner was irate at the call. He argued unsuccessfully. And he was ejected from the game.

Seaver then proceeded to strikeout McCarver.

Seaver next gave up a double to Bernie Carbo but stranded him there when he struck out Bake McBride and got Luis Melendez on a grounder.

And the game went to extra innings.

METS 0 CARDINALS 0 - end of 9 innings

The Cardinals brought in reliever Al Hrabosky to pitch the top of the 10th against the heart of the Mets batting order.

Hrabosky got Rusty Staub out on a routine fly.

Next up was Cleon Jones. Jones hit a deep drive to right centerfield. Playing center was Jones high school buddy, and best friend on the Mets for five years, Tommie Agee.

Agee, who played with the Mets from 1968 - 1972, will be forever remembered by Mets fans for his sensational outfield catches that won game three of the 1969 World Series.

But in the off season, last December, he was mysteriously given up by the Mets for a minor league outfielder.

Now Agee raced for the ball. He caught it on the run. Then he crashed into the wall and smashed into right fielder Jose Cruz. But he held on.

Cleon Jones was out with what would have likely been a triple had Agee not hauled it in.

With 2 outs, Willie Mays came to the plate to pinch hit for Ed Kranepool. And Hrabosky struck him out.

Seaver came back out to pitch the bottom of the 10th. The leadoff hitter, Lou Brock, doubled. And Ted Sizemore moved him to third on a bunt. With 1 out and Brock on third, the Mets pulled the infield in as Jose Cruz stepped in the batters' box.

Cruz hit a chop that bounced on the astroturf infield and bounded 25 feet up into the air. It was a bounce you would never see on grass. Bud Harrelson waited and waited for the ball to come back down. When he got it, he fired home.

But it was hopeless.

Joseph Durso in the New York Times wrote that, ***"Bud Harrelson fielded the ball and hurled it in the general direction of the Mississippi River as Brock crossed the plate."***

The Cardinals won the game 1 - 0.

It was a bitter loss with Tom Seaver having, ***"pitched masterfully,"*** according to Red Foley of the New York Daily News.

But the Mets wasted the effort by not scoring any runs in 10 innings of play.

Mets Unsupportive of Seaver

The Mets have not scored a run for Tom Seaver in the last 24 innings he has pitched. And in those 24 innings, Seaver has allowed just 2 earned runs, one of which was due to the fan interference I mentioned earlier.

Seaver told Durso, *"When you lose it doesn't matter much whether it's 1 - 0 or 10 - 0."*

Seaver also took no consolation from the fact that he had pitched a masterful game, shutting out the Cardinals for nine full innings. He told Jack Lang, *"What am I supposed to do, feel good after I lost... Am I supposed to come in here and say I pitched well, but what the heck?"*

"Shoot, I lost. That's all that matters."

Sensational Seaver

Seaver struck out 9 Cardinals in last night's game, giving him 205 on the season. He has now struck out 200 or more batters in six consecutive seasons. That's every season he's been in the majors except for his rookie year when he "only" struck out 170.

Tom Terrific also reduced his major league leading ERA to 1.70.

But none of those stats make up for the Mets losing a grand opportunity against the 1st place Cardinals.

The Mets are now 10 games under .500 at 61 - 71.

They are back in last place after a one day reprieve.

And now they're 6.5 games behind the Cardinals.

It's getting desperate for the 1973 New Yor Mets.

Here's the standing in the National League East as of this morning:

68 – 65 CARDS

63 – 65 PIRATES   2.5 games back

64 – 67 CUBS   3 games back

62 – 70 EXPOS   5.5 games back

62 – 71 PHILLIES   6 games back

61 – 71 METS   6.5 games back

CHAPTER SIXTY-SIX

Willie Mays to Retire

NEW YORK – August 31, 1973

There was some big news that was informally announced yesterday.

In a special to The New York Times, friends of Willie Mays revealed there will be a **"Farewell to Willie Mays,"** celebration at Shea Stadium on September 25th.

The Mets are allegedly making plans for the event which will take place prior to the Mets next to last home game of the season.

The brief article indicated that, *"Mays has not announced whether he will end his 22-year career, and may not have even decided yet. But a formal announcement was reported under consideration."*

CHAPTER SIXTY-SEVEN

A Six Team Scramble

IT'S THE FINAL MONTH OF THE 1973 BASEBALL SEASON AND THE NL EAST IS IN A FRENZY

INTRODUCTION – REAL LIFE RECOLLECTIONS From The Sports Time Traveler™

We're into the month of September, when baseball drama takes its grip each year.

50 years ago, in real life, I was just turning 10 years old. Summer camp was over. My family had just come back from a 10-hour car trip to Montreal. The school year in New Jersey would begin on the Wednesday after Labor Day.

This was the laziest time of the summer. Nothing to do but watch the Mets on TV - WOR channel 9 in New York. Listening to the Mets announcers, Lindsey Nelson, Bob Murphy and Ralph Kiner was always a great experience. Those guys loved baseball and they loved the Mets just as much as I did. When I was watching a Mets game, it felt like they were my baseball crazy uncles, and the whole world just stopped for a couple of hours.

But it had been dreary time to follow the Mets. They had been in last place since just after school let out. And while they had moved out of the cellar the prior day, I don't recall thinking for a minute that the Mets could leap to the top and take the division.

My friend Charlie says that he never gave up hope that summer. And I suppose anyone a little older, who had experienced the Miracle Mets of 1969, had to believe there was still reason for optimism.

But I was too young to remember 1969. To me the Mets had always been a second-tier team. We just weren't destined to play with the super teams in the playoffs, let alone the World Series. We didn't have the big bats like the Reds and the Pirates had. And the miracle of 1969 was some mystical thing that happened in the ancient past. The kind of thing that happens once in a lifetime. And I had missed it.

And now today's story about the Mets game from 50 years ago last night.

ST. LOUIS - September 2, 1973

The Sports Time Traveler™ is here in St. Louis, virtually, exactly 50 years ago, where later this afternoon Jon Matlack will take the mound for the Mets in the final game of the 4 game set here. A few weeks ago, this game, pitting a last place team against a division leader, would have seemed inconsequential on the calendar. Now it's going to be an important one with the top to bottom in the division separated by just 6 games.

Last night, the Mets sent out George Stone to face the Cardinals lineup. Stone is the surprise starter of the year for the Mets. He has gone 7 - 3 since earning a spot in the rotation at the beginning of June. He has an ERA of 2.96 and has only allowed more than 4 runs in a start just once.

The Cardinals started Alan Foster, who is pitching well at 11 - 6.

Both pitchers got out to strong starts and there was no score after 3 innings.

CARDS 0 METS 0 - end of 3 innings

In the top of the 4th the Mets got to Foster. It started with a walk to Cleon Jones. Rusty Staub then whacked a double, the 1,500th hit of his career, and the Mets had men on second and third with no outs.

Next, Ed Kranepool was intentionally walked to load the bases for rookie catcher Ron Hodges. Hodges hit a bouncer that second baseman Ted Sizemore juggled. Jones scored from third and everyone else was safe.

DON HAHN

Don Hahn came up next. Hahn is a good fielding, light hitting center fielder who is playing because he gets the job done in the outfield. With Willie Mays shoulder leaving him unavailable for outfield duty, Hahn has become a regular center fielder for the 1st time in his career.

At age 24, he had played sporadically with the Expos and the Mets over the past 5 seasons. In 53 games in Tidewater earlier this year, the Mets AAA farm club, he had hit a respectable .274. But in the big leagues it was a different story. He went through a 3 for 29 slump in mid-August and his average dipped to .235.

And then a week ago he finally started hitting. He had a 4 for 4 game and has hit .347 over his last 6 games.

Now with the bases loaded with no outs, Hahn slammed a Foster pitch into left field for a single, driving in 2 runs and putting the Mets ahead 3 - 0.

The Mets added another run in the 5th when Felix Millan doubled to drive in Wayne Garrett and the Mets went up 4 - 0.

Meanwhile George Stone was pitching rock solid. He got the Cardinals 1-2-3 in the 4th and 5th. He finally allowed a run in the 6th, but came back for a strong 7th inning.

METS 4 CARDINALS 1 - end of 7 innings

In the 8th, when Stone opened the inning by giving up a bunt single to Sizemore and then a hard single to left by Tim McCarver, Yogi Berra decided to take him out for Harry Parker.

Parker promptly shut down any rally hopes for the Cardinals. Parker didn't allow a hit in 2 innings of work and the Mets won the game 4 - 1.

It was the Mets 5th win in their last 6 games. The team, which had been as many as 12 games back in mid-July, suddenly were just 4.5 games out of 1st place.

Less than a week ago, the Mets were 12 games under .500 at 58 - 70 and buried in last place. Joe Trimble of the New York Daily News had reported of despair among many players. Now they were in 5th place in the 6 team division, and they were in contention.

Red Foley of the New York Daily News wrote optimistically in the opening paragraph of his story on the game, *"This might be 1969 all over again."* **He ended his article noting that Mets players believe this will be, *'a replay of the 1969 miracle.'"***

Yogi Berra told Doug Grow of Newsday, *"We ain't dead. We ain't been dead all year. And we sure ain't dead now."* It was a classic Yogi Berra quote.

Grow then reported that after winning for the 2nd day in a row in St. Louis, Berra said to one of his coaches, *"Let's go have ourselves a nice big plate of ribs."*

Grow then commented that Berra, *"left the locker room smiling and very much alive."*

The loss for the Cardinals knocked them percentage points out of 1st place. They had been the division leaders since July 22. They had reached 1st place after suffering the worst start in the history of the franchise at 5 - 20 to begin the season.

SPECIAL NOTE From The Sports Time Traveler™

The Cardinals 5 - 20 start to the 1973 season remains the worst start in the 143 season franchise history of the Cardinals going back to 1882.

The Cardinals then went on a 55 - 30 tear to vault from last to first and take a 5 game lead in the NL East. The drive to first landed them a feature story in Sports Illustrated's August 6th issue.

Now they are on an 8 - 17 stretch, nearly as bad as their season opening 25 game flop.

The new division leaders are the Pirates, the team that has owned the NL East here in the early 1970s, winning all 3 division titles so far in this decade and capturing the 1971 World Series. The Pirates have won 9 of their last 13 to take over the division lead. And according to Bob Smizik of the Pittsburgh Press, *"The Pirates are talking championship again."*

The Cubs and Expos, both still ahead of the Mets, can't be dismissed either. The Cubs once held an 8.5 game lead on the division with a 47 - 31 record. At that time, they were saying that their veteran club was ready to hold on and avoid the mistakes of their 1969 collapse. But they went through a calamitous stretch in which they went 9 - 33 with all their regular players healthy. Recently they won 8 of 10, before losing their last 4. And they are now sitting just 3.5 games out.

The Expos, an expansion team in 1969, that has never been this close in their 5 season existence, had the best record in the division in the 5 weeks following the all-star break. They've cooled off a touch, but are also just 3.5 games out.

And even the worst team in baseball last year, the Philadelphia Phillies, were just 4.5 games out of 1st place less than two weeks ago and are still lurking just 6 games back.

It's shaping up to be a mad scramble in September as all the National League teams only play their division rivals the rest of the way.

Here's the NL East Standings as of this morning, September 2, 1973:

66 – 65   PIRATES

68 – 67   CARDINALS

64 – 70   CUBS   3.5 games back

64 – 70   EXPOS   3.5 games back

63 – 71   METS   4.5 games back

62 – 73   PHILLIES   6 games back

CHAPTER SIXTY-EIGHT

Placing Their Bets

THE 1973 NEW YORK METS AND THE OTHER NL EAST TEAMS ARE JOCKEYING TO CAPTURE THE DIVISION TITLE

MONTREAL, CANADA - September 7, 1973

The Sports Time Traveler™ is in Montreal, precisely 50 years ago (virtually, of course), where the Mets play a twilight doubleheader against the hottest team in the NL East, the Expos.

That's right, the Expos, a 1969 expansion team, that have never finished better than 5th place or less than 16 games under .500, have reeled off 6 straight wins and 8 of 10. That's enough to nearly crown them division winners right now in this topsy turvy race where no team seems to have a handle on how to win it.

The Expos surge has put them percentage points ahead of the Pirates for 2nd place in the division.

The Expos are led by 26-year-old Ken Singleton, who they picked up from the Mets in the deal for Rusty Staub prior to the 1972 season. Singleton has been sensational this year. He's the only player in the NL who is in the top 10 in batting and the top 5 in RBIs.

And now the Expos are acting like they're contenders. Yesterday they picked up veteran player Felipe Alou from the fading New York Yankees. Alou is one of just 31 players in history to have amassed 200 home runs and 2,000 hits. The Expos are hoping his leadership may be even more valuable than his bat down the stretch.

The Expos last 3 wins were against the Cubs, which pushed Chicago down into 5th place, crushing the spirit of their fans. The Cubs are now 8 games under .500, the worst they've been this year, after they had been flying high, 8.5 games clear of everyone in the division near mid-season at 47 - 31. The Cubs have now lost 42 of their last 60 games. Desperate Cubs fans, who haven't seen their team play in the post season since the end of the 2nd World War, are ready to give up, even though the team is still just 6 games out.

A fan named Paul DeFrees wrote into the Chicago Tribune this morning, *"It's about that time of the year when old Cubs fans will start saying wait til next year. What for?"*

The newly 4th place Mets, who are 5.5 games back, and have won 8 of 11 in their recent climb after spending over 2 months in last place, are also making bold moves. Yogi Berra announced yesterday that as part of his all-out effort to contend for the division he is moving to a 4 man pitching rotation, a radical departure from the plan that prior manager Gil Hodges had put in place to keep his starters arms fresh in 1969. It's a gamble that Berra feels he has to take.

Jack Lang, in the Jersey Journal, indicated the four Mets starters the rest of the way will be Seaver, Matlack, Koosman and George Stone, which Lang called, *"the four best starters of any club in the East."*

Lang also curiously noted that just one day earlier Berra had told reporters he had no plans of working his pitchers with 3 days rest.

The Mets seem to look like contenders with their 8 - 3 surge. But it could just be more of a mirage than a miracle that is forming. 6 of the 8 wins have come against the NL West last place Padres and the NL East last place Phillies.

The Phillies themselves were right in the thick of the race at 4.5 games back just over 2 weeks ago. But then the Phillies fell flat, losing 11 of their next 16 including

6 of their last 7. It's unofficially over for the Phillies. The last place team from last year isn't going to carry off the division.

But another team is pulling out all the stops to steal the division. The Pirates, the team that has owned this division since 1970, reached 1st place for a day last week, capping off a stretch in which they won 29 out of 50 games. The Pirates looked like they were taking command led by the powerful Willie Stargell, who is having an MVP caliber year, as he leads the NL in home runs (38) and RBIs (98).

And then they came crashing back, losing 4 out of 5 including their last 3 in a row. The Pirates are now in 3rd place, 3 games back.

That little slip was enough to fire their manager, a rare move for a team that is very much in contention in September. In the surprise move they dumped manager Bill Virdon to bring back Danny Murtaugh, the man who previously led them to their only 2 World Series titles in the past 48 years. Murtaugh had stepped down after the 1971 World Series victory due to health concerns, but he's agreed to come back for a drive to the pennant.

All the teams are chasing the St. Louis Cardinals, a team that has had one of the oddest seasons in their storied franchise history. They began with their worst start ever winning just 5 of their first 25 games. Then they went on a tear, that vaulted them from last to 1st, and they took a 5 game lead on the division at 61 - 50. Next, they reverted back to their early season form winning just 7 of 24 to lose their lead temporarily. And now they have gained it back with 3 straight wins over the Pirates.

The Cards have also purchased some expensive insurance on their slim division lead. The Yankees put a sale on Alou brothers this week, and the Cards brought Matty to St. Louis. He didn't come cheap. The Cards will now be responsible for his whopping $80,000 salary.

It's the wild East this year in baseball. And The Sports Time Traveler™ will be following it each day.

CHAPTER SIXTY-NINE

Yogi's Dream

BERRA DREAMS THE METS WILL SWEEP THE MONTREAL EXPOS

MONTREAL, CANADA - September 8, 1973

I'm here in Montreal, virtually, covering the Mets 4 games series against the Expos, exactly 50 years ago. The Mets came here in 4th place, 5.5 games behind the division leading Cardinals and 2.5 games back of the surprising 2nd place Expos.

If the Mets dream of winning the division, the Expos might just be the team to beat. They're the hottest team in the East, having won 6 straight and 8 of 10 to move into 2nd place.

In his article in this morning's New York Times, Michael Strauss, quoted Yogi Berra before the start of last night's twilight doubleheader at Jarry Park, *"I can dream it, can't I? A double win over Montreal and we'll be knocking on 2nd place's door."*

Yogi then loaded his lineup with lefties to face the Expos Steve Renko in the opening game. Renko came into the contest with a 12 - 9 record and a 2.88 ERA.

Berra's dream was palpable when on the first pitch of the opening game from Renko, Mets 3B Wayne Garrett, a lefty, socked it for a home run.

Jon Matlack started for the Mets. Matlack has been a little shaky in his last 3 outings, giving up 4 runs and at least 11 baserunners in each game and only going more than 5 innings in 1 of the 3 starts.

But last night Matlack looked strong. Although he allowed a runner to reach base in every inning. Through 8 innings he had only allowed one runner in the entire game to reach third.

The Mets however could only get 2 runners to third base on Renko in the 2nd through 6th innings. And they struggled against Mike Marshall, who replaced Renko in the 7th. After 8 innings the game remained 1 - 0.

METS 1 EXPOS 0 - end of 8 innings in game 1

In the top of the 9th, Marshall faced the Mets power hitters. First, Rusty Staub grounded out. Second, John Milner struck out looking. And then Ed Kranepool popped to short.

Now the Expos faced Matlack in the bottom of the 9th with their winning streak on the line. Matlack got Ron Woods to strike out looking. Then he got former Met, Tim Foli to fly out to center. One out away from a shutout, Matlack gave up a walk to Pepe Mangual. Next up was another former Met, Mike Jorgensen. He also walked.

Matlack had thrown 147 pitches. He still needed at least one more to get the shutout. But Yogi Berra decided it was time to give the ball to Tug McGraw.

McGraw was struggling most of the year, but in his last half dozen outings he's looked like the old Tug, who was the best reliever in the National League.

On McGraw's first pitch to Ron Hunt, he got him to hit a grounder right back to him. He tossed to Milner at first base and the game was over.

METS 1 EXPOS 0 - FINAL SCORE game 1

The 2nd game started out as another pitcher's duel between the Mets Jerry Koosman and the Expos Mike Torrez.

Each pitcher got through the first 2 innings unscathed.

Then in the top of the 3rd, the leadoff batter was Felipe Alou, who was spending his first night as a member of the Expos, having just been acquired from the Yankees (note that the New York Times incorrectly referred to him by his brother's name, Matty Alou, who had been acquired by the Cardinals from the Yankees on the same day). The 38-year-old Alou had been brought in as much for his clubhouse leadership as his aging bat now that the team is a legitimate contender for the first time.

Alou doubled. He then went to third on Ron Wood's fly out. And he scored when Bob Bailey drilled a shot to shortstop Bud Harrelson and the ball careened off his glove into left field for a single.

The Expos had taken a 1 - 0 lead.

The run ended Jerry Koosman's new club record of 31 and 2/3 scoreless innings.

SPECIAL NOTE From The Sports Time Traveler™

I've come back to the present time momentarily to inform you that Koosman's club record 31 and 2/3 scoreless inning streak stood for the next 39 years, until R.A. Dickey extended the record to 32 and 2/3 scoreless innings on the night of June 12, 2012.

Now back to 1973.

Koosman didn't allow another run and the game was still 1 - 0 Expos when Koosman was taken out for a pinch hitter in the top of the 7th when his place in the order was due up with the bases loaded and 2 outs.

Yogi Berra sent Ken Boswell to face Torrez. Boswell drew a walk, and the Mets tied the game at 1.

And the score remained that way through nine innings.

EXPOS 1 METS 1 - end of 9 innings in game 2

Expos relief pitcher Mike Marshall who had come in for Torrez after he had walked home the tying run in the 7th, stayed in to pitch the 10th. Cleon Jones led off with a single and moved to second on Wayne Garrett's bunt. But Marshall got Felix Millan to hit a grounder back to him.

What ensued is one of the weirdest bits of baserunning in Mets history.

The Expos had Cleon Jones caught in a run down between second and third. While this was taking place, the speedy Millan was dashing around first towards second. Jones, trying to evade being tagged out, ran back towards second only to find Millan was there too. Millan was tagged out. Jones apparently thought that he was also out and started to walk to the dugout. When he walked off the base he was tagged by an Expos infielder.

The umpires were initially confused. But soon ruled it was in fact a double play. The side was retired.

"Berra was enraged," by the call according to Red Foley in the New York Daily News. And he indicated he was playing the rest of the game under protest.

In the bottom of the 10th, Berra sent Tug McGraw to the mound again. He loaded the bases but didn't allow a run.

Neither team was able to score in the next 4 innings as the 2 relief aces were pitching extended innings.

By the top of the 15th, Marshall was entering his 9th inning of relief work. Perhaps he finally was tiring as he gave up a leadoff single to Milner and Ed Kranepool followed up immediately with a double. Two batters later, Don Hahn's sacrifice fly sent Milner home with the go ahead run.

Expos manager Gene Mauch then decided to issue Bud Harrelson an intentional walk so he could get to the pitcher, Tug McGraw. Berra let McGraw bat now that he had a 2 - 1 lead. Besides, McGraw had already singled off Marshall in the top of the 12th.

Passing up Harrelson to pitch to McGraw turned out to be a monumental mistake by Mauch. Tug hit a bloop single to right field and 2 runs scored to put the Mets up 4 - 1.

Tug now came to the mound for the bottom of the 15th to close out the game. But not so quick, McGraw, pitching in his 6th inning, gave up a single, a walk and a double and now the score was 4 - 2 with just 1 out and the winning run at bat.

Berra came out to the mound and catcher Duffy Dyer told him that Tug's stuff was gone.

Berra decided it was time to go to his veteran pitcher Ray Sadecki.

Sadecki walked Bernie Allen to load the bases. The winning run was now on first base with just 1 out. Sadecki next faced Pepe Mangual and struck him out.

Now the old man, and the newest Expo, Felipe Alou, came to the plate. He had been in many pressure situations before having played in over 2,000 major league games. Alou got good wood on a Sadecki pitch and drilled it into centerfield. Don Hahn, an excellent fielder, was there and caught the ball. The game was over.

Yogi's dream had come true. The Mets had swept the doubleheader. And in a strange dream like fashion it took 24 innings to do it.

Mike Marshall, who finished the game as the Expos pitcher, took the loss. But in doing so he set a major league record by finishing his 63rd game of the season.

In other games in the NL East, the Cubs beat the 1st place Cards and the Pirates beat the last place Phillies.

Here's the standings as of this morning, September 8, 1973:

72 – 69 CARDINALS

68 – 69 PIRATES   2 games back

68 – 72 EXPOS   3.5 games back

68 – 73 METS   4 games back

66 – 73 CUBS   5 games back

63 – 78 PHILLIES   9 games back

The Mets have now won 10 of their last 13. But is this surge for real? Six of the wins came against last place teams (the Padres and the Phillies). Two were against the sagging Cardinals who have lost 19 of their last 30 games. And the 2 wins tonight were against the hot, but perhaps starry eyed Expos who suddenly find themselves in the thick of a pennant race and have never been in one before.

One thing is for sure. The Mets need Yogi to keep dreaming.

Tonight Tom Seaver (16 - 8, 1.69 ERA) is back on the mound facing the Expos amazing rookie hurler Steve Rogers (7 - 3, 1.28 ERA).

The 23-year-old Rogers is a major reason for the Expos surge since the all-star break. He came up to the big leagues on July 18th. And in 11 starts he has not allowed more than 3 earned runs in a single outing, and that was just once. He has pitched 3 shutouts including a 1-hitter. And he has pitched into the 8th inning in all but 1 of his starts. He is arguably the hottest starting pitcher in baseball right now.

But he's facing Tom Terrific, and this will be the biggest game of the year for both pitchers.

I can't wait!

CHAPTER SEVENTY

The Franchise vs. The Kid

IT'S A 5 TEAM FRENZY IN THE NL EAST AND THE METS AND EXPOS HAD A CLASSIC DUEL

MONTREAL, CANADA - September 9, 1973

I've been camping out here at Jarry Park in Montreal, 50 years ago, on a virtual time travel trip, because the excitement is building in this incredible pennant race. 5 teams in the NL East entered yesterday's games within 5 games of each other.

Last night, 2 of those teams, the Mets and Expos faced off in a duel for the ages.

Pitching for the Mets was the man whose nickname is "The Franchise" - Tom Seaver. Seaver, at 28, is having perhaps the finest season in his stellar career. He has a 16 - 8 record and leads all major league starters with a 1.69 ERA.

How good is Seaver right now? Rookie third baseman of the Phillies, Mike Schmidt, said this in an AP article that appeared nationally in newspapers this morning, *"He's fantastic. What more can I say? He's the best. He mixes his pitches up and he has good control. His ball just explodes all over the place."*

If the Mets bats supported Seaver better, he would have well over 20 wins. In Seaver's 8 losses, 3 have been 1 - 0, one was 2 - 1, one was 3 - 2 and another was 2 - 0.

And recently, Seaver suffered through a scoreless streak of 24 innings. It was a scoreless streak of the wrong kind in which the Mets didn't score a run for him in 24 innings.

Pitching for the Expos was a rookie phenom, Steve Rogers, who came up from AAA in mid-July and has posted a 7 - 3 record with a stunning 1.28 ERA. In 11 starts he has not allowed more than 3 earned runs in a single outing, and that was just once. He has pitched 3 shutouts including a 1-hitter.

Rogers just might be the toughest starting pitcher in baseball at this moment.

The expected pitchers' duel started to play out as both men breezed through the opening 2 innings.

In the bottom of the 3rd, Seaver struck out Expos second baseman Larry Lintz to open the inning. Then he gave up a single to the veteran left fielder Ron Fairly, who played in 4 World Series with the Dodgers going back to 1959.

This brought up former New York Mets player Ken Singleton. Singleton is one of the reasons Montreal is a title contender this year. Since the Mets traded him in the Rusty Staub deal, the 26-year-old has blossomed into one of the NL's most feared hitters. He comes into this game with a line of 21 HRs / 92 RBIs / .306 average. He is the only NL batter in the top 10 in average and top 5 in RBIs. No one on the Mets comes close to those numbers.

Seaver threw to Singleton with one out and one on and Ken blasted the pitch far over the right field fence. The Expos had an early 2 - 0 lead. Singleton is making the case to be the MVP.

Seaver went right back to business and got the next 2 batters on routine flies.

In the top of the 4th, Rogers walked the Mets first batter Rusty Staub. Then John Milner, the Mets leading home run hitter with 21, hit what New York Times writer Michael Strauss described as an easy grounder to second base. It was a perfect double play ball. But the Expos Larry Lintz muffed it. And now Rogers faced his first trouble with Mets on first and second and no outs.

He got Ed Kranepool to ground out, but that moved the Mets runners to second and third with just 1 out. Next up was catcher Jerry Grote. He singled to score Staub for an unearned run.

Rogers got out of the inning after that with 2 more ground outs and in the middle of the 4th it was Expos 2, Mets 1.

The score stayed that way through 7 innings.

EXPOS 2 METS 1 - end of 7 innings

In the top of the 8th, Felix Millan was hit by Rogers leading off. He then went to second and third on groundouts. With 2 outs, up came Ed Kranepool. At this point it is unclear what happened. But as best as I can tell, it seems that Millan tried to steal home and was out at the plate.

Meanwhile when Tom Seaver came out to pitch the bottom of the 8th, he was working on one of the great streaks of his career. Starting with the 2 outs after Singleton's home run in the 3rd, Seaver had retired every Expos batter. His streak was now at 14. Michael Strauss wrote this morning, *"Seaver, once he had gained his momentum, was particularly outstanding."*

The first batter Seaver faced in the 8th was the pitcher, Rogers, and Seaver got him on a grounder to Bud Harrelson at short. Next was Larry Lintz who hit a grounder right back to Seaver.

Tom Terrific had now put down 16 consecutive Expos batters.

Up came Ron Fairly. Fairly had singled in the 1st and singled and scored in the 3rd. He had 2 of the 3 hits Seaver had allowed in the game. Strauss described the action at this point, *"Fairly, who already had two one-base hits, both of which skimmed through right field, produced his long shot. This long drive came at a time when Seaver seemed to be at his best."*

The drive cleared the fence for Fairly's 16th home run of the year to extend the Expos lead to 3 - 1.

The Mets batters, who had hit feebly against the rookie Rogers all night, now came up for their final chance to support Tom Terrific. Ed Kranepool was up first, and he lined out to the shortstop. Jerry Grote hit a grounder to short. That brought up Ken Boswell, who came in to pinch hit for Mets center fielder Don Hahn. Boswell hit a grounder to Lintz. Lintz made the play cleanly this time. And the game was in the books.

Rogers defeated Seaver 3 - 1.

It was a great duel. Both pitchers had given up just 4 hits. That led to the game being played in just 1 hour and 59 minutes.

It was also the 8th time this season the Mets had scored one run or less when Seaver started a game.

The Mets batters didn't score a single earned run.

Pitching Like It's 1968

Steve Rogers, who pitched 9 innings without an earned run, lowered his ERA to an unbelievable 1.16 in the first 12 starts of his major league career. He's pitching like Bob Gibson in 1968.

Rogers was so spectacular that not one ball all night was hit out of the infield by a Mets batter.

Think about that for a moment.

The loss was particularly damaging for the Mets, since Seaver's starts are always their surest bet to win a game. Since May 7, the Mets are 16 - 8 when Seaver has started and 52 - 66 when someone else has started.

Think about that for another moment.

With the loss the Mets remain in 4th place at 68 - 74, and 4 games back as the Cardinals continued their losing ways, dropping a game to the Cubs.

The Cards have won just 11 of their last 31 games, yet still lead the division by a game over the Pirates.

The Cubs, whose fans seemed to give up on them a couple of days ago, find themselves very much back in the race. They're just four games back in a 4th place tie with the Mets.

The Cubs may be the team to watch out for. They had started the year 47 - 31. They have a veteran team of players, the core of which have been together since 1966 including Billy Williams, Ron Santo, Ferguson Jenkins, Glenn Beckert and Don Kessinger. And then there is Ernie Banks, who is now retired but is still on the field as a coach. Unlike the Cards (1968 World Series champions), Mets (1969 World Series champions), and Pirates (1971 World Series champions), this Cubs team has never won anything. Nor has any Cubs team won anything since 1945. This could be their year if they can regain their early season form.

NL West Update

In the NL West last night, the 5th place Atlanta Braves hosted the division leading Cincinnati Reds. The game was 0 - 0 in the bottom of the 7th when Hank Aaron hit a line drive over the left field fence to put the Braves in front. This was home run number 36 on the year and number 709 in his career for Hank, putting him just 5 behind Babe Ruth's all-time mark of 714.

In the bottom of the 9th, the game was tied at 2, when second baseman Davey Johnson of the Braves hit a leadoff home run to win it 3 - 2. For Johnson it was his National League leading 39th home run of the season. Johnson is just as surprised as everyone else that he leads sluggers like Willie Stargell, Johnny Bench and Bobby Bonds. Davey is now just 3 home runs shy of the all-time single season record for second basemen that has been held by Rogers Hornsby since 1922.

In losing the game, the Reds kept their 2.5 game lead over the Dodgers. The Dodgers, who had command of the NL West nearly the entire season, lost their 9th straight game last night. And the Giants, in 3rd place, are just 4 games back. Those 3 teams have the best 3 records in the NL by a wide margin.

CHAPTER SEVENTY-ONE

This Race Can't Get Much Closer

IT'S SHAPING UP TO BE A WILD FINISH TO THE 1973 BASEBALL SEASON

NEW YORK - September 10, 1973

There's so much excitement going on in baseball here in 1973. I had just turned 10 years old the first time I experienced this in real life in 1973, and it's just as thrilling as I re-live it virtually now. The Sports Time Traveler™ might just have to stay here for the next 3 weeks to take it all in.

Here's a quick run-down of what's happening:

NEW YORK METS

The Mets gave up 13 hits to the Expos yesterday. The Expos had runners on base in every inning, but with clutch pitching from starter George Stone and reliever Tug McGraw, they didn't allow a single runner to cross home plate.

Mets hitters were stymied however and could only manage 5 base hits off Expos starter Balor Moore who came into the game with just a 7 - 14 record.

The Mets are getting no hitting from their power hitters. In yesterday's game the number 3, 4 and 5 hitters, Willie Mays, Cleon Jones and Rusty Staub, went 0 for 10, although Mays did get on base twice, drawing 2 walks.

But the Mets received a gift from a former teammate, infielder Tim Foli. Moments after Foli had made a sensational play throwing out Jerry Grote at home, he had a ground ball hit to him that had the makings of an easy double play. That is until he threw the ball into right field allowing the Mets to score 2 runs.

The Mets went on to win the game 3 - 0.

The win pulls the Mets to within just 3 games of 1st place.

The Mets, winners of 11 of their last 15 were jubilant in the locker room. Manager Yogi Berra told Jack Lang of the Jersey Journal, *"We're still in it, ain't we? If our pitching holds out we still got a chance. The last three weeks we've been playing the best baseball in the league because of our pitching."*

Then Lang heard relief pitcher Tug McGraw, who had two saves and a win this weekend, shout to Ed Kranepool, *"Hey, let's go out and get drunk tonight."* Berra heard that and snapped, *"Not tonight. Wait til we win it. Then we'll all go out and get drunk."*

While Yogi has to temper the enthusiasm of his outstanding pitchers, he needs to find a way to jump start his faltering hitters. Yogi told Lang, *"Do you realize we lost three 1- 0 games? John Milner isn't hitting, and Rusty Staub still has the bad hands. If those 2 come around maybe we can do it."*

The Say Hey Kid Crashes

By the way, no one can say that 42-year-old Willie Mays, who is set to bid his farewell to baseball in 2 weeks at Shea, is just mailing it in. Mays is giving it all he's got.

Yesterday, in addition to being one of only 2 Mets to reach base twice, he tried to make a sensational play on a foul ball hit by his former long time teammate on the Giants, Felipe Alou.

Mays playing first base because his shoulder is too sore to play outfield, raced across foul territory to reach the pop up. In doing so he crashed into the metal railing in front of the Mets dugout. Willie needed 2 full minutes to recover and then he returned and played the entire game.

The Cubs Return to the Pack

When the Cubs arrived in St. Louis 3 days ago to play 3 against the division leading Cardinals, they were on the brink of the abyss, 6 games back in 5th place.

Yesterday, when Billy Williams hit a game winning home run, it capped a 3 game sweep and put them right into thick of the division hunt.

Richard Dozer wrote in the Chicago Tribune, *"In the span of only three days, the Cubs had come off the floor by cutting the breach between the divisional leaders from six games to three."*

"The sweep is something we had to have. Suddenly things seem to have fallen into place," Cubs manager Whitey Lockman told an AP reporter.

The sweep was also another devastating blow for the Cardinals, and although they are still in 1st, they are reeling from a stretch in which they've won just 11 times in their last 32 games. Cards manager Red Schoendienst commented in the Flat River, Missouri Daily Journal, *"Nothing went right for us from the very 1st inning Friday through this game. This race can't get much closer."*

The Pirates are Plundered

The Cardinals loss opened the door for the Pittsburgh Pirates to assume their Eastern throne, their natural position, as they've won this division the past 3 consecutive seasons. They appeared headed for 1st place yesterday when they were leading the last place Phillies 7 - 1 in the 6th inning. Willie Stargell had already clouted 2 doubles and his 39th home run of the season. That gave Stargell a string of 8 consecutive hits.

And then the Phillies scored 6 in the bottom of the 6th to tie the game at 7. And the Phils went on to win it in dramatic fashion with a leadoff home run in the 9th by Willie Montanez.

The loss leaves the Pirates 1 game back in 2nd place.

"You win some like that and you lose some like that. It's going down to the last three games of the season," said Pirates manager, Danny Murtaugh in an AP article that ran nationwide today.

Here's the standings as of this morning, September 10, 1973 in the NL East:

72 – 71 CARDINALS

69 – 70 PIRATES 1 game back

69 – 73 EXPOS 2.5 games back

69 – 74 METS 3 games back

68 – 73 CUBS 3 games back

64 – 79 PHILLIES 8 games back

There are several other stories I'm following in the final three weeks of the season.

HANK AARON

Aaron went 3 for 5 with a double yesterday against the Reds. He's playing well and he needs just 5 more home runs, in the last 19 games of the season, to tie Babe Ruth's all-time mark of 714. Everyone is keeping an eye on The Hammer to see when he will catch the Babe.

NOLAN RYAN

There is also an active watch on Nolan Ryan. He now has 326 strikeouts this season. Sandy Koufax' record of 382 is in sight if Ryan can average one strikeout per inning over his last 6 starts.

BOBBY BONDS

Bonds has the potential to set a standard of combined power and speed never reached in the annals of baseball - 40 homers and 40 steals in the same season. He presently has 38 home runs and 39 steals with 21 games left in the season.

The Mets have an off day today. I'll be getting some much needed rest because the Mets next 3 games will feature Koosman, Matlack and Seaver.

I can't wait!

CHAPTER SEVENTY-TWO

Where's Willie – Part 2

THE 1973 METS ORGANIZATION IS IN DISARRAY AS THEY CAN'T FIND WILLIE MAYS AGAIN

PHILADELPHIA - SEPTEMBER 12, 1973

I'm here virtually in 1973 covering the wild NL East division race in which 5 teams entered yesterday's contests within 3.5 games of each other.

The storylines across these 5 teams are getting too far-fetched to believe if they weren't actually happening. And another twist just took place.

The Mets can't find Willie Mays.

6 months ago The Sports Time Traveler™ reported to you about a similar bizarre spring training situation in which the New York Mets could not find Willie Mays for a couple of days.

Now, it's happened again!

SPECIAL NOTE From The Sports Time Traveler™

I interrupt this article briefly for a special note. For all of you living in 2023, especially those of you under 45 years old, you have to understand, that in these ancient times, in 1973, there are no cell phones, no GPS tracking, and no smartphone cameras that can instantly upload videos to the web every time someone spots a celebrity.

The only form of remote communication that is commonly available in 1973 is an old-fashioned telephone that is connected to a wall by a short cord. They don't even have cordless phones yet.

Now back to 1973.

The Mets Arrive in Philadelphia Minus Mays

All of the Mets players, except one, arrived in Philadelphia yesterday for the first of 3 games against the only division team that seems to be out of it. The Phillies started the day 8 games back in 6th place.

The one player who was not on the field in Veterans Stadium at 7pm was Willie Mays. And Mets manager Yogi Berra had no idea where he was.

When the opening pitch of the game was thrown by Jim Lonborg to Mets' third baseman Wayne Garrett, Berra still did not know where Willie was.

Lonborg, a 22 game winner on the 1967 Red Sox team that went to the World Series, is a righty, so Mays would not have started the game anyway, since Berra is currently only starting Willie against lefties in his platooning system.

But it was still very concerning that Mays was missing.

Meanwhile Lonborg got Garrett to pop up. Then he walked Mets second baseman Felix Millan bringing up Rusty Staub.

Staub is having a tough year as his hands have been hurting all season after he missed most of last year with a broken bone in his hand. He came into the game with a line of just 12 HRs / 62 RBIs / .266 average. At 29 years old, and in his prime, these numbers, for the 5-time all-star slugger, are disappointing compared to his 3 seasons prior to joining the Mets in which he was generally good for 25 HRs / 90 RBIs / .300.

Perhaps tonight Staub's hands felt better, because he blasted a Lonborg pitch over the left field wall for a 2-run shot to give the Mets the early lead.

Meanwhile Mets starter, Jerry Koosman, who came into the game allowing just one earned run in his last 40 and 2/3 innings, kept the Phillies scoreless in the first 2 innings.

In the top of the 3rd, Rusty Staub came up again with 2 outs and Garrett on first. Staub slammed a Lonborg pitch over the wall in right for another 2-run clout.

The Mets were ahead 4 - 0 and were looking very good on the field in this critical game.

Off the field the Mets were still in chaos.

It's one thing for Yogi not to know where Willie was. As Murry Chass of the New York Times reported, *"The manager is often the last person in the Met organization to know things because the organization is often the epitome of disorganization."*

However, in this case, no one in the Mets organization knew where Willie was.

No one that is if you don't count the team's physician, Dr. Peter LaMotte, who himself could not be found either (yes, communication in the mid-20th century was often that fraught with difficulty).

Sometime early in the game, Mets traveling secretary, Lou Niss, called Willie Mays' apartment in New York and reached him on the phone.

Mays explained to Niss that since the last game in Montreal, 2 days earlier, he had been suffering from sore ribs sustained during his 1st inning crash into the metal railing in front of the Mets dugout as he valiantly chased a pop foul ball. As I reported in my last article, Mays had taken 2 full minutes on field to recover. He then played the rest of the game and actually reached base twice.

After the Montreal game, Mays was examined by Dr. LaMotte who told him if the ribs continued to hurt, he needed to get in touch with him and be examined.

With the day off between the Montreal and Philadelphia games, Mays went home to New York and had team permission to travel to Philadelphia himself.

During the off-day Mays couldn't reach Dr. LaMotte. Mays left a message and waited for Dr. LaMotte to return his call. But Dr. LaMotte didn't return the call and could not be located. It turns out his wife needed minor surgery. Meanwhile Willie waited for the doctor to call, since there was no way to be seen if he left for Philadelphia.

An hour after Niss spoke to Mays, Dr. LaMotte finally called Willie and told him to go to Roosevelt hospital so he could examine him. Dr. LaMotte then called Mets trainer Tom McKenna in the Mets locker room in Philadelphia to report that Mays' ribs are sore, but he should be able to join the Mets in Philadelphia for the next game.

Mays later said that he tried to call Lou Niss the night before to inform him he would be staying home to wait for the doctor's phone call. But Mays was unable to reach Niss as well.

Communication in the mid-20th century was often like this.

While the bizarre events off the field were resolved, the magic of Kooz unraveled as young Phillies' sluggers suddenly started to tee off. In the bottom of the 3rd, 22-year-old Greg Luzinski hit his 27th home run of the season. And in the last of the 5th, Luzinski singled to drive in another run. The Mets lead had been cut to 4 - 2.

Lonborg then reverted to his all-star form in the 4th through 6th innings, allowing just one baserunner in breezing through the Mets lineup.

In the bottom of the 6th another young and promising Phillies player, 23-year-old Mike Schmidt, hit a 2 run homer, his 16th of the season and the game was tied at 4.

Lonborg registered his third 3 and out inning in the top of the 7th and Kooz was back on the mound quick - too quick. The 1st batter in the bottom of the 7th, Billy Grabarkewitz hit a sky high fly that landed in the foul pole net in fair territory. It was the 3rd homer off Koosman and put the Phillies in front.

It was not the last home run. Luzinski followed 3 batters later with his 2nd homer of the game. The solo shot gave the Phillies a 6 - 4 lead. Kooz, who had gone 42 innings giving up just one earned run, had now given up 6 earned runs in 5 innings to a last place team.

Lonborg got the Mets 1-2-3 again in the 8th. He had now faced one more than the minimum Mets batters over the past 5 innings.

In the top of the 9th, the Mets got a leadoff single from John Milner. And then Lonborg got the next 3 Mets batters to close out a 6 - 4 win.

Against the last place Phillies this a tough loss for the Mets to swallow.

With the Cards losing, the Mets could have moved to within 2 games of 1st with a victory. Now they remain 3 back, and drop to 5th place at 69 - 75.

The Mets lost ground in the standings because knuckleball pitcher Burt Hooten, of the Cubs, baffled the red hot Pirates hitters, holding them to just 4 hits, all singles, and no walks, in a 2 - 0 win. This was a Pirates team that had rapped out 21 hits in their prior game. That moved the Cubs, a team that looked out of it, just a week ago, to within 2.5 games of the division lead.

And in St. Louis, the Expos beat the Cardinals 4 - 1 to move within 1.5 games of the division leaders. The Cardinals loss dropped them back to .500. They have now won just 11 of their last 33 games.

That's right. None of the 6 teams in the NL East have a winning record right now.

The Mets still have 18 games left on the schedule including 2 more in Philadelphia: tonight with Jon Matlack pitching and tomorrow with Tom Seaver.

It's shaping up to be a wild finish in the NL East. And The Sports Time Traveler™ will be staying here in the past to follow it.

NOLAN RYAN / WILBUR WOOD UPDATES

In a match up against two AL West teams that are out of the pennant race, former New York Mets fireballer Nolan Ryan, now of the Angels, beat Wilbur Wood of the White Sox 3 - 1. Both pitchers went the distance, and the game took just 1 hour and 58 minutes. This great duel was unfortunately only seen by a sparse crowd of 6,727.

Ryan allowed just 4 hits and notched 12 strikeouts raising his season total to 338. He is now 44 shy of Sandy Koufax' single season record of 382 with a projected five starts to go in the season.

Wood, a knuckleball pitcher, who often pitches on short rest, allowed only 6 hits in his 45th start of the season. His record fell to 23 - 19. He won't reach 50 wins as some sportswriters were comically suggesting after he had amassed 13 wins in the White Sox opening 40 games, putting him theoretically on track to reach that absurd mark.

Wood slumped after the month of May. He only won 1 game in June, and only 2 in August. His ERA, which had stood at 1.71 at the end of May is now at 3.32.

While Wood won't get 50 wins, he just might get 50 starts.

OAKLAND vs. KC

The upstart Kansas City Royals, a 1969 expansion team, led by former Met Amos Otis, came into Oakland 2 nights ago with division title hopes. They were 4 games behind the A's in the AL West and a sweep of the A's would have them breathing down the necks of last year's World Series champions. But in the first 2 games of the series Oakland has dominated winning 13 - 0 and 3 - 1. The Royals are now 6 games back with 18 to play.

CHAPTER SEVENTY-THREE

Willie Mays Gets a Ribbing While Rusty Runs

IT WAS ANOTHER BIZARRE NIGHT IN PHILADELPHIA FOR THE 1973 METS

NOTE From The Sports Time Traveler™

Today is another fascinating story from precisely 50 years ago. It's one I never knew about the first time I followed the Mets drive to the division title when I was 10 years old in September 1973.

PHILADELPHIA, PA - September 13, 1973

The Sports Time Traveler™ is here, virtually, at Veteran's Stadium in Philly for one more game tonight in 1973. It's the Mets last trip to the city of brotherly love, but many Mets showed no love for their most esteemed brother when he arrived in the clubhouse last night.

Willie Mays made it to Philadelphia shortly before the game, after having been missing for a day (see yesterday's article). He drove himself from New York, leaving his apartment at 4:30pm.

Murray Chass of the New York Times was there when Willie got to the stadium, *"When he arrived in the clubhouse, he was greeted with the following remarks from his teammates, not all of whom appreciated the special status he enjoys despite repeated denials from the Mets hierarchy that there are no special rules for Willie."*

'Hey, the kidnappers let you go? Who paid the ransom?'

'The weather's nice in Tahoe now, isn't it?'

'What did you shoot today?'"

Mets players may not have been advised that Mets team physician, Dr. Peter LaMotte, delivered a diagnosis that Willie Mays has a *"non-displaced fracture of the 8th and 11th ribs on the left side,"* as noted in the Jersey Journal this morning. Mays told the Journal, *"I was hurt. I couldn't get out of bed,"* as he described why he hadn't shown up in Philadelphia the day before.

This was not reported in the New York Times or the New York Daily News.

Clearly the message is not getting to the Mets players, nor the rest of the media as there appears to be dissension among the players, and perhaps manager Yogi Berra, regarding perceived special treatment for the man who was voted the game's greatest living player 4 years ago.

On the field, Mets starter Jon Matlack allowed the Phillies to crack their bats early. He gave up a leadoff single to Billy Grabarkewitz, walked Mike Anderson and allowed a run to score on Bill Robinson's double to put the Phillies up 1 - 0.

There were Phillies runners on second and third and no outs in what had the makings of a mess of a 1st inning for the Mets.

Then Matlack settled in. He struck out the Phillies' promising young sluggers Greg Luzinski and Mike Schmidt, and got Bob Boone on a fielder's choice to get out of the inning.

In the top of the 3rd, Wayne Garrett tied the game with his 13th home run of the year.

And in the of the 6th, John Milner hit his 22nd to put the Mets in front 2 - 1.

Matlack, after his shaky throwing to the first three batters, didn't allow a run in the 2nd thru 7th innings.

METS 2 PHILLIES 1 - end of 7 innings

The top of the 8th saw a strange play in the Mets turn at bat. With one out, Rusty Staub doubled. The next batter was John Milner. Murray Chass described the action, *"Milner rapped a grounder between first and second, Tommy Hutton, the first baseman, made a diving stop, but Mac Scarce, the pitcher was late covering first, and Milner beat the throw. However, Milner and Scarce tumbled to the ground after colliding at first, and Staub alertly raced around third and headed home. Scarce got up and fired the ball to the plate, but Bob Boone the catcher couldn't hold it as he tried to tag the sliding Staub."*

But Staub also missed home plate on his slide. He finally touched the plate and was safe with the run.

Rusty' running, perhaps the least notable part of his game, had put the Mets ahead 3 - 1.

NOTE: Staub has stolen 1 base and been caught stealing twice in the past 2 seasons.

Rusty told Jack Lang of the Jersey Journal, *"Once I looked over there and saw Milner and the pitcher colliding and going down on the play at first, I had to come home."*

METS 3 PHILLIES 1 - middle of the 8th inning

Matlack came to the mound in the bottom of the 8th with a 2 run lead. But when leadoff batter Mike Anderson homered, the lead was cut to one.

This prompted Yogi Berra to go to the bullpen and bring in his trusted reliever, Tug McGraw.

McGraw gave up a couple of singles, but struck out Luzinski, Schmidt and Tommy Hutton to keep the Mets lead at 3 - 2 after 8 innings.

In the bottom of the 9th, McGraw struck out the leadoff batter, Larry Bowa. He then got Terry Harmon to pop up. The next hitter was Billy Grabarkewitz. Grabarkewitz was 2 for 4 in the game and had 7 hits in his last 15 at bats. Since coming over from the Angels to the Phillies in August he's been looking like his former all-star self from 1970. But McGraw struck him out. Game over.

Mets win 3 - 2.

Tug McGraw had recorded his 6th save, to go along with 3 wins in his last 10 appearances. Five of the 6 outs he made were by strikeouts.

McGraw told Jack Lang of the Jersey Journal, *"I can pitch three or four days a week if they need me. Look there's nothing else if we don't win it these last three weeks... I'm not tired. I'll pitch whenever he wants me."*

Matlack got the win, his 13th of the season and the Mets 70th.

The Mets moved to within 2.5 games of the East division lead and moved up to 4th place. However, the 2.5 games seems closer than it really is as the Mets are still 4 games back in the loss column from the division leader.

That division leader is now the Pittsburgh Pirates, who are in sole possession of 1st place for the 1st time since April 24th, after having fallen 10.5 games behind in mid-July. They reached the top by beating the Cubs 4 - 2.

The Pirates also benefited from the Expos 2nd straight defeat of the Cardinals in St. Louis. The surprising Expos were tied with the Cards 1 - 1 in the 9th, when 12-year veteran Bob Bailey, who is enjoying his finest season, whacked his career high 24th home run of the year to put the Expos ahead 2 - 1.

And rookie sensation, Steve Rogers, pitched a complete game 6-hitter to raise his record to 9 - 3 and lower his ERA to an unbelievable 1.15.

This was Rogers' 13th start in the majors after coming up from triple A in mid-July. And his win puts the Expos just 1 game out of 1st.

The Expos, an expansion team from 1969, have never been in a pennant race before, and now they're right in the thick of this one.

Here's the NL East Standings as of this morning:

71 – 71 PIRATES

72 – 73 CARINALS   0.5 games back

71 – 73 EXPOS   1 game back

70 – 75 METS   2.5 games back

69 – 75 CUBS   3 games back

65 – 80 PHILLIES   7.5 games back

CHAPTER SEVENTY-FOUR

Pirates Take Command of the East

IN THE 1973 NL EAST IT'S TIME TO MEET THE NEW BOSS; SAME AS THE OLD BOSS

NEW YORK - September 15, 1973

The Sports Time Traveler™ is back in New York, virtually, here in 1973, where the Mets will take on the Cubs in a doubleheader starting at 2:05pm ET today at Shea Stadium.

The Mets and Cubs were rained out last night. The Cubs will send Ferguson Jenkins and Burt Hooton to the mound to face George Stone and Ray Sadecki of the Mets.

I can't wait!

While the Mets were not playing last night, the Pirates were in St. Louis opening a 3 game series pitting the top 2 teams in the division. The Pirates had edged a half game ahead of the Cards the night before. The winner of last night's game would be the division leader.

The Pirates jumped out quickly in the top of the 1st. Two of the first 3 batters reached base and the clean-up hitter, Willie Stargell, drove in the first run of the game. Stargell, a leading MVP candidate, is the only NL player in the top 10 in all three of the main offensive categories as he is 2nd in HRs, 1st in RBIs and 10th in batting average.

The Pirates went on to score 3 in the 1st inning. They held a 3 - 1 lead going into the bottom of the 4th when the Cardinals Joe Torre came up with 1 out and drilled a ball right back to pitcher Nelson Briles. The ball hit Briles glove and fell to the ground. Briles needed a moment to locate the ball and then hurriedly threw to first. But his throw was way off and sailed into right field, into the territory that had been roamed by Roberto Clemente from 1955 until his untimely death in a plane crash on a relief mission last New Years' eve.

NOTE From The Sports Time Traveler™ - Roberto Clemente still holds the major league record for most games played as a right fielder.

Now back to 1973.

Playing right field last night was a Pirates rookie, Dave Parker, who had come up from triple A for the first time 2 months ago.

Torre knew the book on Parker was that he didn't have a great arm, so he raced past second and sprinted towards third.

But the book on Parker's arm was wrong.

Parker got to the ball in foul territory near the on-field bullpen. Perhaps inspired by the memory of The Great One, Parker planted his back foot on the side of the pitcher's mound, and he threw off balance to Dave Cash covering third base.

"It wasn't even close," Dave Cash told Bob Smizik in the Pittsburgh Press.

Parker had gunned down Torre.

Now instead of a runner on third and 1 out, there were no runners on base and 2 outs.

Pirates manager, Danny Murtaugh, told Smizik, *"It was the key play of the game for us. If you remember the next two batters followed with singles. It had to be the key play. Without it the game is 3 - 2 and they have runners on first and third with 1 out."*

The Pirates went on to win the game 3 - 1.

The Pirates now lead the NL East by 1.5 games. They have won 6 of their last 8. They're hitting well. They have Danny Murtaugh, their 1971 World Series championship manager back at the helm. And they look like they're finally taking command of the division that they won easily by 6 games, 7 games and 11 games in 1970, 1971 and 1972.

And the Pirates have all the pieces of the puzzle. They're one of the top hitting teams, they have the 2nd most HRs of any team in baseball, they have 4 solid starters and one of the top relievers in the game in Dave Giusti.

The Pirates own the NL East.

The Cardinals which had looked like they would run away with the division back on August 5th, when they were in 1st by 5 games and had just played a stretch of two-and-a-half months with a 50 - 26 record, have now lost 6 straight and 24 of their last 35 games. The loss drops them to 3rd as the Expos moved into 2nd place with a win over the Phillies last night.

The Expos beat Steve Carlton 3 - 2 last night in Montreal to move into 2nd and remain 1.5 games behind the Pirates, thus keeping their hopes very much alive as the possible Cinderella team.

And the Mets are in 4th, 3 games back, but 4 off in the loss column.

It's getting more interesting every day and there's still nearly three 3 weeks to go in the season.

Chapter Seventy-Five

Hope and Despair

Each day the 1973 Mets teeter on the brink in their dream to drive from last to first

NEW YORK - SEPTEMBER 19, 1973

I've returned to New York in 1973, on a whirlwind of virtual trips, as we're coming down the stretch in this incredible multi-team drive for the division title in the NL East.

The ups and downs have been so turbulent in the last few days that even as a visitor from the future, who knows the final outcome, I'm feeling the stress of this close 5 team pennant race.

I'm feeling the same pangs of hope and despair that I felt as a child who had just turned 10 and was living for the New York Mets as I started my 3rd week of 5th grade.

Here's a recap of the 4 days running up to last night in 1973.

SATURDAY, SEPTEMBER 15

Four days ago, on Saturday, the Mets lost the nightcap of a doubleheader against the Cubs 7 - 0, leaving the Mets in a dire situation. Not only did their ineptitude at the plate bode badly for any chances to catch fire and win the division, but the loss left them 5 games behind in the loss column with just 14 to go.

SUNDAY, SEPTEMBER 16

The Mets squeezed out a win, quite literally on Sunday in the final game of the Cubs series at Shea.

With the score tied at 3 in the bottom of the 8th, the Mets Jerry Grote executed a perfect squeeze bunt, scoring John Milner for the go ahead run.

Then Tug McGraw shut down the Cubs in the 9th allowing no hits in 1 and 1/3 innings to seal a 4 - 3 squeaker.

McGraw won NL Player of the Week for this and his other great relief performances in the past 7 days.

Then the Mets got the news that the division leading Pirates had lost, due in large part to the beloved former Mets legend, Tommie Agee. His home run for the Cardinals broke a 3 - 3 seventh inning tie in that game on the way to a 7 - 3 Cards victory.

The New York Mets were suddenly right back in the mix, just 2.5 games behind the division leader.

And although the Mets remained 4 behind in the loss column with just 13 games remaining, they were headed to Pittsburgh to play the Pirates for 5 consecutive games.

The first 2 of the 5 games took place on Monday and Tuesday in Three Rivers Stadium.

UPDATE ON TOMMIE AGEE

I'm interrupting this story for an update on Tommie Agee, one of the heroes of the 1969 Miracle Mets, who was shamefully discarded by the Mets brass last December 1972, in a story I reported on previously titled, "They Didn't Want Me Anymore."

Agee was traded to the Houston Astros where he played lackluster ball all summer. But the St. Louis Cardinals, desperate for veteran help in their division title battle, picked up Tommie Agee in mid-August and gave him a chance.

As noted above, on Sunday, Agee socked a home run in the 7th inning that changed the complexion of the game for the Cardinals. A few more moments like that and Tommie Agee might become one of the heroes of 1973 for the Cards. The Cardinals are very much in the thick of the five team battle for the NL East.

By the way, Agee is batting .233 with 9 home runs in 240 at bats this season. That's a whole lot better than the Mets current center fielder, Don Hahn, who has almost an identical batting average, but just 2 home runs in 239 at bats.

UPDATE ON THE MONTREAL EXPOS

Another team that is in the thick of the NL East battle is the Montreal Expos.

Going into their game on Sunday, September 16th they sat at .500 with a 73 - 73 record, good for 2nd place and just 1.5 games behind the division leading Pirates.

On Sunday, they set a franchise record by winning their 74th game. They did it with an 8th inning come from behind rally, scoring 3 runs to turn a 2 - 1 deficit into a 4 - 2 lead and ultimately the victory. The win gave the Expos a tie in the win column with the Pirates.

Never before have the Expos been above .500 after the month of May. And never before have they been even close to being a contender this late in the season, but that's precisely what they are right now with as good a chance as any team to take the title.

MONDAY, SEPTEMBER 17

Tom Seaver took the mound in Pittsburgh on Monday night, knowing that a win would put the Mets just 1.5 games out of 1st place.

Seaver has been a sure thing for the Mets most of the year even through their dreary summer in last place. Now he was pitching on 3 days rest, part of the Yogi Berra plan to go for broke down the stretch in a bid to win the division.

Pirates slugger and MVP candidate, Willie Stargell, had other plans. The hot hitting slugger boomed a run scoring triple off Seaver in the 1st. Then after Seaver gave up another run in the 2nd on 2 doubles, Stargell came up again in the 3rd with a man on and hit a long home run over the centerfield fence. It was Stargell's 40th of the year. The next batter, Richie Hebner, also homered off Seaver, who gave up 5 earned runs in 3 innings and was knocked out of the game.

It was the first game all season that Seaver had gone less than 6 full innings (and even in that game Seaver had pitched well but was taken out for a pinch hitter in the 7th).

The Pirates went on to win it 10 - 3. Stargell had 2 doubles after Seaver was out. That gave Stargell 4 extra base hits. It was the 4th time in his career he had a game with 4 extra base hits.

And that was a new National League record.

Stargell is having a sensational September. And cutting down the best starting pitcher in baseball this season had to give the Pirates a huge boost in their efforts to wrap up their 4th straight NL East title.

For the Mets the loss was a killer. Not only had their best pitcher been soundly beaten, but they fell 3.5 games back, were still in 4th place, and once again were 5 games behind in the loss column, now with just 12 games left on the schedule.

Yogi Berra's go for broke strategy of pitching his starters on 3 days rest had proved a catastrophe as Seaver and Koosman have both faltered in the last several days.

TUESDAY, SEPTEMBER 18

The depths of despair reached their height last night in Pittsburgh.

Jon Matlack took the mound for the Mets. He was pitching fortunately on 5 days rest.

Yet the Pirates still bolted ahead to a 4 - 1 lead in the 3rd inning, knocking Jon Matlack out of the game, in one of his worst starts of the season.

Ray Sadecki came in to pitch the 4th. Berra couldn't have hoped for much from Sadecki who had given up 5 runs to the Cubs in just 3 innings in his last trip to the mound. He was now going up against a Pirates team in full attack mode, having plundered Mets pitching for 14 runs and 19 hits in their last 11 innings of play against the Mets vaunted pitching staff.

But the veteran Sadecki came through. He pitched a 1-2-3 inning in the 4th and another one in the 5th. In the 6th he allowed a walk and a single, but shut down the Pirates after that.

Ray Sadecki had pitched 3 brilliant innings.

But the Mets were still down 4 - 1 as they couldn't touch Pirates starter Bob Moose who had allowed just 4 hits through 6 innings.

Sadecki came out for a pinch hitter in the 7th and the Mets loaded the bases on 3 singles by Wayne Garrett, Felix Millan and Rusty Staub. And there was just 1 out. Pirates manager Danny Murtaugh took Moose out and brought in reliever Ramon Hernandez.

Ramon Hernandez had not allowed a run in his last 6 appearances.

Facing John Milner, Hernandez got the Hammer to hit into an inning ending double play.

That double play was a crusher. The Mets were now down to their last 6 outs, and they had just blown their chances with the top of the order. The bottom 5 batters would be coming up in the 8th and 9th.

A loss would drop them 4.5 games back and 6 back in the loss column with just 11 to play.

It was a near hopeless situation.

To have any chance they had to first continue stopping the Pirates hitters. Berra called for Tug McGraw to go to the mound against the top of the Pirates order. He gave up a leadoff single to Dave Cash. Then he got Al Oliver and Willie Stargell to both pop-up. And he got Richie Zisk on a grounder.

In the top of the 8th, the Mets 5, 6 and 7 batters went down 1-2-3 to Hernandez.

In the bottom of the 8th, McGraw did his job again. A 1-2-3 inning for Tug.

Now it was the top of the 9th. The Mets were down to their final 3 outs. And they had their 8, 9 and leadoff batters coming to the plate.

Bud Harrelson popped up for out number 1.

Two outs left in what effectively might be the end of the season for the Mets.

Jim Beauchamp came in to pinch hit for Ed Kranepool. Beauchamp singled.

Next up was Wayne Garrett. Garrett came through with a double. Now there were men on second and third and 1 out for Felix Millan.

Millan tripled! Beauchamp and Garrett both scored. The Mets had pulled to within 1 run at 4 - 3 with 1 out.

Next up was Rusty Staub. Unsurprisingly he drew a walk.

Now pinch hitter Ron Hodges came up for Tug McGraw. The rookie Hodges singled scoring Millan.

The game was tied at 4!

Next, Cleon Jones was walked, loading the bases.

The light hitting center fielder Don Hahn now came to the plate. Hahn told Jack Lang of the Jersey Journal, *"I was looking for a ball to hit and there it was."*

He singled driving in 2 runs and the Mets had taken a 6 - 4 lead with one of the most unlikely rallies in franchise history.

The Pirates got out of the inning after that, but they were down by 2 going into the bottom of the 9th.

And then the game got even more interesting.

With McGraw and Sadecki both out of the game, and Harry Parker unable to pitch, Yogi Berra was thin on relievers. He had Buzz Capra available, but he decided to bring in rookie Bob Apodaca to pitch in the big leagues for the very first time.

Apodaca walked the first 2 Pirates he faced. The winning run was now at the plate. There were no outs and the Mets had to face the top of the Pirates fearsome lineup.

Berra took out Apodaca and brought in Buzz Capra.

Dave Cash bunted and moved the runners to second and third with 1 out.

Al Oliver hit a grounder and the runner on third scored. The game was 6 - 5 Mets with 2 outs.

Next up was Willie Stargell. Berra wisely elected to give Stargell first base.

There were runners on first and third with 2 outs.

The next batter was Richie Zisk, and he drew a walk.

Bases loaded. 2 outs. Pirates down by 1.

Up came Manny Sanguillen. Sanguillen is one of the best hitting catchers in baseball. He had already driven in 2 runs in the game. The 3-time all-star had once finished 8th in the MVP voting.

The count on Sanguillen reached 3 - 1. A walk would tie the game and leave the bases loaded.

Buzz Capra described the next pitch to Jack Lang in this morning's Jersey Journal, *"It was the biggest pitch of my career."*

Sanguillen hit the pitch, a fly ball to left field. Cleon Jones caught it. And the game was in the books.

The Mets had won the game 6 - 5!

Jack Lang's headline in The Jersey Journal read, **"An In(Capra)ble Met Win!"**

Lang also stated something that had to be on the minds of all Mets fans last night, *"Why Berra brought in a raw rookie like Apodaca is something that stretches the imagination."*

In the Hackensack Record, Ron Drogo got some interesting quotes from Tug McGraw, *"The bottom of the 9th was the most exciting thing I've ever experienced in baseball. I mean that could have been it for us and Buzzie came through."*

Drogo went on to finish his article with this, *"The effect of the victory was quite obvious in the Mets locker room. They knew they had made another miraculous recovery when the situation was critical."*

The win puts the Mets back to 2.5 games behind. They're still 4 games back in the loss column with 11 to play. And they're still in 4th place. But the Mets play the Pirates at Shea the next 3 nights. If they can win 3 straight, they would pass the Pirates in the standings.

There is still hope.

NOTE From The Sports Time Traveler™

In my 5th grade classroom at Warnsdorfer elementary school in central New Jersey, this morning, 50 years ago, someone announced the score of last night's game and all the boys in the class erupted in cheers.

CHAPTER SEVENTY-SIX

You've Got to Believe

TUG MCGRAW IS QUOTED FOR THE FIRST
TIME IN A NEW YORK NEWSPAPER WITH
HIS ICONIC PHRASE

VERY SPECIAL NOTE From The Sports Time Traveler™

I have to share what is a seminal moment in the short history of The Sports Time Traveler™.

I've been waiting patiently, all year, for my eyes to spot the phrase, "Ya Gotta' Believe," in a 1973 newspaper archive.

For non-Mets fans, "Ya Gotta' Believe," is the legendary phrase most associated with this 1973 Mets team.

It's a mantra for the ages.

Each day for the past month I have searched newspaper after newspaper from precisely 50 years ago searching for those three magical words.

I still haven't seen it.

That is, I still haven't seen it spelled out in the colloquial version that is how the phrase was canonized.

However, yesterday, in the September 19, 1973, issue of Newsday, a Long Island newspaper, writer Joe Donnelly wrote something that definitely qualifies as the birth of the phrase.

And it did indeed come from the lips of the man who made it famous.

I can't describe how excited I was to find this.

It was my Mets equivalent of discovering the holy grail.

I found it in Donnelly's piece about the Mets inspirational victory over the Pirates at Three Rivers Stadium the prior evening. In that game, the Mets were on the brink of practical elimination. Down 4 - 1 in the 9th, a loss would have put the Mets 6 back in the loss column with just 11 games left, and 3 teams in front of them.

It would have been a deficit no team could recover from.

And in almost divine fashion, against 2 of the best relievers in baseball, this sparse hitting team scored 5 runs in the top of the 9th to take a 6 - 4 lead.

And then they held on for dear life in the bottom of the 9th as Buzz Capra was pitching to Manny Sanguillen with 2 outs and the bases loaded and the Pirates down by 1.

Tug McGraw was on the bench, having already pitched 2 superb innings before being lifted for a pinch hitter.

Donnelly then wrote these words about McGraw:

"The end came with the bases bulging with Pirates and Manny Sanguillen swinging on Buzz Capra's 3 and 1 pitch and flying softly to left. The end? The Mets viewed it as a beginning."

"Tug McGraw, the sturdiest of all the Mets in this September song nearly flew off the bench to meet Capra, who came off the mound with a leap and a bound."

"McGraw, who had been shouting, 'You've got to believe!' from the bench, grabbed Capra and told him, 'Hey, that jumping around off the mound is reserved for left handers.'"

The victory and the save were the property of these two."

My eyes popped off the page and a shrill went down my spine as I was seeing those words, *"You've got to believe,"* on my screen for the first time in this year long journey, 50 years into the past.

At the close of the article Donnelly wrote this:

"The 1973 Mets have had so many bad innings, it's rather incredible that hope is still alive."

"'You've got to believe,' McGraw said one more time."

"As questionable a team as this is, from manager to benchwarmer, they still own the right to share that belief."

So there it is.

"You've got to believe."

It wasn't in the New York Times.

It wasn't in the Daily News.

It wasn't in the Jersey Journal or the Hackensack Record.

It wasn't in any other newspaper in the country.

It was only in Newsday.

It was only put there in print by Joe Donnelly.

It's the first time Tug McGraw was quoted saying anything that approaches the iconic phrase that is now canonized as,

"Ya Gotta' Believe."

Wow!

And now let's go back in time again 50 years for today's article on last night's game at Shea stadium against the Pirates.

NEW YORK - SEPTEMBER 20, 1973

The Mets were home last night for the first of 3 games against the Pirates at Shea.

They received a shot of adrenaline the night before with their dramatic 5 run 9th inning rally to defeat the Pirates in Pittsburgh and move to within 2.5 games of 1st place.

The Mets quickly came back to Earth when the first batter of the game, Rennie Stennett, smashed a long home run over the centerfield fence off starter George Stone.

Cleon Jones got the run back and put the Mets in the lead when he hit a 2-run homer in the bottom of the 2nd. For Jones, who has suffered through injuries all season and still has inflamed feet, it was his 1st home run at Shea since April.

Meanwhile after giving up the leadoff homer, Stone blew through the Pirates next 8 batters until he faced Stennett again, and the leadoff man tripled and scored on a Dave Cash single. The game was tied at 2.

The Mets got another run in the 3rd and then Stone himself got an RBI on a groundout in the 5th to give himself a 4 - 2 lead.

In the 6th, Stone gave up a home run to Willie Stargell, the big man's 41st of the year. And that tightened the game to 4 - 3 Mets.

It was time for Tug.

Yogi Berra brought in McGraw to pitch in the top of the 7th. He allowed a walk and a single and faced runners on first and third with 1 out, but he got out of the inning.

In the 8th he faced just 3 batters, and got Stargell to ground out.

Then in the bottom of the 8th, Cleon Jones gave McGraw breathing room as he hit a 3-run homer, his 2nd of the game, off Dave Giusti, one of the top relievers in baseball, to put the Mets up 7 - 3.

McGraw then put the Pirates down in order in the 9th for his 22nd save of the season.

Tug McGraw has emerged as the MVP of the team over the past month. And in that time the team has surged. After they reached an August low at 58 - 70, Tug has had 4 wins and 9 saves in his last 13 appearances and the Mets are now in the midst of a 17 - 7 run that has seen them improve from last place to a 3rd place tie. And McGraw has figured in each of the Mets last 10 wins.

Hank Lowenkron of the Herald-News in New Jersey, said that McGraw told him, *"The feelings of fun in 1969 are starting to creep into his thoughts."*

The win puts the Mets just 1.5 games back with 10 games remaining on their schedule. They are right in the thick of this race.

Cleon Jones, the hitting hero of the game, told Jack Lang in the Jersey Journal, *"If we win it this year it would be even better than '69."* When Lang asked him how could anything be better than '69, Jones replied, *"But we were down 12 games at one point this year. It would really be something if we won this one."*

Four teams are now within 1.5 games of the NL East division lead.

It's the closest division race in history.

Here's the standings in the NL East as of this morning, September 20, 1973:

75 – 74 PIRATES

75 – 76 EXPOS   1 game back

75 – 77 METS   1.5 games back

75 – 77 CARDS   1.5 games back

72 – 79 CUBS   4 games back

67 – 85 PHILLIES   9.5 games back

Willie Mays Officially Retires

Yesterday Willie Mays made it official. He is retiring from baseball.

Mays is suffering from 2 swollen knees, an inflamed shoulder and 2 fractured ribs and he hasn't played since September 9th after he broke the ribs chasing a foul ball and running smack into the railing in front of the Mets dugout in Jarry Park in Montreal.

It is unclear if he will play in any of the final 10 games on the Mets schedule.

"I want to play as long as I can help," Mays was quoted in the New York Times recently.

The Times also quoted Mets chairman Donald Grant about the decision, *"The only thing he's known was his life as a ballplayer. And he didn't relish the idea of facing the world otherwise. But Herman Franks and other people have convinced him it's basically time to quit."*

Herman Franks was Mays former manager with the Giants. Franks piloted the Giants during one of Mays best seasons in 1965 when he hit 52 home runs.

CHAPTER SEVENTY-SEVEN

An Off-the-Wall Thriller

THE 1973 METS ARE BATTLING THE PIRATES AND 3 OTHER TEAMS FOR THE NL EAST TITLE

SPECIAL NOTE From The Sports Time Traveler™

My friends who know their Mets history better than me have been urging me for months to make sure I write an article about the game that took place at Shea against the Pirates on September 20, 1973.

One of the rules of Sports Time Travel is that I can never "look ahead." I have to systematically follow the sports day-by-day, exactly 50 years ago, to maintain the illusion that I'm actually back in 1973.

This morning in real life, September 21, 2023, I could finally open the New York Times from September 21, 1973. I could finally have the same experience I would have almost certainly had this morning 50 years ago as I sat down to my routine of a bowl of Life cereal before I walked to Warnsdsorfer elementary school.

And I could finally find out why it is that I inexplicably have no recall of the game from September 20, 1973.

Here's my article about the game from 50 years ago last night.

SHEA STADIUM - SEPTEMBER 21, 1973

The Mets came into last night's game feeling a divine presence in their midst.

They had somewhat miraculously defeated the Pirates in Pittsburgh 3 nights ago, with a 5 run rally in the 9th, and then beat them again 2 nights ago here in New York to pull within 1.5 games of the division leader.

Last night, the Mets sent Jerry Koosman to the mound, working on just 3 days rest. This strategy didn't work the last time Kooz came out on 3 days rest. In that outing on September 11th he gave up 6 runs, 4 by homers, and lost to the Phillies.

Then on 5 days rest, last Sunday, Kooz gave up 3 runs in 5 innings to the Cubs. But Berra decided to go for broke again last night because he needed one of his top pitchers to face the frightening Pirates.

Kooz responded.

He struck out Rennie Stennett to start the game. This was big. Stennett had hit a home run to leadoff the game 2 night ago.

Kooz then gave up a single to Dave Cash, but he got Al Oliver to fly out and Willie Stargell to strike out.

It was a great start.

Kooz continued to throw well. He gave up a couple of walks, but no hits, in the 2nd and 3rd and the score was nothing to nothing after 3 innings.

In the 4th, Kooz walked the dangerous Stargell to open the inning. With 1 out, Manny Sanguillen singled and Stargell made it to third. Kooz got Bob Robertson to strikeout looking. And Kooz looked like he was out of the inning when Dal Maxvill hit a grounder to Bud Harrelson at shortstop, but Harrelson couldn't handle the ball and Stargell scored. It was ruled an error.

PIRATES 1 METS 0 - middle of the 4th inning

Koosman got the Pirates in order in the 5th.

In the 6th Kooz struck out Stargell again and allowed just one base runner on a walk.

Through 6 innings Jerry Koosman had allowed just 2 hits and no earned runs. But he was behind 1 - 0.

Then the Mets finally gave Kooz some support when Cleon Jones, who had homered twice and drove in 5 to secure the Mets win last night, singled home the Mets 1st run of the game.

PIRATES 1 METS 1 - end of 6 innings

In the 7th, Kooz was cruising. He got the first 2 batters out and then a pinch hitter, Richie Hebner came up to replace Stennett who had left the game with a pulled muscle. Hebner homered and the Pirates were back in the lead 2 - 1.

The Mets went down in order in the 7th.

Kooz shrugged off the homer he gave up in the 7th, only his 3rd hit allowed in the game, and mowed down the Pirates 3, 4 and 5 batters in the 8th, getting Stargell on a grounder, striking out Richie Zisk and then getting, Sanguillen, one of the best hitting catchers in baseball history, to pop up.

Koosman had pitched 8 innings allowing just 4 hits and one earned run against the powerful Pirates batters.

PIRATES 2 METS 1 - middle of the 8th inning

Going into the last of the 8th however, things were starting to look dire for the Mets. Down a run, the Mets could not afford a defeat that would push them 3 back in the loss column with only 9 to play.

But Jim Beauchamp, pinch hitting for Kooz, gave the Mets hope with an opening single in the 8th. This was a good sign. It was Beauchamp who had kicked off the Mets 1 out, 5 run rally, 3 nights ago in Pittsburgh.

Teddy Martinez came in to run for Beauchamp and Wayne Garrett bunted him over to 2nd. Then Felix Millan, the steady hitting second baseman, singled Martinez home and the game was tied again.

But the Mets power hitters could do no further damage and the game moved on to the 9th.

Harry Parker came on to pitch the 9th for the Mets, and he gave up a run on a double by Dave Cash and suddenly the Mets were facing the abyss again, down 3 – 2, as the Mets had their last turn at bat and with the bottom of their order.

Leading off for the Mets was Ken Boswell, pinch hitting for catcher Jerry Grote. Boswell came through with a single. Then Don Hahn moved Boswell to second on a bunt. But the Mets next batter, pinch hitter George Theodore struck out.

The Mets were down to their last out. An out that would severely dent their division title hopes.

Up to the plate came yet another pinch hitter, the back-up catcher, Duffy Dyer - a man without a hit in 27 days.

Dyer doubled!

The game was tied again at 3.

And that's where it stayed.

PIRATES 3 METS 3 - end of 9 innings

Ray Sadecki now came in to pitch for the Mets and he was as good as he's ever been.

Sadecki got the Pirates in order in the 10th. Then he struck out the side in the 11th.

In the bottom of the 11th the Mets were able to put a man on third base with 2 outs via a couple of walks and a grounder.

Now Yogi Berra had a big decision to make. Sadecki was due up, but he was pitching brilliantly, and Berra had few pinch hitters left. He decided to let Sadecki hit. And he grounded out.

PIRATES 3 METS 3 - end of 11 innings

Sadecki proved Berra right however as he mowed down the Pirates in order again in the 12th.

He had pitched 3 perfect innings racking up 5 strikeouts.

The Mets stranded Rusty Staub after he singled in the 12th and the game moved on to the 13th.

Sadecki opened the inning with a statement as he struck out Stargell.

But then he gave up a single to Zisk. After he got Sanguillen to fly out to right, up came rookie Dave Augustine to the plate with 2 down.

Augustine was a 23-year-old who had shown some promise as an outfielder in the minors. He had just come up in September, and he was coming to the plate for just the 4th time in the big leagues.

Let's take a look at Augustine's at bat. Bob Murphy the Mets long time broadcaster is on the call for WOR Channel 9 in New York.

This is 19 seconds of must see baseball.

Type this into the YouTube search bar and watch:

Ball On The Wall Play, Pirates @ Mets, Sept. 20th, 1973

It was nothing short of miraculous.

Augustine's long fly to left appeared to be on a trajectory to land in the bullpen.

Cleon Jones, with his badly inflamed feet, stopped running towards the wall and watched.

He later told Ron Drogo of the Hackensack Record, *"I knew it was going to hit the top. But it hit directly on the corner."*

The ball then unbelievably bounced right back to Jones.

Cleon Jones alertly whirled and made a quick throw to a perfectly positioned Wayne Garrett in short left field.

Garrett whirled and threw a one hopper to third string, rookie catcher, Ron Hodges, a man who had gone straight from AA to the majors earlier this summer.

Hodges adeptly applied the tag, like a veteran, to Richie Zisk.

Zisk was out at the plate.

The Mets had survived.

The game continued on into the bottom of the 13th.

It was now midnight.

NOTE From The Sports Time Traveler™

At home in New Jersey, I was long asleep on this school night, and it was too late for the New York Times to have their game write up in time for the paper that would be delivered just 5 hours later on my driveway.

I finally know what I never knew about this game.

Remember this is 1973, and there is no seeing the tape on ESPN or the viral video on social media the next day.

Now back to the game.

Leading off in the bottom half of the 13th was John Milner. The Hammer walked. So did Ken Boswell. The Mets had runners on first and second and no outs.

The Pirates had Dave Guisti on the mound. While Tug McGraw might be the best relief pitcher in baseball at this moment. Giusti has been the best across the entire season. He got Don Hahn to pop up for the 1st out.

Next up was the man who had applied the tag that saved the game in the top of the inning, Ron Hodges. Giusti got ahead on the count 0 and 2.

Hodges described the next pitch to Ron Drogo, *"The first two pitches were really good fastballs. Then I decided to just stick the bat out and I was really lucky to get the hit. It was a high fastball and once I hit it, I started praying that it would just drop in somewhere."*

His prayer was answered.

Hodges line drive fell into left field and Milner scored.

The Mets had done it!

Final score: Mets 4 Pirates 3.

In a late edition of the Hackensack Record the headline of the sports section read, *"Somebody up there must like the Mets."*

Three times the Mets had come from behind against the division leader on the same night.

Twice in the last 3 days they'd been behind in the 9th inning to the Pirates and pulled it out.

And now they've taken 3 straight from Pittsburgh - the best team in the NL East for the past 3 years.

The New York Mets, in last place just 3 weeks ago, are now in 2nd. And they're just 1/2 game behind with 9 games on the schedule to play.

Four teams remain within just 1.5 games of the lead, including the Expos and the Cardinals, and a 5th team, the Cubs are just 3 back.

It's been a crazy and wonderful experience and there's still plenty left to go.

The Mets are right in there now. And they have momentum.

Ray Sadecki told Ron Drogo, *"You look back two games to that 9th inning rally and that's where momentum comes in. It really exists. You can't define it. But you're damn aware that it's all happening for you."*

In an AP article, Mets 3rd baseman Wayne Garrett was quoted saying, *"You've got to believe that somebody is watching over us. And I hope he stays there."*

That quote appeared in hundreds of newspapers around the country. It was the first time the phrase *"You've got to believe,"* was seen in print outside of Long Island.

But the first time that phrase made it in print with regard to the Mets was in Newsday, two days earlier, which had quoted Tug McGraw, when he was shouting it maniacally, at the top of his lungs, from the dugout to his teammates in the last game in Pittsburgh.

CHAPTER SEVENTY-EIGHT

The Frenzy in Flushing

THE LARGEST CROWD OF THE 1973 SEASON AT SHEA WATCHED THE FINAL BATTLE AGAINST THE PIRATES

SHEA STADIUM - September 22, 1973

I'm back here in 1973 virtually to see the Mets play the Pirates for the final time this season in a battle for 1st place in the NL East.

The Mets dramatic 13th inning **"ball off the top of the wall"** victory 2 nights ago has energized the Mets fan base to a level not seen since their miracle season 4 years ago.

The New York Daily News proclaimed, *"It's like 1969 all over again. It's like watching a television re-run."*

As a result, a crowd of 51,381 came to Shea last night, the largest of the season, to watch Tom Seaver pitch against Pittsburgh. The Mets, winners of 3 straight against the Pirates coming into last night, started the game just a half game back with 9 games left on the schedule.

A win would put the Mets on top of the division.

This was a startling turn of events.

Four nights ago in Pittsburgh the Mets were facing practical elimination, trailing 4 - 1 in the 9th, a loss would have left them for dead, in 4th place, 4.5 games back and 6 games behind in the loss column with 11 games to go.

But a miraculous 5 run rally, fueled by Tug McGraw screaming, *"You've got to believe,"* from the dugout triggered the 3 straight wins that have sent Mets fans into a full frenzy last night.

Steve Jacobson of Newsday wrote, *"the electricity from the largest crowd of the season (was) crackling from Seaver's first pitch."*

Tom Seaver responded by retiring the Pirates in order in the top of the 1st including strike outs against Dave Parker and Al Oliver.

Then the Mets batters, who seldom support Seaver at the plate, blasted Pirates pitcher Steve Blass right out of the game, nailing him for 4 runs in the bottom of the inning on a pair of 2-run doubles by Cleon Jones and Jerry Grote. Jones now has 8 RBIs in his last 3 games.

With a 4 - 0 lead, New York Daily News writer Phil Pepe wrote, *"Tom Seaver and a four run lead may be the safest bet in baseball."*

But these are the Pirates, a great hitting ball club, and they came right back at Seaver for 2 runs in the top of the 2nd.

Pepe was proven right though as Seaver settled in and allowed just 4 singles and no runs the rest of the way.

The Mets meanwhile continued pounding Pirates pitching. They scored 2 more in the 3rd and 1 in the 6th to take a 7 - 2 lead.

By the 7th inning, the fans around the stadium were all celebrating.

Joseph Durso wrote in the New York Times, *"Fans were jamming the aisles and even dancing on the dugout roof."*

Jack Lang of the Jersey Journal wrote, *"the fans began the rhythmic championship chant - "We're no. 1!, We're no. 1!... the Mets still needed six outs to make it the top, but that never bothered the season's largest crowd."*

The Mets not only got those last 6 outs, they also put up 3 more runs to make it a 10 - 2 rout.

When the game was officially over, Lang wrote, *"The wildly ecstatic fans let out a tremendous roar, 'We're no. 1! We're no. 1!' The chant continued for several minutes."*

"The ballpark was a madhouse. The Mets. The Miracle Mets... Yogi's little bears were back on top."

The win raised the Mets record to an even .500 at 77 - 77. They were now 19 - 7 over the past 26 games. They had risen from last to first in just over 3 weeks.

While the fans were in a state of delirium, the Mets players, coaches and especially manager Yogi Berra were not doing any celebrating. Berra told Lang, *"It's been a long time coming. Now we got to worry about staying there."* And he told Durso, *"Even Chicago is only 2 and a 1/2 games out and they're 5th."*

But it is still a pennant race - a crazy pennant race with 4 teams now breathing down the backs of the new division leading Mets.

Phil Pepe of the Daily News echoed the feeling of the fans when he wrote, *"With only eight games to play, you have to believe in the Mets. You have to believe they have enough to carry on. You have to believe because they have made you believe."*

Here's the standings in the NL East as of this morning, September 22, 1973:

1. 77 – 77 NEW YORK METS

2. 75 – 76 PITTSBURGH PIRATES   0.5 games back

3. 76 – 78 ST. LOUIS CARDINALS   1 game back

4. 75 – 78 MONTREAL EXPOS   1.5 games back

5. 74 – 79 CHICAGO CUBS   2.5 games back

6. 68 – 86 PHILADELPHIA PHILLIES   9 games back

The Mets now play 2 games against the Cardinals this weekend at Shea. They will have Monday off and then 2 more home games against the Expos. And they finish the season at Wrigley Field with 4 games against the Cubs. I can't wait!

Chapter Seventy-Nine

Mets Pennant Fever

The front page of the September 24, 1973, NY Times declared, "Pennant Fever Rises."

INTRODUCTION From The Sports Time Traveler™

50 years ago this morning, on Monday September 24, 1973, I started my walk to Warnsdorfer elementary school, and I didn't feel my usual self. I was slightly lightheaded.

My energy level was not the same - it was elevated.

I was a little giddy, almost excited.

This was quite odd for a Monday morning, since I was facing 5 straight days of school, an unbearably long time when you're 10.

I knew what was wrong with me.

I had caught the disease.

It had started infecting people around Shea Stadium a couple of weeks ago. And it had reached an epidemic level in the metropolitan New York area in the last 72 hours.

I had acquired a case of full blown pennant fever.

My New York Mets were in 1st place. The team that had been in last all summer, the team I had staked my identity with, was now on top of the National League's Eastern Division. Me and millions of other fans around the New York area were completely caught up in this amazin' story.

NOTE From The Sports Time Traveler™

50 years later, in the present time, as The Sports Time Traveler™ I've been staked out at Shea Stadium all weekend, virtually, to experience the Mets take on the Cardinals. And I'm caught up with pennant fever again.

Here's my report on Sunday afternoon's game in 1973.

NEW YORK - September 24, 1973

It took just 6 days. Six days ago the Mets woke up with a headache. They were in 4th place, 5 games behind the Pirates in the loss column. Tom Seaver, "The Franchise," had just been routed the prior night by Pittsburgh in his worst start of the season. The Pirates were in total command of the NL East.

And then in a stunning and magical turn of events, the Mets took 4 straight games from the Pirates and then another from the Cardinals, and suddenly this rag tag team with struggling hitters, none of whom bats over .300, none of whom have driven in more than 72 runs, along with their sometimes stellar pitchers, whose star starters have all been rocked recently, suddenly this team was on top, yes on top of the division with a 1 game lead going into yesterday's game.

This stirring string of 5 straight wins caused a fever to spread like wild over the New York area. A front page story in the New York Times had the headline, *"Met Pennant Fever Rises."*

The article started out with this description of the madness that is associated with this malady as witnessed by New York Times reporter Murray Shumach at Shea Stadium yesterday, *"Shrieking Mets fans stampeded down the elevated ramp to Shea Stadium, used ladders to scale fences, perched in trees and stood in mammoth lines outside ticket windows... pennant madness had invaded the city for the 1st time since 1969."*

54,701 fans jammed Shea on a Sunday afternoon for the game against the Cardinals yesterday, and according to Steve Jacobson in Newsday, *"There were 54,701 counted in the house, and that didn't include those agile ones who had scaled rope ladders and air conditioning fins after the ticket sale was closed 45 minutes before the game."*

5,000 fans had to be turned away after ticket sales were shut off.

Many of them found a spot to watch the game from outside the stadium. Joseph Durso wrote in The New York Times, *"small boys shinnied up a tree beyond the centerfield fence, people jammed the subway ramp to watch."*

And Durso also wrote this about the pre-game fervor inside Shea, *"two nuns behind home plate hoisted a sign that read, 'You Got To Believe.'"*

EXTRA From The Sports Time Traveler™

The nuns "You Got To Believe" sign is the 1st mention in a New York newspaper of a sign inside Shea Stadium bearing the now iconic slogan.

Now back to 1973.

Tug McGraw told the Hackensack Record, *"They* (the fans) *feel the same things we feel. And they want to help us win"*

THE GAME

Yesterday the Mets and Cardinals played for the last time this season. The Cardinals had already experienced their own bizarre 1973 journey of abysmal depths followed by a methodical rise to the top. They had begun the season with the worst start in franchise history at 5 - 20. Then they reeled off a stretch of 56 - 30, to take a 5 game lead. This was on August 5th when they stymied the Mets at Shea in a doubleheader allowing only 3 runs in the 18 innings of play and beat Seaver in the process. It dropped the Mets to a seemingly hopeless 11.5 games out. And kept them buried in last place.

Now, just 7 weeks later the Mets came into Sunday's game 2 games ahead of the now 3rd place Cardinals who have gone just 15 - 29 since reaching their apex in early August.

But despite their collapse, the Cardinals were still very much in this whacky NL East race which has a week to go.

As soon as the game got underway, it was going well for one of the New York Mets greatest legends - the hero of game 3 of the 1969 Miracle, Tommie Agee, now a member of the Cardinals flock, smashed a 2-run homer, driving in Ted Sizemore who had just singled.

Unfortunately for current Mets fans, Agee had been unceremoniously dumped by Mets management 10 months ago and he was now the starting center fielder for St. Louis. And his home run, off Mets starter George Stone, put the Cardinals in front 2 - 0.

The Cardinals made it 3 straight hits off Stone when he gave up a single to Ted Simmons after Agee's home run. But Stone got out of the inning, when Joe Torre hit into an inning ending double play.

In the bottom of the 1st, the Mets batters faced Cardinals starter Mike Thompson. The 23 year old Thompson was starting his 1st game for the Cardinals, his 1st game in the National League, and his 1st in the majors since he had started 12 games for the old Washington Senators in 1971, winning just 1 of them.

Thompson lasted for just 2 batters. After he walked Wayne Garrett, and Felix Millan singled, he was removed for Rich Folkers.

Mets manager Yogi Berra must have been as confused as everyone else regarding why Cardinals manager Red Schoendinst had started Thompson in such a big game. Berra told the Jersey Journal, ***"Gee, I don't think Red Schoendinst planned it that way. Hey, maybe he didn't want me making out a left-handed hitting lineup."***

Folkers, a righty, held the Mets without a hit and got out of the inning.

In the bottom of the 2nd, Berra was already concerned with his team down 2 - 0 and decided to pinch hit for pitcher George Stone. The move didn't pay any immediate dividends, but it sent Harry Parker to the mound for the 3rd inning.

Parker pitched stellar, allowing just 1 hit in 4 innings.

Meanwhile the Mets chipped away at the Cardinals lead. They scored a run in the 3rd on 3 walks and a sacrifice fly. And another in the 5th on a single, bunt and another single. And after 5 innings the game was tied at 2.

In the 6th, Wayne Garrett supplied the power, as he's been doing all month. His triple scored 2 runs to put the Mets up 4 - 2.

Now Berra brought in Tug McGraw, who was well rested, having not pitched since Wednesday. With 3 days off he had as much down time as Tom Seaver had this week.

Tug had a 1-2-3 inning in the 7th.

In the bottom of the inning, Cleon Jones homered. It was his 10th RBI in his last 5 games and the Mets were now up 5 - 2.

McGraw allowed 2 walks to the top of the order in the 8th. There was 1 out and Cardinals on 1st and 2nd when Tommie Agee came to the plate against his former teammate. McGraw got him into an inning ending double play.

In the 9th, McGraw again put 2 men on via singles, but he got Mike Tyson to hit a fly ball to Cleon Jones to end the game.

Tug McGraw got his 10th save to go along with 4 wins in his last 14 appearances.

And the Mets were winners of their 6th game in a row.

The Mets remained in 1st place, but their lead was actually cut in half as the Pirates swept a doubleheader from the Expos to move to just 1/2 game out of 1st.

After the game, Wayne Garrett described how pennant fever is impacting even the Mets players. He told Mike Dyer of the Jersey Journal , *"Everybody is keyed up. The adrenaline is flowing. We just have confidence."*

The Mets now stand at 79 - 77. They have won 21 of their last 28 games. They're 17 - 6 in September. But they must keep winning to capture the division.

Today is an off day for the Mets and then they host 2 games against the Expos before going to Chicago for 4 games against the Cubs.

Here's the standings in the NL East as of this morning, September 24, 1973

79 – 77 NEW YORK METS

77 – 76 PITTSBURGH PIRATES   0.5 games back

76 – 80 ST. LOUIS CARDINALS   3 games back

75 – 80 MONTREAL EXPOS   3.5 games back

75 - 80 CHICAGO CUBS   3.5 games back

69 – 87 PHILADELPHIA PHILLIES   10 games back

The Mets have 6 games left on the schedule.

I can't wait.

I've got the fever.

And I don't want the cure.

Thanks for reading!

CHAPTER EIGHTY

The Pirates Stash & the Double Doubleheader

THE 1973 PIRATES ARE IN 2ND PLACE BUT HAVE A SECRET STASH THAT COULD DASH THE METS THE NL EAST TITLE DREAMS

NEW YORK - September 25, 1973

The Sports Time Traveler™ is still hanging out in New York in 1973 following one of the great pennant races of all-time.

Going into the games on September 23rd, 5 teams were inside of 2.5 games of each other in the National League East.

The Mets had a 1 game lead over the Pirates. This was a stunning turnaround as the Mets had been in last place just a little over 3 weeks earlier at the end of August. But while pennant fever had overtaken Mets fans, they may not have realized that their 1st place standing was part miracle and part mirage.

That's because the Pirates have a secret stash that could carry them to their 4th straight NL East title.

The Pirates were still a game ahead in the loss column with a record of 75 - 76 to the Mets 78 - 77.

The Pirates also had 11 games left on their schedule to the Mets 7.

That meant that the 2nd place Pirates held the keys to the loot. If the Pirates could win out, they would win the NL East, not the Mets.

And the Pirates secret stash was a rich one. They were set to play the 3 worst teams in the National League over the past 4 years for all their final 11 games - the Expos, the Phillies and the Padres.

All the Pirates had to do was plunder these 3 teams to capture the East.

They started with the Expos.

Every baseball man knew there was nothing exceptional about these 1973 Expos, even though they had gotten within a half game of 1st place in the past week.

The Expos were pretenders. Their manager, Gene Mauch, had engineered the biggest collapse in baseball history in 1964, when he was piloting the Phillies. With a 6.5 game lead and 12 games to go, the 1964 Phillies lost 10 straight to finish 2nd to the Cardinals. And now his 1973 Expos had lost 5 straight before they had to host the Pirates.

The Pirates had a golden opportunity against the Expos. A snow out in April and a rain out the prior week in Pittsburgh had served them up a unique platter, a double doubleheader against the Expos - 4 games in 2 days.

The first 2 games were on Sunday, September 23rd. While the Mets were winning their 6th straight game, the Pirates took 2 from the Expos by a combined score of 13 - 7. That enabled the Pirates to pick up a half game on the Mets and retain their 1 game lead in the loss column.

Willie Stargell, already a clear MVP candidate, hit his 42nd home run and his 43rd double. He now had 87 extra base hits on the season (including 2 triples) for a new Pirates franchise record.

Then on Monday, September 24th, the Bucs had their chance for the real bounty with the 2nd doubleheader. Winning both games, while the Mets had an off day would put the Pirates back on top. The Pirates would be in command and on their way to a 4th straight division title.

But in game 1, Pirates long time starter Bob Moose was awful, giving up 4 runs inside of 3 innings.

A host of Pirates relievers subdued the Expos after that allowing just 1 run and 4 hits the rest of the way.

And the Pirates batters got them back in the game.

When Stargell smacked his 43rd four-bagger to lead off the 8th, it pulled the Pirates to within a run at 5 - 4.

In the 9th, the Pirates made their bid. A single and a double put runners on 2nd and 3rd with 2 outs for the always dangerous Al Oliver. Mauch brought in Mike Marshall to pitch to Oliver.

Oliver hit a hard one hopper. The ball went right to shortstop Tim Foli, a former Mets player, and he threw the ball to 1st base and got Oliver to save the game.

In game 2, the Pirates Nelson Briles and Dave Giusti combined to shut out the Expos, while Stargell provided the Pirates power with his 44th homer of the year, in a 3 - 0 victory.

Stargell also provided the on field heroics with a running one handed catch that took a home run away from Ken Singleton.

The Pirates had taken 3 of 4 from the Expos and they left Canada a half game out of 1st with a record of 78 - 77 to the Mets 79 - 77.

Stargell had played like a true MVP. He reached base 10 times in 16 plate appearances, hit 2 homers, a double, drove in 5 runs and crossed the plate himself 7 times.

But all of that wasn't enough.

The Pirates needed to sweep both doubleheaders to take over 1st and retain their 1 game lead in the loss column.

The Mets were still in front.

Yet the Pirates still have an extra game to play in their stash with a feast against the Phillies the next 3 days, followed by 3 more against the Expos and 1 against the Padres.

The Pirates are still the fearsome band to beat in the East.

CHAPTER EIGHTY-ONE

Willie Mays Says Goodbye to Baseball

THE SAY HEY KID HAS A TEAR FILLED FAREWELL AT SHEA

SPECIAL NOTE From The Sports Time Traveler™

Before I start the article on the Willie Mays farewell and the Mets game from Tuesday, September 25, 1973, I have an important note to share.

On the morning of Monday, September 24, 1973, on page 29 of the Hackensack Record, there appeared this headline about the New York Mets:

"You Gotta Believe"

This is the 1st time that the iconic slogan appeared in a headline.

Writer Ron Drogo was responsible for penning the headline. Drogo explained that the 2 nuns who held the sign behind home plate that read, "You Gotta Believe," during Sunday's game (on September 23rd), were actually friends of Mets relief pitcher Tug McGraw, whose maniacal clubhouse chants of "Ya Gotta Believe," are at the core of the Mets rise from last to first over the past 4 weeks.

Even though there is a week to go in the season, and even though at the time of that writing, the 1st place Mets were actually a game behind the Pirates in the loss column, Drogo wrote, *"There is talk of miracles and mysticism at Shea Stadium, where the home team seems to be getting every clutch hit, clutch play and clutch break they need... The Mets seem destined to win the National League East... and the miracle of 1969 looks pale in comparison."*

The Mets players are being spurred on by the Shea Stadium fans who are willing the team to the top. Tug McGraw described the atmosphere to Ron Drogo as he entered the game on Sunday, in which he registered his 23rd save of the season, *"Everybody's been talking about the electricity of the crowd and I felt it. When I was walking to the mound it was like putting my finger in a socket and having a chill run through my body."*

McGraw went on to describe the Mets magic, *"Because everything is going in the right direction, it just picks you up and carries you along downstream, even when you're not at your best... But You Gotta Believe. That phrase is catching on around here."*

Yes, Tug, your phrase is catching on.

And now, today's article.

SHEA STADIUM - September 26, 1973

Last night was as special a night as there ever was at Shea Stadium.

It started with the farewell of Willie Mays.

The 42 year old Mays has identified himself only as a baseball player his entire life. But his diminished play, due to severely debilitating injuries this year, and the urging of several close friends, led him to agree to call it quits and have the Mets hold an evening in his honor last night.

Watch Willie Mays farewell address to the New York fans here:

https://www.youtube.com/watch?v=hEHdrV9i43w

Or, you can search for the video in YouTube by entering this in the search, "Willie Mays Farewell at Shea Stadium (1973)."

Mays, who hasn't played in over 2 weeks since suffering 2 cracked ribs while chasing a foul pop in Montreal, stood near home plate and addressed the packed house, *"This is a sad day for me... to hear you cheer and not be able to do anything about it."*

Then he looked at his teammates in the dugout and said, *"I hope you go on to win a flag for the New York people."*

That sentence generated a long cheer from the crowd, all of whom were on their feet for Mays.

Willie then lamented about his un-Mays like .211 batting average.

He praised how the Mets were playing, and he indicated he knew it was his time to depart.

He closed with, *"Willie say goodbye to America."*

Then he stepped back from the microphone and he shed enough tears to make his cheeks visibly moist on television as he waved his cap.

The crowd remained on their feet and cheered endlessly for the Say Hey Kid, who had once electrified this city nearly as much as Thomas Edison had 90 years earlier when he it up lower Manhattan for the first time.

It had been a 55 minute ceremony. It included Joe DiMaggio and Duke Snider and many other former stars. There was an estimated $100,000 in gifts lavished upon the Say Hey Kid.

And then it was over.

Yet, there was still a game to play.

ANOTHER SPECIAL NOTE From The Sports Time Traveler™

The game on September 25, 1973, was not originally scheduled to be on WOR Channel 9 in New York. But Channel 9 agreed to televise the game. And watching at home, as a 10 year old boy in East Brunswick, NJ, that evening, it was one of the most stirring moments I had ever seen.

It's still one of the most stirring moments I've ever seen.

I had come to be a Willie Mays fan these past 2 seasons since it had been announced in May, 1972 that the Mets had traded for Mays. And I was very sad to see him go. I also felt, probably as all Mets fans did, that the Mets just had to win this game and the division title for Willie.

Willie had come into baseball in 1951 and had been a part of a miracle at that time. He had been the rookie-of-the-year and the Giants center-fielder during their drive from 13 games back to beat the Dodgers on Bobby Thomson's shot-heard-round-the-world, the home run that won the pennant. Mays was on deck behind Thomson in that game.

Now the Mets just had to win the division, and cap another miracle, so Mays could go out a winner just like he came in.

THE GAME

Yes, they played a game last night against the Expos.

The crowd was as amped up as it's ever been at Shea. Joseph Durso in the New York Times wrote that it was a *"riotously noisy evening."*

Cleon Jones, a fellow Alabama native to Mays, told Ron Drogo of the Hackensack Record, *"It was a very emotional night for me... I just couldn't wait to go out and do something important for the team and Willie."*

And he did.

Jones reached base 3 times in 5 trips to the plate including his 9th home run of the season in the 6th inning to put the Mets in front 2 - 1. Jones has been on a tear during the Mets last 6 games, batting .333 with 11 RBIs.

In the top of the 7th, starter Jerry Koosman, who had allowed no earned runs, got into trouble. With 2 men on and 2 outs, Berra decided it was time for Tug.

McGraw came in to pitch to the veteran Felipe Alou. Alou, a long time team-mate of Mays on the Giants, had been recently acquired by the Expos as part of their division drive efforts. Now Alou had a big opportunity

Alou crushed a line drive to left-center. Jack Lang in the Jersey Journal described the hit, *"a ball that appeared certain to drop in for a double until Jones caught up with it."*

Ron Drogo, in the Hackensack Record wrote, *"Jones got a quick jump on the ball and ran it down in the alley. He gloved the ball on the dead run with his arm fully extended."*

Cleon Jones had just made a catch that would make Willie Mays proud of him.

McGraw was out of the inning, but not out of trouble. He put the first 2 runners on in the 8th before he retired 3 straight batters to escape.

In the 9th, with the Mets clinging to the 2 - 1 lead, McGraw took the mound again. He got Tim Foli to pop up and Pepe Frias to ground out. This brought up Ron Fairly. Fairly was a veteran player who had played on 4 Dodgers' World Series teams going back to 1959. He had been the hero at the plate on the Dodgers' 1965 World Series championship team.

Tug got him to hit a foul pop to Wayne Garrett at third base.

The Mets had won their 7th game in a row!

And the scoreboard watchers saw that Steve Carlton had shut down the Bucs in Pittsburgh 2 - 1 on 5 hits.

The New York Mets now had a 1.5 game lead on the NL East with just 5 games remaining on the schedule.

What's more, it was now the Mets, not the Pirates, who had a 1 game lead in the loss column.

The Mets, for the 1st time, could control their own destiny.

And it was beginning to appear to everyone that 1st place was their destiny.

After the game, the hero of the day, Cleon Jones, described his feelings to Joseph Durso in the New York Times, *"When I saw Willie crying I felt bad.*

It was a sad day for all of us. And all I wanted to do was get out there and play the game."

He told Phil Pepe in the Daily News, *"I wanted to go out and do something big for Willie Mays tonight."*

Chapter Eighty-Two

Destiny Waits

Tom Seaver takes the mound as the Mets control their destiny with 5 games remaining

SHEA STADIUM - September 27, 1973

I've been camping out at Shea Stadium for a week now (virtually, of course), trying to soak in the most exciting race to the finish in Mets history. I remember the arc of the story from 50 years ago, when I had just turned 10, but none of the details. And that's what makes this virtual experience so exciting.

When the Mets took the 1.5 game lead 2 nights ago after Willie Mays' farewell, it seemed like it was just about over, even though there were still 5 games left on the schedule. I knew that Tom Seaver was pitching the next night against the Expos, on 4 days rest, and that was as about a sure thing as there is in baseball.

Last night Seaver opened the game by throwing 2 strikes to former Met Mike Jorgensen.

A typical Seaver start at Shea.

And then he couldn't get strike 3.

Seaver, the master of control, threw 4 consecutive balls.

Next up was Larry Lintz. Lintz tried to bunt, and Wayne Garrett came charging in at third, as he should have. But Lintz' bunt sailed over Garrett's head for a little bloop double.

Then Ron Fairly inadvertently hit a soft liner on a check swing. The ball went to Seaver, but it bounced off his glove and a run scored.

The Mets suddenly weren't getting any of the breaks that divinely seemed to go their way in the prior 7 games in a row they had won.

Seaver then pitched carefully to the powerful Ken Singleton, another former Met, and walked him.

When Jerry Grote allowed a passed ball, that put runners on second and third, Berra ordered an intentional walk to Jim Lyttle so that Seaver could get out of this nightmarish start with a double play.

The strategy backfired.

Seaver walked the veteran Bob Bailey.

Tom Terrific had walked in a run.

What's more, he had issued 4 walks in the 1st inning.

Now the bases were loaded with Expos. And there was still only 1 out.

It got worse.

Former Met Tim Foli singled and 2 runs scored.

Tom Seaver had allowed 4 runs in the 1st inning at Shea in one of the biggest starts of his career.

Seaver was so off that in the 1st inning, in which he threw 38 pitches, 19 of his throws were balls.

Where was the Mets magic from the past week?

Some fans even started to boo.

And remember this, it was Seaver who had pitched the game in Pittsburgh before the 7 game winning streak started. In that game he had his worst outing of the year lasting just 3 innings in a 10 - 3 drubbing by the Pirates.

On this night Seaver was even more dreadful. He let another run score in the top of the 2nd.

Berra pinch hit for Seaver in the bottom of the 2nd. He was out of the game after just 2 innings, and he had left with the Mets down 5- 0.

The disastrous performance raised Seaver's stellar ERA from 1.88 up to 2.00.

After Seaver was on the bench, the Mets scrapped all the way back to tie the game at 5. But the Expos Bob Bailey homered off Harry Parker in the 7th and the Mets lost 8 - 5.

40,363 fans went home without a chance to experience any sense of the miracle that Mets devotees had witnessed for 5 straight days at Shea.

After the game Seaver openly discussed his failed performance.

He told Joe Donnelly in Newsday, ***"I'm frustrated and discouraged. I've really pitched 2 terrible games in the last 3. I should have had enough rest. There was nothing there. There was plenty of rest. The right amount of sleep. The ball just felt like a shot put. The only thing I can think of is the innings I have pitched."***

Seaver has now pitched 284 innings. The only year he pitched more was when he threw 291 in 1970. In that season he struggled late in the season and the Mets lost ground down the stretch as the Pirates pulled away to win by 6 games.

"It has to take its toll," commented Mets pitching coach Rube Walker on the high volume of innings Seaver has pitched this season.

Seaver is now 3 - 2 in September, while the rest of the Mets are 15 - 5. That's a complete role reversal from earlier in the season, when Seaver was winning most of his starts and the rest of the Mets were deeply under .500

The loss tonight was especially concerning as the Pirates were pounding the Phillies all evening and won that game 13 - 2.

The Pirates win combined with the Mets loss trims the Mets lead to a slim 1/2 game with 4 games to go on the schedule for the Mets. The Mets are off tomorrow and then they go to Chicago to play all their final games of the season.

The Pirates still have 5 games to play, all against the Phillies, Expos and Padres.

The Mets may still need another miracle to win the division.

Here are the NL East standings as of this morning - September 27, 1973:

80 – 78 METS

79 – 78 PIRATES 0.5 games back

77 – 81 CARDS 3 games back

76 – 81 CUBS 3.5 games back

77 – 82 EXPOS 3.5 games back

70 – 88 PHILLIES 10 games back

Chapter Eighty-Three

Unintentional

Five teams remain in contention in the 1973 NL East going into the final weekend of the season

CHICAGO, IL - September 28, 1973

I'm going to be spending the remainder of the 1973 regular season virtually at Wrigley Field in Chicago where the Mets have their final 4 games on the schedule beginning tonight.

Yogi Berra is suffering from a headache, no doubt brought on by the failure of the ace of his pitching staff, Tom Seaver, in the final game at Shea 2 nights ago. Seaver was knocked out in just 2 innings. That didn't happen all year. And it hadn't happened since July, 1969.

The Mets subsequent loss 2 nights ago opened the door back up for the Pirates who went into their game at home last night, against the last place Phillies, with the opportunity to move into a 1st place tie with a victory.

That was their intention.

In the Pirates-Phillies game last night, both teams scored 2 runs in the 1st and then didn't score again until the 13th inning.

In the top of the 13th, Pirates pitcher Chris Zachary, who has been a pro for 11 years, threw a ball, designed for an intentional walk, that unintentionally came within reach of batter Bob Boone. Boone reached out and hit the ball into centerfield for a clean single. Greg Luzinski, the Phillies baserunner on second, was so surprised that he was only able to advance to third base.

With runners on first and third, Zachary then threw a ball that unintentionally bounced before home plate. Pirates catcher Manny Sanguillen couldn't handle the ball, and this time Luzinski was alert enough to score the go ahead run.

Mets magic was at work at a distance as the last place Phillies knocked off the Pirates 3 - 2.

That gave the Mets a full game lead on the division going into tonight's games.

But the schedule is not kind to the Mets, even though it's all unintentional.

The Pirates now play 3 games at home against the Expos, a team they have gone 11 - 4 against this year. The Expos have won only 1 time in Three Rivers Stadium.

Even the Expos themselves recognize how sharp an advantage the Pirates have. Bob Bailey of the Expos was quoted saying, ***"The Pirates have the edge. We play terribly against them."*** And this is coming from a key player on a team that is theoretically still in the race themselves.

If the Pirates are still within reach of the Mets after the Expos series, then they will play 1 make-up game against the Padres, a team that has already lost 100 games this season.

Meanwhile the Mets play 4 games against the Cubs in the windy city. The Mets have gone 5 - 9 against the Cubs. The Cubs, a veteran team, need to win all 4 games against the Mets to have a chance to win the division. And the Cubs are hungry. They blew it in 1969 and they haven't won anything since 1945. This could be their time if they can win 4 straight.

Lamenting about where the Mets play their final games of the season, writer Ron Drogo in the Hackensack Record concluded, ***"The simple fact is the Mets must win and not be concerned about home field advantages, winds or past records."***

"This is a do or die situation," said Tom Seaver.

Seaver is scheduled to pitch the last game of the season on Sunday.

The whacky thing about the 1973 NL East right now is that 5 teams all have the possibility of finishing tied. There is a scenario in which the Mets, Pirates, Cards, Expos and Cubs can all finish at 80 - 82.

And no one is quite sure what would happen if it comes to that.

It would be quite unintentional.

CHAPTER EIGHTY-FOUR

The Five Team Tie

THE NL ANNOUNCED PLANS IN CASE THE WHACKY 1973 NL EAST ENDS IN A FIVE TEAM TIE

WRIGLEY FIELD - September 29, 1973

I'm here virtually in Wrigley Field where last night the Mets and Cubs were rained out. Now they will play 2 today and 2 tomorrow to conclude the season.

Cubs coach Ernie Banks, who coined the phrase, "Let's play two," while he was a player, must be loving it. Banks' Cubs are still mathematically in the race, as are 5 of the 6 teams in the NL East.

That led the National League to announce their plans in case of the never before conceived possibility of a 5 way tie at the top.

The only way for the 5 way tie to happen is for the Mets to get double swept today and tomorrow by the Cubs. But we've seen stranger things happen this season already.

Here's the current plan in the event of the 5 way tie:

TUESDAY October 2nd

Pirates at Mets; Expos at Cardinals; Cubs have a bye

WEDNESDAY October 3rd

Cubs at Expos/Cardinals winner

THURSDAY October 4th

Pirates/Mets winner at Cubs/Expos/Cardinals winner

In last night's other action, the Pirates were hosting the Expos. The game was delayed half an hour due to rain and the outfield was very wet when the game finally started.

The Pirates entered the contest just 1 game behind the Mets. They had Dock Ellis on the mound, one of their top starters over the past few seasons. And they were facing the Expos, a team they'd beaten 11 of 15 times this year.

A win would pull the Pirates to within half a game of the Mets.

Ellis got into early trouble with a walk and single. The lead runner reached third base, but Ellis got out of it with an inning ending double play.

And then Ellis went to work facing the minimum number of batters and allowing no hits in the 2nd through 6th innings.

Dock Ellis was working on a 1 hit shutout, but in all that time, the powerful Pirates could only put up 1 run.

PIRATES 1 EXPOS 0 - end of 6 innings

In the top of the 7th, Ellis allowed 2 singles. With runners on first and second and 1 out the batter was Jim Lyttle. He hit a bouncing ball to Al Oliver at first base. It was a double play ball.

But Oliver threw the ball past Dal Maxvill at second base and on into left field. That allowed the lead runner to score and tie the game.

A few minutes later, with 2 outs, John Boccabella hit a short liner into center-field. The speedy Gene Clines was playing too deep. As he raced in for the ball he skidded a long way on the wet grass. The ball fell in for a double and 2 more runs scored.

The Expos were up 3 - 1, all on runs that should not have happened.

The gift runs allowed the Expos to upset the Pirates in Pittsburgh 3 - 2, for just their 2nd win of the season in Three Rivers.

It kept the Expos slim hopes alive.

More importantly it pushed the Pirates to 1.5 games back of the Mets.

Two nights in a row the Pirates have been done in by mistakes.

On 2 consecutive nights, if the Pirates would have executed sound baseball and beaten weaker teams at home, they would have found themselves with a half game lead in the NL East and in the captain's seat for the rest of the way. They would have been staring at a 4th straight division title.

Chalk it up to "MET-a-physical" spooky action at a distance.

Almost every break that could have, has gone the way of the New York Mets over the past week.

Here's the standings in the 1973 NL East as of the morning of Saturday, September 29th:

80 – 78 METS

79 – 80 PIRATES 1.5 games back

79 – 81 CARDINALS 2 games back

78 – 82 EXPOS 3 games back

76 – 82 CUBS 4 games back

71 – 89 PHILLIES 10 games back

The Mets are pitching Matlack and Koosman in the doubleheader today. I can't wait!

CHAPTER EIGHTY-FIVE

The Daily Double

SLOPPY FIELDS FOILED MULTIPLE CONTESTS YESTERDAY IN 1973

WRIGLEY FIELD – September 30, 1973

The Mets and Cubs were rained out of their doubleheader yesterday at Wrigley Field. *"The field is absolutely bad, almost a quagmire,"* said chief umpire Augie Donatelli in the New York Times.

The Mets and Cubs doubleheader will be attempted today and then they may still have to play another doubleheader tomorrow.

This means the Mets and Cubs might be the only teams in modern major league baseball history to have been scheduled to play doubleheaders on 3 consecutive days.

In this whacky NL East division, the games could go on for several days to sort out a winner. That's because 5 teams are still in contention to capture the division title as we enter what was originally scheduled to be the last day of the regular season.

In Pittsburgh yesterday, a game was played between the Pirates and the Expos that took 6 hours and 15 minutes from the scheduled start until the conclusion. The game started after a 2 hour and 22 minute rain delay and then took nearly 4 hours to play including more rain delays.

In the top of the 2nd inning the Pirates had their next in a series of bizarre plays that have derailed their division dominance in the past week.

With a runner on 1st and no outs, Expos batter John Boccabella swung at a pitch and his bat hit the forearm of Pirates catcher Milt May. May was charged with interference and Boccabella was awarded first base. With 2 runners on and no outs, the Expos feasted on Pirates pitching. They scored 5 runs in the inning as the Pirates used 3 pitchers to try and stop the flooding of baserunners.

On the mound for the Expos, the wonder rookie, Steve Rogers, was not at his best, but he was good enough in teaming with iron man reliever Mike Marshall, pitching in his major league leading 91st game of the year, to hold the Pirates to 7 hits and 3 earned runs for the game.

The Expos, for the 2nd straight day, had shocked the Pirates winning the game 6 - 4. And it was the Pirates 3rd loss in a row in games they were heavily favored to win. Had they won all 3 they would have a 1 game lead on the Mets with 2 to play.

Instead the losses pushed the Pirates to 2 games back.

In St. Louis, where the weather was dry, Bob Gibson made his 1st start since a knee injury, suffered against the Mets in early August, had kept him sidelined. Gibson pitched well, throwing 6 innings and allowing 5 hits and 1 run in a 7 - 1 victory over the Phillies. That moved the Cardinals to 1.5 games behind the Mets.

TIED FOR 1ST

In one way of counting, the Cardinals win moved them into a 1st place tie with the Mets as both teams have now won 80 games.

4 teams are within 1 game in the win column. And the 5th place team, the Cubs, still control their own destiny.

It's the last day of the regular season and there can still be a 5 team tie.

Here's the standings of the top 5 teams in the NL East on what was supposed to be the final morning of the baseball season:

80 – 78 METS

80 – 81 CARDINALS 1.5 games back

79 – 81 PIRATES 2 games back

79 – 82 EXPOS 2 games back

76 – 82 CUBS 4 games back

The Mets are sticking with the same scheduled starting pitchers today, Matlack in game 1 and Koosman in game 2. They will go against Rick Reuschel and Ferguson Jenkins of the Cubs.

I can't wait!

CHAPTER EIGHTY-SIX

And Then There Were Three

THE 1973 NL EAST RACE WAS CUT FROM 5 TO 3 TEAMS ON THE LAST SCHEDULED DAY OF THE SEASON

WRIGLEY FIELD - October 1, 1973

The Mets and Cubs finally played yesterday after being rained out 2 straight days. And I was there virtually to experience the games.

The field was still very soggy. The Mets had to play yesterday without taking batting practice. They have not had batting practice since leaving New York 4 days ago.

In the opener, it was a pitching duel between Jon Matlack of the Mets and the Cubs' Rick Reuschel. Both men allowed no runs thru 7 innings.

In the top of the 8th, Reuschel came out of the game with a blister on his pitching hand. But reliever Bob Locker picked up where Reuschel left off and stifled the Mets.

In the bottom of the 8th, Matlack gave up a single to rookie leadoff batter Dave Rosello. Don Kessinger then bunted. Matlack got to the ball and tried to get the lead runner at second. But his throw was late and now the Cubs had runners on first and second and no outs.

Matlack got the next 2 batters, Rick Monday and Billy Williams out. That brought up Ron Santo, the Cubs reliable third baseman since 1960. Santo is as much the heart of this Cubs team as anyone. He knew this was a do or die game as the Cubs needed to sweep the 2 doubleheaders (yesterday and today) to get into a tie for the division.

Santo came through. He singled to left to score Rosello and give the Cubs a 1 - 0 lead.

That was all Matlack let up.

Going into the 9th, the Mets needed a run to tie the game. They got men on first and second with 2 outs for Ed Kranepool. Kranepool is the only player to have been on the Mets since their very 1st year in 1962. He hit a home run in the one game he started in the 1969 World Series. But unlike Santo, he was not able to deliver the clutch hit on this day. He grounded out and the Cubs won it 1 - 0 to stay alive.

The loss meant that the Mets lead was now cut to 1 game over the Cardinals, whose game against the Phillies had not yet ended. The Cards and Mets came into today tied in a sense as they both have 80 wins.

GAME 2

In the 2nd game, it was Jerry Koosman for the Mets vs. 1971 Cy Young Award winner Ferguson Jenkins of the Cubs. And although Jenkins was not in his Cy Young form for much of this year, he had just pitched an 8 inning, 4 hit win over the Cardinals 5 days ago.

The potential for the Cubs to pull off the 1st doubleheader sweep had to seem very realistic. The Cubs were very much alive.

That is, until the game started.

Jenkins walked Wayne Garrett, the Mets leadoff hitter. Felix Millan bunted Garrett over to second. Rusty Staub then singled and advanced to second on a poor throw. The Mets had runners on second and third and 1 out.

John Milner was then intentionally walked to load the bases.

Next up was Cleon Jones. He hit a grounder to Santo at third base who threw wildly to the plate and 2 runs scored. And then another run scored on a Jerry Grote ground out.

The Mets were up 3 - 0 before the Cubs even came to bat.

Then Mets magic took over. Jerry Koosman was pitching very nicely, but he got help on some plays that could not have possibly happened via any other explanation other than "somebody up there," was looking out for the Mets.

Oh, how I wish there was video tape of this game. But until one surfaces we'll have to make do with the eye witness descriptions of the Mets' beat writers.

Joseph Durso in the New York Times described a play by Cleon Jones in left field in the 2nd, *"Jones misjudged a fly to the wall, pirouetted, fell on the wet grass and finally grabbed the ball one-handed while flat on his stomach."*

My gosh, I'd have loved to see that.

Phil Pepe in the Daily News described the miraculous catch this way, *"Jones made a catch in left field after circling under the ball that was swirling in the wind. He finally caught it with a dive, landing on his chin and lay there for several moments."*

In the 3rd inning Jones did it again. Durso wrote nonchalantly, *"He grabbed another while sliding past Bud Harrelson,"* as though these kind of catches are routine. Pepe described it like this, *"Jones made another catch on his belly in the 3rd."*

Next it was right fielder Rusty Staub's turn. Durso described Staub's stabs in the 4th inning, *"Staub made a diving catch and followed that by hauling down a long one in the ivy vines."*

But that wasn't all. In the 7th inning, second baseman Felix Millan, *"robbed Ken Rudolph of a hit with a racing overhead catch,"* according to Durso.

The great defensive plays kept the Mets in the game, and it was 3 - 2 Mets going into the 6th inning. Jenkins had pitched 1-2-3 innings in the 2nd, 3rd and 4th and allowed just a single in the 5th.

At about this time, scoreboard watchers would have seen the Cardinals leading the Phillies. A win would pull the Cardinals to just a half game back of the Mets and put them ahead in the win column by 1.

In the 6th, Cleon Jones came up with 1 on and 1 out and blasted a Jenkins pitch to deep left for a 2-run shot that extended the Mets lead to 5 - 2.

And that was all Jerry Koosman needed. The 2 runs he had allowed early in the game were unearned. He only gave up 6 hits and pitched a complete game which the Mets won 9 - 2.

The win spelled the end for the Cubs. They're officially out. But they will have to come back to Wrigley today to play another scheduled doubleheader against the Mets.

The win kept the Mets in 1st place. But it wasn't enough to clinch the division. They will need to win 1 of the 2 games today to be the NL East champs. And the Mets are now assured of at least a tie.

The Mets will send Tom Seaver to the mound for game 1 and George Stone for game 2.

I can't wait!

And now updates on the other teams in the NL East race.

THE PIRATES

The Pirates finally beat the Expos as they were supposed to. They did it with an all-around performance befitting their franchise that has won the NL East crown in each of the past 3 seasons. They pounded 10 runs while starting pitcher Jim Rooker pitched a complete game, allowing just 2 runs.

The Pirates are still in the race. They must beat the San Diego Padres at home in Three Rivers stadium today. The Padres are the worst team in the National League with 102 losses. What a gift for the Pirates.

The Pirates also need the Mets to lose both games in today's doubleheader in Wrigley to force a tie with the Mets.

THE EXPOS

The loss in Pittsburgh yesterday spelled the end of a near Cinderella season for Montreal. An expansion team in 1969, the Expos had never even come close to contending for the NL East title prior to this run.

Two weeks ago, on Sunday September 16, the Expos drew to within a half game of the division leading Pirates.

They were 2 full games up on the Mets and 3 ahead in the loss column.

And then they were done in by a string of 7 straight losses and 9 losses in 10 games immediately after getting so close to the top.

For manager Gene Mauch it must have been deja vu, as he was the manager of the Phillies 9 years ago, in 1964, when they collapsed similarly in the final week of the season.

THE CARDINALS

The Cardinals beat the Phillies in their final game of the season 3 - 1. It was the Cardinals 5th straight win and it gave them a record of 81 - 81 for the year. At the moment they won the game, the Cardinals were just a half game behind the Mets and 1 ahead in the win column.

This caps one of the craziest seasons in their long franchise history. The team started with their worst ever opening. They lost their 1st 5 games in a row and got out to a 5 - 20 start. They were as much as 11.5 games back on May 14th when their record was 8 - 23.

Then they were sensational going on a 53 - 27 run (a 106 win pace) to take the division lead. They were up by 5 games and appeared to be on their way to their 1st NL East title. And then they collapsed. They lost 8 straight and 11 of 12. They lost 31 of 46 games after reaching their apex to fall 4 games back with 5 to play.

And then they won their last 5 in a row to possibly salvage a season that had seemed hopelessly lost twice already.

If the Pirates lose today and the Mets lose both games of the doubleheader, then the Cardinals will tie for the NL East.

Here are the standings in the NL EAST as of this morning, October 1, 1973

81 – 79 METS 2 games left to play

81 – 81 CARDINALS 1 game back - season complete

80 – 81 PIRATES 1.5 games back - 1 game left to play

79 – 83 EXPOS 3 games back - season complete

77 – 83 CUBS 4 games back - 2 games left to play

71 – 91 PHILLIES 11 games back - season complete

HANK AARON

In other baseball news, Hank Aaron went into yesterday's final game of the season in Atlanta with 713 career home runs, 1 behind Babe Ruth's all-time record. A crowd of 40,517 came out hoping to see history made.

Aaron described what happened in The New York Times, *"The 1st pitch the 1st time up he threw a fastball right down the middle. I took it. And it was the last one I saw down the middle... I only got one good pitch all day."*

The Astros pitchers didn't give Aaron anything to hit and so Hammerin' Hank will remain stuck on 713 for the next 6 months until the start of the 1974 baseball season when he will be 40 years old.

NOLAN RYAN

Nolan Ryan got his last start of the season 4 nights ago on September 27th. He started the game 15 strikeouts behind Sandy Koufax's record 382 strikeouts in a single season.

Ryan was facing the Minnesota Twins, the best hitting team in the American League and the team with the second lowest number of strikeouts.

When the game began, Ryan couldn't get anyone out. He issued a walk, 2 singles and a double leading to 3 Twins runs.

Koufax' record sounded safe.

Then Ryan started striking out Twins. He got out of the 1st inning by striking out 3 Twins.

Ryan got 8 more strikeouts in the 2nd through 5th innings, and didn't allow another run until the 6th.

In the top of 7th, Ryan registered 3 more strikeouts. His total for the game was now 14, and his season total was now 381. He needed 1 to tie Koufax and 2 to set a new MLB record.

ANGELS 4 TWINS 4 – Ryan at 381 strikeouts – end of 7 innings

In the top of the 8th, Ryan got a little shaky. He issued a walk and threw a wild pitch to open the inning. Then he settled down, got a couple of ground outs and finished off the Twins with a strikeout.

Ryan had tied Koufax at 382.

In the top of the 9th, Ryan had to face the Twins 3 great hitters, Rod Carew, Tony Oliva and Harmon Killibrew. He got Carew and Oliva to fly out. But Killibrew hit a single to center. Ryan stranded pinch runner Rich Reese at first when he got Jim Holt to fly out.

The Angels now had the opportunity to win the game in the bottom of the 9th, but they went down with just with just the minimum 3 batters.

At this point, Angels manager Bobby Winkles allowed Nolan Ryan to stay in the game to pitch the top of the 10th inning to give him a chance at the record.

After coming off the mound in the top of the 9th, Ryan had suffered a leg cramp and required the services of trainer Freddie Federico.

Ryan told Dave Distel in the Los Angeles Times, *"They left it up to me,"* regarding the decision to go back out for the 10th.

Ryan gave up 2 singles in the top of the 10th, but got out of the inning with no runs scored. However, he did not get another strikeout.

The Angels went down in order in the bottom of the 10th and Ryan had another opportunity as he came back out for the top of the 11th.

He got Steve Brye to ground out for the first out.

Then Rod Carew walked and stole second.

Ryan then got Tony Oliva to hit a fly to center for out number 2.

Next up was Rich Reese, who stayed in the game after he pinch ran for Killibrew.

Reese was the 11th batter since Ryan had thrown his last strikeout. Perhaps the Ryan Express was out of gas.

Fortunately for Ryan, Reese was batting just .151 on the year.

Ryan blitzed Reese with 2 straight fastballs for strikes.

Ryan then threw a 3rd fastball. Reese swung. And he missed.

It was strikeout number 383 for Ryan!

Dave Distel wrote, *"Ryan hesitated for a moment after Minnesota Twins' Rich Reese swung and missed for the historic strikeout, almost unbelieving that it had finally happened."*

The Angels scored in the bottom of the inning and the game was over.

Nolan Ryan had won his 21st game of the season.

And he was the new single season strikeout king.

BOBBY BONDS

Bobby Bonds came into the final game of the season yesterday in Cincinnati with 43 steals and 38 homers. He had hit his 38th home run all the way back on September 9th, but he was stuck on that number for the past 3 weeks.

No player had ever had a "40-40" season, and Bonds needed 2 home runs in the final game to reach that milestone.

Bonds led off the game by striking out.

In his next at bat, in the 3rd inning, Bonds hit number 39, a solo shot to deep right field.

In the 4th inning Bonds came up again and slashed a single.

Bonds was up again in the 6th, and struck out again.

Bonds had one more chance in the top of the 9th. He led off and connected. It was a fly ball to center. But it was caught by Ed Armbister.

The Giants closed out a 4 – 3 win in the bottom of the 9th and Bobby Bonds season was over. He had just missed the "40-40" season.

THE YANKEES

The Yankees hit a high point on July 27th, at which time they had the best record in the American League at 59 – 44, and held a 1.5 game lead in the AL East.

Then they promptly plummeted, losing 10 of their next 12 games, and suffering through 3 walk-off losses.

In late August they went on another losing binge, dropping 10 of 11 games.

The Yankees finished the campaign 17 games behind the AL East division winners – the Baltimore Orioles.

That's it for today.

Tomorrow is the big day. It's overtime in the NL East.

CHAPTER EIGHTY-SEVEN

The Tale of Tug

TUG MCGRAW HAS THE METS BELIEVING THEY CAN WIN THE 1973 NL EAST

CHICAGO - October 2, 1973

The day began with a whimper. It was drizzling when I arrived here virtually yesterday, at Wrigley Field, where just 1,913 fans showed up to watch a double-header featuring the home town Cubs against the Mets.

The games meant nothing for the Cubs who had been eliminated the prior day.

But they meant everything for the Mets who started the day with a 1 game lead over the Cardinals and 1.5 games over the Pirates, both of whom could tie the Mets depending on the outcome of the day's games.

The Cardinals season was done, but with 81 wins, they were tied with the Mets in the win column. The Mets needed to win 1 today to eliminate the Cardinals.

The Pirates had a make-up game to play. Their game against the Padres in Three Rivers Stadium was set to start at 1:35pm ET. The Pirates had 80 wins. They needed to beat the Padres and hope the Mets would lose both games to enable a tie for the NL East.

The 1st game between the Mets and Cubs started at 12:20pm ET after a short rain delay.

The Cubs sent knuckle ball pitcher Burt Hooton to the mound. Hooton had pitched 4 strong games against the Mets already this year. He shut them out on 3 hits in April. He threw a complete game 4 hitter in June. He lost a complete game 5 hitter 2 - 1 also in June. But in a game 2 weeks ago at Shea, he gave up 10 hits and lost.

Yesterday Hooton started out looking like the version of himself who had shut down the Mets earlier in the season as he retired the first 4 batters.

Then in the top of the 2nd Cleon Jones, the hero of yesterday's win, clubbed another homer to deep right to put the Mets on the scoreboard first.

For Jones it was his 6th homer in the last 10 games.

In the 4th, Hooton got into trouble as he loaded the bases with no outs. Jerry Grote then singled driving in 2 runs and the Mets were up 3 - 0.

In the 5th, Hooton started the inning allowing a double and a single and that was it for him.

Reliever Mike Paul couldn't hold the runners and 2 more scored on Rusty Staub's single and John Milner's sacrifice fly.

The Mets were ahead 5 - 0 in the middle of the 5th.

Tom Seaver was doing his job through the opening 4 innings. He wasn't dominating though. He allowed 5 hits and had only 1 strikeout. But he didn't let anyone get past second.

Then in the bottom of the 5th the Cubs got to Seaver. Tom Terrific allowed 4 singles to the first 5 batters in the inning and the lead was cut to 5 - 2. With men on first and third and only 1 out, it could have gotten much worse, but Seaver got Ron Santo to pop up and struck out Jose Cardenal to end the inning.

The score remained 5 - 2 going into the 7th. In the top of the inning, Rusty Staub singled, reached third base on a walk and a ground out and scored on an error by Santo.

That padded the Mets lead to 6 - 2.

They needed it.

Tom Seaver opened the bottom of the 7th by giving up a single to Dave Rosello and a home run to Rick Monday. That drew the Cubs to within 2 at 6 - 4, with no outs.

Seaver had now given up 11 hits and 4 runs. Massive numbers for the Cubs against the normally over powering Seaver.

Yogi Berra decided it was time to take out The Franchise, who had now faltered for the 3rd time in his last 4 outings.

TUG TO THE RESCUE

Berra brought in the heart and soul of the Mets drive to the top over the past month, Tug McGraw.

The ball was now literally in Tug's hands to win the division title. If he could hold on and save this game, the New York Mets would be the NL East Champs.

McGraw came in and immediately had to face the heart of the Cubs order. He got Don Kessinger, a 5 time all-star to ground out. He got Billy Williams, the man who nearly won the triple crown last year to ground out. And then he struck out Ron Santo.

In the top of the 8th, McGraw was the leadoff hitter, and pitcher Jack Aker hit him. Was this intentional? It might have been. McGraw had an old feud going with Aker according to Dick Young in the Daily News. And Aker hit McGraw, a lefty, on the left shoulder. McGraw shouted at Aker as he strode to first base, *"You got better control than that."*

Would the sore shoulder thwart Tug's save attempt? McGraw told Dick Young that as the bottom of the 8th inning was ready to begin, *"I was walking toward the mound. I could feel the shoulder. Then I said to myself 'the heck with it. Don't let it bother you. This is too good a day to let them ruin it for me.' Two months ago I might have tried to blast every batter or start swinging at Aker."*

McGraw kept his cool, and in business like fashion he mowed down the Cubs 1-2-3 in the 8th, striking out the last 2 batters.

Then in the 9th, with the score still 6 - 4, McGraw went back to the mound.

At about this time a look at the scoreboard in the outfield revealed that the Padres had unthinkably opened a 2 - 0 lead on the Pirates in the top of the 4th in Pittsburgh. A loss would mean the Pirates were out.

Then in the bottom of the inning the Pirates scored 3 and pulled ahead. A Mets double loss today and a Pirates win would mean the Mets, Pirates and Cardinals would all be tied at the top and a 3 way playoff would be required.

Tug McGraw however, could end it all right here.

Three outs and the Mets would be division winners no matter what happened in Pittsburgh.

The 1st batter was Ken Rudolph who was batting just over .200. He singled. The tying run was now at the plate with no outs.

Next up was Dave Rosello. Rosello was playing in just the 21st game of his major league career.

McGraw struck him out.

Now Glenn Beckert came up as a pinch hitter. Beckert had batted .342 in 1971, when he was 11th in the MVP voting. But this year he was only hitting .255.

Beckert got the count to 3 and 2 and McGraw threw his favorite pitch, the screwball.

Durso described the action as Beckert swung, *"Beckert pinch-hit a looping fly behind first. Milner grabbed it and stepped on the bag to double off Rudolph."*

That was it!

The New York Mets had won the game!

Tug had done it again!

He had allowed 1 hit and no runs in 3 innings for his 25th save.

The umpires then made the decision to cancel the 2nd game which was now meaningless for everyone.

The Mets were division champions!

The impossible drive from last to first had happened.

Ron Drogo in the Hackensack Record reported that Tug McGraw jumped up on a bench in the clubhouse, waved a bottle of champagne, and yelled, *"1-2-3, Ya Gotta Believe! Ya Gotta Believe! Ya Gotta Believe!"*

SPECIAL NOTE From The Sports Time Traveler™

"Ya gotta believe" is the iconic phrase that will forever be associated with this version of the 1973 Miracle Mets.

The phrase was coined by Tug McGraw and his legacy will always be his maniacal chanting of this famous mantra.

McGraw's spirit was almost singlehandedly responsible for willing the Mets to believe they could achieve the impossible.

Tug inspired his teammates to do what has never been done before or since - a fairy tale last to first place division title drive in the final month of the season. Tug had 12 saves and 5 wins in his last 19 appearances over the final 5 weeks of the season. That means he had a direct impact on 17 of the Mets last 24 wins. And Tug had no blown saves or losses in any of those final 19 games in which he pitched.

Now back to 1973.

Yogi's biggest thrill

Yogi Berra described this division title as the biggest thrill he's ever had in baseball in an interview with Durso, *"I was on 14 Yankee teams that won, but this has to be a big thrill because we jumped over 5 clubs to do it. We were 12 games back and hurt."*

The New York Times reported that Mayor John Lindsay declared in a statement released shortly after the game, *"The Mets are the best. This miracle tops '69."*

Tom Seaver had a different take on comparisons to 1969. He told The New York Times, *"Nothing will ever be like 1969. We were all so young then. Anyhow, we've only taken one step of the three. We still have to win a playoff and World Series to match 1969. But in a way this was more earned."*

Catcher Jerry Grote had another point of view, *"It was just like 1969 in that it was a team thing. All the pitchers, Harrelson, Cleon, Garrett - everybody did something."*

The win also meant that Willie Mays goes out a winner.

Still on the roster, even though he bid farewell last week and hasn't played in 3 weeks due to cracked ribs he sustained in the game on September 9th, Mays was in the clubhouse when the champagne was flowing yesterday.

Mays, who doesn't drink alcohol, reportedly had 3 sips and passed out. This led Tug McGraw to declare Mays the MVP of the champagne contest.

The Mets have done it!

Ron Drogo titled his story in the Hackensack Record with a headline that read, *"Are there any non-believers out there?"*

The Mets won the division with the worst record in history for a 1st place team. But they had finished with a flash, winning 24 of the final 33 games to come from last place on the morning of August 31 to division champions a month later.

A short while later when the Padres came from behind and beat the Pirates 4 - 3, all regular season activity for the 1973 season finally ceased.

Here are the final standings in the 1973 National League East

82 – 79 METS

81 – 81 CARDINALS   1.5 games back

80 – 82 PIRATES   2.5 games back

79 – 83 EXPOS   3.5 games back

77 – 84 CUBS   5 games back

71 – 91 PHILLIES   11.5 games back

The National League Championship Series begins on Saturday, October 6 in Cincinnati. It is a best of 5 game series for the National League pennant.

I can't wait!

CHAPTER EIGHTY-EIGHT

Conflicted

THE METS ARE SET TO START THE 1973 NLCS AGAINST THE CINCINNATI REDS

IMPORTANT NOTE From The Sports Time Traveler™

All this week I have been thinking about my memories from 50 years ago of Saturday, October 6, 1973. I was 10 years old and my New York Mets were going to be in the National League Championship Series. But it was going to be played on Yom Kippur, the most holy day of the year for the Jewish people. I was somewhat conflicted.

On that morning, I was in synagogue as were most Jews around the world. I was supposed to be in the kids' service, but I recall I was out in the hallway with my friends when I heard the grim news.

Israel had been attacked, on the holiest day of the year for the Jews, by the Syrian and Egyptian armies, from both the north and the south.

Caught completely off guard, it was an existential moment for the tiny country.

I raced into the main sanctuary to tell my parents.

The adults already knew.

In another unreal and awkward moment, as I sat next to my dad, he whispered in my ear, *"The man sitting in front of you is Mr. Spock."* What my dad meant was that actor Leonard Nimoy, who played Mr. Spock on Star Trek, one of my favorite shows of all-time, was literally sitting right in front of us in the synagogue.

This is one more oddity that added to the surreal nature of one of the seminal days of my childhood. And no, I didn't wonder why his ears weren't pointy.

Later that day the Mets were scheduled to play the Cincinnati Reds in game 1 of the NLCS. Luckily for most Jewish fans in the New York area, who were not orthodox, the game would start after services had ended at 4pm ET. That meant I could still see the game on TV.

My grandparents came over the house for the traditional break fast meal at the end of Yom Kippur which is a fasting holiday. I tried to fast as long as I could that day, although I don't remember if I made it all the way till game time.

It was very special having both my dad and grandpa there for this momentous game, the biggest game the New York Mets had played in since I had become a fan in 1970.

Once the game began I selfishly forgot about the Jewish holiday or the war in Israel. At 10 years old, I was focused on the Mets.

It was surreal to see the Mets players, who I was so familiar with, Tom Seaver, Bud Harrelson, Wayne Garrett, Jerry Grote, Cleon Jones, etc. on national TV on NBC, in the National League Championship series against the Big Red Machine with Pete Rose, Johnny Bench, Joe Morgan and Tony Perez.

The Reds had made it to the 7th game of the World Series the prior year in 1972, where they had lost a 1 run game to the Oakland A's.

The Mets in 1972, had finished 13.5 games out of first and had spent nearly the entire summer in the cellar the 1973 season.

I kept having the feeling, *"we're not supposed to be here."*

Even to this day it still feels surreal that my Mets from the early 1970s played in the National League Championship series.

For the past year, since I began this Sports Time Travel odyssey, it's all been a virtual fantasy. I don't really believe I'm traveling back in time, although I do think I get a sense of what it was like 50 years ago because of the way I systematically follow sports day-by-day in the newspapers, and never look ahead.

But today, for the 1st time in this journey, on October 7, 2023, the actual feelings of 50 years ago seem eerily real.

When I awoke on this day in 2023 my initial thoughts were about the plan I had to watch the tape of game 1 of the 1973 NLCS and then to read the newspaper accounts of the game.

I would be watching the game for 1st time since I had seen it live on TV, 50 years ago, with my dad and my grandpa.

I couldn't wait.

And then I turned on the TV and saw the live news in 2023.

Israel was under attack. Now.

Just like 50 years ago, it was a surprise attack on an important Jewish holiday. Although it is not the most solemn of all holidays, Yom Kippur, it is the double high holiday of Shmeni Atzeret and Simchat Torah - two major holidays that take place together in Israel (and on two consecutive days outside of Israel).

And so my plans to watch the game were delayed as I am conflicted with similar feelings to those I had precisely 50 years ago.

As a result, I will watch game 1 of the 1973 NLCS tomorrow and report on the game a day late.

CHAPTER EIGHTY-NINE

1973 NLCS GAME 1 – Seaver vs. the Big Red Machine

IN A BEST OF 5 SERIES THE METS SENT OUT THEIR ACE, TOM TERRIFIC TO BATTLE THE REDS

IMPORTANT NOTE From The Sports Time Traveler™

On "50 year tape delay" I watched the NBC broadcast of Game 1 of the 1973 NLCS between the Mets and the Reds at sold out Riverfront Stadium in Cincinnati.

This was the 2nd time I watched the game.

The first time was exactly 50 years ago, when I watched the game live on television. The result was the same of course, but my 50 year memory of the outcome of the game was blank.

As a result, my virtual experience, watching the game on YouTube today, had all the suspense of the original live broadcast. It was the closest experience I can ever have of actual sports time travel when watching a major sporting event.

And now, I take you back 50 years.

Cincinnati - October 7, 1973

The Mets won the NL East division last Monday, one day after the season had been originally scheduled to conclude.

3 teams were still in contention as rained out make-up games took place on October 1st.

When the Mets beat the Cubs to finish with an 82 - 79 record they clinched 1st place.

The Mets victory capped one of the greatest stories in the history of American professional sports. Just about a month earlier, on the morning of August 31st, the Mets were in last place and their situation looked hopeless. But fueled by the maniacal *"Ya Gotta Believe"* mantra of Mets reliever Tug McGraw, and a few minor miracles, the Mets passed every team in the NL East to reach the top.

The poor season long play of every team in the division led some onlookers to call it, **"The National League Least."** But the Mets did play like champions posting a record of 24 - 9 over the final 5 weeks of the season.

Despite their hot finish to the season, the Mets are substantial underdogs against Cincinnati's Big Red Machine.

The Reds lineup is daunting. Take a look at the first 6 batters:

1. PETE ROSE - .365 average / .405 OBP since July 1st

2. JOE MORGAN - 26 HRs / 90 RBIs / .405 OBP average / 67 steals

3. DAN DRIESSEN - .301 average with Reds since June; .409 in AAA prior to that

4. TONY PEREZ - .347 average / .409 OBP since July 1

5. JOHNNY BENCH - MVP in 1970 & 1972; "off year" in 1973 - 25 HRs / 104 RBIs

6. KEN GRIFFEY - .384 average in 86 at bats since being called up from AAA

The Big Red Machine got off to a slow start to the season and then blasted past the Dodgers to capture the NL West by posting an extraordinary 60 - 26 record after July 1st (a 113 win pace). Their record for the entire 162 game season was 99 - 63, the best across all major league baseball.

The Reds have been one of the best teams in baseball since 1970. They lost 2 of the past 3 World Series, including game 7 of last year's Fall Classic to the Oakland A's.

The Reds are ready. This is their year to finally win the World Series with their present core group of players.

They plan to pounce on the Mets.

The Mets, despite their miracle finish, have a big question mark that will be resolved in game 1. Is Tom Seaver healthy?

Seaver pitched God like for most of the season. His ERA got as low as 1.69 after his September 4th win.

But he struggled in last 4 starts, posting a 6.75 ERA. As a result, his major league leading ERA for starters over the full season soared to 2.08. That was still the lowest ERA for a NL starting pitcher by a large margin over Don Sutton of the Dodgers at 2.42.

Seaver was by far at the top of the class for the season. He was the dominant starter in all baseball this year. But suffering from shoulder soreness, would he be the real Tom Terrific against the Reds? That was the question all week.

From my perspective, the culprit for Seaver's soreness is most likely the game he pitched September 13th in Philadelphia. He went 11 innings, striking out 12 and allowing just 2 runs in a 4 - 2 win. The first of his poor performances occurred when he was called on by Berra to start again on just 3 days of rest, after that extra inning game.

It was a recipe for disaster.

In his September 17th start, Seaver lasted just 3 innings and gave up 5 earned runs.

Seaver last pitched in the final game on Monday. In that game, with the division title on the line, Seaver allowed 4 earned runs in 6 innings. Tug McGraw bailed him out and the Mets won it and won the division by a 6 - 4 score.

Coming into today's game, he's now had his normal 4 days' rest. He claims his shoulder feels fine now.

The Mets really have no choice. They have to live or die with The Franchise.

In a 5 game series if you can win game 1 on the road, your chances of winning the series increase exponentially.

A Reds loss in game 1 at home would be a disaster for the Big Red Machine. It would mean they would have to beat the Mets twice at Shea and win 3 of the final 4 games to earn the spot they feel they already deserve in the World Series.

But the Reds have strong reason to believe, even if Seaver is perfectly healthy. That's because Seaver has not beaten the Reds this year.

One of Seaver's losses to the Reds was in a strange game right here at Riverfront against the same starter he will face today, Jack Billingham. In that July 13th game, Billingham held the Mets to 2 hits and beat Seaver 2 - 1. The game only took 1 hour and 37 minutes, the shortest game in the majors this year.

To be fair to the Mets, they did show they can play with the Reds late in the season. After losing their first 5 matchups early, the Mets won 4 of the final 7. And in their final 3 games against the Reds at Shea in August, the Mets took 2 of 3. In the 2 victories, the Mets erupted for 14 runs while starters Jon Matlack and Jerry Koosman each pitched complete games in which they held the Reds to a single run. Although the Reds did manage to put 22 men on base in those games.

The Reds are well deserving of the Big Red Machine nickname.

The top two-thirds of the Reds offense is simply scary. The team scored 741 runs, 2nd in the NL. The Mets managed just 608, only better than the 102 loss Padres.

And while the book on the Mets is they have a superior pitching staff, the fact is the Reds staff is nearly as good when looking top to bottom. The Mets team ERA was 3.26 while the Reds was 3.40. If you subtract Seaver's stats from the Mets, the Reds pitchers would have the better ERA. It was the Reds, not the Mets who led the NL in team shutouts with 17 (to the Mets 15).

Despite all of this, the Mets beat writers are optimistic. Both Phil Pepe in the Daily News and Hank Lowenkron of the Passaic Herald News are picking the Mets in 4!

They're banking on the Mets core starters: Seaver, Jerry Koosman, Jon Matlack and George Stone, and their fanatical reliever, Tug McGraw, to shut down the machine.

Koosman had a 1.95 ERA in 7 starts in September.

Matlack had a 2.43 ERA in 6 starts in September

Stone had a 2.15 ERA in 5 starts in September

And then there is Tug. The man who was arguably the best reliever in baseball from 1969 - 1972. He started the season with an inexplicable 6.17 ERA in his first 35 games in relief.

In his last 25 games Tug McGraw had an ERA of 1.64.

And in 14 games down the stretch in September, McGraw had an ERA of 0.57 in 31 innings.

He won 3 games and saved 10 in September, accounting for 13 of the Mets 19 victories.

In the 14 games in September in which McGraw got the call to pitch, the Mets won 13.

No wonder the Mets beat writers are confident.

This is all tempered by the Mets lack of hitting and baserunning.

The Reds had 3 hitters with 25 or more HRs. The Mets had none. Willie Mays was the 5th leading HR hitter on the Mets with just 6.

The Reds had 4 hitters with 40 or more extra base hits. The Mets had 1.

The Reds had 2 batters that drove in over 100 runs and another that drove in 82. The Mets leading RBI man, Rusty Staub, had just 76.

The Reds had 148 steals, to lead all of baseball, and were only caught 55 times, for the best ratio of any team in the majors. The Mets stole 27 bases and were caught 22 times.

The Mets are going up against a Goliath.

WATCH THE GAME

You too can watch the game on YouTube at this link:

https://www.youtube.com/watch?v=1prox0xCz1k

Or search on this phrase in YouTube: "1973 NLCS Mets Reds game 1."

My commentary on the game is below.

The video starts with the WOR Channel 9 broadcast of the game and then switches to the NBC broadcast of the game in the bottom of the 1st.

Mets fans will love seeing their long time home team announcers, Bob Murphy, Lindsey Nelson and Ralph Kiner at the beginning.

We learn early on, that in game 1 of the ALCS, Jim Palmer of the Baltimore Orioles shut out the defending World Series champion Oakland A's 6 - 0.

The Mets opened the game well with Wayne Garrett singling off Reds starter Jack Billingham. Felix Millan bunted Garrett to second and Rusty Staub drew a walk. John Milner then got the Mets 2nd hit and the bases were loaded with 1 out for Cleon Jones.

Jones had been the Mets batting hero down the stretch in September with 6 HRs and 14 RBIs in the Mets last 10 games. But Jones grounded into a double play to end the threat.

In the bottom of the 1st it was the big moment of truth. Tom Seaver took the mound, and the baseball world was about to see if he would be Tom Terrific or Tom Terrible.

Seaver had said earlier this week that the key to beating Cincinnati was to get their opening 2 batters out: Rose and Morgan. He got both of them to pop up. Then he got Dan Driessen to ground out to finish off a 1-2-3 inning.

At the 16:20 mark on the tape you can hear the NBC announcers, Curt Gowdy and Tony Kubek describe the shadow problem on the field due to the late afternoon start. A shadow is cast between the pitcher's mound and the batter's box making it more difficult for hitters to pick up the ball. This was a concern all week with the 4pm starting time that was dictated by NBC.

At the 18:24 mark you can see Mets centerfielder Don Hahn have a pathetic strikeout. The Mets are in a quandary in the postseason with the centerfield position. Hahn, a good fielder offers nothing at the plate. While Willie Mays has 2 broken ribs and a chronically sore shoulder.

Hahn's strikeout was the 2nd out of the inning. With no one on base, Bud Harrelson drew a walk.

At the 19:25 mark I enjoyed hearing the great fielding Tony Kubek say that Harrelson may be the best fielding shortstop in baseball.

This brought up Seaver. Many times this year Seaver has provided his own offense when the team wasn't hitting. And this proved to be yet another case.

Watch Seaver hit a double that rolls all the way to the outfield wall at the 21:50 mark. Harrelson scored on the hit and the Mets took a 1 - 0 lead.

In the bottom of the 2nd Seaver got into a bit of trouble when he gave up a double to Johnny Bench and walked Ken Griffey. But then he looked brilliant striking out the next 2 batters.

At the 27:17 mark watch as Kubek says Seaver's pitches are *just exploding.*

At the 28:20 mark watch as Seaver gets 2 swings and misses in a row.

Seaver looks like he is in his "terrific" form.

At 36:12, Seaver continues to pitch outstanding as he gets Rose and Morgan to both fly out again.

METS 1 REDS 0 - end of 3 innings

At 42:40 Cleon Jones loses a ball in the sun and Dan Driessen has a leadoff double that should have been a routine fly out.

Seaver then gets Perez to fly out and strikes out Bench and Griffey.

Watch at 44:25, as Seaver gets Bench to swing and miss 3 times!

At 47:50, NBC does a great slow-motion replay of Seaver's pitching form. He is putting on a clinic!

At 58:30, Seaver faces Rose in the 5th with a man on second and 2 outs. He gets Rose looking on a full count. Seaver has a shutout through 5 innings.

Meanwhile Billingham retires the Mets 1-2-3 in the top of the 6th. He has now retired 10 straight Mets. It's a classic pitching duel.

In the bottom of the 6th, Seaver gets Morgan to pop up. Rose and Morgan are now 0 for 6 against Seaver, which Seaver said was the key to the game.

Seaver then fools Dan Driessen badly at the 1:06:50 mark on the tape.

At 1:07:20, Seaver throws 2 vicious curves for strikes on Tony Perez and then gets a big swing and a miss for another strikeout. Seaver has 9Ks through 6 innings.

METS 1 REDS 0 - end of 6 innings

Billingham puts the Mets down in order in the 7th. He has now retired 13 consecutive Mets. And he hasn't allowed a hit since Seaver's double in the 2nd.

At 1:10:50 Don Hahn has another pathetic looking strikeout. The Mets are just not going to get much offense with a hitter like Hahn.

In the bottom of the 7th, Seaver gives up a single to Bench. But he strands him there and picks up 2 more strikeouts.

METS 1 REDS 0 - end of 7 innings

Billingham retires the Mets in order again in the 8th. It's his 5th consecutive 1-2-3 inning.

Jack Billingham has now retired 16 consecutive Mets batters.

THE BIZARRE STOPPAGE

In the bottom of the 8th there was a bizarre incident that I've never seen in a baseball game.

Seaver opened the inning by striking out Hal King. It was Seaver's 12th strike-out. He was having a truly magnificent game. And he needed just 5 more outs for the shutout.

Next up was Pete Rose. But at this point, Seaver informed the umpire that he had to go into the dugout to fix his shoe.

Watch at the 1:27:15 mark as Seaver is in the dugout working on his shoe.

Back on the field, Seaver gets Rose to a 2 and 2 count. Then he throws a belt high fastball inside. The pitch has no movement on it at all. Rose is tracking it all the way. And Pete Rose turns hard on it and crushes it over the right field fence.

Shutout gone.

Pete Rose who led the NL in hitting, but had only 5 home runs all season, has tied the game at 1 with a blast off baseball's best starting pitcher, who was in the midst of one of his greatest performances.

You can see the home run at the 1:29:25 mark on the tape.

The NBC announcers note that the ovation for Rose's home run is the longest they've ever seen in postseason play. The Reds fans just won't sit down.

Seaver recovered quickly. He struck out Joe Morgan on another vicious curve. And he got Driessen to fly out.

But the damage was done. The game was tied.

METS 1 REDS 1 - end of 8 innings

Pedro Borbon, one of the top relievers in baseball in 1973 with a 2.16 ERA came on to pitch the 9th for the Reds. Rusty Staub led off with a walk. But the Mets could do nothing after that.

The Mets have not had a hit since Seaver's double in the 2nd and have just 3 hits in the game.

Now Seaver comes back to the mound for the bottom of the 9th.

At this point, the video tape is unavailable. But you can continue to listen to the radio call from the Mets announcers on the same YouTube video.

Seaver gets the leadoff man Tony Perez to ground out. Next up is Johnny Bench. Bench has 2 of the 5 Reds hits off Seaver.

Bench hits a game winning home run.

Seaver loses 2 - 1.

The loss is crushing for the Mets.

Tom Seaver has just played one of the best games of his career. He struck out 13 Reds. He walked none. He had a shutout going into the 8th inning. He hit the only Mets extra base hit. He drove in the Mets only run. He had done almost everything he could.

Tom Seaver was terrific.

And he still lost.

Now the Mets are in a big hole. They have lost with their best pitcher, and they will need to win 3 of 4 to take the series. And they will have to do that against the Big Red Machine that can smell a World Series title that they've been so close to snaring over the past 3 seasons.

After the game, Seaver was distraught. He wouldn't talk to reporters for quite a while. Finally, beer in hand, he tried to explain the 2 pitches that lost the game.

In a special to the New York Times, Seaver said *"Rose hit a pretty good pitch... above his waist, a fastball inside, a good pitch... Bench hit a nothing pitch. Nothing on it... It was supposed to be a fastball, but there didn't seem to be much on it."*

Seaver was asked if he got tired. *"I didn't feel like I was tired. But I might have been."*

When told he had 13 strikeouts Seaver replied, *"I had a good fastball, but big deal, we lost 2 to 1."*

A reporter asked him, *"Were you ever better for 7 innings?"* If you watch the game, it's a great question, because I thought Seaver looked incredible. I can't recall seeing so many swings and misses against a top hitting ball club. It was Tom Seaver in his prime (he's 28) and at his best.

Seaver, ever the competitor, replied to the compliment, ***"What difference does it make. If it was a 7 inning game I would have won 1 - 0."***

Game 1 is in the books. It's a sad story for the Mets.

The Sports Time Traveler™ will continue following the NL Championship Series.

Chapter Ninety

1973 NLCS Game 2 - Matlack vs. The Reds

Jon Matlack pitches his first post season game

INTRODUCTION From The Sports Time Traveler™

The Mets lost game 1 of the 1973 NLCS in a heartbreaker 2 - 1. Johnny Bench's home run in the bottom of the 9th won the game for the Reds in front of their home town fans.

The dramatic homer wiped out a championship series strikeout record performance by Tom Seaver who had whiffed 13 Reds, and held a 1 - 0 lead going into the 8th inning.

Game 2 would now be a critical one for the Mets as this is just a best of 5 game series. Going into a 2 - 0 hole against the Reds, the team with the top record in baseball, would pretty much spell the end of the Mets season, way too fast, after they had won the division title in a miraculous finish less than a week ago.

Going to the mound for the Mets on this day was 23 year old Jon Matlack, the 1972 Rookie-of-the-Year, a season ago, who would be pitching in his 1st post season game.

The lineup he would have to face was just plain scary.

The first 4 batters all either reached, or should be in, the Hall of Fame:

Pete Rose

Joe Morgan

Tony Perez

Johnny Bench

All 4 of them had been in the top 10 in the MVP voting in 1973.

Of course I had to travel back in time virtually to Cincinnati in 1973 to experience this game.

The impossible dream of a last place team at the end of August reaching the World Series was now in peril. And the big, young lefty, Matlack, now held in his hands, the hopes of all Mets fans from across the vast New York area.

RIVERFRONT STADIUM, CINCINNATI - October 8, 1973

I'm here in Cincinnati in 1973, virtually, for game 2 of the National League Championship Series between the 99 win Cincinnati "Big Red Machine" and the 82 win New York Mets.

It's Jon Matlack of the Mets vs. Don Gullett of the Reds.

Early in the season, Matlack was struck on the forehead by a line drive that fractured his skull. While he only missed a brief time recovering, his pitching form didn't return to his Rookie-of-the-Year level until late in the season. In his last 14 starts since the All-Star break he's had a 7 - 4 record with a 2.85 ERA and in September he reduced his ERA to 2.43 over 6 starts.

But all the stats mean nothing now. Matlack was headed out to pitch his first ever playoff game.

The Reds starter Don Gullett is a formidable pitcher. He had a record of 18 - 8 with 4 shutouts.

You can listen to the entire game with the New York Mets radio announcers at this link below. You'll hear Ralph Kiner call the first 3 innings, Lindsey Nelson call the middle 3 innings and Bob Murphy call the last 3:

https://www.youtube.com/watch?v=KBHIgwiDTvk

You can also find this broadcast by entering this search term on YouTube: 1973 10 07 NY Mets vs Reds NLCS Game 2 Complete Radio Broadcast.

Here's my account of the game.

The Mets went down in order in the top of the 1st.

Now Matlack had to face the Reds.

He got off to a great start as he struck out Pete Rose. And then he got Joe Morgan and Tony Perez on easy outs.

And the pitching duel was on.

The score was nothing to nothing through 3 innings.

Matlack had allowed just 1 baserunner on a single by Andy Kosco. Gullett had allowed just 1 baserunner, a walk issued to Matlack.

In the top of the 4th, Rusty Staub came up for the 2nd time. In the 1st inning, Staub had hit a Gullett pitch to the warning track. Now he hit a towering high fly that went just a little further. It cleared the fence to give the Mets a 1 - 0 lead.

Meanwhile, Matlack wasn't giving an inch to any of the Reds famous sluggers. In the bottom of the 4th he notched his 2nd 1-2-3 inning of the game. This time the names were Morgan, Perez and Bench.

In the bottom of the 5th there was a scare for Matlack. Andy Kosco, the veteran right fielder, who was a strong hitter at .280, but not one of the fearsome Reds near the top of the order, hit a deep fly ball down the line that just hooked foul. Reds manager, Sparky Anderson, raced out to dispute the umpire's decision, believing it had been a home run. But on the radio call of the game, Lindsey Nelson explained that from his vantage point in the press box, he had a perfect line on the ball, and it was clearly foul.

Spared of having the game tied at 1, Matlack ended up issuing a walk to Kosco. Kosco then reached 2nd base when Darrel Chaney walked. But Matlack got out of the inning when he struck out pinch hitter, Phil Gagliano, for his 5th K of the game.

The Mets were now stymied by another pitcher. Reliever Clay Carroll got the Mets in order in the 6th and 7th and didn't allow a hit in the 8th.

Matlack, was also not allowing any hits, except for the one by Kosco. When Andy got his 2nd single in the 7th, putting him on base for the 3rd time, it ended a streak of 17 Reds batters without a hit.

At this point Jon Matlack did the same thing Tom Seaver did yesterday. He left the pitching mound and walked into the Mets dugout in the middle of the game. Yesterday Seaver had to fix a problem with his shoe. On this day, Matlack needed attention to a blister that had formed on his pitching hand. Although I could only listen to the call on the radio, it was incredible to hear of the same unusual time out in 2 consecutive games and at about the same point in the game. Even more unusual was that Matlack was allowed to throw a warm-up pitch when he came back on the field.

With the blister fixed, Matlack didn't allow Kosco past first base. And after 7 innings the score was the exact same as it had been the day before.

METS 1 REDS 0 - end of 7 innings

Phil Pepe of the New York Daily News wrote, *"It was like a television rerun. The Mets were leading, 1 to 0, just like Saturday, and the Reds were coming to bat in the 8th."*

And Pete Rose, the man who tied Saturday's game in the bottom of the 8th by belting a home run off Tom Seaver, was coming to the plate.

Matlack got him to ground out. Rose was now 0 for 4. And Jon Matlack was through 8 innings holding on to a 1 - 0 lead.

The Mets had now played 17 innings in this series and their batters had gotten only 5 hits, including just 2 in this game.

The Mets just don't make it easy on their pitchers.

To begin the 9th inning, the Reds brought in reliever Tom Hall. Hall got the leadoff batter, Wayne Garrett to ground out. Then Felix Millan became the 1st Mets batter since the 5th inning to get a base hit when he singled. Hall then walked Rusty Staub and gave up a run scoring single by Cleon Jones.

With the Mets up 2 - 0 now and still only 1 out, Sparky Anderson decided to bring in his best stopper, Pedro Borbon. But Borbon couldn't contain the suddenly prolific Mets batters. Singles ensued by bottom of the line up players Jerry Grote, Don Hahn and Bud Harrelson in succession, and the New York Mets opened up a 5 - 0 lead.

Unlike Tom Seaver who had to provide his own offense yesterday in losing 2 - 1 (the 1 run coming on a Seaver double), Jon Matlack was now the beneficiary of an envious 5 run lead going into the bottom of the 9th.

But he had to face the heart of the Reds lineup. He got Joe Morgan to fly to Hahn in center. Then Tony Perez flied to Staub in right. Now it was up to Johnny Bench - the 2-time MVP who hit the game winning home run the day before. Matlack struck him out. It was his 9th strikeout of the game.

Game over.

Mets win 5 - 0.

Mets radio announcer Bob Murphy exclaimed, *"A brilliant 2 hit shutout."*

A minute later, Murphy, who has been calling Mets games since the beginning, in 1962, told the audience that Matlack had given up only 2 hits, both of them to Andy Kosco, and allowed only 2 men to reach second base, with neither of them getting there via hits.

The top of the Reds order, Rose, Morgan, Perez and Bench had gone a combined 0 for 16. None of them had reached based.

Matlack had pitched a masterpiece.

Excited about Matlack's performance, Murphy proclaimed, *"This is the most brilliant game of his career."*

Jon Matlack had done it. He had pulled the Mets back to even in the National League Championship Series. Once again, the Mets had come back from the depths after losing game 1.

"The miracle lives. The believers still believe," wrote Phil Pepe in the New York Daily News.

Jon Matlack's picture appeared on the front page of the New York Times getting a kiss from his wife after finishing his 2-hit shutout of the Big Red Machine.

The same picture appeared on the front page of The New York Daily News.

Matlack had just made himself into a Mets legend.

Now the series heads to New York, with no day off. All of the rest of this 5 game series will take place at Shea Stadium.

Jerry Koosman, the man who won both of his starts in the 1969 World Series, including the decisive game 5, will pitch for the Mets tomorrow.

I can't wait!

CHAPTER NINETY-ONE

The Mighty Mets Machine

BUD HARRELSON AND PETE ROSE RUMBLE IN THE BIGGEST FIGHT IN THE HISTORY OF SHEA STADIUM

NOTE From The Sports Time Traveler™

It's time for game 3 of the 1973 NLCS.

This will be the 1st time I've experienced this entire game.

On Monday, October 8, 1973, when the game actually took place, I was in a 5th grade classroom in Warnsdorfer elementary school in New Jersey. All of the league championship games in 1973 were day games.

After school, the game was still going on. But I had a dentist appointment. In the dentist chair I was listening to the game. And on the ride home I heard the fight.

When I got home I raced into the house, turned on the TV and saw the pleas from Willie Mays to the fans to calm down. It was one of 2 indelible impressions of Willie Mays pouring his heart out for the Mets in the 1973 post season. It is one of the most enduring images I have of Willie Mays, who was now a true blue & orange Mets believer.

Naturally, I had to go back and experience the entire game.

Although there is no videotape of the entire game that is publicly available, we do have something very precious - the tape of the live radio broadcast by the New York Mets announcers.

This morning I listened to the entire game - for the 1st time, on 50 year tape delay.

What an incredible and surreal experience. It's surreal because even after 50 years, I still can't believe my last place Mets from the long summer of '73 were playing the Big Red Machine for the NL pennant.

Here's my story from 50 years ago. The byline as always is based on the day the story ran in the newspapers.

SHEA STADIUM - October 9, 1973

I've traveled back in time, virtually, 50 years to the Mets 1st home game of this 1973 National League Championship series which is tied at 1 game apiece.

You can experience the entire game as I did at this link:

https://www.youtube.com/watch?v=2T6Xypd6CHM&t

You can also find it by searching on YouTube for 1973 10 08 Mets vs Reds NLCS Game 3.

Here's the highlights:

Jerry Koosman was on the mound for the Mets to start the game. For the 3rd straight day the Mets starting pitchers got the Reds 1-2-3 in the 1st inning.

In the bottom of the 1st, the lefty Reds pitcher Ross Grimsley, got 2 quick outs and then faced the left handed hitting Rusty Staub.

Staub homered. And the Mets took a 1 - 0 lead for the 3rd consecutive game.

You can hear the call on Staub's homer at the 21:15 mark on the audio above.

Kooz got the Reds in order in the 2nd.

In the bottom of the inning, the Mets loaded the bases with 1 out on a walk and 2 singles. Wayne Garrett then drove in a run with a sacrifice fly. And Felix Millan hit a single to drive in another run.

The Mets were up 3 - 0.

At this point on the audio, at about the 48:20 mark, you can hear Mets announcer Bob Murphy comment on the "Ya Gotta Believe" signs that fans were holding in Shea Stadium.

Immediately after that on the tape, Murphy makes the call as Rusty Staub blasts a 3 run homer that hits the auxiliary scoreboard in right field.

The Mets now lead 6 - 0 in the 2nd inning.

Staub has 3 home runs, all against lefties in his last 5 at bats across 8 innings of play in the series.

Rusty Staub had finished the season on a tear with 7 hits in last 10 at bats against the Cubs last week and a 15 game hitting streak. For the full month of September he had batted .307 with 16 RBIs. After 2 full seasons the Mets finally had the Rusty player they had traded for prior to the 1972 season.

And Staub has helped transform the Mets. The weak hitting Mets, who had just 5 hits and 2 runs in the first 17 innings of this series, suddenly have scored 10 runs in the last 3 innings going back to their 4 run burst in the 9th inning of game 2.

METS 6 REDS 0 - end of 2 innings

You can see both of Staub's home runs at this link:

https://www.youtube.com/watch?v=ALuExrO8iF8

Or you can search for it on YouTube by typing this into the search bar: Staub homers twice in Game 3 of the '73 NLCS.

In the top of the 3rd Kooz got into trouble. The Reds Denis Menke, playing for the 1st time in the series, led off with a home run.

Kooz got an out, but then gave up 3 consecutive singles, the last of which drove in a run.

The Big Red Machine was coming back. The score was now 6 - 2, there was only 1 out, 2 runners on base and Tony Perez and Johnny Bench were coming up, the Reds 2 biggest sluggers. A home run would put the tying run at the plate. You can lose a 6 run lead fast against the Machine.

But Kooz was clutch and he got Perez to fly out and Bench to hit a grounder and he got out of the inning with a 4 run lead at 6 - 2.

In the bottom of the 3rd, at the 1:17:10 mark on the tape, Kooz comes to bat. In the tradition of what seems to be BYOB for the Mets pitchers (bring your own bat), Kooz singles and drives in a run to pad his lead to 7 - 2.

And in the bottom of the 4th the Mets got 2 more runs to make it a 9 - 2 game. The Mets have now scored 13 runs in their last 5 innings of play.

METS 9 REDS 2 - end of 4 innings

In the top of the 5th, Kooz struck out pinch hitter Roger Nelson to open the inning and then Pete Rose got a single.

You can watch what happened next on this short video:

https://www.youtube.com/watch?v=k8xKLnO4hOs

You can search for that video in YouTube with this phrase: NLCS Gm3: Harrelson and Rose scuffle at second base.

At the 1:51:40 mark on the audio tape (from further above), you can also listen to the Mets radio broadcast of the fight between the bantam weight Bud Harrelson and the light heavyweight Pete Rose.

The Fans Put the Game in Jeopardy

At the 2:04:50 mark on the audio tape, the Mets are up for the bottom of the 5th, when fans start throwing bottles at Pete Rose in left field. Rose leaves the field and then Sparky Anderson pulls his whole team off.

This is a crisis. National League President Chuck Feeney, Commissioner Bowie Kuhn and the umpires all meet.

A Possible Forfeit

There is real concern that if the fans don't calm down, the Mets could forfeit the game, even though they are leading 9 - 2.

The Mets giant scoreboard in right centerfield posted this message, *"Interfering with a game can lead to a forfeit. If we must lose let us be beaten by our rivals rather than by our fans. Keep the game in play for fair play."*

At the 2 hours and 7 minute mark on the audio tape you can hear the umpire address the crowd on the PA system indicating the game will not resume until order is restored.

Bob Murphy then describes how Tom Seaver, Cleon Jones, Rusty Staub and Willie Mays are going out to left field to attempt to get the fans to calm down and stop throwing bottles and debris on the field.

This is the first time since his farewell 2 weeks earlier that Willie Mays is on the field in a Mets uniform in Shea Stadium.

NOTE From The Sports Time Traveler™

By this time in real life in 1973, I was home from the dentist office, and I witnessed the incredible value that Willie Mays provided to the Mets that day.

I'll never forget seeing him pleading with the fans in left field.

The fans listened to Willie. They stopped throwing stuff on the field.

There would be no forfeit.

On the tape at the 2 hour and 10 minute mark, Mets announcer Bob Murphy says this will be the big story of the game for a long time to come.

Well, Bob, wherever you are, it's been 50 years and we're still talking about this game and this incident. Thanks for all you did for the Mets.

After Willie Mays, and the Mets other stars, got the fans to calm down, the game resumed.

At the 2:36:37 mark on the audio tape, Bud Harrelson comes to the plate and gets a huge ovation and then has a verbal spat with catcher Johnny Bench.

The game is comparatively dull after that. There was no more scoring in the game.

But at the 2:44:40 mark, Don Hahn loses a ball in the sun and Johnny Bench gets a double.

It doesn't make a difference. The Mets win it 9 - 2.

Jerry Koosman has pitched a complete game victory with 9 strikeouts. He allowed just 4 hits and no runs in the final 6 innings.

Mets pitchers have now held the Reds to 4 runs in 3 games. They have struck out 31 Reds batters.

And most remarkably, the Mets have not had to use the bullpen.

Seaver, Matlack and Koosman have done all the pitching.

The New York Mets are now up 2 games to 1 over the Cincinnati Big Red Machine.

With their 13 run outburst in 5 innings, from the 9th inning of game 2 to the 4th inning of game 3, combined with diminutive Bud Harrelson holding his own in the brawl with Pete Rose, perhaps it's time to call New York the Mighty Mets Machine.

CHAPTER NINETY-TWO

The Last Place Team That Could

GAME 4 OF THE 1973 NLCS IS A CHANCE FOR THE METS TO WIN THE PENNANT

NOTE From The Sports Time Traveler™

Right now I'm completely "METS-merized," as I'm re-living the experience of my youth when I first followed the 1973 version of the Miracle Mets 50 years ago.

I've now reached game 4 of the National League Championship Series and the Mets lead the best of 5 series 2 games to 1.

The 2 to 1 lead means that the Mets, a team that had been in last place in the NL East on the final day of August, less than 6 weeks earlier, could win the National League Pennant with one more win.

It has the makings of one of the greatest stories in the history of American professional sports.

I'm also eerily facing the same day in, day out anguish that I did, exactly 50 years ago, as Israel was at war then and is at war now and facing another existential crisis.

I had not bargained for this "re-living" of the 1973 Mets season to become so real.

As I write this I have just learned a cousin-in-law, 83 year old Oded Lifshitz and his wife Yocheved, are 2 of the hostages taken by Hamas on October 7ᵗʰ.

Wikipedia states that Oded and his wife are, *"peace activists who worked for Israeli organization, On the Way to Recovery, which helps aid Palestinian citizens in need of medical care in getting transportation to Israeli hospitals across the border."*

UPDATE: As of the writing of this draft of the book in the summer of 2024, Yocheved has been released, but Oded is one of the over 100 hostages that still remain in Gaza.

And now my report on game 4 of the 1973 National League Championship series.

SHEA STADIUM - October 10, 1973

Shea Stadium was rocking yesterday. I was in attendance virtually and I listened to the live radio broadcast of the game.

Below is the link to the live radio broadcast featuring the Mets announcers if you would like to have the incredible experience I did:

https://www.youtube.com/watch?v=jfMHcda0_GA

You can also access this tape on YouTube by typing in this search term: 1973 10 09 NY Mets vs Reds NLCS Game 4.

Here are the highlights:

The Mets came into the game leading the series 2 games to 1 due to stellar starting pitching and suddenly heroic hitting.

Mets starters Tom Seaver, Jon Matlack and Jerry Koosman had all pitched complete games. They collectively allowed just 4 runs and struck out 31. And

Mets hitters, who were silent for most of the first 17 innings of the series, in which they amassed just 5 hits and 1 run, managed to score 13 runs in a 5 inning stretch from the 9th inning of game 2 through the 4th inning of game 3.

And because of that, the Mets came to the ballpark today with a chance to be the National League Champions with a victory at Shea.

At the beginning of game 4, one of the Mets announcers said that Pete Rose, who instigated the fight with Bud Harrelson in game 3, entered Shea Stadium from centerfield from to escape the wrath of the Mets fans. Rose told them that now he knows how Nixon feels.

Mets starter George Stone made Rose feel even worse when he got Rose to hit a little grounder right back to him for the easy out to open the game. Then Stone got Joe Morgan and Tony Perez to ground out too.

For the 4th consecutive game, the Mets starting pitchers had gotten the fearsome first 3 batters of the Big Red Machine to go down in order in the opening frame.

The game quickly became a pitchers' duel with Stone and Reds starter Fred Norman combining to retire the game's first 15 batters.

In the bottom of the 3rd, Mets centerfielder Don Hahn broke the ice with a walk. George Stone then became the latest Mets pitcher to supply his own offense when he also drew a walk. And a couple of minutes later the Mets scored the first run when Felix Millan singled, driving in Don Hahn.

For the 4th consecutive game the Mets took a 1 - 0 lead.

And the game stayed that way through 5 innings.

In the top of the 6th with 1 out, Sparky Anderson sent in pinch hitter Larry Stahl to bat for the pitcher Norman. Stahl hit a long drive into the right field corner. Rusty Staub raced to the wall and made a sensational overhead one handed grab just before bracing himself against the fence.

The catch helped Stone collect his 5th 1-2-3 inning.

METS 1 REDS 0 - end of 6 innings

In the top of the 7th, Tony Perez came up with 1 out. Perez was 0 for 14 in the series. But he teed off on a Stone pitch for a home run to tie the game at 1.

Yogi Berra decided it was time to bring in his first relief pitcher of the series. Tug McGraw entered the game having not seen action since the final game of the season 8 days earlier.

At the 1 hour and 13 minute mark on the audio tape of the game you can hear the huge ovation for George Stone as he leaves the game.

As McGraw warms up, Mets announcer Bob Murphy says on the tape at 1:13:40 that McGraw was the one who sounded the battle cry, *"You Gotta' Believe,"* when the Mets were still in last place.

McGraw got out of the 7th inning easily. And he had a 1-2-3 inning in the 8th.

METS 1 REDS 1 - end of 8 innings

But Tug ran into trouble in the top of the 9th. Pete Rose led off with a single. Joe Morgan tried to bunt Rose over to second, and ended up reaching first base safely when Tug couldn't field the bunt.

Now McGraw had runners on first and second and no outs.

He got Tony Perez to pop up for out number 1. But then he walked Johnny Bench to load the bases.

Tug got Andy Kosco to strikeout. And then he had to face Denis Menke, who had homered off Koosman in game 3. Tug got Menke to pop up.

He was out of the inning.

On the tape you can hear the crowd roar at 1 hour and 39 minutes when Tug gets out of the jam.

The game was going to the bottom of the 9th tied at 1.

Now the Mets, in last place 40 days ago, stood on the precipice of a pennant which they would possess if they could score a run.

At 1 hour and 40 minutes on the tape, I got chills as I listened to Bob Murphy say, *"Now the Mets can win the National League Championship."*

At 1:41:30 on the tape, Felix Millan singles bringing up Rusty Staub. An extra base hit by Staub would win the pennant.

But Yogi Berra called on Staub to bunt.

I was stunned listening to the tape.

Staub is the Mets leading RBI man. He had hit 2 home runs in game 3. And Berra is asking him to bunt?

Staub's bunt attempts resulted in a 2 strike count. Now he had to swing away. But behind on the count he struck out.

Then Cleon Jones and John Milner didn't hit the ball out of the infield and the game went to extra innings.

Tug McGraw came out to pitch the 10th, his 4th inning of relief. And he got into trouble again. Again the bases were loaded. This time he got Tony Perez to fly out to Staub in right field to end the scare. You can hear the roar of the crowd at 1 hour and 59 minutes after Staub ends the inning.

Once again the Mets came to bat in the bottom of the 10th needing 1 run to win the pennant. But Grote, Hahn and Harrelson went down in order.

In the 11th, it was right back to another jam for Tug, who was now pitching his 5th inning in relief. He gave up 1 out singles to Andy Kosco and Denis Menke. Tug struck out Cesar Geronimo and that brought up the dangerous Dan Driessen.

At the 2 hour and 11 minute mark on the audio you can hear Bob Murphy on the call - it's a classic.

"The pitch to Dan Driessen. And a fly ball hit deep to right, way back, Staub going back, going back, he's got it! ... Rusty Staub made a magnificent catch, crashed into the wall, fell back, but he held on to the ball. And the side is retired. Staub is on his feet. Listen to the roar. They are standing and cheering and roaring for Rusty Staub. No runs. Middle of the 11th game tied 1 - 1."

At this point on the audio tape the broadcast changes to a new set of announcers that I don't recognize. At the 2:12:20 mark these announcers continue to praise Rusty Staub's sensational overhead catch and crash into the wall, *"He knew he was going to crash into the fence. In 1969, we saw Agee and Swoboda make great plays, none of them involved simply running head first into a wall like we saw right there."*

Watch Staub's 2 great catches in the game on this video. The one in the 11th inning is the 2nd of the 2 catches:

https://www.youtube.com/watch?v=_HV4bBdhKfI

You can also see this on YouTube by typing in this search: Staub's two fantastic catches in Game 4 of the NLCS.

NOTE From The Sports Time Traveler™

In my opinion, the 11th inning catch and crash by Rusty Staub was the moment that forever endeared Mets fans to Staub who was forever after one of most beloved Mets players in franchise history.

The game marched on to the bottom of the 11th inning. McGraw finally came out of the game for a relief pitcher. Tug had had his troubles, but he didn't allow a single run in 5 innings of work.

Unfortunately the Mets couldn't get a run either in the bottom of the 11th, and the game went to a 12th inning.

In the top of the 12th the Mets brought in Harry Parker, only the Mets 6th pitcher to take the mound in the 4 games.

Parker got leadoff batter Ken Griffey to fly out. Next up was Pete Rose, the villain of game 3. Rose got one back on the Mets crowd, who had booed him all game. He took Harry Parker deep for a home run to give the Reds a 2 - 1 lead. It was Rose's 2nd clutch home run of the series (he had hit one in the 8th inning of game 1 to tie it up), after he had only hit 5 homers all year.

Parker didn't allow another hit, getting Perez to fly out and Bench to pop up. But the damage was done.

REDS 2 METS 1 - middle of the 12th inning

Sparky Anderson still had his best reliever available, Pedro Borbon, and he brought him in to pitch to the heart of the Mets order in the bottom of the 12th. Staub led off. With a sore shoulder, Staub flew out. Then Cleon Jones did the same. It was now up to the Hammer, John Milner. But he grounded out.

The game was over. The Mets had lost a chance to go to the World Series.

The Cincinnati Reds, the heavily favored Big Red Machine, had now tied the series at 2 games each.

The next game would be a winner takes all affair for the National League Championship.

The Mets who were riding high after their 13 run barrage in 5 innings, now have a problem. They've reverted back to their non-hitting norm. They have just 3 hits and have scored just 1 run in their last 16 innings of play. The 3 hits were all singles (2 by Felix Millan). And the Mets last 12 batters in this game went down consecutively in the 9th through 12th innings yesterday.

They have another problem. Tom Seaver will be pitching on just 3 days rest. And Seaver faltered several times on 3 days rest at the end of season.

This time it will be the biggest game of Seaver's life. He's never pitched a must win game.

Game 5 will be epic.

I can't wait!

CHAPTER NINETY-THREE

The "A–MAYS-in" Mets & Russ Hodges Reincarnated

THE 1973 NLCS COMES DOWN TO A WINNER TAKES ALL GAME 5

BACKGROUND

I have made a personal discovery about the magical feeling of sports radio broadcasts. They seem timeless. They have the ability to transport your mind to another age and almost convince you that you're actually there.

This was the experience I had this past week.

The video tape of games 2 - 5 of the 1973 NLCS are not publicly available. However, the original Mets radio broadcasts are up on YouTube.

I originally was not looking forward to just listening to 4 entire baseball games. But I knew it was the only way to have the virtual experience of these games.

In the current era we live in, in the 2020s, we are accustomed to experiencing sports on giant TV screens enriched with a perpetual barrage of statistics, graphics and in-depth analysis in addition to constant updates on other games and other sports. It's almost impossible to focus on the actual game itself.

As I listened to the Mets games from 1973, I realized that nothing in my journey as The Sports Time Traveler™ had been as close to transporting my mind back in time as this experience. Nothing else had let me feel totally immersed in the games as though they were actually taking place now.

The voices of the Mets radio broadcasters, Bob Murphy, Ralph Kiner and Lindsey Nelson, the original 3 Mets broadcasters, brought back the familiar sounds of my childhood when these three men were almost like uncles to me as they were the broadcasters for every New York Mets game on TV on channel 9 WOR in New York, which was how I had "gotten to know them" when I was a kid.

And the fact that the Mets announcers focused solely on the game helped as well. When there was down time they told stories related to the game instead of streaming endlessly sterile stats. And these broadcasters were fans of the Mets themselves, so there was a folksy feeling that we're following the contests together.

The radio broadcast of game 5 of the 1973 NCLS was the most epic experience I've had yet as The Sports Time Traveler™ and I can't wait to share it with you.

NEW YORK – October 11, 1973

Yesterday, I was back in Shea Stadium for the decisive winner-takes-all game 5 of the 1973 National League Championship Series between the New York Mets and the Cincinnati Reds.

It's all tied at 2 games to 2.

For this Reds team, it's the biggest game they've played in since they lost game 7 of the 1972 World Series last year.

For the Mets it's the first time they've ever played in an elimination game. In 1969, they only lost 1 game in the entire post season when they cruised to the World Series title in their only prior franchise playoff appearance.

I experienced game 5 of the 1973 NLCS via the radio broadcast and you can too at this link:

https://www.youtube.com/watch?v=VgAKtAEtLk4&t

Or you can find the radio broadcast via this search on YouTube: 1973 10 10 NY Mets vs Reds NLCS Game 5.

Here's my account of the game:

Prior to the game we learned that Rusty Staub would not be able to play. He severely bruised his shoulder when he ran at full speed into the right field wall making his sensational 11th inning catch that saved 1 and possibly 2 runs in game 4.

Staub has all 3 Mets home runs in the series.

This is a huge blow for the Mets hopes.

Replacing Staub in the outfield is Ed Kranepool, the only original Mets player from 1962, the first year of the Mets existence. Kranepool batted just .239 and hit only 1 home run in 1973.

At the beginning of the radio broadcast, you can hear the Mets theme song. Listening to this not only brought back great memories for me, it got me pumped up for this win or go home contest.

Immediately after the song, you hear Bob Murphy setting the stage, ***"Today's game is for the National League Championship."***

Those words, spoken by the man who I had listened to in nearly every Mets game I had watched in the 1970s, sounded totally surreal.

How was it that these Mets, "my Mets," were playing for the National League Championship? These Mets were the epitome of mediocrity. They had been mired in the cellar for most of the summer of '73. They had one of the worst offenses in the game. And yet Bob Murphy just said, *"Today's game is for the National League Championship."*

Even 50 years later, it was just mind boggling.

Taking the mound for the Mets was Tom Seaver, the Franchise. Seaver was easily the best starting pitcher in baseball in 1973. He led a Mets pitching staff that was held in high regard by everyone. It was the Mets pitching that had the team in this position to be a game away from the National League Title.

But there was a major question mark hovering around Tom Seaver. He had been experiencing a sore shoulder and he was clearly off over the past 3 weeks since Yogi Berra had started pitching him on just 3 days rest down the stretch in the regular season.

Seaver had pitched poorly in 3 of his final 4 games in the regular season, and after pitching 7 strong innings in the series opener, he gave up 2 home runs including the game winner to Johnny Bench. The Bench homer came on a pitch that Seaver admitted had *"nothing on it."*

Now Seaver was again pitching on just 3 day's rest.

But there was no choice for manager Yogi Berra. Seaver was their ace, and you have to live or die with your ace in this type of game. Seaver himself was eager for the opportunity. This was quite clearly the most important game of his career. For back in 1969, the Mets were never in such a critical position as this when Seaver was starting.

Seaver faced Pete Rose to open the game. The last time he had faced Rose, in the 8th inning of game 1, Rose had hit the home run that tied the game which Seaver would eventually lose.

This time Seaver got Rose to ground out. And thus the Mets got Rose out to leadoff in every game of the series.

The Mets had also gotten the 2nd batter, Joe Morgan, out in each of the first 4 games of the series. But this time Seaver allowed Morgan to get on with a walk.

Now the Big Red Machine went to work. Dan Driessen singled. And a moment later, pitching too carefully to the powerful Tony Perez, Seaver, the master of control, threw a wild pitch and let the count get to 3 - 0 on Perez.

A nervous quiet enveloped Shea Stadium.

Seaver, their top pitcher, was already appearing shaky as he had men on second and third with just 1 out in the 1st. This already didn't look like the typical Tom, who blew the ball by batters and maintained zeroes on the scoreboard deep into games.

In the bullpen the Mets had Ray Sadecki start warming up. This was almost certainly the first time this season, maybe the first time this decade, that a Mets reliever started to warm up in the 1st inning with Tom Seaver on the mound.

Seaver then collected himself. He threw 5 straight strikes to Perez, getting the count to 3 and 2, as Perez fouled off several pitches before Seaver finally got him to miss for a strikeout.

It was a big out, but it was only out number 2.

Up came Johnny Bench, the 1970 and 1972 MVP, who had hit the game winning blast in the opener off Seaver.

The Mets decided to give Bench first base, thus loading the bases for a force out and taking away the threat of a 3 run homer that might have put the Mets in a deficit from which their bats might never recover.

This brought up the rookie Ken Griffey.

Seaver got Griffey to fly out.

No runs scored.

It was already a sit-on-the-edge of your seat type game, and it was just the middle of the 1st inning.

In the Mets half of the inning, Reds starter Jack Billingham got leadoff batter Wayne Garrett to ground out. But the Mets next 3 hitters got to Billingham for 2 singles and a walk, and the Mets had their own threat going with the bases loaded and just 1 out.

This brought up Ed Kranepool for his first postseason plate appearance since the 8th inning of game 3 of the 1969 World Series. In that time at bat, in the only game he played in that series, he homered.

Now he was up with a chance to be a hero again.

At the 23:50 mark on the audio tape below, you will hear pandemonium as Kranepool comes through. Bob Murphy yells, *"a line shot to left field."*

It's a 2 run single for the original Met.

For the 5th straight game the Mets have scored first.

The next significant moment on the audio is at 30:35, when the broadcast is interrupted for a breaking news announcement. Vice President of the United States, Spiro Agnew, has resigned.

Back to the action on the field, Seaver gets the bottom of the Reds lineup in order in the 2nd, but he is not pitching like Tom Terrific.

In the top of the 3rd, Morgan doubles and Driessen drives him in on a sacrifice fly.

Seaver gives up another double in the 4th before getting out the inning.

Uncharacteristically, Seaver has just 2 strikeouts in his first 2 times through the Reds order. But he still has the Mets in the lead.

METS 2 REDS 1 - end of 4 innings

The 5th inning of game 5 turned out to be the most eventful of the series.

At the 1 hour and 5 minute mark on the audio you will hear another official announcement as a newscaster breaks into the game to let us know that former Vice President Agnew has pleaded no contest to tax evasion.

Seaver then gives up his 3rd double in 3 innings as Pete Rose is safe on second to start the 5th. A few minutes later Rose scores as Tony Perez drives him in with a single.

The game is tied.

Ray Sadecki again starts warming up in the bullpen.

But Seaver shuts down any hopes of a big Reds inning when he gets Bench on a pop up.

Seaver is again out of a jam and still has just 2 strikeouts through 5.

In the bottom of the 5th, Billingham opens just like Seaver did in the top of the inning, allowing a leadoff double to the Mets leadoff hitter Wayne Garrett.

Next up is the Mets crafty batter, Felix Millan. With the game tied, the weak hitting Mets are just trying to manufacture a run and Millan bunts to try and move Garrett to third base.

Just before the 1 hour and 16 minute mark on the audio, listen as the Reds rookie third baseman, Dan Driessen, makes a monumental mental error. Covering third base, he receives the throw on the fielded bunt in plenty of time to catch the lead runner Garrett. But Driessen doesn't apply the tag. He apparently thought it was a force play, which it was not. And Garrett is safe at third, Millan is safe at first and there are no outs.

The next batter is Cleon Jones. Jones had finished the season with a flurry, driving in 14 runs in the final 10 games. And he came through again with a double that scored Garrett.

Next to the plate comes John Milner, the Mets leading home run hitter with 23 this year. The Reds decide to walk Milner to avoid his big bat and set up a possible double play.

A Magical Mets Moment to Remember

At the 1:21:45 mark on the audio tape comes a magical Mets moment. If you listen to nothing else, listen to this.

The bases are loaded with Mets and there are still no outs. The Mets are ahead by a slim margin, 3 – 2 in this do or die game.

Lefty hitter Ed Kranepool is due up to bat.

Suddenly the crowd goes wild. The noise is not for Kranepool however.

Bob Murphy says, ***"Listen to the roar. Kranepool is being called back. It's Willie Mays!"***

Yogi Berra is sending right handed batter Willie Mays to the plate to hit against the lefty Don Gullett who has replaced Billingham.

Mays has not been in a game in over a month. His last time on field was September 9th in Montreal. In that game he started at first base and giving it everything he had, he crashed into metal railing in front of the dugout racing to catch a fly ball. Mays had fractured 2 ribs from which he is still not fully recovered.

Sparky Anderson counters the move by bringing in righty Clay Carroll.

Now Mays is at the plate and Bob Murphy said, ***"The Mets have a glorious opportunity."***

Lindsey Nelson says, ***"This is the biggest moment in Mets history because in 1969 they never had to play with anything on the line."***

At 1:24:30 Mays comes through. He hits a ***"Baltimore chop down the 3rd base line."***

It's an infield hit that just stays fair and Millan scores.

Nelson says this is ***"a moment to remember in sports history in New York."***

It's 4 - 2 Mets.

Mays hit leads to 2 more hits and the "Say Hey Kid" scores on a Bud Harrelson single.

The Mets are up by 4 after 5 innings of play and Tom Seaver is still pitching.

Willie Mays has helped the Mets break open the game.

METS 6 REDS 2 - end of 5 innings

At 1:33:30 on the audio tape, Willie Mays is playing centerfield for the first time since August 25th. He makes a catch to close out a 1-2-3 inning for Seaver, his first one since the 2nd inning, and the crowd noise is unbelievable.

At 1:36:10 Seaver comes to the plate. He continues his strong hitting and gets a double.

At 1:40:45 on the tape, Seaver scores on a Cleon Jones single.

METS 7 REDS 2 - end of 6 innings

At 1:51:50 Seaver gets a standing ovation as he comes to bat again in the 7th.

It's beginning to seem like a festive atmosphere at Shea as the Mets are only 6 outs away from the title.

METS 7 REDS 2 - end of 7 innings

At 2:04:50 Mays comes up to bat and there is another roar.

Mays flies out, but the Mets are still up by 5 runs.

Imagine how Willie Mays must feel.

He thought his playing days were over.

He had in fact retired.

He had his farewell celebration on this same field 2 weeks ago.

And now he has been responsible for 2 of the Mets runs that gave them the lead in this decisive game.

And he is back in the field playing his old position in center.

METS 7 REDS 2 - end of 8 innings

The Mets are now just 3 outs away from the National League Championship and Tom Seaver is still pitching.

Although Seaver has only managed 4 strikeouts, he has only allowed 1 baserunner in the past 3 innings. It's only the 3rd time all year that Seaver has pitched into the 9th inning with 4 or less strikeouts.

At 2:08:30 on the tape, Cesar Geronimo lines out to Milner at 1st base.

There is 1 out in the 9th.

Next up Larry Stahl singles.

At the 2 hour and 15 minute mark on the tape several fans come onto the field. There is still only 1 out.

Tom Seaver has to plead with the fans to stay off the field.

Lindsey Nelson describes how 2 old ladies, who had come out of the stands onto the field, were being escorted by police officers into the Mets bullpen. Nelson says, *"I've never seen that before."*

More fans come on to the field.

At 2:17:40 Nelson describes how 2 blonde women have gotten into the Reds dugout.

There is some concern, like there was in the game 3 melee, that the Mets could forfeit the contest if they can't get the fans under control.

But the game is finally able to resume.

Seaver walks pinch hitter Hal King and then he walks Pete Rose.

The bases are loaded. There is just 1 out.

The Big Red Machine is poised for a rally.

It's time for Tug

Berra removes Seaver who admits he was tired. And it's going to be up to Tug McGraw to save the game.

McGraw pitches to Joe Morgan and the count runs to 2 - 1. A walk would score a run and then the 3, 4 and 5 hitters would be coming up.

It could be catastrophic.

But Tug gets Morgan on a pop fly and there are now 2 outs.

The next batter is Dan Driessen.

At 2:26:45, Nelson sets the stage for the radio listeners.

It's a moment that gives me chills even though I'm listening on a 50 year tape delay.

"The Mets were in last place, they were 13 games below .500 on August 17th, now they are 1 out away from the National League Championship."

The count goes to 2 strikes.

Here's the next pitch:

It's a grounder to Milner deep behind 1st base.

In the most fitting moment possible for this miracle to finish, it's Tug McGraw who gets the flip from Milner and races to touch first base.

Tug is there in plenty of time.

He steps on the bag.

The Mets are the 1973 National League Champions.

At 2:27:55 Lindsey Nelson chants repeatedly, *"The New York Mets have won the pennant. The New York Mets have won the pennant. The New York Mets have won the pennant."*

Nelson must have been thinking of the famous call by Russ Hodges 22 years earlier when he maniacally screamed, *"The Giants win the pennant,"* over and over after Bobby Thomson hit the shot heard round the world to beat the Dodgers 5 - 4 at the Polo Grounds.

In that game, Willie Mays was on deck. He was a scared rookie. But he was also a National League Champion.

Now Willie Mays was running in from centerfield, trying to avoid being mobbed by the fans, as he is ending his career as a National League Champion again.

Nelson says, *"It's a mad scene. Fans are pouring out onto the field. They're digging up home plate. They're on top of the dugout."*

On the scoreboard there is a message, *"Guess who is National League Champion... Would you believe the NY Mets. Well you better believe."*

This morning the front page of the New York Times story on the game started with this, *"The New York Mets completed their 6 week odyssey from last place to the National League pennant yesterday."*

It's one of the great stories in American professional sports history.

50 years later I still find it hard to believe. But you've got to believe. Because it actually did happen.

And it happened in stunning fashion. The Mets outscored the Big Red Machine 23 - 8 in the series.

Mets pitchers combined for a 1.33 ERA across the 5 games.

On page 61 of the New York Times was a story about the city of New York's instant celebration. *"Sirens went off on 5th avenue. Bus drivers on Queens boulevard blew their horns. Tabloids were shredded and dropped from East side apartment windows... shouts of 'you gotta believe' filled the air."*

On page 62, Willie Mays was asked about being on the field in both 1951 and 1973 for the National League titles. *"When Thomson hit* **(in 1951)** *I was on deck and scared to death. Today I was hoping to be up when something was happening... I like the pressure."*

He might get to feel the pressure at least one more time because the New York Mets are going to the 1973 World Series!

I've got to write that again - The New York Mets are going to the 1973 World Series.

I can't wait!

CHAPTER NINETY-FOUR

Oddities & Errors in Oakland

THE OPENING GAME OF THE 1973 WORLD SERIES COULDN'T HAVE HAD MORE STRANGER THINGS

BACKGROUND From The Sports Time Traveler™

Fifty years ago this week I felt like I was living in a dream. The most surreal thing was taking place. The New York Mets were in the World Series.

I found this hard to fathom. I couldn't comprehend it when the Mets were introduced as the National League Champions at the start of NBC's World Series broadcast.

I repeatedly had this feeling that we're not supposed to be here.

Decades later when I read Stephen King's novel titled, 11/22/1963, a story about time travel, in which the "yellow card man" repeatedly tells the time traveler, *"you're not supposed to be here,"* I could relate to that line very well.

I still to this day feel like someone played a "MET-a-physical" trick in space-time to put the Mets in the 1973 World Series. It's like Tug McGraw knew something nobody else did when he kept chanting, *"Ya Gotta Believe!"*

After all, the team I had followed so closely the prior 2 summers were more deserving of the nickname the "Mediocre Mets" than the "Miracle Mets."

1972 and 1973, when I was 8 and 9 years old, was the prime time of my childhood. In June, July and August, I was at the golden moment to be a baseball fan, when nothing else in the world matters more than your team. And in those summer months over 2 seasons, my team, the Mets, had won just 75 games and lost 96.

And yet now my Mets were in the World Series. Unbelievable!

I was now getting to experience what I had missed in 1969 because I was too young to be a Mets fan in the year of the Miracle.

And now that we were here I wanted desperately for us to win.

Of course, I had to get in the Sports Time Travel machine and travel back 50 years to experience the 1973 World Series again.

Below is my story of game 1, written as though I had just read the newspaper account of the game the day after it was played.

OAKLAND, CALIFORNIA - WORLD SERIES GAME 1 - October 14, 1973

Yesterday was game 1 of the 1973 World Series pitting the Miracle New York Mets against the defending 1972 World Series champion Oakland A's.

PRE-GAME ANALYSIS

The Mets got here by getting hot, winning 24 of their last 33 games to go from last place to first place in the NL East and then defeating the team with baseball's best record, the Cincinnati Big Red Machine, 3 games to 2 for the National League pennant.

The A's got off to a slow start to the season too, but took over the lead in the AL West in late June and spent nearly the entire summer in 1st place. They had the division comfortably locked up in mid-September and cruised home winning just 4 of their last 11 games, yet still finishing with a 6 game lead.

The A's scored 758 runs, the most in the American League. And they had a deep pitching staff with three 20 game winners. Their top pitchers were among the most famous and feared in baseball: Catfish Hunter, Vida Blue, Ken Holtzman and Rollie Fingers. They also had great team speed finishing 2nd in stolen bases. And they had Reggie. Reggie Jackson had just completed an MVP worthy season with 32 HRs and 117 RBIs.

The Mets meanwhile lived solely on pitching. Their batters were 2nd to last in average and last in slugging percentage during the season. And their baserunners were 2nd to last in steals and last in stolen base %.

But the Mets pitchers were some of the most highly regarded in baseball. Tom Seaver had been perhaps the best starting pitcher in both leagues. Jon Matlack and Jerry Koosman, who both had ups and downs over the course of the season, had pitched stellar down the stretch and in the NLCS. And their reliever Tug McGraw was becoming a legend for both his on field performance, a 0.57 ERA in his final 14 appearances of the season, as well as his clubhouse leadership. It was Tug McGraw's maniacal chants of, *"Ya Gotta Believe,"* that more than anything else had willed the Mets from the cellar to the pennant.

The Oakland A's were favored. Jimmy the Greek set the odds at 13 - 10. But in New York they believed in the Mets after what they had seen over the past 6 weeks. Phil Pepe in the New York Daily News predicted the Mets in 6 games in yesterday's paper.

SPECIAL SECTION About Ted Kubiak of the Oakland A's

I return to the present time for this special section on Ted Kubiak.

In 1973, Kubiak was not one of the Oakland A's players that was a household name like Reggie Jackson, Catfish Hunter or Rollie Fingers. But Kubiak was one of just 13 A's players to appear in both the 1972 and 1973 World Series.

Ted played professional baseball for 16 years including 10 years in the majors. He was on all 3 of the Oakland A's World Series championship teams. He then spent several decades as an instructor and a minor league manager. And he is the author of 2 books on baseball.

On the A's World Series teams he was a utility infielder, often used in defensive situations late in games.

Sportswriter Mike Hall of the Berkeley Gazette wrote an article on July 11, 1974 in which he called Kubiak, *"possibly the best fielding shortstop in the American League."*

Tony La Russa, the hall of famer manager, and a former A's player, once said this about Ted Kubiak:

"I always thought Kubiak was the most valuable player on that team (Oakland A's) because he could fill in for Dick Green at second, or Campy Campaneris at short, or Sal Bando at third, and the team would go on winning."

TED KUBIAK - FAMILY FRIEND

Ted Kubiak is also friend of my family.

He grew up in Highland Park, NJ, where my family lived before I was born. One of Ted Kubiak's best friends in high school was my cousin Alan, and they stayed in touch when Ted became a major league baseball player.

When I was 10 years old in the summer of 1974, and my cousin Alan lived in the Boston area, we traveled to New England to visit. Alan took us to Fenway Park to see the Oakland A's play the Red Sox. And I got to meet Ted Kubiak on the field. He gave me a baseball signed by all the A's. What a thrill this was.

Before going into the Sports Time Travel machine to experience the 1973 World Series again, I asked Ted whether the Oakland A's players thought they could repeat as champions in 1973.

Ted said, *"It was just an ongoing mindset that you go out there and you win. The defense was good. The pitching was excellent. And we had just enough to always come out ahead."*

Then I asked Ted if the A's players preferred playing the Mets or the Reds in the World Series. He replied, *"I never thought about that. We had no say over that. You want to just get in there yourself. Who the opponent is, who cares? We'll deal with it when it happens. I don't remember ever thinking I'd rather play the Mets instead of the Reds. It didn't matter to me."*

Now back to 1973.

THE WORLD SERIES BEGINS

You can watch the entire game 1 of the 1973 World Series on YouTube at the link below as I did yesterday.

https://www.youtube.com/watch?v=h2Q9nnV7tU8&t

You can also find the tape by entering this search in YouTube: 1973 World Series Game 1 OAKLAND 10/13/73.

Here's my commentary on the game.

At the 5:40 mark Willie Mays is introduced to a standing ovation. Mays played for 14 years across the bay in San Francisco and still lives in the area.

The standing ovation goes on for quite a long time. It is remarkable considering he is a player on the opposing team. It's a fitting way for Willie Mays to have his farewell from baseball.

Willie Mays is starting in centerfield because Rusty Staub is out, and Don Hahn, the Mets starting center fielder in the NLCS is covering right field.

Staub's shoulder is still too sore from his crash into the fence in game 4 of the NLCS and he can't swing the bat to Yogi Berra's satisfaction.

This is a surreal situation. Mays had retired from baseball and had not played at all from September 9th, when he cracked 2 ribs in a game, until the final game of the NLCS 4 days ago, in which he drove in the run that broke open the deciding game. And now he's starting in the World Series.

The A's are missing an outfielder as well. Center fielder Bill North is injured. Reggie Jackson is starting in centerfield for the 1st time all season. This is also Reggie's first ever World Series game as he missed the entire 1972 World Series with an injury.

At the 13 minute mark the national anthem is sung by "Gomer Pyle," actor Jim Nabors.

At 14:50 on the tape, Hank Aaron throws out the ceremonial 1st pitch. This is the first time that an active player has ever thrown out the 1st pitch in a World Series.

At 19:53 Willie Mays comes to the plate with 2 outs in the top of the 1st. It is May first appearance in a World Series game since 1962. None of the other players in the starting lineups for either team was playing in the major leagues in 1962, while Willie played in his first World Series 22 years ago, in his rookie year of 1951.

Facing Ken Holtzman, a 21 game winner with a 2.97 ERA and 4 shutouts, Willie Mays has a great at bat. He hits a long foul down the right field line. Then he runs the count to 3 and 2. And on the next pitch he slams a hard grounder between short and third for a base hit. It's the first hit of the 1973 World Series. Mays is now 2 for 4 in the post season.

Willie Mays single turns out to be the only hit by either club in the opening 2 innings.

Holtzman and Mets starter Jon Matlack are shutting down the batters on a day in which it is exceedingly difficult to see the ball.

In the bottom of the 1st, at 26:35 on the tape, Bud Harrelson makes a spectacular catch on a Joe Rudi liner. Harrelson had to race behind second base and leap to grab the ball.

NO DESIGNATED HITTER

Here is another oddity of this World Series. Even though the American League has adopted the designated hitter here in 1973, and played with the DH all season, there will be no DH in the World Series.

This should be an advantage for the Mets as most of the A's pitchers, including today's starter Ken Holtzman, have not come to the plate all season.

At the 48 minute mark on the tape, Holtzman comes to bat with Dick Green on first base having reached on a walk to become the A's first baserunner of the series. Holtzman tries to move the runner up by bunting, but his attempt is laughable as the ball skies up and out of play behind home plate.

Holtzman tries to bunt again and misses. But Dick Green was running on the play and Mets catcher Jerry Grote fires him out at 2nd.

Now Holtzman can swing away with 2 outs and nobody on. He looks at a curve and a fastball both of which barely miss the strike zone. Holtzman looks again as Matlack throws one outside. With a full count the .158 career hitter fouls off a low fastball.

Matlack needs 1 strike against the pitcher Holtzman to get out of the inning. The next pitch is the 7th one of the at bat. It's another low fastball and Holtzman drills it. He hits a shot down the third base line for a double.

So much for the Mets advantage of the A's pitchers being required to bat.

The next batter is the leadoff hitter Bert Campaneris. Watch at the 52:40 mark as Campaneris hits a ground ball to the Mets Felix Millan at second base. It's a routine grounder and Millan is squarely in front of it and gets one knee down on the dirt.

But the ball rolls right between his legs and into centerfield.

Holtzman comes around to score.

The Mets should have been out of the inning. But now they're behind 1 - 0.

Campaneris, who had more steals in 1973 (34) than the entire New York Mets team (27), then steals second base and scores when Joe Rudi singles to right.

Both runs are unearned for Matlack, but that's of no solace to the Mets who are behind 2 - 0 after 3 innings.

A big picture of the Felix Millan error appeared on the front page of the Sunday New York Time this morning.

In the New York Daily News today, Felix Millan told Phil Pepe, *"I can't remember ever letting a ball go through my legs like that."*

Dick Green, the A's starting second baseman had an explanation about Millan's error that also appeared in the Daily News. He told Pepe, *"This is not a true infield. You have to battle every ground ball. We have an advantage playing here. We learn to be careful. I thought he should have charged the ball more. But he let it play him."*

TED KUBIAK'S ASSESSMENT of the Felix Millan Error

I interrupt this article to tell you that after I came back to 2023, I contacted Ted Kubiak to get his perspective, 50 years later, on the Felix Millan error.

I started out by letting Ted know that he can see himself being introduced on field at the 11:10 mark on the video tape.

Here's what Ted shared with me:

"Thanks for the memories, Len. When someone attempts to field a ground ball by going down on one knee as Millan almost did, I always felt they were unsure of themselves. That happens because the infielder has been, maybe not a little lazy getting to the right position but was just not as aggressive as he should have been to get "in front of" the ball properly. Basically, he just "misread" the ball. I remember thinking that as he maneuvered to field it.

There are a number of little maneuvers that go into fielding the different types of ground balls that affect the outcome: your aggressiveness, the angle you initially use, your speed, how you control your upper body and head....Millan never got those things into the play."

I then shared with Ted the quote from his teammate Dick Green from 50 years ago today. I asked Ted what he thought about Green's comment that, *"This is not a true infield."*

Here was Ted's reply:

"Interesting and Greenie is basically correct that he 'let the ball play him.' That's everyone's answer because no one has studied the movements like I have. And yes, the Oakland infield was horrible; it would break up into 'clumps' of crusty dirt, but all the infields were bad in those days. Not the rock quarries I played on in the minor leagues, but you had to battle them all in one way or another."

TED KUBIAK'S BOOK ON FIELDING

Ted recently wrote an instructional book for infielders titled, "How to Field a Ground Ball: An Ultimate Guide for Infielders."
  I thought the book was absolutely fascinating.
  You can order "How to Field a Ground Ball" on Amazon.
  Now back to game 1 of the 1973 World Series

A's 2 METS 0 - end of 3 innings

At the 1:03:40 mark on the video, John Milner comes to the plate with 1 out and Cleon Jones on second. Jones had doubled for the Mets 2nd hit of the game. Milner hits a single to short center and Reggie Jackson makes a terrible throw to the plate. Jones scores and the Mets are within a run at 2 - 1.

On the next pitch, Jerry Grote hits a long drive into deep left centerfield. Jackson races over and makes a spectacular catch on the run at the warning track to save a run.

THE WARM CALIFORNIA SUN

Jackson made that catch despite the great difficulty the outfielders are having seeing the ball. At the 1:12:45 mark, NBC play-by-play announcer Curt Gowdy begins to show the TV audience why. An outfield camera, from the left fielder's point of view, pans upwards to see the hazy sunshine.

Just as Gowdy is explaining this, Jesus Alou belts a long high drive to deep left field. Gowdy thinks the ball is going out, because Mets left fielder Cleon Jones does not appear to be trying to catch the ball. But Jones has lost the ball in the sun. Suddenly he sees the ball and makes a great catch in front of the wall. Gowdy and Tony Kubek speculate the ball must have been held up in the wind as they can't fathom that Jones simply couldn't see the ball at all.

A's long time announcer Monty Moore, who is in the booth with the NBC announcers, explains that the field in the Oakland Coliseum is actually 90 feet below sea level and wind was not the issue. He knows that Cleon Jones simply couldn't see the ball.

THE SUN PROBLEMS PERPETUATE

At the 1:20:20 mark on the tape, A's left fielder Joe Rudi completely loses a routine fly ball in the sun on a Felix Millan drive to left. Millan ends up on third base. But Willie Mays coming to the plate with 2 outs can't drive Millan home. Mays does have a strong at bat, running the count to 3 and 2 before flying out to right. It's Mays 3rd solid at bat.

At the 1 hour and 27 minute mark, Angel Mangual pinch hits for Holtzman. It's only the 5th inning and Holtzman would probably have stayed in the game if they were playing with the DH. This is an advantage for the Mets as Holtzman has allowed just 1 run on 4 hits through 5 innings.

Matlack gets Mangual to line out and then strikes out Campaneris to end the 5th.

A's 2 METS 1 - end of 5 innings

At the 1:38:30 mark Don Hahn strikes out, but the ball gets by catcher Ray Fosse and Hahn is safe at first. The Mets now have runners on first and third with 2 outs in the top of the 6th with the A's Rollie Fingers now pitching. Next up is Bud Harrelson and Fingers strikes him out to retire the side. Gowdy had brought up the famous 1941 passed ball by Mickey Owen of the Brooklyn Dodgers that enabled the Yankees to win a game and ultimately the World Series. But the passed ball didn't lead to a Mets run and they're still behind 2 - 1.

At the 1 hour and 42 minute mark on the tape, Joe Rudi explains why it's so hard for hitters to see during the World Series games, as the tarps on the outfield bleachers are removed and the bright clothing of the fans makes for a difficult back drop for batters.

In the top of the 7th, Yogi Berra had Ken Boswell pinch hit for Jon Matlack. Matlack left the game having pitched 6 innings with no earned runs. Combined with his shutout of the Reds in game 2 of the NLCS, Matlack has now pitched 15 innings in the post season without allowing an earned run.

Berra sends Tug McGraw to the mound for the bottom of the 7th. For Tug McGraw this is his first appearance in a World Series game. Despite being the Mets top bullpen man in 1969, he was never needed in the World Series that year.

At the 1:56:55 mark on the tape Curt Gowdy says, *I think it was McGraw that coined the Mets slogan, 'Ya Gotta Believe.'*

A MOST UNUSUAL PLAY

At the 2:07:25 mark on the tape is one of the most unusual plays I've ever seen. Campaneris bunts down the first base line. Milner fields the ball about 15 feet down the line towards home. Milner dives to tag Campy who is racing towards first base. Campy slides under Milner, then gets up and runs on to first base.

Neither the first base nor home plate umpire make a call initially.

And the announcers question whether Campaneris ran outside the baseline.

Slow motion replays show Campy stayed inside the line and that he slid under the tag.

But umpires in 1973 can't refer to the replay.

The umpires eventually called Campaneris safe.

Joe Rudi bunts Campy over to second, but McGraw is able to retire the side and completes 2 strong innings.

A's 2 METS 1 - end of 8 innings

In the top of the 9th, the Mets got a baserunner when Ron Hodges walked with 1 out.

The Mets then had the pitcher spot coming up and Yogi Berra initially sent Rusty Staub to the plate. But when the A's changed pitchers to bring in a lefty, Berra called Staub back and sent up Jim Beauchamp. He hit a pop fly to short and Dick Green made a great catch at the 2:20:35 mark. Then Wayne Garrett flied out to end the game.

The A's won it 2 - 1.

The Mets are down 1 game to 0 in the 1973 World Series.

Phil Pepe wrote in The New York Daily News this morning, *"Believers are reminded not to be of such little faith. A week ago they lost the 1st game of the National League playoff... also by the score of 2 - 1."*

Game 2 is today at 1pm PT / 4pm ET. It's Jerry Koosman vs. Vida Blue.

I can't wait!

CHAPTER NINETY-FIVE

The Last Heroics and Hiccups for Willie Mays

GAME 2 OF THE 1973 WORLD SERIES WAS PERHAPS THE ZANIEST IN HISTORY

OAKLAND, CA - October 15, 1973

The Sports Time Traveler™ was thrilled to be in northern California yesterday on a virtual trip back in time 50 years ago to experience the 2nd game of the 1973 World Series. No matter how many times I say it to myself, I still can't believe that the New York Mets are in the World Series.

Anyone who experienced this game will agree it deserves some type of qualifier not often associated with a World Series contest. Some that I've seen in the sports pages today include *"crazy," "embarrassing,"* and *"wild."* But my favorite was from Ron Drogo, in the Hackensack Record, who called it, *"The zaniest."*

Drogo opened his article on the game by writing, ***"Is this the World Series or the Ringling Bros. Circus."***

The weather was sensational for the fans.

But on the field the ball players were tormented by a hazy sunshine pervading the entire playing surface of the Oakland Coliseum.

Several of the A's players stressed how difficult the conditions were.

Left fielder Joe Rudi told the New York Times, *"The seeing out there is just terrible in the field, at bat, all over."*

The A's captain and third baseman, Sal Bando, told the Times, *"It's just a shame that World Series games have to be played under such conditions."*

And the A's superstar and MVP candidate, Reggie Jackson, said after the game, *"It's just really brutal. The ball that Cleon Jones hit I just never saw."*

Jackson was referring to a play in which he stumbled and fell flat on all fours while trying to field a fly to center by Jones. It was ruled a hit. But in normal conditions, Jackson would have certainly made the catch.

You can see this play at the 1:23:20 mark on the video tape of the game below.

https://www.youtube.com/watch?v=u5uwrvtMDFk&t

Or find it by searching on YouTube for, "1973 World Series Gm 2 New York Met's at Oakland A's."

Note that this video tape has most, but not the entirety, of game 2 of the 1973 World Series.

Here's my commentary on the game in case you don't have time to watch the entire video tape.

Just 2 minutes and 30 seconds into the tape you can see Joe Garagiola's pre-game show as Joe Rudi explains how he lost a ball in the sun in game 1. You can see a video of Rudi falling flat on the ground after he loses his footing trying to follow the ball's path.

Before the game began we learned that Rusty Staub was back in the lineup after missing game 1 due to his sore shoulder from his crash into the wall on his spectacular catch in game 4 of the NLCS. That's big for the Mets as they need Staub's bat. The Mets scored only 1 run in game 1 and Staub hit 3 homers in the NLCS. And those are the only homers for the Mets entire ball club in the 6 post season games so far this October.

With Staub in right field, Don Hahn returned to his normal position in centerfield and Willie Mays went back to the bench.

At the 30 minute mark on the tape it appears questionable how much help Staub will actually be able to provide the Mets. NBC's Tony Kubek explains Staub couldn't throw the ball at all in warm ups and then you see Staub ground out weakly to finish a 1-2-3 inning for A's starter Vida Blue, who won 20 games and threw 4 shutouts this season.

In the bottom of the 1st, Jerry Koosman took the mound for the Mets. Kooz has been clutch in the postseason. In 1969, he won both games he started in the World Series. And this year he beat the Reds in game 3 of the NLCS as he went the distance allowing the Big Red Machine just 2 runs.

But Kooz immediately got into trouble minutes into the game. At the 35:30 mark on the tape, Joe Rudi hits a high fly deep to left. The announcers clearly think it's gone as Cleon Jones just stands next to the left field wall. What the announcers don't know is that Jones has no idea where the ball is. He literally could not see the ball in the sun. The ball drops near his feet and Rudi winds up on second base. It is ruled a double.

On the very next pitch, Sal Bando drives a ball to right centerfield. Don Hahn misplays the ball and takes a long time getting to it allowing Bando to get all the way to third base.

Even if his outfielders had played perfectly, Kooz has been rocked by 2 long balls from the first 3 batters and the A's are up 1 - 0.

Kooz settles in and gets Reggie to strikeout. But he can't get out of the inning. He walks Gene Tenace and gives up another double to Jesus Alou. The A's are up 2 - 0 and already Ray Sadecki is warming up in the bullpen.

Kooz finally gets the side retired when he strikes out Dick Green.

At the 49:15 mark on the tape, the hot hitting Cleon Jones takes Vida Blue deep for a home run to pull the Mets within 1. Jones is now hitting .360 in 25 at bats in the post season.

In the bottom of the 2nd, the A's continue to pound the ball against Koosman. Bert Campaneris triples. And at the 57:35 mark you can see Joe Rudi drill a single up the middle to drive home the run and put the A's up 3 - 1.

The announcers question the defensive strategy of the Mets manager Yogi Berra who had ordered the infield to play in. The ground ball would have been an easy one to play with the infield at normal depth. Curt Gowdy says, *"There's an old saying that when you pull the infield in you make a .300 hitter a .400 hitter."*

In the top of the 3rd, watch at the 1:05:50 mark as Wayne Garrett homers to pull the Mets back within a run at 3 - 2. Garrett has hit .336 in his last 31 games.

At the 1:11:50 mark on the tape NBC shows a view from left field towards the infield which demonstrates how hard it is to see in the sunny haze. At the 1:12:20 mark, A's announcer Monty Moore explains that normally from that angle you could see the Oakland Hills outside the stadium, but in the haze they can't be seen at all.

In the bottom of the 3rd, Kooz loaded the bases and that was enough for Berra to go to the bullpen. Kooz is taken out of the game after just 2 and 1/3 innings for the veteran Ray Sadecki. Sadecki gets out of the jam and keeps the Mets just a run behind.

A's 3 METS 2 - end of 3 innings

At the 1:23:20 mark on the tape, Cleon Jones comes to the plate with 1 out and hits a soft fly to straightaway center. Reggie Jackson can't see the ball and falls flat on all fours as noted at the beginning of the article.

The fielding woes continue at the 1:27:20 mark when Jerry Grote hits a grounder that Sal Bando can't handle at third base and Mets are safe at first and second. But Blue gets Don Hahn out to end any threat.

The video tape then skips ahead to the top of the 6th with the score still 3 - 2 A's.

Vida Blue walks Cleon Jones and gives up a single to John Milner. This is enough for A's manager Dick Williams to take Vida Blue out and bring in Horacio Pina. Pina then hits the first batter he faces, Jerry Grote, and the Mets have the bases loaded for Don Hahn.

At the 1:40:20 mark on the tape, Hahn hits a slow roller towards third that Bando charges but misplays and Jones scores with the tying run.

Then at 1:42:30 with the bases still loaded with Mets, Bud Harrelson drills a single to right that drives in another run and the Mets are up 4 - 3. And that's all for Pina who leaves without getting anyone out.

But the next A's pitcher, Darold Knowles, can't do any better. He gets Mets pinch hitter Jim Beauchamp to hit an easy double play ball right back to him. But Knowles throws the ball away, 2 runs score, and the Mets are up 6 - 3.

METS 6 A's 3 - end of 6 innings

In the bottom of the 7th at the 1:57:30 mark, Tug McGraw is on the mound for the Mets. He hits Campaneris and walks Rudi and the A's have 2 on and 2 outs with Reggie at the plate. Jackson drills a ball into right field, but Staub can barely throw the ball, tossing it almost under handed, and the A's get a run.

In the top of the 9th at the 2:01:05 mark, Willie Mays has entered the game as a pinch runner after Rusty Staub singled. Staub apparently can't play any longer with his sore shoulder and is a liability in the outfield.

John Milner hits a hard grounder into right field and Mays stumbles, as he's looking to the right at the ball that has just shot past him, and trying to adjust his steps to reach the bag at second. He then misses second base and has to go back and hold on second.

Mays explained the stumble around second base to Jack Lang in the Jersey Journal, *"I missed the bag at 2nd. I remembered what Leo Durocher told me years ago. He said, 'Willie, when you miss the bag, stop and go back or you could run us out of a big inning.' I guess I was trying to watch*

*the ball at the same time. Was I embarrassed. Are you kidding? I've been
around too long to be embarrassed."*

NOTE From The Sports Time Traveler™

For decades after the game, Mays stumble on the basepaths has been
brought up as a sign that he was over the hill, washed up, tarnishing his
legacy and embarrassing himself on the field by playing in the World Series
at age 42.

But if you watch the slow motion replay and listen to A's announcer
Monty Moore, he explains that Mays found himself off stride to touch
second base after he had been looking at the ball, which shot right past
him. Mays tried to adjust his steps to touch second while making the turn
and skidded on the infield dirt.

Now let's recall what Ted Kubiak had to say about the Oakland infield
in the prior chapter, *"The Oakland infield was horrible; it would break
up into 'clumps' of crusty dirt."*

And think about this. This was just the second time Willie Mays ever
played a game in Oakland.

Given all the other mishaps to players who fell to the ground in this
game, including Reggie Jackson who was in his prime, it's simply ridiculous to belittle Mays for this play.

Now back to 1973.

In the bottom of the 9th inning at the 2:06:30 mark, Deron Johnson comes to
the plate for the A's who are still down 2 runs. He hits a soft fly into left centerfield.
Mays has a long run to get to the ball. He has to reach down to get it and he can't
grab it. The ball gets by Mays and Johnson is on with a leadoff double.

Curt Gowdy then pontificates that Willie Mays, *"can't seem to get his coor-
dination together today."* And Monty Moore says, *"This is the thing that*

all sports fans hate to see, a great one, playing in his last years, having this kind of trouble."

Gowdy does say that he thinks the sun bothered Willie but then sets the expectation that May should have easily caught the ball when he says, *"10 years ago he would have put that ball in his hip pocket underhanded with blindfolds on him."*

NOTE From The Sports Time Traveler™

This incident was also damaging to Mays legacy, but again I feel it was totally unwarranted. Watching the video, it was a tough play for anyone in any conditions. And we know that Jackson had lost a ball in similar fashion as reported above in this article.

Yet no one suggested Reggie Jackson was washed up.

Willie Mays had been unfairly criticized by the announcers.

Now back again to 1973.

Willie Mays told Jack Lang in today's Jersey Journal, *"I just lost Johnson's ball. I didn't even see it."*

The A's go on to tie the game in the bottom of the 9th at 6 - 6 as Reggie Jackson and Gene Tenace hit singles off McGraw.

And on this odd game goes to extra innings.

A's 6 METS 6 - end of 9 innings

At the 2:28:00 mark on the tape comes the signature play of the game and one of the most memorable moments in World Series history.

The Mets have Bud Harrelson on third base and Wayne Garrett on first with 1 out in the top of the 10th inning. Felix Millan is at the plate and Willie May is in the on deck circle.

Millan hits a high fly to shallow left field.

Joe Rudi catches is for the 2nd out and Bud Harrelson tags and races home.

Rudi's throw is in time, but it's up the third base line about 10 feet from home.

Harrelson comes barreling by and bends away from the catcher, Ray Fosse, eluding the tag and seemingly scoring the go ahead run.

But the home plate umpire Augie Donatelli calls Harrelson out to end the inning.

Willie Mays, who had maneuvered himself towards home plate from the on deck circle, had a better angle on the play than Donatelli, and he immediately drops to his knees to plead with Donatelli.

Yogi Berra then comes racing frantically out of the dugout to argue the call with Donatelli to no avail.

In the New York Times this morning, Dave Anderson wrote, *"Mays was the closest Met to the game's most controversial moment... Mays leaped in protest."*

Anderson then quotes Willie Mays on the play saying, *"I thought Fosse didn't tag him. I thought Buddy jumped over his glove."*

NOTE From The Sports Time Traveler™

The picture of Willie Mays on his knees pleading with the ump in vain is one of the greatest pictures in sports history in my opinion.

This enduring image of the legendary Willie Mays, on his knees, supplicating, begging the umpire to change his call, is a remarkable scene.

Here was a heroic figure at the highest rung of baseball royalty, a player revered as the greatest of his generation, a man who had long ago attained an almost mythical status in the minds of millions of baseball fans, and he was down on the ground, looking up, holding his arms in the air, appealing from the depths of his soul to the on field authority.

It was the most heartfelt possible show of support a player could provide for his teammates. Here was Willie Mays on the world stage, at his most humble, unashamed to display his emotions, unembarrassed to be seen with a pained, almost teary eyed expression.

I was already a Willie Mays fan before that moment, but after seeing it I became a Willie Mays fanatic forever.

Who wouldn't want that kind of man on your team no matter what age or condition he was in.

He had heart.

Here's another look at the play:

https://www.youtube.com/watch?v=RHNnoQg1ccA&t

You can also find it with this YouTube search, "1973 WS Gm2: Mets argue after Harrelson out at home."

Now back again to 1973.

Monty Moore recognized the historical nature of the moment and on the tape at 2:37:37 he says, *"I think that shot we have of Willie Mays down on his knees pleading with Donatelli is as dramatic a shot as I've ever seen."*

At the 2:39:35 mark on the tape the A's are up in the bottom of the 10th, with the game still tied at 6. There are 2 outs and Rollie Fingers is batting. He hits a fly into short centerfield. Mays comes dashing in a long way. He momentarily loses the ball in the sun, but he recovers and makes a great running catch.

A's 6 METS 6 - end of 10 innings

NOTE From The Sports Time Traveler™

In the 50 years since the game was played, I've never heard anyone comment on this catch by Mays to end the 10th inning. It was one of those typical Willie Mays plays in which he made a very difficult fly ball, especially under the horrifying conditions that day, look like a routine catch.

Back again to 1973.

At the 2:53:07 mark on the tape Willie Mays is up in the top of the 12th in a critical situation. The Mets have runners on second and third with 2 outs. They might not get another chance like this.

Mays is facing one of the best relief pitchers in the game. Rollie Fingers had an ERA of 1.92 this year. For Mays it's the only time in his entire 22 year career that he has come to the plate in extra innings in a World Series game with 2 outs and runners in scoring position. In addition, the Mets are in a must win situation. They can't fall behind 2 games to none against the defending World Champions.

Fingers throws an inside fastball and Mays hits a hard grounder over the mound and into centerfield driving in Bud Harrelson with the go ahead run.

Willie Mays has come through with the big hit the Mets needed.

At 2:53:35 on the tape John Milner hits a grounder that goes through the legs of A's 3rd string second baseman Mike Andrews. Tug McGraw and Willie Mays score. The Mets are up 9 - 6.

Andrews then makes a poor throw to first base on Jerry Grote's grounder and the error gives the Mets their 10th run of the game.

In the bottom of the 12th, Reggie Jackson leads off and hits a high fly at the 2:54:04 mark on the tape. Mays can't see the ball and it drops to the ground right next to him for a triple for Jackson.

Mays told the New York Daily News, *"The sun hit me right in the face. I couldn't see the ball at all... I might have caught Jackson's ball, but I didn't want to take the chance. In a close game I might have, but we were 4 runs ahead... we couldn't afford to lose another outfielder."*

Willie was referring to the fact that with Staub and Beauchamp out of the game the Mets couldn't afford to lose another outfielder if he got injured by the ball hitting him on the head.

Cleon Jones also explained that it was, *"The worst sun I've ever seen. An outfielder has no chance. You gotta know it's bad because if anybody can handle it you know Willie can."*

Jackson scored a few minutes later, when Mets pitcher George Stone, who took over after McGraw had gone 6 full innings, gave up a single to Jesus Alou. But Stone didn't give up another hit and the Mets closed out the win.

It was the longest game in World Series history up to this time, taking 4 hours and 13 minutes.

METS 10 A's 7 - FINAL SCORE

The World Series is now tied at one game all.

The game brought out the best in many of the men who make their living writing about the game.

Some focused on the comical aspects of this crazy contest. Ed Comerford in Newsday wrote, *"The longest day in World Series history seemed like a week at a film festival commemorating the Marx Brothers."*

Many focused on the heroics of Willie Mays who drove in the go ahead run.

Steve Jacobson in Newsday praised Willie Mays for, *"the ability to find - somewhere in the midst of almost total embarrassment - the spark to be great one more time. And win a World Series game with it."*

Jim Murray in the Los Angeles Times wrote, in his nationally syndicated column a flattering piece about the legend, *"William Howard Mays is to baseball what William Howard Taft was to 1910, what Oliver Wendell Holmes was to law, what the Archbishop of Canterbury is to the church. He is the French aristocracy, Charlemagne. He is the House of Lords. He is 42 years old, can't see too well and his feet hurt. But he knows commoners when he sees them. MAYS SENT an 0 and 1 fastball into centerfield. And that was the old ballgame."*

And Willie Mays got some headlines too.

The back page of the New York Daily News had a banner headline, *"Willie Mays bat foils A's."*

The top of the front page of the New York Times had the picture of Willie Mays hitting the single that drove home the go ahead run.

An impassioned Willie Mays told the New York Daily News, *"It's a helluva way to go out. I'm very excited. I guess I'm just an emotional guy, but I try not to show it on the field. A week ago I didn't think I'd be in a World Series. Now this."*

FINAL THOUGHTS From The Sports Time Traveler™

After experiencing this contest for the 2nd time, 50 years after I first watched it live, I'm of the opinion that a new branch of psychoanalysis could be devised that categorizes people by how they interpret Willie Mays' performance in game 2 of the 1973 World Series.

Did you think Willie Mays was a washed up "has been" or was he the hero of the game?

Did you think he was a man who selfishly couldn't admit his own fading skills or was he a man who selflessly sacrificed for the good of the team?

Did you focus on his hiccups or his heroics?

I chose the heroics.

By the way, Jimmy the Greek has revised his odds. He now rates the Mets 6 - 5 favorites to win the 1973 World Series.

Games 3 to 5 will take place in New York. They will be the first ever night games in a World Series in New York.

I can't wait!

CHAPTER NINETY-SIX

The Andrews Affair

1973 OAKLAND A's OWNER CHARLIE FINLEY "FIRED" SECOND BASEMAN MIKE ANDREWS AFTER GAME 2 OF THE 1973 WORLD SERIES

BACKGROUND From The Sports Time Traveler™

The final tumultuous 12th inning of game 2 of the 1973 World Series was filled with heroics, most notably Willie Mays' 2 out single to drive in the go ahead run for the Mets.

It was also filled with hiccups, most impactful were the 2 errors by the A's 3rd string second baseman, Mike Andrews. The Andrews errors led directly to 3 Mets insurance runs in New York's 10 - 7 victory which tied the series at 1 game apiece.

After the game a brouhaha developed that clouded the A's organization going into game 3.

The short story is that Oakland A's owner Charlie O. Finley tried to rid the team of Mike Andrews and the A's players revolted.

To get a full understanding of what happened requires some insight into the cohesiveness of the Oakland A's players.

To gain this understanding I called my friend Ted Kubiak recently.

Kubiak was a utility infielder on the A's. He was one of just 13 A's players to appear in both the 1972 and 1973 World Series. He had an important role as a back up to Dick Green at second base, Bert Campaneris at shortstop, and the team captain Sal Bando at third base.

Ted often entered games as a late inning defensive specialist as he did in the top of the 7th inning of game 2.

Kubiak was then taken out of the game in the bottom of the 8th when Mike Andrews pinch hit for him and took over playing second base in the field.

THE A's AS A FAMILY

In a recent interview, Ted Kubiak described to me how the A's players were like a big family.

"I spent 13 years in that organization. I grew up with a lot of those guys. We played together in the minor leagues, in winter ball instructional leagues. It was kind of like a family. We just had a reunion this summer and a fan asked who was the inspiration on the club? I said, 'Each guy individually was the leader. I knew they were individually going to take care of themselves and do the job.' "

"It was a special time for me to participate in that. They all feel like family to me."

Understanding how close the players felt to each other and how they had literally grown up together in professional baseball, it is easier to understand their reaction to Finley's rash move after game 2.

The Andrews Affair Summarized by Ted Kubiak

Here's how Ted Kubiak described the incident 50 years later in my interview with him:

"The game ends (game 2) *and we're getting on the plane and the plane's not taking off and we're wondering what's going on. And then the news starts coming in that Finley wants to get rid of Mike."*

"Then we go to New York and the next day we're working out and we all have an arm band on with Mike's number like he died. And the press was all over everything."

As Ted Kubiak indicates, The Mike Andrews story was the big news on the day off between games 2 and 3 of the 1973 World Series.

Ted piqued my interest so much about this incident that I just had to go back in time to experience it for myself.

Here's my report from the day off in between games 2 and 3 of the 1973 World Series.

NEW YORK - October 16, 1973

It's close to game time here at packed Shea Stadium for the 3rd contest of the 1973 World Series between the A's and the Mets.

It's a brisk night with the temperature at 56 degrees and expected to drop during the game.

It will be the first ever night game in a World Series in New York.

The teams' 2 aces will be on the mound - Catfish Hunter for the A's and Tom Seaver for the Mets.

But those are not the big stories this evening.

The big story is whether the A's will actually take the field.

There is some doubt because the players are boiling mad at A's owner Charlie O. Finley's decision to "fire" reserve second baseman Mike Andrews after his 2 errors in the 12th inning of game 2.

The Dubious Beginnings to the Affair

Ron Bergman of the Oakland Tribune reported yesterday that, *"The A's said a doctor's examination showed Andrews right shoulder was in no condition for him continue to play in the Series and he was sent home."*

However, Bergman also noted that when game 2 concluded, *"There was no announcement made after the game that Andrews was disabled."*

The injury story appears to have been a complete ruse engineered by Finley to replace Andrews on the roster in the middle of the series - effectively firing him.

A's pitcher Vida Blue told Bergman, *"I was in the training room when it happened. Andrews came in in a daze. He said, 'there's nothing wrong with me.' They took him into another room for a phone call. I can't believe he signed without any pressure."*

Blue was referring to a statement that Andrews was apparently forced to sign indicating that he was injured.

The Players Are at Near Mutiny in Their Response

Catfish Hunter told Bergman, *"This is bush horsemeat. That's the worst thing Finley can do. I can't believe that Mike would quit during a World Series."*

And Bergman also spoke to Reggie Jackson who described the A's players in a state of *"near mutiny"* over the Andrews situation. Jackson said, *"I've never seen the players more riled up over anything."*

Team captain, Sal Bando, told Bergman, *"Knowing Mike the way I do, I don't think we're getting the true story. It's a very low-class thing to be done, very non-professional."*

Finley appears to have recruited manager Dick Williams to go along with the injury ruse because Williams told Bergman on the plane ride to New York last night, *"Mike was really feeling down after the game. He was just thinking of the team, thinking that perhaps we could add another player if he left."*

That other player is Manny Trillo, a player that Finley had wanted to add to the roster prior to the World Series but was denied so by the commissioner's office.

In this morning's New York Times, Joseph Durso reported that A's union player representative, Reggie Jackson told him that removing Andrews from the team, *"It's grounds for a grievance."*

A Possible Boycott

Then Jackson told Durso, *"There could be a possibility of refusing to play."*

Durso then noted that later in the day Jackson walked back that statement saying, *"There are a bunch of guys who are close to that point."*

Durso also noted that during practice at Shea, *"The A's players stuck adhesive tape to their sleeves with the notation, 'No. 17,' and they said they did it, 'in memory of Mike Andrews.'"*

Charlie O Speaks

In the Jersey Journal this morning, Jack Lang reported that he spoke to Finley at the Americana hotel near midnight last night. Finley told him, *"We're not concerned about this."* Finley told Lang he would convene a team meeting before game 3. Finley said, *"There is no doubt in my mind the A's will be on the field a hootin' and a tootin' after the meeting."*

Lang indicated Finley admits some of his players are upset but doesn't expect a boycott.

Finley Lies

Regarding Mike Andrews, Finley told Lang, *"We invited him to come east with us for the series along with his wife. But he told us he would rather go to his home in Boston."*

But the Finley story doesn't add up as Lang noted that he saw Andrews' bags were in the Americana hotel even though Andrews himself was not on the plane.

Thus indicating Andrews was removed from the flight at the last minute by Finley.

The New York Daily News also noted that A's manager Dick Williams told them that he never ordered Andrews' shoulder to be examined. When they asked Williams who ordered the exam he replied, *"Maybe it was Mike himself, or maybe it was our owner."*

Boycott Now Seems Unlikely

Although the players are very upset, the prospect of a boycott seems unlikely.

Phil Pepe, in a rare joint article with Dick Young in the New York Daily News today, ran a headline that read, *"A's Cancel Mutiny for Love of Mike."* They quoted A's players saying they had decided to go ahead with the World Series, *"for the fans, for our families, for ourselves as men."*

They also noted that the, *"firing of Mike Andrews, considered a heartless act by the Oakland players, triggered a torrent of vitriol against their boss, and an overt act of hostility at their afternoon workout."*

The Daily News reporters spoke to Reggie Jackson yesterday who told them his side of the story, *"Jackson said he first realized something was up when he counted heads on the team bus enroute to the Oakland airport, 'Where's Andrews?' somebody said. Then everybody realized what had happened, and you should have heard the comments by the nucleus* (Jackson's term for the team's starting players).*"*

The bottom line is that Mike Andrews is no longer with the Oakland A's and the A's players will be playing game 3 of the World Series albeit with a heavy heart for their former teammate.

It will be Seaver vs. Catfish tonight.

I can't wait!

Thanks for reading.

CHAPTER NINETY-SEVEN

Kubiak in the Clutch

IN GAME 3 OF THE 1973 WORLD SERIES TED KUBIAK PLAYS THE THINKING MAN'S GAME

NEW YORK - October 17, 1973

The Sports Time Traveler™ was in Shea Stadium last night (virtually, of course) for the first World Series night game in New York history.

The series is tied 1 - 1 after the wild game 2 in Oakland in which the Mets won 10 - 7, scoring 5 unearned runs after Jerry Koosman was knocked out in the 3rd inning, and getting the go ahead run on a clutch single by Willie Mays.

Now instead of the blazing California sun, game 3 was being played in the cold and darkness of a night in Gotham.

Prior to the game the controversy over the Mike Andrews affair was still the big story dominating this World Series.

A's owner Charlie Finley, who had "fired" Andrews after game 2 and had said the day before he would preside over a team meeting, did not enter the clubhouse before the game. Instead, A's manager Dick Williams held a team meeting to inform his players of two things:

- Mike Andrews is back on the team, having been reinstated by commissioner Bowie Kuhn. Andrews told a UPI reporter by telephone that Finley had, *"threatened to destroy me in baseball and end my career,"* if he didn't falsely sign the statement, that his shoulder was injured, so that he could be removed from the team. Andrews is flying to New York today and will join the team for game 4.

- Williams told his players that he is leaving the A's after the World Series. Although he requested the players not leak this news, an AP reporter was informed, and the story ran nationwide this morning. There is speculation that Williams may have been complicit with the owner, Finley, in the Mike Andrews affair.

Reggie Jackson, the A's union player representative, has been particularly vocal with the press about the Andrews affair. He told Jack Lang in the Jersey Journal, *"I'm a marked man,"* and, *"I wouldn't mind being traded."*

Meanwhile 2 of the best starting pitchers in baseball were warming up for the game - Catfish Hunter for the A's and The Franchise, Tom Seaver, for the Mets.

Hunter, who only lost 5 games all season while winning 21, blanked the Orioles 3 - 0 in the decisive game 5 of the ALCS last Thursday to put the A's in the World Series for the 2nd year in a row.

Seaver was the winning pitcher in game 5 of the NLCS when he held the Big Red Machine to 1 earned run in 8 and 1/3 innings last Wednesday.

Both pitchers were now well rested for this contest.

Most of the game can be seen on this video tape.

https://www.youtube.com/watch?v=ZLN_UAjhc54

You can also find the video on YouTube with this search: 1973 World Series Game 3 NEW YORK 10/16/73.

Here's my recap of the game.

At 11:10 on the video the crowd roars as Seaver gets Bando to swing and miss on a beautiful curve ball for his first K of the game.

Seaver then gets Reggie to swing and miss at 2 over powering high fastballs. Then he strikes him out looking at a brilliant pitch that moved from the inside to the center of the plate.

After striking out Jackson, Seaver walks nonchalantly off the mound at the 13:10 mark, like it's just another day in his office.

In the bottom of the 1st, watch at the 14:20 mark as Wayne Garrett hits the 2nd pitch from Catfish Hunter down the right field line and just over the wall to put the Mets up 1 - 0.

Felix Millan then singles on a grounder through the left side of the infield and already John "Blue Moon" Odom is up throwing in the A's bullpen.

As Rusty Staub comes to the plate, Mets announcer Lindsey Nelson, who is in the booth with Curt Gowdy and Tony Kubek doing the play-by-play on NBC, informs us that Staub is still not swinging the bat normally due to his shoulder injury.

But at 17:45 Staub drills a single and the Mets have runners at first and third and still no outs.

At 19:20, Hunter throws a wild pitch and the Mets have their 2nd run.

Hunter faces 7 batters before he finally retires the side.

METS 2 A's 0 - end of 1st inning

At 25:25 on the video, Seaver picks up right where he left off as he blows his 1st pitch of the 2nd inning by Gene Tenace who swings and misses.

Seaver is looking fantastic.

Curt Gowdy informs the TV audience, *"he looks like he might be in for one of those overpowering games."*

A minute later Seaver strikes out Tenace.

Then at 28:30, he notches his 4th K on a called strike on the outside corner to Vic Davalillo.

Seaver's pitch placement is perfect.

At 29:05 Seaver's 1st pitch to Ray Fosse is a fantastic curve for another called strike. And at 30:20 he gets Fosse swinging.

Seaver now has 5 straight strikeouts.

He looks as good as he has in his entire career.

Tom Seaver is putting on a show on the world's biggest stage.

In the top of the 3rd, Dick Green grounds out to end Seaver's strikeout streak, 1 shy of the World Series record.

At the 40:20 mark, Catfish Hunter flies out to Don Hahn, Hunter's career batting average of .227 is just 2 points shy of Hahn's batting average of .229 this season.

The next batter is Bert Campaneris. At the 40:50 mark, Seaver's 1st pitch is a vicious curve for a swing and a miss.

Gowdy remarks, *"That's Seaver's best curve ball."*

But on a 1 - 2 count Seaver tries to get Campy with a heater over the middle and Campy hits it between first and second for the 2nd A's hit of the game.

Seaver strands Campy at first however to keep the A's scoreless through 3.

In the bottom of the 3rd the Mets get no hits and 1 walk and Catfish Hunter has settled into a groove.

METS 2 A's 0 - end of 3 innings

In the 4th, at the 52:20 mark, Reggie is up again.

It's power against power.

Watch at 52:35 as NBC shows the slow motion replay of Seaver's big breaking curve. Reggie swings wildly and misses for another strikeout.

Nelson remarks that Seaver is *"really sharp tonight."*

At 55:50, Seaver gets some help from his roommate on the road, shortstop Bud Harrelson, who makes a great pick up and throw to first on a grounder over the mound to end the inning.

In the bottom of the 4th, with Don Hahn on second base and no outs, there is a perfect strike thrown. But it's not by A's pitcher Catfish Hunter.

Watch at 1:00:50 as Reggie Jackson catches Bud Harrelson's fly to right and then guns the ball to Sal Bando at third base.

Watch it again at 1:01:20 on the slo-mo replay. It's as good a throw from right field to third base as any ever made by the late Roberto Clemente.

Gowdy describes Jackson's incredible strike from right field to 3rd base as a *"frozen rope."*

Jackson's throw holds Hahn at second and saved a run as Felix Millan singled a couple of minutes later and Hahn could not get past third. Catfish then holds the Mets in check again.

At 1:09:35, Seaver continues to show off his crushing curve as he strikes out Dick Green for his 7th K.

After striking out Catfish, Seaver pitches to Bert Campaneris at the 1:13:45 mark, and he gets him to swing and miss on an impossible curve that started in the strike zone and faded left and low.

Campy had no chance on that ball and Seaver has struck out the side. He has 9 Ks through 5 innings.

COMMENT From The Sports Time Traveler™

I spent my whole childhood watching Tom Seaver pitch and I never remember him being better than this. He's putting on a masterful display.

Seaver continues to get great back up support in the field in the 6th inning. At the 1:19:30 mark Don Hahn makes a leaping catch at the wall in centerfield to rob Joe Rudi of an extra base hit, if not a home run, as the ball appears it may have been over the top of the wall on the slow motion replay.

Hahn's catch is nearly as good as the famous one Joe Rudi made the year before in the 1972 World Series.

On the replay, Tony Kubek says, *"Hahn actually thought he was closer to the wall than he was when he was on the warning track."* As we will find out in a minute, this was a very perceptive comment by Kubek.

The long drive by Rudi is a first sign that Seaver is tiring. Watch at the 1:20:12 mark as Seaver's next pitch to Sal Bando goes completely wide of Jerry Grote and runs all the way to the back stop behind home. It's not a wild pitch however since no one is on base.

Then Seaver's next pitch is high and inside and Bando has to duck out of the way.

This is not typical Seaver control.

With the count at 3 and 1 on Bando, he belts a long ball to deep center. At the 1:21:25 mark watch as Hahn appears to be confused with the position of the ball and where he is in the outfield. The ball falls in for a double.

It's a critical mishap as Bando scores moments later on another double by Gene Tenace.

Seaver's lead is down to 1 run in the middle of the 6th.

Jack Lang in the Jersey Journal provided an extra insight about Hahn's play in centerfield on the long drive by Bando. Lang admonished the fans who had stormed the field after the Mets won the NLCS and destroyed the playing surface. Lang wrote, *"Maybe it was the fans' fault... because they needed extra sod to repair the damage to the rest of the field, the Mets' groundskeepers extended the warning track an extra 3 feet. They took some of the outfield sod and moved it to the infield... the extended warning track had (the Mets centerfielder) Hahn mixed up."*

METS 2 A's 1 - end of 6 innings

In the 7th inning, Seaver regroups, and at 1:36:30 he finishes a 1-2-3 inning by getting pinch hitter Deron Johnson, batting for Catfish Hunter, to strikeout looking.

But in the 8th inning, Seaver gets off to a rocky start. Bert Campaneris leads off with a single and steals second. Then at 1:49:15 Joe Rudi singles into right field. Rusty Staub, whose shoulder makes a normal throw impossible, flips a little underhanded ball back to the infield as Campy scores the tying run.

Seaver collects himself and gets the next 2 batters out and then at the 1:53:20 mark he gets Gene Tenace to swing and miss for his 12th strikeout.

Seaver Exits

In the bottom of the 8th, Seaver leaves the game for a pinch hitter.

It's a tough call for Yogi Berra to take your best pitcher out in a tie game in the World Series. But the consensus was that it was the right decision.

Joe Rudi told reporters after the game, *"Seaver was awfully tough, but he lost something off his fastball after the 5th inning."*

Jack Lang in the Jersey Journal, who has followed the Mets all season, wrote that Seaver, *"is the best pitcher in the National League, maybe the best in baseball, but after 8 innings in which he struck out a dozen batters, Seaver had to leave... he was tired, he was out of gas."*

Seaver himself told reporters that the cool night air had stiffened his arm. He also told Newsday, *"I wanted to keep pitching; I felt I was pitching well, but I didn't want to get myself to the point where I can't pitch for the rest of the series."*

Seaver was certainly well aware that Berra will be calling on him to pitch game 6 on 3 days rest on Saturday if the series goes back to Oakland. That must have impacted his decision to exit the game, as Seaver has struggled on 3 days rest in the past month when he was called on to do that several times.

The Mets didn't score in the 8th, so Seaver left without a decision. It's a shame because he pitched a great game. He gave up 7 hits, 1 walk and just 2 runs in 8 innings, while striking out 12 in a dominant display.

It's not Seaver's best game ever, but in parts of the game he looked as good as he's ever been. And it was awesome to watch what he did to one of the best hitting teams in baseball in one of the biggest games of his career.

The Mets Feel the Stress

At the 2:06:10 mark as Tug McGraw is warming up for his 3rd appearance in 3 games in the series, outfielder Cleon Jones is visibly showing the stress of this tie game as he gets sick in the outfield.

McGraw keeps the A's from scoring in the top of the 9th and now the Mets can win the game in the last of the 9th.

At 2:22:30 Rusty Staub is at the plate with 2 outs and no one on. The count is full and it's the 7th pitch to Staub. He drills one in the gap in left and it bounces over the fence for a ground rule double. The A's elect to walk Cleon Jones to enable a force out at third and John Milner comes to the plate.

At 2:25:50 there are 2 strikes to Milner, and he hits a blast to deep right. On the run, just shy of the warning track, Reggie Jackson spears the ball for the final out of the 9th.

Reggie Jackson has just saved the game for the A's. If the ball fell in, the Mets would have won the game 3 - 2 and taken a 2 games to 1 World Series lead.

METS 2 A's 2 - end of 9 innings

In the top of the 10th, McGraw allowed a runner to reach third and then got out of the jam.

In the bottom of the 10th the Mets again had a chance to win the game.

Willie Mays Has One More Opportunity

With Bud Harrelson on first base and McGraw due up, Yogi Berra sent up Willie Mays to pinch hit.

At the 2:39:35 mark on the tape, the video has cut out, but you can hear the crowd roar as Mays comes to the plate. An extra base hit would win the game.

But there are no more heroics for Mays who grounds out to end the 10th.

METS 2 A's 2 - end of 10 innings

In the top of the 11th the Mets sent Harry Parker to the mound. He gets the first batter out and then Ted Kubiak comes up.

Kubiak had entered the game to play second base in the 7th inning.

Kubiak draws a walk. He told Barry Levine of the New Brunswick Home News, *"Those pitches Parker threw me weren't even close."*

With 1 out and Kubiak on first base, Angel Mangual comes to bat.

At the 2:46:30 mark the video has come back and Mangual swings and misses at the 2 strike fastball down the middle.

It's a strikeout for out number 2.

But Jerry Grote, one of the finest defensive catchers in baseball, loses the ball. It rolls about 15 feet to the left of home.

Ted Kubiak alertly races to second base.

Kubiak had a good view of the pitch on the passed ball. He told Levine, *"The pitch that got by Grote appeared to move sharply on him and it surprised him. It was a perfect strike, but it just bounded off his glove."*

The memory of the famous passed ball by Mickey Owen in the 1941 World Series comes to mind again.

At 2:49:46 on the tape, Bert Campaneris lines a base hit about 10 feet over the head of the shortstop into shallow left centerfield.

Watch as Ted Kubiak gets a great jump on it and dashes from second base towards home.

Mets third baseman Wayne Garrett cuts off the throw to the plate and fires the ball to second as Campaneris is going for 2.

Campaneris is out at second for the 3rd out.

But running at full steam, Ted Kubiak crosses the plate just before Campy is called out.

The run counts.

The A's are ahead 3 - 2.

In the bottom of the 11th, Wayne Garrett led off with a single and got to second on Felix Millan's bunt. But Rusty Staub and Cleon Jones could not bring him home and the A's had escaped with a victory to take a 2 games to 1 lead.

A's 3 METS 2 - FINAL SCORE

Ted Kubiak told Barry Levine of the New Brunswick Home News, *"I've scored winning runs before during my career, but none were as important as this one."*

Kubiak also explained why he slid at the plate even though there was no play on him, *"Our scouting reports said that Grote is a master at faking a possible cutoff and then tagging a runner. I heard him yell to have the throw cutoff and I heard Joe (Rudi) yell to keep my feet, but the run was just too important to take any chances."*

For the A's it was good that Kubiak got the great jump, ran hard all the way and slid into home, because if Campaneris had been out at second prior to Kubiak touching home, the run would not have counted.

Analyzing the video, Kubiak touches home plate not more than 1 second before Campy is tagged at second.

The A's have not only won game 3, they've won the game the Mets were most likely to win, with Tom Seaver starting at home.

It's a crushing loss for the Mets.

EXCLUSIVE From The Sports Time Traveler™

Back in 2023, I called Ted Kubiak to ask him about his recollection of scoring the winning run in game 3 of the 1973 World Series.

Below is Ted Kubiak's fascinating account of how he used his head, and the lessons he had learned from baseball coaches many years before the game, to put himself in position to score the run that won a World Series game.

"You never how what you're learning as a youngster about the game is going to show up later. The coaches used to tell us when you're on

base always know where the outfielders are. I remembered that. I get to second base on the wild pitch. Campy is the hitter. And I check the outfielders. I know where they're all positioned. Campy hits a line drive over Harrelson's head. And I immediately took off. I surmised I had made the right decision as to where the left fielder was and I didn't have any qualms that the center fielder could catch the ball. I decided I've got to score. I don't even remember the third base coach, Irv Noren, telling me to stop or go. I was going and I wound up scoring the run. If I didn't have that good jump I never would have scored. If I had turned around to look to see where the ball was going we don't score and who knows who would have won the game."

"I scored the winning run. That's my claim to fame."

"If I didn't know where those guys were positioned I would have at least had to look over my shoulder and it might have kept me from scoring."

A picture in Ted's hometown newspaper, the New Brunswick Home News, from October 17, 1973, showed him scoring the winning run.

This World Series has not been short on drama. It's one of the most exciting in history so far.

The teams will be back in action right away for game 4 tonight.

I can't wait!

CHAPTER NINETY-EIGHT

The Heart & Soul of the Mets

GAME 4 OF THE 1973 WORLD SERIES IN NEW YORK HAS THE METS IN A MUST WIN SITUATION

SHEA STADIUM - October 18, 1973

I was back at Shea Stadium again last night, 50 years in the past, on a virtual trip, to experience game 4 of the 1973 World Series.

The air was brisk, 50 degrees at game time and quickly diving colder.

Fortunately the Mets were sending Jon Matlack, their hottest pitcher, to the mound on this night where they desperately needed a win. The Mets were down 2 games to 1 in the series.

Matlack had already pitched 15 innings in the post season and not allowed a single earned run. And going back to the regular season he had allowed only 1 earned run over his past 32 innings. His presence gave the Mets and their fans reason to believe.

Oakland sent the game 1 winner Ken Holtzman to the mound. Holtzman had allowed the Mets just 1 run in the 2 - 1 A's victory in that game.

This had all the makings of another pitcher's duel.

BACKGROUND ON THE TITLE OF THIS ARTICLE

I interrupt this article to explain the title I chose for this article.

THE HEART OF THE METS

The heart of the Mets right now is embodied by slugger Rusty Staub. In just his 2nd year with the team, Staub has endeared himself to the fans despite the fact that he's had 2 injury plagued, statistically underwhelming seasons.

Rusty has won over Mets fans because, despite a painful injury, he is playing his heart out for the team. Staub's shoulder is so sore he can barely throw the ball. This was evidenced by his underhanded flip from right field on a key play in game 3 after Joe Rudi lashed a single with Bert Campaneris on second. If a healthy Staub could've mustered a bullet strike throw like the one Reggie Jackson made from right field in game 3, Staub could've possibly gunned down Bert Campaneris at the plate and preserved the 1 run lead Seaver had at that time in the 8th inning.

However, no one is blaming Staub on that play (throwing out the speedy Campaneris would've been difficult even for the great Roberto Clemente), because he got that sore shoulder by willingly running at full speed into the right field wall in game 4 of the NLCS after he had made a spectacular catch on a Dan Driessen drive. Staub could only have been grabbed that ball by having no fear of the impending crash.

And then we found out this morning that after game 2 in Oakland, Staub was so dedicated to winning that he devised a way to get in the extra batting practice in New York that he needed to get ready for the next game. Staub found a way to fly back east ahead of the team, with Yogi's permission, by taking the red eye from Oakland with the New York press corps.

Jack Lang of the Jersey Journal joked in his article this morning, *"If the Mets win the World Series they* (the press) *may ask to be cut in for a share."*

Rusty Staub has as much heart as any player in the game, and he has captured the hearts of Mets fans.

THE SOUL OF THE METS

The soul of this Mets team, as all Mets fans know, is their pitching staff.

Tom Seaver, Tug McGraw and Jerry Koosman have been the core of the staff since the Miracle of 1969. Jon Matlack first joined them in 1971, but he's been in the Mets family since being drafted as a 17 year old in 1967. Now he is an integral piece of the vaunted staff.

Right now the soul of the Mets pitching staff is embodied best in Jon Matlack, the only one of the three starters to hold the A's to no earned runs in this year's World Series.

In fact, Matlack, at this moment in 1973, is on one of the great streaks in post season history as he has allowed no earned runs in his first 15 innings of post season play. Including his final 2 regular season starts, he has allowed just 1 earned run in his last 32 innings.

And like Seaver, McGraw and Koosman, Matlack is a home grown Mets pitcher. He was drafted with the 4th pick in the 1st round of the 1967 draft, and had 115 starts in the Mets minor league system. In 1972, he earned a spot in the Mets starting rotation and won the NL Rookie-of-the-Year award.

And now he has reached the zenith with his current unearned run streak.

Now back to game 4 of the 1973 World Series.

You can experience game 4, just as I did this week, by watching the video of the start of the game below, and then cutting over to the radio broadcast, also included in another link below, when the video cuts out.

https://www.youtube.com/watch?v=Y4jDK3oJjeo

You can also find the video on YouTube with this search: 1973 World Series Game 4 NEW YORK 10/17/73.

Here's my account of the game.

At the 21 minute mark on the video watch as a player from the Pittsburgh Pirates takes the field at Shea. Nelson Briles, was a top starter in 1973, winning 14 games with an ERA of 2.84. But on this night he's not in uniform on the mound, he's in a suit in centerfield singing the Star Spangled Banner. It turns out Nelson Briles has as good control over his voice as he does his pitches. His rendition of the National Anthem is every bit as strong as Jim Nabors, who sang before game 1.

At the 21:50 mark on the tape is another special moment for Mets fans. Bill Shea, the man for whom Shea Stadium was named for, throws out the ceremonial 1st pitch.

As the game begins, Jon Matlack is sharp from the outset. At 35 minutes watch as he gets Reggie to swing and miss for a strikeout to retire the A's in the 1st. Just prior to that moment, Lindsey Nelson, the Mets play-by-play man, explains that the only player Matlack followed growing up was Sandy Koufax. Koufax, no surprise, was also a lefty who wore #32, the number Matlack selected.

Following the strikeout Mets fans will enjoy the Sears commercial featuring Tom Seaver selling a suit for $64.97.

At 40 minutes watch as the Mets first 2 batters reach base and then Rusty Staub comes to the plate.

Staub crushes a Ken Holtzman pitch over the left field wall for a 3 run homer.

The Mets lead 3 - 0 and they still have no outs in the 1st.

At the 46 minute mark, after Jerry Grote singles, Ken Holtzman is removed from the game after getting just 1 batter out. It's a stunningly poor start for Holtzman, the winner of game 1.

After the game, Holtzman told Joseph Durso in the New York Times, *"I just didn't have it. No control. No speed. No nothing."*

At the 1:04:25 mark, Matlack registers his 4th K as he gets the A's pitcher Odom on "Blue Moon's" 1st at bat of 1973. It was a big sweeping curve that landed smack in the middle of the strike zone. It's a beautiful pitch to see.

METS 3 A's 0 - end of 3 innings

At 1:13:15 Mets fans will enjoy seeing a **"Ya Gotta Believe"** button on a fan's hat.

A minute later at 1:14:40, Matlack completely fools Joe Rudi for his 5th K on another big sweeping curve.

An error by Wayne Garrett then leads to an unearned run as the A's make it a 3 - 1 game.

At 1:20:00, the tape skips ahead to the bottom of the 4th with Felix Millan at the plate. Millan hits a slow roller to second base that Dick Green can't handle, and the Mets score their 4th run.

A moment later Rusty Staub singles driving in 2 more runs and the Mets are up 6 - 1.

Staub now has 5 RBIs in 4 innings.

At this point the video tape cuts off.

Now switch over to the radio broadcast

https://www.youtube.com/watch?v=G0YM8Ah6eAU

You can also find the recording on YouTube with this search: 1973 World Series Game 4 Oakland Athletics vs Mets (AUDIO ONLY).

At 1:14:50, the A's radio announcer Monty Moore notes that all 3 Mets runs in the 4th inning should have been unearned because Green's error could have been a double play ball to get the A's out of the inning.

At this point in the series the Mets have scored 19 runs in the 4 games and 8 of them could be considered unearned, although only 6 are being scored as unearned.

At 1:31:20, Monty Moore wonders if the Mike Andrews affair has distracted the team's on field performance.

The A's can't get any offense going against Matlack, and after 7 innings the Mets still hold a 5 run lead.

METS 6 A's 1 - end of 7 innings

At the 1 hour and 59 minute mark Dick Williams sends in a pinch hitter for the pitcher. It's Mike Andrews.

Andrews was the player who was "fired" from the team by A's owner Charlie Finley and missed game 3 only to be reinstated by commissioner Bowie Kuhn.

The Mets fans give Andrews a standing ovation as he walks to the plate.

Andrews then gets an even bigger ovation after he grounds out and heads back to the A's dugout.

In today's New York Times, Andrews was quoted saying, *"It was great, just great. I don't think I've ever had an ovation like that before."* This is coming from a man had been an all-star in 1969 and was the starting second baseman on the 1967 Red Sox World Series team.

Andrews was also quoted in the New York Daily News today, *"Believe me, it gave me a big lift. I knew their reaction was in support of my position. It made me feel great."*

At 2:10:30, Rusty Staub got his 4th hit of the game to tie the record of 4 hits in a single World Series contest. Note one of the players who Staub tied for the record is NBC pre-game show host Joe Garagiola.

Matlack came out of the game after the 8th inning having given up just the 1 unearned run.

Jon Matlack's post season performance now consists of 23 innings without giving up an earned run.

After the game Matlack told Joseph Durso in the New York Times, *"My shoulder started getting stiff from the 6th inning on. It was very cold out there."*

In the top of the 9th, Mets reliever Ray Sadecki loads the bases. But at 2:21:50 he strikes out Bert Campaneris to end the game.

METS 6 A's 1 - FINAL SCORE

The 2 heroes of the game for the Mets were the heart and soul of the team tonight.

The Heart

Rusty Staub drove in 5 of the Mets 6 runs on a World Series record tying 4 hits.

After the game Staub told Durso, *"When you've been in the league 11 years, to have a night like this is unbelievably satisfying."*

Staub also told Durso that even with all the extra batting practice he got in after coming back early to New York following game 2, he had not been able, with his sore shoulder, to hit a single home run in practice. Thus making his 3 run blast in the 1st inning even more remarkable.

Jack Lang wrote in the Jersey Journal that Staub told him this game, *"was the result of a lot of work and a lot of concentration and a lot of batting practice too,"* and, *"it was the greatest thing that ever happened to me. I just can't explain the thrill I have experienced."*

He also explained, *"I adjusted to the conditions. I studied what I would have to do to compensate for my shoulder."*

Lang indicated in his article that the Mets had actually considered putting Staub on the disabled list, but Staub argued against it. Lang wrote, *"All he had left was determination. Rusty was never short on that."*

The Soul

Jon Matlack had just pitched one of the great games of his career, allowing just 3 hits and no earned runs in 8 innings, and most importantly adding another page to the mystique of Mets pitching with a masterful World Series victory.

Bud Harrelson authored an article that appeared in the Jersey Journal this morning. He shared the following about Matlack, *"Jon Matlack was so strong last night that in the 7th inning, Rube Walker* (the Mets pitching coach) *came out to talk to him because he was overthrowing the ball. He just had so much stuff the ball was jumping all over the place. The harder he threw the more it moved... his pitching this past month has been absolutely fantastic."*

Going back to late September, Matlack now has a stretch of 40 innings in which he's allowed just 1 earned run.

And now thanks to Rusty's great heart and Matlack's stirring display of the Mets' soul, the World Series is tied again at 2 game apiece.

Game 5 is tonight at Shea.

It will be Jerry Koosman against Vida Blue.

It will be a chiller again as temperatures are expected to drop from an afternoon high of 60 into the upper 40s at night.

The winner will be in the driver's seat to capture the World Series title.

I can't wait!

CHAPTER NINETY-NINE

Chiller Thriller at Shea

GAME 5 OF THE 1973 WORLD SERIES TAKES PLACE IN THE COLD CONFINES OF SHEA STADIUM

INTRODUCTION From The Sports Time Traveler™

In the mid-1970s on WOR Channel 9 in New York, the station that aired all the Mets games, there was a Saturday morning kids show called, *"Chiller Thriller."*

As I watched and listened to game 5 of the 1973 World Series yesterday, I kept thinking about *Chiller Thriller,* since the temperature at Shea Stadium was in the upper 40s for most of the game, and the game turned out to be a thriller.

This was an enormously important contest as the winner would be 1 victory away from a World Series title.

Now let's go back to 1973.

SHEA STADIUM, FLUSHING, QUEENS, NY - October 19, 1973

I was back again at Shea Stadium last night, virtually, for the 5th game of the 1973 World Series which is tied up at 2 games to 2.

The game was a re-match from the wildly entertaining game 2 in Oakland featuring Jerry Koosman against Vida Blue.

You can experience the game as I did via this YouTube link which takes you to a combination video / radio broadcast of the game.

https://www.youtube.com/watch?v=xhr6Ksznn8k

You can also find the game on YouTube by searching for, 1973 World Series game 5 Reconstruction.

Here's my account of the game.

At the beginning of the broadcast we found out that Cleon Jones is very ill with flu like symptoms. He hasn't eaten in 2 days. But he is determined to play.

Joe DiMaggio throws out the 1st pitch. You can see a good view of Joltin' Joe looking dashing at the 11:45 mark on the video.

As the game got underway, Jerry Koosman, who is from Minnesota, and still lives there in the winter months, must have felt right at home in the cold weather.

Koosman walked Sal Bando in the top of the 1st, but otherwise had no trouble with the A's and struck out Reggie to retire the side.

Vida Blue got the Mets 1-2-3 in the bottom of the 1st.

And a pitching duel was on.

In the bottom of the 2nd, Cleon Jones didn't show any effects of illness as he led off with a double. Then at 33:00 on the tape, which is extremely grainy at this point, the next batter, John Milner slashes a hard grounder through the right side of the infield and Jones races around third and easily scores the 1st run of the game.

But Vida Blue clamps down and gets the next 6 Mets batters out in a row.

METS 1 A's 0 - end of 3 innings

Kooz had to face the heart of the A's order in the top of the 4th. He got Joe Rudi to pop up. Then Sal Bando hit a hot grounder down the third base line that took a bad hop and Wayne Garrett couldn't handle it.

While the official scorer ruled it a hit, it should have been an error on the Mets fans, as the entire infield had to be re-constructed after thousands of Mets fans stormed the field in an out of control celebration after the Mets won the pennant 8 days ago.

With Bando on first and 1 out, the leading home run hitter in the American League, Reggie Jackson came to the plate. Kooz got him to hit a double play ball from Millan to Harrelson to Milner and the A's were done in the 4th.

In the bottom of the 4th the Mets started out with 2 singles and loaded the bases with 2 outs on a rare error by the A's shortstop Bert Campaneris. But Blue got Bud Harrelson to pop up to end the threat.

Kooz continued to cruise in the 5th. After walking Gene Tenace to open the inning he got the next 3 A's on fly balls. One of them was a sensational catch by second baseman Felix Millan on a fly to shallow right field.

The New York Times' Joseph Durso described the grab, *"(Millan) running full tilt with his back to the infield, made a sparkling catch over his right shoulder... it was the kind of ball that drops 99 times out of a 100."*

You can see aftermath of the play in slow motion replay at the 1:10:13 mark on the video. After Millan has caught the ball, Rusty Staub, who was running in from deep right, nearly collides with Millan.

In the top of the 6th, Kooz gave up a walk to Bert Campaneris with 1 out. Then Joe Rudi hit a foul pop behind the plate that was caught by the catcher Grote, while John Milner, the Mets the first baseman, ran towards the mound to be in position for a possible cut off throw if the speedy Campaneris tried to tag up.

In a smart move, Rusty Staub raced in from right field to cover first base and the Mets almost doubled up Campy who managed to get safely back to first base.

You can hear this fascinating play at the 1:24:08 mark on the tape. And you can see the replay at the 1:24:42 mark.

A moment later at 1:28:00 on the tape you can hear as Sal Bando hits a grounder to third that again bounces oddly. This one is ruled an error on Garrett, but you have to wonder if he would have fielded it cleanly if the playing surface was in better shape.

Now Reggie Jackson came to the plate with 2 on and 2 outs. At 1:30:20 listen as Jackson hits a grounder up the middle. Bud Harrelson is positioned perfectly behind second base and grabs the ball, steps on second base for the force out, and Kooz is out of the jam.

After the game, Jackson and the A's praised the fielding of Bud Harrelson who has been brilliant throughout the series.

Reggie told the Hackensack Record, *"That little shortstop is all over the place."*

Sal Bando also was impressed by Bud, *"He's the best fielding shortstop I've seen. I thought (Baltimore's) Belanger was the best, but Harrelson is better... He knows where to be."*

Even A's manager Dick Williams had kind words to say about the opposing shortstop, *"He's in the right spot all the time."*

In the bottom of the 6th, the supposedly sick man, Cleon Jones, came to the plate. Jones had 2 of the 4 hits off Vida Blue. Now in his 3rd time at bat, Cleon hit a deep fly ball to left field. The ball went all the way back to the wall just in front of the 358 foot sign before Joe Rudi leaped and speared it for a spectacular catch, reminiscent of his famous catch in the 1972 World Series.

You can see the catch in a slow motion replay at the 1:32:53 mark on the tape. NBC's Tony Kubek called it, *"the play of the series so far."*

Every Don Has His Day

A minute later Blue gave up a single to Jerry Grote and then Don Hahn came to the plate.

Watch at the 1:40:00 mark as Don Hahn steps in against Vida Blue. The TV graphic indicates Hahn is just 3 for 20 in the series at this point. But he's actually

3 for 21 for a .143 average. And including the NLCS, Hahn is batting just .184 in the playoffs in 38 at bats.

Stick with the video as Hahn drives the 1st pitch from Blue into deep left center field. It bounces all the way to the wall at the 396 foot mark. Grote scores easily and Don Hahn ends up at third with a stand up triple.

It was the 1st triple of 1973 for Don Hahn and just the 2nd of his career in over 200 major league games.

Hahn benefitted from the fact that Reggie Jackson, playing centerfield, was shifted over towards right center as the A's apparently thought Hahn could not pull the ball on Blue. This created a huge gap where Hahn hit the ball and Jackson had a long run to pick it up.

Phil Pepe of the New York Daily News was so excited for Don Hahn, who batted just .229 on the season, that he wrote a couple of paragraphs about him in his article on the game in this morning's paper, including this:

"Hahn is there for his glove. He plays because he can throw and Willie Mays can't, and he can catch baseballs in centerfield. He catches baseballs very well, so well that some people have suggested he should take a glove to home plate for all the good he does with his bat."

Hahn's triple after Jones nearly hit one out of the ballpark was enough for A's manager Dick Williams to decide it was time to take Vida Blue out of the game.

Blue had pitched well going 5 and 2/3 innings and giving up 6 hits and 2 runs.

METS 2 A's 0 - end of 6 innings

In the 7th, Ray Fosse hit a hard grounder past Garrett at third base to put runners on second and third with 1 out. This was the 1st time an A's runner had reached third base in the game.

And Yogi Berra decided it was time to bring in Tug McGraw.

Koosman said after the game to Ron Drogo in the Hackensack Record, *"I was battling myself all night and I felt unsteady at times. The cooler weather tends to keep me stronger, so I was able to survive despite not being at my best."* Nevertheless Kooz had pitched a great game, going 6 and 1/3 innings and allowing just 3 hits and no runs.

Tug immediately loaded the bases on a walk to Deron Johnson, who is normally the A's designated hitter, but was now pinch hitting for Dick Green. McGraw clearly pitched around Johnson, who with 19 homers on the season, and 212 for his career, could have given the A's the lead with one swing of the bat.

Now Tug went to work and got Angel Mangual to pop up and Bert Campaneris to strike out to end the threat.

Tug is pitching magnificently on this night. The radio announcer explains at 2:02:00 that McGraw, *"throws a curveball that breaks into the right handed hitter and a screwball that breaks away, and he's got a good fastball. So, you can't guess on him."*

At the 2:09:00 mark on the tape Cleon Jones comes up for his 4th at bat and the radio announcer says, *"Cleon Jones has scorched the ball 3 times tonight."* But on this trip Jones grounds to the shortstop.

At the 2:21:30, the video is back on, with good quality, as Jesus Alou is at the plate with 2 outs in the 8th. Alou hits a bullet down the third base line that Wayne Garrett snags a la Brooks Robinson style to end the inning.

METS 2 A's 0 - end of 8 innings

In the top of the 9th, Cleon Jones, flu and all, makes a nice sliding catch at the 2:32:40 mark on the video for the 1st out of the inning.

Jones has played as good a game as anyone on the field. And yet the New York Times reported that team Dr. Peter LaMotte ordered Jones to go home after the game and stay in bed until the team departs for Oakland. *"He's very ill,"* said Dr. LaMotte.

At 2:34:30, Ted Kubiak, on the 7th pitch of his at bat, takes a called 3rd strike, as McGraw fools him on the outside corner, and there are 2 outs.

At 2:35:40 McGraw blows a fast ball by Billy Conigliaro for strike 2, and a moment later gets him on a called 3rd strike to seal the save.

Game over. Mets win.

The New York Mets have taken a 3 games to 2 lead in the World Series.

Tug McGraw pitched 2 and 2/3 innings without allowing a hit, as he combined with Jerry Koosman to shut out the Oakland A's.

Yogi Berra told the New York Times, *"I think I've got the best relief pitcher in baseball. And I think he proved it tonight."*

Mets pitchers have held the A's to 8 hits and 0 earned runs in the past 18 innings!

And the New York Mets pitching staff now have a post season team ERA of an incredible 1.65.

The back cover of the New York Daily News had a banner headline this morning, *"Ya Gotta Believe"* and a picture of Tug McGraw after he got the final called 3rd strike.

Phil Pepe of the Daily News wrote, *"One more completes the miracle, the trilogy of division title, National League title, world title. One more makes believers out of everybody."*

In the Hackensack Record, Tug McGraw was quoted saying, *"I should've copyrighted that damn slogan and I'd be rich right now. This whole damn city believes now. I've seen bumper stickers, buttons, all kinds of stuff with 'You Gotta Believe' on it."*

In the New York Daily News, Phil Pepe also celebrated one of the other heroes of the night, Don Hahn, with this humorous paragraph, *"There were only 2 runs scored at Shea last night and half of them were driven in by Don (Hondo) Hahn. Think of it. All those big sluggers - Reggie Jackson, Sal Bando, Rusty Staub, Joe Rudi, Cleon Jones, Gene Tenace and Bud Harrelson - and Hahn drives in half the runs."*

It's off to Oakland now for game 6, and game 7 if necessary.

The Mets are in the driver's seat needing to win just 1 game to be World Series champions for the 2nd time in 4 years.

The A's know they need to start hitting. Leonard Koppett in the New York Times reported this morning that the A's have petitioned baseball commissioner

Bowie Kuhn to put a green tarp in centerfield to improve the batter's view in Oakland.

Koppett also reported that despite the 2 straight losses, the A's are confident. Bando told him, *"We never do anything easy. We never have. Now we just have to win 2 games."*

Bando is also confident the team will play better at home, *"There's nothing wrong with Shea Stadium, but in a strange park you just don't feel sure of yourself, your step may be a bit hesitant, your movements not quite as relaxed as they are at home, where everything fits into place and feels right."*

Things are feeling right for the Mets right now. Very right. The fans are feeling it too.

And right hander, Tom Seaver, will be the starting pitcher in game 6 in Oakland, where he will have a chance to make the Mets the 1973 World Series champions.

I can't wait!

The Hahney-moon Ends in Oakland

GAME 6 OF THE 1973 WORLD SERIES SHIFTED BACK TO OAKLAND WITH THE METS AHEAD 3 GAMES TO 2

EXCLUSIVE From The Sports Time Traveler™

In 2023, Ted Kubiak shared his recollections with me about the mood of his Oakland A's team as they went into game 6 at home, down 3 games to 2.

"The Andrews affair kind of messed up the whole thing. Those middle games, I can't even say my head was in those games because of what was going on. It took away from the series, all that rigamarole."

"That whole series was kind of a mess because of the Andrews situation. But when we got home it was the A's again coming in to do what we had to do.

I used to ride in to the ballpark with Catfish and Holtzman, and on the way to the stadium for game 6, I thought we're going to win.

Our mindset was that we were going to win."

INTRODUCTION From The Sports Time Traveler™

After game 5 of the 1973 World Series the back page of the New York Daily News celebrated Don Hahn's big hit that helped seal the 2 - 0 Mets victory that gave them a commanding 3 games to 2 lead on the A's.

Phil Pepe of the Daily News joyfully made light of the unexpected run driving triple by the humble hitter Hahn. That run gave the Mets breathing room for Tug McGraw to weather a late inning challenge by the defending World Series champion A's.

When game 5 ended, there was a sense of destiny among the Mets beat writers in New York. The Mets had just limited the A's to 3 hits and no runs a day after they had held them to 5 hits and no earned runs. 18 innings of Mets pitching, and some stellar defense had the Amazins' on the brink of a 2nd miracle in 4 years.

Phil Pepe, in his back page article in the Daily News, also went to great lengths to note that it's Don Hahn's glove in centerfield that is the only reason he's in the lineup of instead of Willie Mays. Mays sore shoulder makes it impossible to throw the ball well.

Well in the 1st inning of game 6 in Oakland, the Hahneymoon abruptly came to a quick end.

Let's go back to 1973 and experience the Mets big opportunity to close out the A's.

OAKLAND, CA - October 21, 1973

Yesterday afternoon I was in Oakland on a virtual trip back in time to experience game 6 of the 1973 World Series.

The pitchers were the aces of the 2 pitching staffs - Catfish Hunter for the A's and Tom Seaver for the Mets. Both men would be pitching on just 3 days rest as they were the game 3 starters in New York.

Seaver has given up just 4 earned runs in 24 and 2/3 innings in the post season while striking out 29. He beat the Reds in game 5 of the NLCS on 3 days rest allowing just 1 earned run in 8 and 1/3 innings.

Now Seaver would be pitching on 3 days rest again.

There is some concern because he stiffened up at the end of his 12 strikeout 8 inning performance in game 3, and he faltered on 3 days rest in several games down the stretch in the regular season.

Yogi Berra told Joseph Durso in the New York Times the day before the game, ***"I had a long talk with Tom last night and he said he felt great and wants to go."***

Catfish Hunter pitched even stronger than Seaver on 3 days rest last week when he shutout the Orioles in game 5 of the ALCS to send the A's to the World Series. Hunter also pitched on 3 days rest with great success during the regular season many times, going 11 - 2 in those outings.

You can see a portion of game 6 in this video. Sadly there is no complete game video of this game.

https://www.youtube.com/watch?v=ObP0ao0RVN4&t

You can find the video on YouTube with this search: 1973 World Series Game 6 OAKLAND 10/20/73 Original NBC Broadcast.

Hunter opened the game by issuing a walk to the leadoff batter Wayne Garrett.

He then got Felix Millan to hit a pop foul to the right side. Watch at the 1:05 mark on the tape as Dick Green races a long way in foul territory and makes a nice catch for the first out.

Oakland's stadium has an enormous amount of space between the foul lines and the stands.

At Shea Stadium that ball would have been halfway up to the mezzanine and Millan would still have been at bat.

If Millan could have reached base, putting runners on first and second with no one out, the Mets likely would have scored a run, especially since the game's 3rd batter, Rusty Staub, singled.

Instead Hunter stranded Garrett on second and Staub on first.

The home field advantage for the A's could be seen on the tape at the 1:43 mark when NBC showed the vast stretch of grass on the right side of the playing surface.

In the bottom of the 1st Seaver got the leadoff batter, Bert Campaneris, to fly out to center.

Then he gave up a hard single to right field to the 2nd batter, Joe Rudi. Rudi was able to follow the flight of Seaver's down the middle fastball all the way, and drove it well over Felix Millan's head.

Joe Rudi told Red Foley of the New York Daily News after the game that Seaver, *"didn't have that good curve he had the other night."*

Seaver did get the A's captain Sal Bando to strikeout for out number 2. And then he faced Reggie Jackson. Seaver had struck out Jackson the first 3 times he came up in game 3, in which Jackson ended up 0 for 5. Across the 3 games in New York, Reggie had gone 1 for 12.

But back in his home park, Reggie drilled a Seaver pitch into the gap in left center. The ball rolled to the wall and Cleon Jones slipped on the warning track trying to retrieve it. Then Don Hahn collected the ball, but his throw sailed over the cutoff man's head and Rudi was able to score from first base standing up.

If Jones hadn't slipped, or if Hahn's throw had been on the money to Bud Harrelson, it is conceivable that Bud could have fired to Jerry Grote and nailed Rudi at the plate.

Rudi was not known at all for speed on the basepaths. On the American League's 2nd leading team in steals, Rudi had not attempted to steal a base all season.

Allowing Rudi to score from first base was a minor catastrophe in a battle of ace pitchers, as Hunter was mowing down the Mets in order in both the 2nd and 3rd innings.

After Seaver got through the 2nd inning without giving up a hit, and then getting the first 2 batters out in the bottom of the 3rd, Sal Bando singled to center. This brought up Jackson again with a man on first base.

This time Seaver couldn't get his fastball by Jackson. He belted it into right field. Staub got to the ball quickly on 1 hop, but with his sore shoulder he could only muster an underhand flip to Felix Millan who had run far out into right field to retrieve it. Millan couldn't handle the unconventional toss and his relay throw to the plate was not in time.

Sal Bando scored from first base.

Bando is another A's player not known for speed. He attempted just 4 steals in 1973 and was caught twice. Yet he scored from first base on Jackson's 2nd double of the game.

A's 2 METS 0 - end of 3 innings

In the 4th, Catfish put the Mets down quietly 1-2-3 again. He had now retired 11 consecutive Mets. While Seaver gave up his 5th hit of the game in the bottom half of the inning to Dick Green, the second baseman who had been 0 for 9 in the series coming into the game.

Jerry Grote broke Hunter's streak when he led off the 5th with a single.

After Hunter got the next 2 batters out, Tom Seaver came to the plate.

As Seaver has often had to do all season when the Mets bats weren't supporting him he played BYOB (bring your own bat). Seaver hit a long fly to deep left. Joe Rudi went back to the warning track. The ball looked like it had a chance to go out according to the radio announcers. But it stayed in the park. Rudi caught it at the warning track to end the top of the 5th.

Hunter took down the top of the Mets lineup in order in the 6th, garnering his 4th 1-2-3 inning of the game.

On the mound for the Mets, Seaver allowed just 1 single across the 5th and 6th to Deron Johnson. Johnson, the DH during the regular season, had been inserted into the starting lineup at first base by A's manager Dick Williams in an effort to produce more offense.

While Seaver was getting the A's out, he wasn't striking out batters as he usually does. After striking out 4 A's in the opening 3 innings, he didn't register a single strikeout in the 4th - 6th innings.

A's 2 METS 0 - end of 6 innings

In the top of the 7th, after John Milner had singled, breaking another Hunter streak of 6 straight Mets retired, Jerry Grote drilled a long high fly to deep left. But Joe Rudi made the catch just in front of the wall.

A few more feet and Grote would have tied the game.

Seaver started the bottom of the 7th nicely striking out Hunter and leadoff hitter, Campaneris. But then he walked Joe Rudi and threw an uncharacteristic wild pitch to Sal Bando before getting him to fly out to end the inning.

That was Seaver's last batter, as Yogi took him out for a pinch hitter in the 8th.

Seaver had pitched well. He had only allowed 6 hits and 2 earned runs in 7 innings. However he wasn't his usual overpowering self, as he only struck out 6, exactly half the number of batters he whiffed in game 3.

Yet with a little better outfield help he still could easily have been working on a shutout.

Reggie Jackson told Red Foley in the New York Daily News after the game, *"He just wasn't Tom Seaver today and I give him a lot of credit for pitching the kind of game he did today."*

Sal Bando, in the same article, commented on Seaver's arm, *"I think it's dead... his arm must be bothering him because he threw much harder in the game at Shea."*

Seaver himself was terse in his comments to the press after the game. Joe Donnelly of Newsday got the most from him, *"I didn't have the same fastball. But I wasn't hurting... I've pitched shutouts with worse stuff than I had today."*

In the top of the 8th, Mets pinch hitter Ken Boswell came through with a single.

Dick Williams then took out Catfish Hunter for relief pitcher Darold Knowles.

Hunter had pitched 7 and 1/3 innings and allowed just 4 hits and no runs.

Knowles gave up a single to the 1st batter he faced, Wayne Garrett, and the Mets had the tying run on first with just 1 out.

Next, Felix Millan singled.

Boswell scored on the play.

And suddenly the Mets had pulled to within a run and still had runners on first and third with 1 out and their power hitters coming to the plate.

A Magical Moment

Rusty Staub steps in at the 14:55 mark for what is arguably the biggest at bat of his career.

Staub is playing solely for his bat as he can barely throw a ball with his sore shoulder. And his bat had been good. He was hitting .444 for the series.

The 5 time all-star had hit as many as 30 homers in a single season. He had led the NL in doubles back in 1967, and he had averaged above .300 over a 6 year stretch from 1967 - 1972.

But he'd never been in the post season till this year.

And now it was his time.

And he knew it.

A home run in this situation would likely win the World Series for the Mets. Staub already had 4 home runs and 10 RBIs in 9 post-season games.

Staub took 3 vicious swings, clearly trying for a 3 run shot.

And he missed on all 3.

Rusty Staub had struck out.

After the game he told Joe Donnelly, ***"I was just trying to lay the bat on it."***

But the video tape clearly shows Rusty was trying to be the World Series hero with one big swing.

And if he had connected, he would have been.

It could've been a magical moment for Staub, even greater than his big moments from game 4 when he drove in 5 of the Mets 6 runs.

Now the sly manager Dick Williams brought in Rollie Fingers to pitch to Cleon Jones with 2 outs. Fingers got him to fly out to retire the side.

The Mets had squandered a huge opportunity by not getting the runner home from third to tie the game with their big hitters at bat in the 8th.

Tug McGraw came in to relieve Seaver in the bottom of the inning. The first batter he faced was Reggie Jackson.

Watch at the 16:35 mark to see one of the big plays of the game. Jackson drives McGraw's pitch into straightaway centerfield. Don Hahn pulls up to get the ball on 1 hop. But he completely misjudges the hop and the ball rolls behind him all the way to the wall while Jackson, who does have great speed, races all the way to third.

This was an enormous blunder by Hahn. NBC's Tony Kubek said that Hahn, *"had a chance for a shoestring catch."*

Instead of possibly having an out or just a man on first, the A's suddenly had the leadoff runner on third base.

A moment later Jesus Alou lifted a fly ball to left and Jackson scored easily on the sacrifice fly.

The A's were up 3 - 1 with an important insurance run.

All 3 A's runs had come on outfield mishaps.

It is quite conceivable that the Mets could have shut down the A's offense yet again if Staub had a healthy arm in right and if Don Hahn had done his job in center.

Perhaps if Willie Mays had been in centerfield he might have caught the ball with a classic basket catch.

And regarding his own mishap in right field, after the game, Rusty Staub told Phil Pepe of the New York Daily News, *"If I can throw there's no way they get that 2nd run."*

A's 3 METS 1 - end of 8 innings

The Mets couldn't mount a comeback in the 9th as Rollie Fingers retired the side in order to close out the A's victory.

The New York Mets who had looked golden before the game, with Tom Seaver, a central California native, pitching to try to win the World Series, suddenly found themselves going to a game 7 on the road.

Fortunately for the Mets, the scheduled pitcher for the deciding game is the hottest pitcher in all baseball, Mr. Jon Matlack.

And Matlack is scheduled to go up against Ken Holtzman, who the Mets knocked out in the 1st inning in game 4.

At the 11:30 mark on the tape, Curt Gowdy said, *"**Matlack very definitely will start... his ERA is 0.00."***

It's the Mets vs. the A's at 4:30pm ET on Sunday, October 21, 1973.

The game will be broadcast in the New York area on both NBC Channel 4 and the WOR Channel 9.

All of you reading this in the future can find the game on YouTube.

I will wait until tomorrow to watch it.

I can't wait!

Mr. October and Midnight for the Mets

GAME 7 OF THE 1973 WORLD SERIES WAS A LEGACY MAKING OPPORTUNITY

Background From The Sports Time Traveler™

Last year I set out on the ambitious goal of re-living the 1973 New York Mets baseball season. I was determined to follow every single game from spring training through to the World Series 50 years ago to the day.

Following sports 50 years ago to the day is one of the basic rules of sports time travel.

Now I am proud to share my story on game 7 of the 1973 World Series. I remember the day in real life but not all the details.

It was Sunday, October 21, 1973. I was 10 years old, and I was at home in New Jersey. My grandpa Joe was there with me. Before the game started at 4:30pm ET, he predicted that Oakland would win it 5 - 2. I was so angry at him for predicting the Mets would lose. I couldn't understand why he would say such a thing when he knew I lived for the Mets.

I wonder now if Grandpa Joe was secretly rooting for Ted Kubiak of the A's who was from Highland Park, NJ, where my grandfather lived. He had likely followed Ted when he was the star player on the Highland Park high school team in 1960. Grandpa Joe was a big Highland Park high school sports fan and he used to take me to see their home football games.

I've been waiting for this virtual trip all year. It would be the first time since the game was actually played 50 years ago that I would get to see it. This time I would have a slightly different experience as I would be watching it with the NBC announcers - Curt Gowdy, Tony Kubek and Monty Moore. In 1973, I watched the game on the New York station, WOR Channel 9, which had the familiar Mets announcers.

Now let's go back to the decisive game 7 of the 1973 World Series.

OAKLAND, CA - October 22, 1973

Yesterday was game 7 of the 1973 World Series between the Oakland A's and the New York Mets. I still had a hard time believing that my New York Mets, the team that had been in last place on the last day of August, were now in the final major league baseball game of 1973 - the decisive game 7 against the defending World Series champs.

You can watch the entire game as I did at the link below:

https://www.youtube.com/watch?v=zME6PLJ1Txs

You can also find the game on YouTube with this search: 1973 World Series Game 7 OAKLAND 10/21/73 Original NBC TV.

Here's my account of the game.

The starting pitchers were the same that had started game 1 and game 4. Ken Holtzman for the A's and Jon Matlack for the Mets.

Both men were going on just 3 days rest and doing so for the 2nd time in the series.

But there was a big difference. Holtzman had pitched less than 1 inning in game 4, as he was knocked out by the Mets when he gave up 4 hits and 3 runs while only getting 1 out.

Matlack had given up just 3 hits and no earned runs in 8 innings in a brilliant performance as the Mets won the game 6 - 1.

The 23 year old Matlack comes into game 7 with an incredible streak in which he had not yielded an earned run in all 23 innings he has pitched in the postseason. But he has rarely ever started on 3 days in rest in his short career with the Mets. And doing it for the 2nd time in this series raises the question about whether his arm will hold up.

Holtzman made it through the 1st inning much better than in game 4. He got Wayne Garrett to strike out looking to open the game. Then Felix Millan grounded out and Rusty Staub flew out.

In the bottom of the 1st Matlack got Bert Campaneris to ground out. But then he walked Joe Rudi on 4 pitches. Next up was Sal Bando and although he got him to strike out, Bando wasted a lot of pitches. And then Reggie Jackson grounded out to end the inning. Matlack had gotten out of the inning without allowing a hit. However he had already thrown 17 pitches.

In the top of the 2nd, Cleon Jones nearly put the Mets ahead when he sent a long fly ball to warning track in left field for out number 1. You can see it at the 16:00 mark on the tape.

At 18:30 on the tape watch as Jerry Grote is robbed of an extra base hit on Reggie Jackson's diving catch in centerfield.

The Mets had some good shots off Holtzman but still had no hits in the middle of the 2nd.

In the bottom of the 2nd, Matlack opened by getting Gene Tenace to strikeout looking and then quickly retired the side in order.

Jon Matlack now had 25 innings in the postseason without an earned run. He was through 2 innings in this game, but had already thrown 30 pitches.

METS 0 A's 0 - end of 2 innings

In the top of the 3rd, after Don Hahn got the Mets 1st hit, Bud Harrelson hit a fly to deep left that Joe Rudi almost lost in the sun. You can see it at the 28:10 mark.

Then Matlack came up and bunted into a double play to end the side.

In the bottom of the inning, Holtzman, who hit a double off Matlack in game 1, did it again.

So much for the A's being at a disadvantage with no designated hitter.

Next up was Bert Campaneris. At the 35:30 mark, Campy connected on the first pitch and blasted it over the right field fence.

It was the A's 1st home run of the entire World Series. It gave them a 2 - 0 lead and it destroyed Matlack's 25 inning no earned run streak.

After the game Matlack told Vinnie Ditrani in the Hackensack Record that Campaneris had been, *"swinging and missing at curve balls the whole series. I gave him a pretty good one where I wanted it. It was my pitch, but he hit it."*

The next batter, Joe Rudi hit a Matlack curve for a line drive single to left. Suddenly Matlack was looking vulnerable, and Monty Moore and Curt Gowdy made note of the fact that Matlack was throwing a lot more breaking balls. Tony Kubek suggested that in games 6 and 7, the A's batters were doing a lot more thinking at the plate and forcing the Mets pitchers to change their pitching patterns.

Now Reggie Jackson came up. At the 41:00 minute mark Jackson waited on Matlack's high curve and belted it with everything he had.

Reggie then stood at the plate and relished the sight of the ball sailing deep into the right field bleachers.

The home run by Jackson was his first ever in a World Series.

It was a classic Reggie Jackson moment.

He had just become Mr. October.

The A's were ahead 4 - 0.

Matlack was knocked out of the game.

He told DiTrani, *"I thought I had pretty good stuff when I was warming up in the bullpen. I may not have been as strong as I would like, but I thought I was throwing pretty well. But Jackson hit a good old-fashioned hanging curve ball."*

Matlack knew he had made a fatal mistake. He told Sports Illustrated, *"When the ball left my hand I knew it was going out of the park."*

On the replay you can see that Jackson was locked in on the ball and simply waited for the moment to uncoil and smash it with all his power.

A's 4 METS 0 - end of 3 innings

The Mets bubble had burst. Their chances of being the Cinderella team that went from last place to become World Champions was over barring a real miracle.

NOTE From The Sports Time Traveler™

Baseballreference.com indicates the Mets chances of winning the game dropped from 50% at the start of the 3rd inning to 10% after Jackson's home run.

50 years ago, watching the game live in real time, it felt like there was even less chance than that. I had a sour feeling in my stomach after the 3rd inning.

Now back to 1973.

At the 49:00 mark watch as Reggie Jackson, now moved to right field for defensive purposes, makes yet another sensational catch off a Felix Millan deep fly ball in foul territory.

The Mets couldn't mount any offensive challenge against Holtzman. The Mets had no base runners get past 2nd in the first 5 innings. And then the A's scored another run in the 5th.

A's 5 METS 0 - end of 5 innings

The Mets finally got on the board with back-to-back doubles by Millan and Staub.

And that prompted Dick Williams to go to his top reliever, Rollie Fingers.

Listen to Curt Gowdy and Tony Kubek at the 1:22:30 mark talk about the innovation of the relief pitcher in baseball over the past several years. Relief pitchers are now key players on the team rather than being the 2nd class citizens of the pitching staff.

Fingers locked down the Mets in the 6th - 8th innings, allowing only singles to Don Hahn and pinch hitter Ken Boswell and not allowing any runner past second base.

Boswell's pinch hit, his 3rd of the series, tied the World Series record for most pinch hits.

The Mets brought in George Stone to pitch and he held the A's in check in the 7th and 8th.

A's 5 METS 1 - end of 8 innings

NOTE From The Sports Time Traveler™

Back in 2023 I interviewed Gene Tenace who was the starting first baseman and back-up catcher on the 1973 A's.

I was curious to ask Gene about Mets pitcher George Stone.

Stone got Tenace to fly out in the 8th inning in game 7.

George Stone had been the Mets regular 4th starter during the season. He pitched great with a 12 - 3 record and 2.80 ERA. But he didn't get a start in the World Series, and prior to game 7, he had seen just 1 inning of relief work.

Here is what Gene Tenace had to say about George Stone.

"We couldn't hit him. He had nasty stuff. When he came in out of the bullpen we were like 'who is this guy?'"

We couldn't figure out why they didn't pitch him because honest to God we couldn't hit him. We were in the dugout saying we can't hit this guy.

We were puzzled that he didn't get a start. He had some of the best stuff that we'd seen."

It really makes you wonder what George Stone could have done if he had started one of the middle games of the series and given the big three - Seaver, Matlack and Koosman, an extra day of rest.

Now back to 1973.

Time for Miracles

In the top of the 9th, the Mets John Milner opened with a walk as Rollie Fingers was now pitching in his 4th inning.

After Jerry Grote flew out, Don Hahn collected his 3rd single of the game and moved Milner to second.

Next up Bud Harrelson bunted the runners over to second and third.

But now the Mets were down to their last out.

Ed Kranepool, the original Met, came up to pinch hit. He hit a bouncer to first base and the fans in Oakland started streaming on to the field as it looked like an easy out. But Tenace bobbled the ball. Kranepool was safe and Milner scored.

Now the Mets were down 5 - 2, with 2 outs in the bottom of the 9th.

The field was cleared of fans. And play resumed.

Wayne Garrett came to the plate. Garrett had hit 2 home runs in the series.

He was the only player on either team to hit 2 home runs in the series.

A home run right at this moment would tie the game.

At 2:17:40 on the tape Garrett connects.

But it's a short fly into shallow left. Bert Campaneris moves back and catches the ball.

The Oakland A's are World Series champions for the 2nd year in a row.

And midnight has struck for the Mets' Cinderella season.

A's 5 METS 2 - Final Score

In this morning's Hackensack Record, Ron Drogo wrote, *"The inevitable had happened. The Oakland A's had come to life and the Mets dream of another miracle championship had been shattered."*

NEVER SEEN A TEAM AS HIGH

The A's gained confidence when the series moved back to Oakland and the fans came out strong for them.

Sal Bando told Ron Drogo in the Hackensack Record, *"I've never seen a team as high for a game as we were today."*

And Bando told the New York Times, *"We really got into high gear the last 2 games. The people came out and rooted for us, and that makes a big difference."*

Ken Holtzman, the game 7 winning pitcher, told the Times, *"In New York, that home crowd really helps the Mets. I think they were higher than we were. Here, the crowd really gave us a lift."*

Joe Rudi told the Times, *"We got the adrenalin flowing from the crowd reaction yesterday, and it was still higher today."*

And in the clubhouse after the game, the A's could not have been happier with their 2nd consecutive World Series victory.

Barry Levine wrote in the New Brunswick Home News that a *"glass eyed Ted Kubiak after devouring a bottle of champagne said, 'I thought all along we were a better club... We went into last year's World Series as underdogs but this year we were the favorites and wanted to prove we deserved to be.'"*

Kubiak was one of just 13 A's players on both World Series championship teams.

Ted Kubiak Described How the A's Won The Final 2 Games

Back in 2023, I asked Ted Kubiak how the A's won the final 2 games and what was the mindset of the team.

"I remember thinking that we were going to win game 6 and 7. Our team seemed to win every game during the season by one run; we never had it easy. In the late 60's we would lose those games by one run; we were up and coming during those years. I think everyone could see good things coming. When everyone improved, we were on the plus side of that one run. I think that is why being down 3 games to 2 was not that big a deal vs. the Mets. All our games were close, so we were used to the pressure.

Reggie had a knack for coming up big. One thing about him, he played hard. And he ran every ball out hard.

All I can say is everyone approached those 2 final games the same way they did every other one."

Gene Tenace also described how the A's came from behind 3 games to 2 to win the World Series:

"We had confidence we could come back in our home park in Oakland. We felt comfortable there. We just had some guys, Campy and Reggie come up big for us and our pitchers did a pretty good job."

COULD THE METS HAVE WON THE 1973 WORLD SERIES?

There is no doubt the New York Mets could have won this hard fought World Series.

The key statistics were nearly all in the Mets favor. Across the 7 games the Mets scored more runs (24 - 21) and out hit the A's (.253 to .212).

The Mets also left a World Series record 72 men on base in the series.

And there were many plays that if they went the other way, the Mets would have won the World Series.

TOP 4 PLAYS THAT COST THE METS THE 1973 WORLD SERIES:

Here are my picks for the top plays that could have changed the outcome of the 1973 World Series.

NUMBER 4 - Staub's Swings For the Fences

In the 8th inning of game 6, with the Mets leading the series 3 games to 2, Rusty Staub came to the plate with men on first and third and 1 out with the A's ahead by a score of 2 - 1.

Staub was having a sensational series at the plate batting .444 through the first 5 games.

Staub took 3 crushing swings.

Each swing was forceful enough to send the ball out of the park.

But he missed all 3 times.

If he had connected on one of those swings, and hit a homer, the Mets would have gone up 4 - 2 and Tug McGraw would have certainly held on for the Mets win and capture the series in 6 games.

Watch Staub's swings here starting at the 14:53 mark:

https://www.youtube.com/watch?v=ObP0ao0RVN4&t

You can also find it on YouTube using this search: 1973 World Series Game 6 OAKLAND 10/20/73.

NUMBER 3 - Milner's Near Game Winner

John Milner narrowly missed being the hero of game 3 when his deep fly to right in the bottom of the 9th of a 2 - 2 game was caught on the run by Reggie Jackson.

If Jackson doesn't make this catch then Rusty Staub, who was on second base, would have trotted home with the winning run.

Reggie himself said after the World Series that if Milner's ball had gone a foot more then Rusty Staub would have scored from second base with the winning run.

If the Mets won game 3, they likely would have gone on to win the World Series 4 games to 1 as Matlack and Koosman shut down the A's in games 4 and 5, allowing not a single earned run.

Watch Milner's blast here at the 2:25:55 mark on the tape:

https://www.youtube.com/watch?v=ZLN_UAjhc54

Or you can find it by typing in this search on YouTube: 1973 World Series Game 3 NEW YORK 10/16/73.

NUMBER 2 - Hahn's Misdirection

In game 3, Tom Seaver was pitching brilliantly, overpowering the A's with 12 strikeouts. Seaver had a 2 - 0 lead in the 6th inning when Sal Bando hit a ball to deep centerfield.

Watch at the 1:21:25 mark on the tape as Don Hahn in centerfield misplays the ball and it falls in for a double.

https://www.youtube.com/watch?v=ZLN_UAjhc54

Or you can find it by typing in this search on YouTube: 1973 World Series Game 3 NEW YORK 10/16/73.

It's a critical mishap as Bando scores moments later on another double by Gene Tenace.

As noted in Sports Illustrated, Hahn was confused by the additional length of the warning track at Shea Stadium as groundskeepers had to transfer turf from the outfield to repair the badly damaged infield after the wild celebration by Mets fans following the final game of the NLCS victory over the Reds 6 days earlier.

Without that run the Mets might have won game 3 by a 2 - 1 score as Seaver only allowed 1 other run on one of his sharpest nights. Again, the Mets would likely have won the series 4 games to 1 if they had taken game 3.

NUMBER 1 - KUBIAK's BIG JUMP

In the 11th inning of game 3, Ted Kubiak was on second base with 2 outs and Bert Campaneris at the plate.

Kubiak got a big jump on a short liner by Campy to left centerfield. Kubiak, knowing where the outfielders were positioned, knew the moment Campy hit the ball that it was going to drop in for hit. So he put his head down and raced for home on the play. He scored the go ahead run just a split second before Campy was tagged out trying for second base.

If Kubiak had not had the awareness of the Mets fielders to know that he could race home without hesitating to look at the ball, or his third base coach, he would not have scored before Campy was out at second, and the run would not have counted.

Ted Kubiak's smart play won game 3 for the A's.

If Kubiak did not score, and the game remained tied the Mets had an enormous advantage because Dick Williams had already used 18 of the 23 players on his roster, while Yogi Berra still had 11 players on his bench. The longer the game continued, the higher the probability the Mets would have won.

And a Mets victory in game 3 would have meant the Mets, in all likelihood, would have taken the World Series in 5 games, since they didn't allow the A's a single earned run in their games 4 and 5 victories.

Watch Kubiak's heads up baserunning to win game 3 here at the 2:49:46 mark on the tape.

https://www.youtube.com/watch?v=ZLN_UAjhc54

Or you can find it by typing in this search on YouTube: 1973 World Series Game 3 NEW YORK 10/16/73.

Here are Gene Tenace's recent comments about Ted Kubiak's smart play 50 years ago:

"When Ted had a chance to play, he played hard. He was always one of the smartest ballplayers we had on the team. He had his head in the game at all times. He put himself in that position to get that good jump. And that turned out to be critical.

Ted was the original super utility guy. He was the first guy that could do multiple things. Switch hitter. He could substitute Bando at third base, Campy at short and Green at second. He could play the outfield if we needed it."

EXTRA NOTES ON THE 1973 WORLD SERIES

Several records were set in the 1973 World Series. Most notable was Gene Tenace tying Babe Ruth's record for walks in a World Series with 11. Tenace had nearly half the walks issued by Mets pitchers in the series. And none of the walks to Tenace were intentional.

THE METS PLAYERS' REACTIONS

The Mets were naturally disappointed by losing the World Series. But there were many different takes on it.

Tom Seaver told the Hackensack Record, *"You can never feel bad about losing a World Series. If you told me 2 months ago that we'd even be in the World Series I'd have told you that you were crazy."*

Tug McGraw was a little less philosophical saying, *"It's just a bummer to come all this way and lose. Second best doesn't mean a thing."*

Mets GM Bob Scheffing told Joseph Durso in the New York Times, *"The only guy who seemed really sad was Matlack. I told him on the plane though, that he had 1 bad inning since the middle of August and how many 23 year old kids even get to pitch 3 games in the World Series."*

Arthur Daley in the New York Times summed it up with this: *"Defeat is never easy to accept, and it came harder for the Mets, perhaps, because they had let themselves be carried away by the gospel of their spiritual leader and faith healer, Tug McGraw. He kept insisting with mystical fervor that 'you gotta believe.' The Mets believed."*

THE FINAL GAME IN UNIFORM FOR WILLIE MAYS

Game 7 was also the final game in a baseball uniform as an active player for Willie Mays.

Although he didn't get to play in games 4 - 7, he had no regrets. He told the New York Times, *"just because it was my last game it didn't make any difference to me if I played or not. If it was to help the ball club fine, but not because it was my last game. I didn't come in that way. I don't want to go out having people feel sorry for me."*

Then Mays said, *"The big significance was winning the playoff, that was more exciting than the World Series."*

And of course it was Willie Mays who had one of the big RBI hits that put the Mets up 4 - 2 in that final game against the Big Red Machine and help the Mets advance to the 1973 World Series.

Mays was 3 for 10 in the 1973 post season with 2 RBIs. And he played in 4 games

In 1962 he was .250 with 1 RBI in 7 games

In 1954 he batted .286 in the series

In 1973, Mays batted .300 in the post season and 2 of his hits contributed to victories.

It may be hard to believe, but 1973 was the best postseason in the legendary career of Willie Mays.

FINAL NOTE From The Sports Time Traveler™

The game 7 loss crushed me when I was 10 years old.

The 1973 World Series took place at the prime moment of my childhood, when baseball was the most important thing to me, and I was devastated that the Mets lost the World Series. Many of my friends from that time feel the same way.

For 50 years, I could not get over the loss of the 1973 World Series. This journey to re-live the 1973 season was a form of therapy for me. I had to reach some closure over the biggest event in my childhood.

Now that I've completed the journey I can finally look back now and realize what a gift it was to have my team go on a dream like run from last place to the World Series.

No team in American professional sports history has ever experienced anything like it. And I got to experience it as a fan at the perfect age, at a time when it was the most important thing in my life.

Looking back, it is now obvious that the A's were the better team, and not just because they won game 7 of the 1973 World Series.

The A's were the team of the decade, winning 3 consecutive World Series, more than any other team in the 1970s. The only other contender for the title of team of the decade would be the Big Red Machine with 4 World Series appearances and 2 wins.

And think about it, the 1973 Mets, "my team," almost took down both of them, in their prime, in the same postseason.

Also 2 of the A's big stars Reggie and Catfish would become household names, Reggie would have a candy bar named for him, and the pair were instrumental in the leading Yankees to 2 additional World Series titles in the late 1970s.

When you think about it that way it makes it easier to take the game 7 loss.

Another perspective I've gained that has "cured" me comes as a direct result of talking to my friend, Ted Kubiak, who played on the Oakland A's in the 1973 World Series.

It's comforting to now know that one of the big moments in Ted's career was also what I believe to have been the key moment in the entire 1973 World Series.

Now that we've become friends, and I've heard him say that winning game 3 was one of the great highlights of his career, it gives me enormous satisfaction to know that if the Mets had to lose the World Series, at least they lost it because of something my friend did. I can accept that. It even makes me feel good about the outcome of the 1973 World Series.

It also occurred to me that I'm not friends with anyone on the 1973 Mets. So, I should be happy for the one friend I have that played in and won the 1973 World Series.

In the prior chapter, I analyzed the key moments in which the Mets lost the World Series. I wrote that the number one reason was Ted's heads up play to score the winning run in game 3.

I really believe this was the most important moment that led the A's to win the series. On the video tape it's clear that Ted needed the jump he got off second base when Campy hit the ball for him to score before Campy was thrown out at second. And if Ted didn't score in the 11th, the Mets most likely would have won the game later on because the A's had used up most of their players, while the Mets were playing at home and still had most of their bench available.

If the Mets would have won game 3, they would have gone up 2 games to 1. And Matlack and Koosman shut down the A's in games 4 and 5 completely, not allowing a single earned run. So the Mets would have won it 4 games to 1.

Once Ted scored the winning run of game 3, with his heads up base running, the Mets fate was sealed, because as Ted has indicated, the A's were in haze over the Andrews affair in New York, and once they went back to Oakland there was no way they were going to lose.

The only path for the Mets to win the 1973 World Series was to sweep all 3 games at Shea. Ted Kubiak prevented that with his heads up base running to score from second on a short hit to left field in the 11th inning of game 3.

Finally, the Mets losing game 7 in many ways was a blessing for me. It taught me a valuable life lesson at just 10 years old, that you can't always get what you want. And that you can never take anything for granted.

If the Mets had won game 7, I might have perhaps become complacent about the accomplishment and not sought to strive for excellence in other areas of my own life.

It also made the Mets only subsequent World Series triumph, also performed in miraculous fashion, in 1986, sweeter than it ever would have been if the Mets had not lost in 1973.

And in all likelihood if the Mets had won game 7 in 1973, I might also not have seen the need, 50 years later, to take this amazing journey as The Sports Time Traveler™.

A Magical Holiday Story

The experience of following the 1973 Mets day-by-day, 50 years after it all took place for real, was a magical one for me. It was the closest thing to real time travel I will ever experience.

The Mets team mantra down the stretch in September, 1973 was, *"Ya Gotta Believe."* Mets relief pitcher Tug McGraw had adopted the phrase and chanted it maniacally in the bullpen, the dugout and the Mets clubhouse.

The phrase quickly caught on with fans, and placards with *"Ya Gotta Believe,"* could be seen in Shea Stadium as the Mets made their improbable drive from last to first in the NL East over the final month of the 1973 season.

I remember this time nostalgically from when I first lived through it when I had just turned 10 years old.

On my virtual journey, half a century later, I was wild with anticipation as I entered September, 2023. Each day as I scanned the archives of all the New York area papers from precisely 50 years ago, I knew that sometime soon I would spot that phrase, *"Ya Gotta Believe,"* in print.

I finally found it in the Long Island paper, Newsday, in an article by the sportswriter Joe Donnelly. That was on September 19, 2023, exactly 50 years after Donnelly had written the article on September 19, 1973. As best as I can determine, Donnelly was the first sportswriter to use that phrase, or anything else like, *"Ya Gotta Believe,"* in print as referring to the New York Mets.

Joe Donnelly mentioned the phrase as he recapped the Mets inspirational victory over the Pirates at Three Rivers Stadium the prior evening. The Mets had come back from a 4 – 1 deficit in the 9th inning to win the game in divine like fashion by scoring 5 runs in the 9th inning to stave off a loss that would have put them on the brink of elimination.

Donnelly wrote that Tug McGraw, who was in the Mets dugout having already pitched 2 superb innings, *"had been shouting, 'You've got to believe!' from the bench."*

My eyes popped off the page and a shrill went down my spine as I was seeing those words, *"You've got to believe,"* for the first time in my year long virtual journey.

On September 20, 2023, I wrote a Substack article about this experience. I titled it simply, **"You've Got to Believe."** You can read that article in this book in the chapter with that same name.

In my article I wrote, *"It was my Mets equivalent of discovering the holy grail."*

Then 3 months later, something else magical, perhaps even mystical, came about as a result of my virtual journey back in time.

On Christmas Day, 2023, I received a comment on my Substack article about the first time I had seen the words, *"You've Got to Believe,"* in a newspaper archive.

The message writer was Joe Donnelly's son, Mike Donnelly. He wrote, *"My sister shared this with me today on Christmas morning. My father, Joe Donnelly, passed away a little over a year ago. However, there are times when I feel him with me. So viewing this for the first time on Xmas morning, a holiday my father loved. I can say most assuredly....yes, You've got to believe!"*

Needless to say, I had chills when I read that message.

I was so enthralled by the message that I reached out to Mike and his sister Julie to learn more.

Julie and Mike shared that their father Joe had passed away a couple of weeks before Christmas in 2022. Grieving from their loss, they couldn't celebrate the holiday in 2022 without their father.

Over the next year Julie was interested in finding articles via Google searches that discussed how her father had impacted other people's lives via his writing. On Christmas morning, 2023, Julie was really missing her father as they prepared to celebrate the holiday for the first time without him. So she decided to do one more search.

On that search, on Christmas morning, Julie found my article, **"You've Got to Believe,"** and listened to the audio version that I had narrated.

Julie told me, **"what struck me was the title, 'You've Got to Believe,' since it was Christmas morning and it's all about believing. I was just floored. I sent it to my brother. I said to him, 'the title is not lost on me.'"**

Julie went on to tell me, **"the biggest thing about it was your enthusiasm. You said something like it was the holy grail. You were so excited that you were searching for something and you found it. And it was something that my dad had written."**

"Writing was such an art form to my dad. To know that he was providing joy, so many years later, in the way he loved the most, it felt like he was living on."

"That was such an incredible gift to us," Julie told me. **"My dad had 5 children, we all talked about it and shared it that day. It was huge. It felt like he was with us."**

In my conversation with Julie's brother Mike he shared that he had a deep connection with his dad. He told me he was not a very spiritual person, but when his dad passed he hoped to see some signs from his dad. Mike told me that over the past year and-a-half since his dad's passing, **"I've had what my family calls winks. My dad was famous for having this big smile and this incredible little wink. My dad was a big fan of Christmas. He loved the gift of giving.**

So this past Christmas morning when my sister sent me your article, it was one of my dad's winks."

"My dad lived an amazing life and there is so much stuff I'm still uncovering. I didn't realize that he was the one that was the first to put, 'You've Got to Believe,' in a story about the Mets."

Mike finished telling his story by saying, **"So Len, you definitely have me believing."**

And now this journey finally comes to a conclusion. I hope you enjoyed the experience as much as I did.

Thanks for reading.

Please share your comments with me at Len@Fermaninnovation.com

www.ingramcontent.com/pod-product-compliance
Lightning Source LLC
Chambersburg PA
CBHW020427130626
46549CB00001B/18